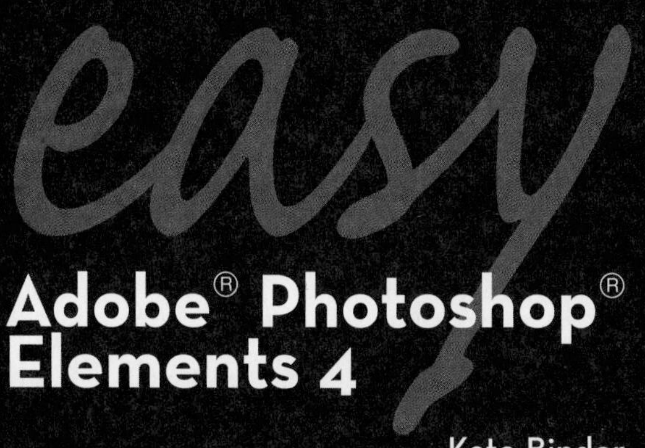

Adobe® Photoshop® Elements 4

Kate Binder

Contents

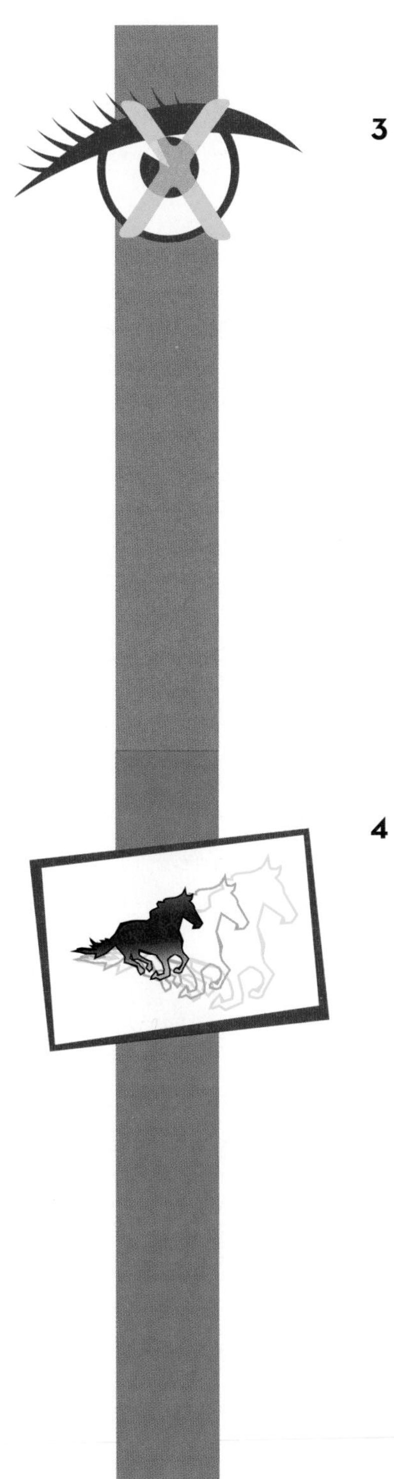

EASY ADOBE® PHOTOSHOP® ELEMENTS 4

International Standard Book Number: 0-7897-3467-2

Library of Congress Catalog Card Number: 2005932884

Printed in the United States of America

First Printing: October 2005

08 07 06 05 4 3 2 1

U.K. International Standard Book Number: 0-7897-3524-5

First Printing: October 2005

08 07 06 05 4 3 2 1

TRADEMARKS

All terms mentioned in this book that are known to be trademarks or service marks have been appropriately capitalized. Que Publishing cannot attest to the accuracy of this information. Use of a term in this book should not be regarded as affecting the validity of any trademark or service mark.

Adobe and Photoshop are registered trademarks of Adobe Systems, Inc.

WARNING AND DISCLAIMER

Every effort has been made to make this book as complete and as accurate as possible, but no warranty or fitness is implied. The information provided is on an "as is" basis. The author and the publisher shall have neither liability nor responsibility to any person or entity with respect to any loss or damages arising from the information contained in this book or from the use of the CD or programs accompanying it.

BULK SALES

Que Publishing offers excellent discounts on this book when ordered in quantity for bulk purchases or special sales. For more information, please contact

U.S. Corporate and Government Sales
1-800-382-3419
corpsales@pearsontechgroup.com

For sales outside of the U.S., please contact

International Sales
international@pearsoned.com

Associate Publisher
Greg Wiegand

Acquisitions Editor
Michelle Newcomb

Development Editor
Laura Norman

Managing Editor
Charlotte Clapp

Project Editor
Dan Knott

Indexer
Lisa Wilson

Technical Editor
Doug Nelson

Publishing Coordinator
Sharry Lee Gregory

Multimedia Developer
Dan Scherf

Book Designer
Anne Jones

Page Layout
Michelle Mitchell

ABOUT THE AUTHOR

Kate Binder is a design and graphics expert who works from her home in New Hampshire. She has written articles on graphics, publishing, and photography for magazines including *Shutterbug, Publish, eDigital Photo, PEI,* and *Desktop Publishers Journal*. Kate is also the author of several books, including *Easy Mac OS X v10.4 Tiger, The Complete Idiot's Guide to Mac OS X*, and *Easy Adobe Photoshop 6*, and she is the coauthor of books including *Teach Yourself Photoshop CS2 in 24 Hours, Microsoft Office: Mac v.X Inside Out, Easy Mac OS X, The Complete Idiot's Guide to Mac OS X, SVG for Designers*, and *Get Creative: The Digital Photo Idea Book*.

Kate's website is http://www.prospecthillpub.com.

DEDICATION

To the Knitwits, my true help and haven, who have taught me much more than knitting—your value is far beyond pearls.

ACKNOWLEDGMENTS

My thanks go first to my family, as always: my husband and partner Don, who makes me lunch every day; our son Mack, who amazes me every day; and my parents Richard and Barbara, without whom ... well, that's pretty obvious. And thank you once more to Laura Norman and Michelle Newcomb at Que, for walking me through another one. The rest of the gang at Que deserves kudos, too, especially project editor Dan Knott, production editor Megan Wade, and technical editor Doug Nelson.

Many of the models for the photos in this book are retired racing greyhounds—a most extraordinary breed of dog. To learn more about how greyhounds make wonderful pets, visit www.adopt-a-greyhound.org.

—Kate Binder

WE WANT TO HEAR FROM YOU!

As the reader of this book, *you* are our most important critic and commentator. We value your opinion and want to know what we're doing right, what we could do better, what areas you'd like to see us publish in, and any other words of wisdom you're willing to pass our way.

As an associate publisher for Que Publishing, I welcome your comments. You can email or write me directly to let me know what you did or didn't like about this book—as well as what we can do to make our books better.

Please note that I cannot help you with technical problems related to the topic of this book. We do have a User Services group, however, where I will forward specific technical questions related to the book.

When you write, please be sure to include this book's title and author as well as your name, email address, and phone number. I will carefully review your comments and share them with the author and editors who worked on the book.

Email: feedback@quepublishing.com

Mail: Greg Wiegand
Associate Publisher
Que Publishing
800 East 96th Street
Indianapolis, IN 46240 USA

For more information about this book or another Que Publishing title, visit our website at www.quepublishing.com. Type the ISBN (excluding hyphens) or the title of a book in the Search field to find the page you're looking for.

IT'S AS EASY AS 1-2-3

Each part of this book is made up of a series of short, instructional lessons, designed to help you understand basic information.

1. Each step is fully illustrated to show you how it looks onscreen.
2. Each task includes a series of quick, easy steps designed to guide you through the procedure.
3. Items that you select or click in menus, dialog boxes, tabs, and windows are shown in **bold**.

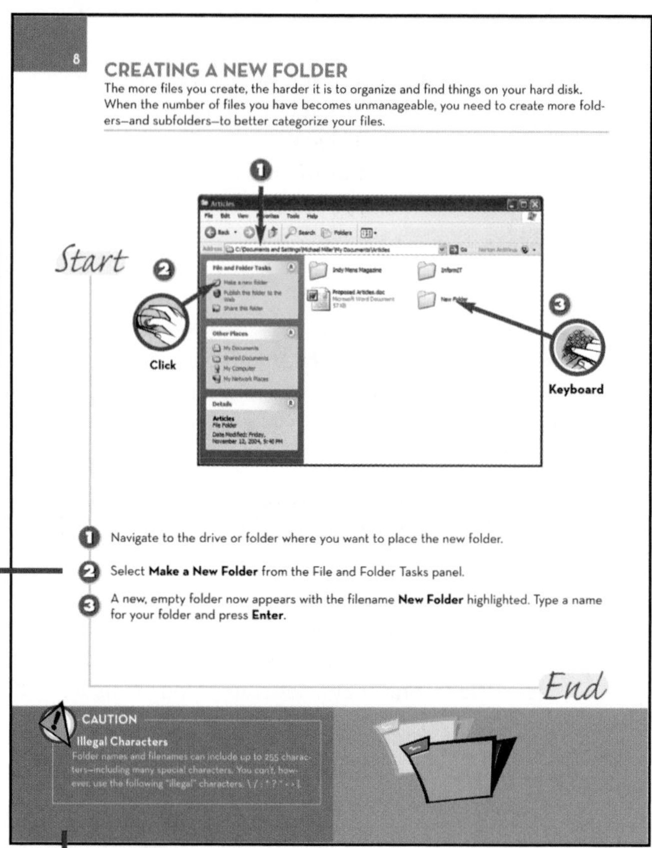
8

CREATING A NEW FOLDER

The more files you create, the harder it is to organize and find things on your hard disk. When the number of files you have becomes unmanageable, you need to create more folders—and subfolders—to better categorize your files.

1. Navigate to the drive or folder where you want to place the new folder.
2. Select **Make a New Folder** from the File and Folder Tasks panel.
3. A new, empty folder now appears with the filename **New Folder** highlighted. Type a name for your folder and press **Enter**.

End

CAUTION

Illegal Characters

Folder names and filenames can include up to 255 characters—including many special characters. You can't, however, use the following "illegal" characters: \ / : * ? " < > |.

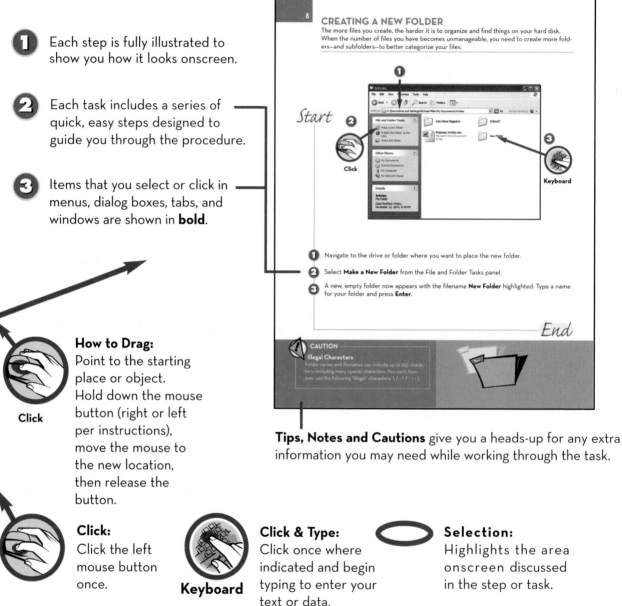

Tips, Notes and Cautions give you a heads-up for any extra information you may need while working through the task.

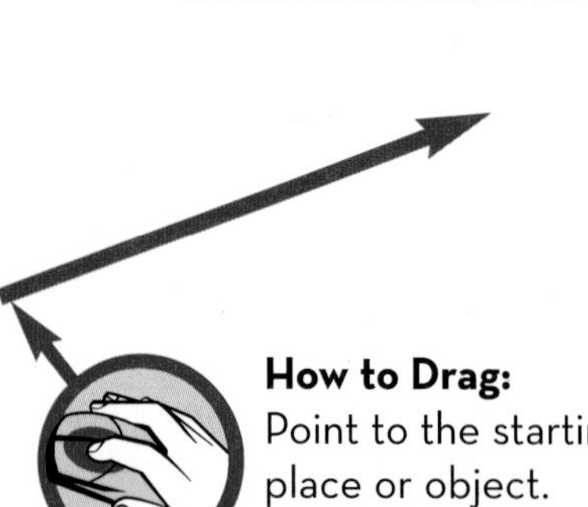

Click

How to Drag:
Point to the starting place or object. Hold down the mouse button (right or left per instructions), move the mouse to the new location, then release the button.

Click:
Click the left mouse button once.

Keyboard

Click & Type:
Click once where indicated and begin typing to enter your text or data.

Selection:
Highlights the area onscreen discussed in the step or task.

Double-click:
Click the left mouse button twice in rapid succession.

Right-click:
Click the right mouse button once.

Pointer Arrow:
Highlights an item on the screen you need to point to or focus on in the step or task.

INTRODUCTION

I love Photoshop Elements, I really do.

Now, that's a statement that may surprise people who know me—in other words, people who know that I make a lot of my living working with "Big Photoshop" and its professional-level siblings in Adobe's powerful Creative Suite. Nonetheless, Photoshop Elements has a special place in my heart. And I'm sure you'll feel the same way by the time you're finished reading this book.

Look at it this way. You've got a digital camera, and probably a scanner too. You've got this desktop PC that's hundreds—no, thousands of times more powerful than the computers of just a few decades ago. Maybe you even have a cell phone that can take photos. How about your PDA? I bet it can do the same.

You've got all the gadgets—but let's face it; one thing you don't have is a lot of time.

And if you did find some time, you'd pick up a real book by Elizabeth Peters or Tom Clancy, kick back, and enjoy yourself.

Who wants to read about computers?

Not me, that's for sure. I'm a lot like you. I love my digital camera. I look forward to sharing my pictures, but I don't want to spend hours "playing" with them. I spend enough time sitting at a computer when I'm working—when it comes to my family photos, vacation snapshots, and eBay listing photos, I just want to get them looking good as quickly as possible so I can get on with my life.

And that's exactly where Photoshop Elements fits into my plans. Now, I'm a huge fan of "Big Photoshop's power and breadth of features. It's just that, as I said earlier, I don't feel like getting out the big guns after hours. But I'm used to the power of Photoshop—after all, it's the industry standard image editor, and there's just not much it can't do. Given that, is it really possible for Photoshop Elements to keep me happy?

The answer, it turns out, is emphatically yes. With Photoshop Elements, you get maximum results with minimum effort. And version 4 offers more of the same, only better, with automatic skin tone adjustments and red-eye repair, a new Straighten tool, and a Magic Selection Brush that's, well, truly magical. Elements' Organizer component is more powerful than ever, with new ways to import, sort, and label your photos so you can always find the ones you want. And built-in wizards do all the heavy lifting involved in creating everything from photo album pages and greeting cards to wall calendars and Web galleries.

So here's hoping that you love Photoshop Elements as much as I do[md]and that this book enables you to use the program to create images you'll love even more.

May you enjoy this book, thrill as I did at the tricks you can do with Photoshop Elements, and not spend a minute more than you need to with either of them.

part 1

LEARNING THE ROPES

Back when ships needed favorable winds to get anywhere, new recruits had to learn which ropes to pull to carry out the captain's orders and set sail. This first part of the book is for novice sailors—people who feel more comfortable if they can begin at the beginning, while their ship is still safely docked. Just turn the page to sign on for a brief orientation session: You'll quickly learn the commands, controls, and features of the Photoshop Elements work area. For example, you'll find out what a *tool* is and how to choose one from the *toolbox*. After you have your bearings, we can shorthand the steps in later parts and just say, "Click the **Crop** tool," and move on and you'll know exactly what to do.

If you're feeling adventurous, don't worry about sailing ahead to another part of the book. You can do most of the tasks in any order, and you can always come back to this part if somehow you get turned around.

Welcome aboard, and fear not: You have nothing to lose but your old film cameras and the tiresome wait for your prints to come back from the lab.

THE PHOTOSHOP ELEMENTS WORK AREA

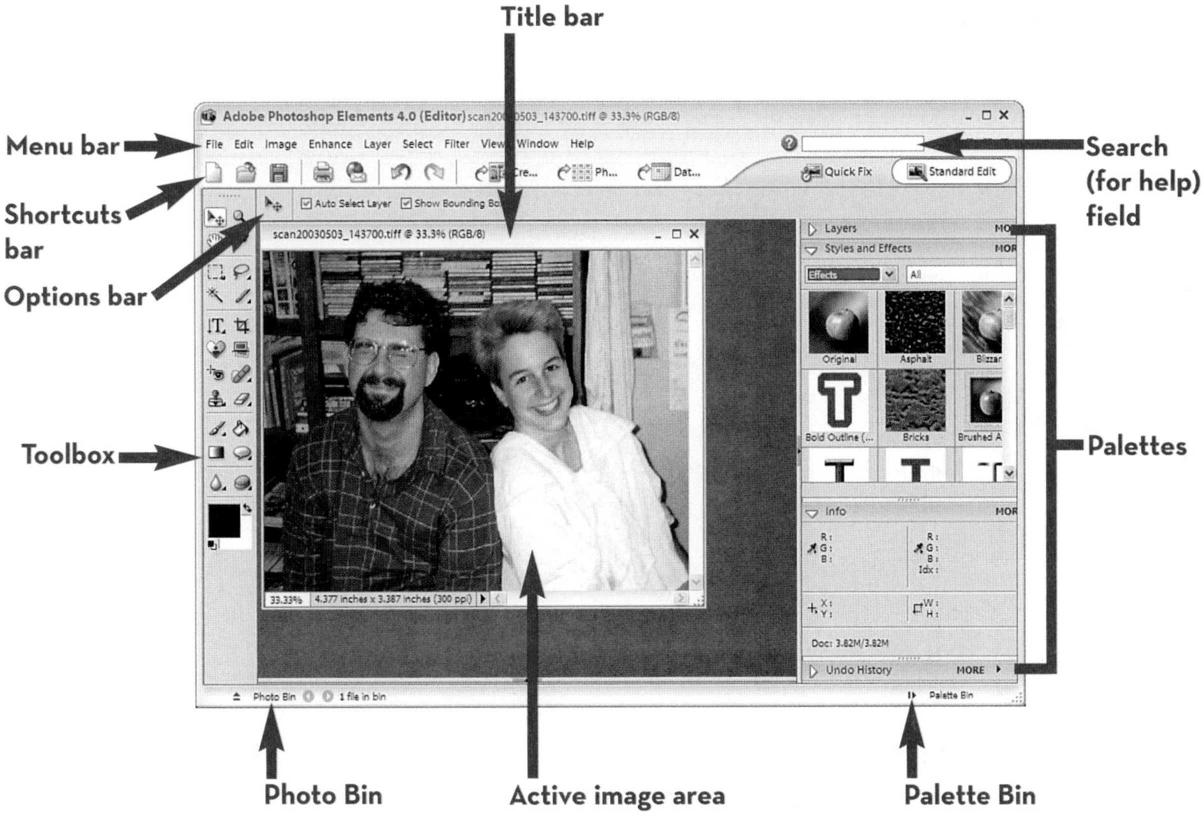

STARTING PHOTOSHOP ELEMENTS AND OPENING A PICTURE

Photoshop Elements has two working modes: Quick Fix mode, for making instant automated image corrections, and Standard Edit mode, for more complex operations. To use either, you first have to start Elements and open your image.

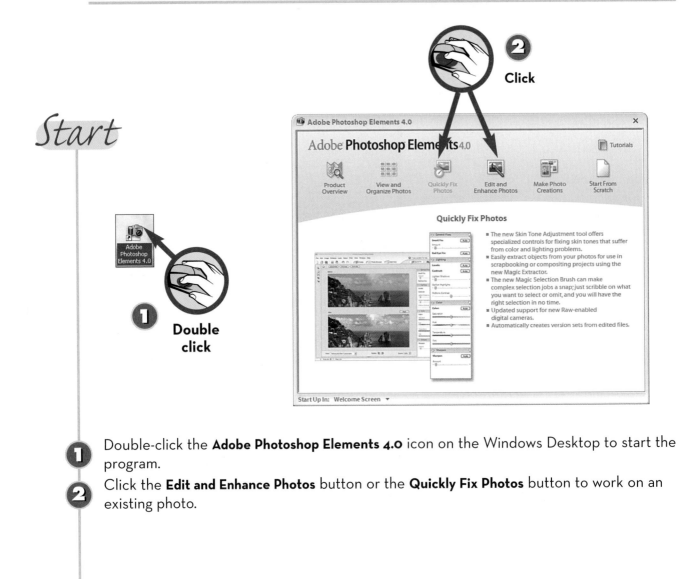

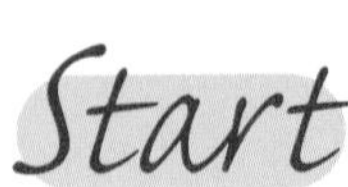

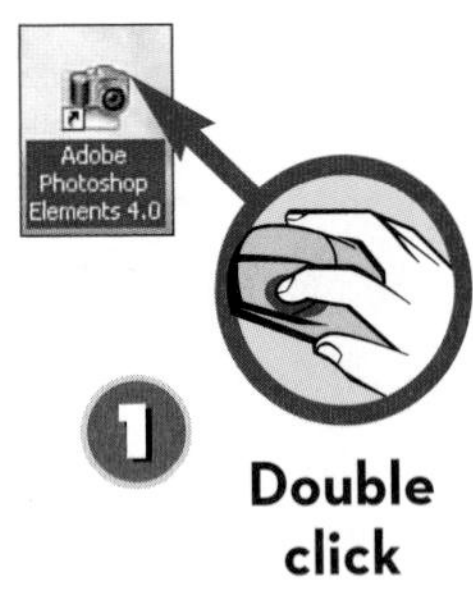

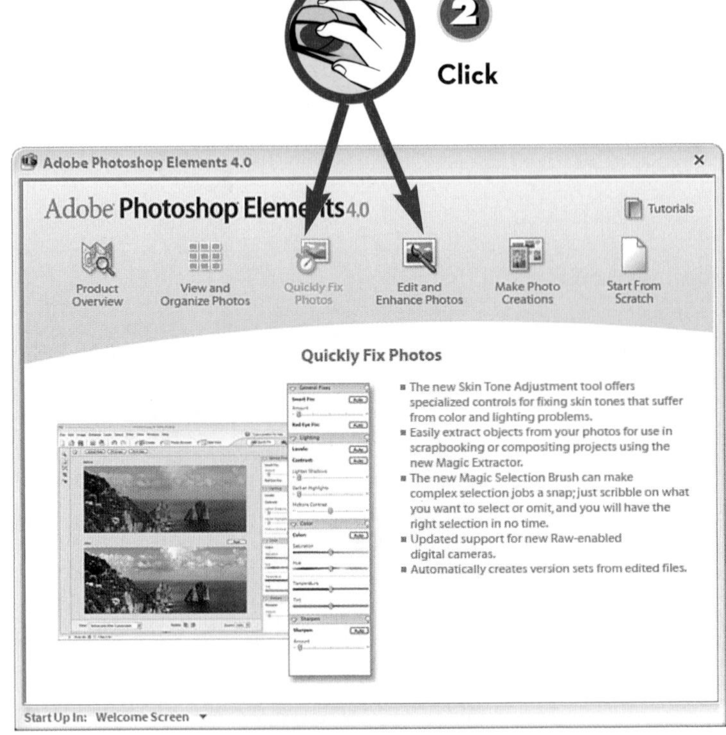

1. Double-click the **Adobe Photoshop Elements 4.0** icon on the Windows Desktop to start the program.
2. Click the **Edit and Enhance Photos** button or the **Quickly Fix Photos** button to work on an existing photo.

Continued

TIP

Welcome Back

Click the arrow next to **Start Up** in to choose a different startup option. You can have Elements open the Editor or Organizer rather than showing the Welcome screen. If you want it back, choose **Window, Welcome** from the menu bar.

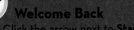

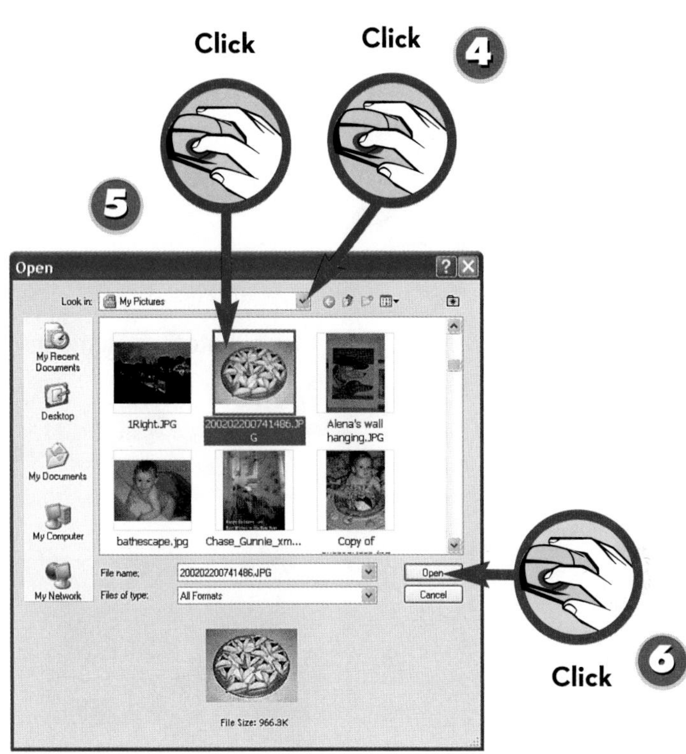

3. Choose **File, Open** from the menu bar.
4. Navigate to the folder where your image files are stored.
5. Click the file you want to open.
6. Click the **Open** button. The picture opens in the active image area.

End

TIP

Hide and Seek

Don't see your shots? Either you didn't load them from your camera or scanner yet or you stored them in a different folder. You might need to navigate the filesystem on your hard drive or CD to find the images you want. Turn to the next task, "Browsing for a File," to learn how.

STARTING WITH A BLANK CANVAS

Not all images start out as photographs. Sometimes, you just want to paint. For that to happen, you need to start with a blank document, rather than opening an existing file. You can choose the size and resolution of your new image file.

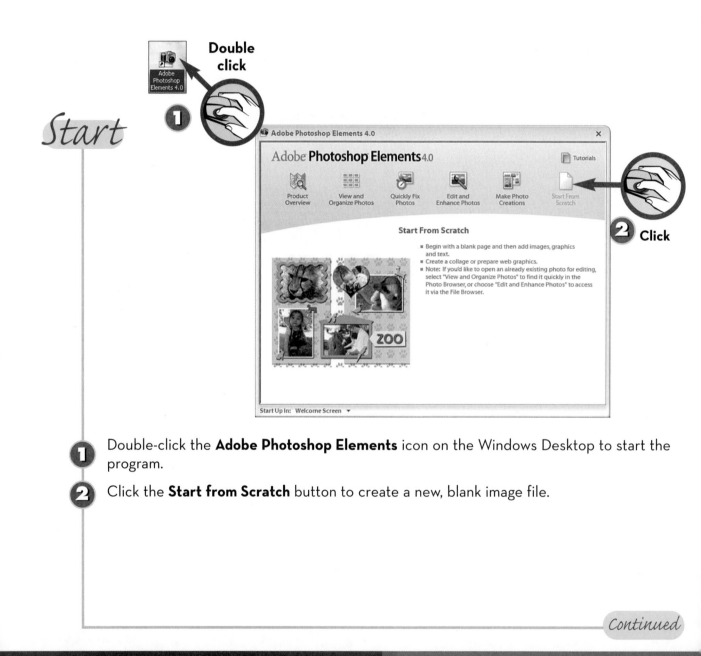

Start

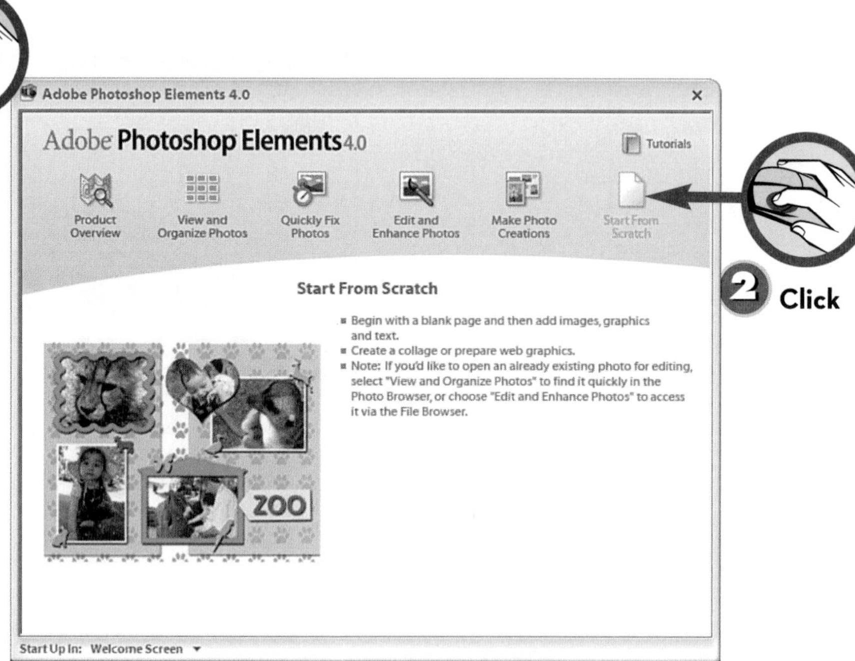

1. Double-click the **Adobe Photoshop Elements** icon on the Windows Desktop to start the program.
2. Click the **Start from Scratch** button to create a new, blank image file.

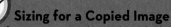

Continued

NOTE

The Color of the Canvas

Choose a background from the Background Contents pop-up menu. White gives you a white "page", and Background Color makes the canvas the current background color. Choose Transparent to overlay your drawing on another image.

TIP

Sizing for a Copied Image

If an image is on the clipboard, Photoshop Elements automatically inserts the size and resolution of that image in the New dialog box. Click **OK**; then press **Ctrl+V** to paste the image into the document.

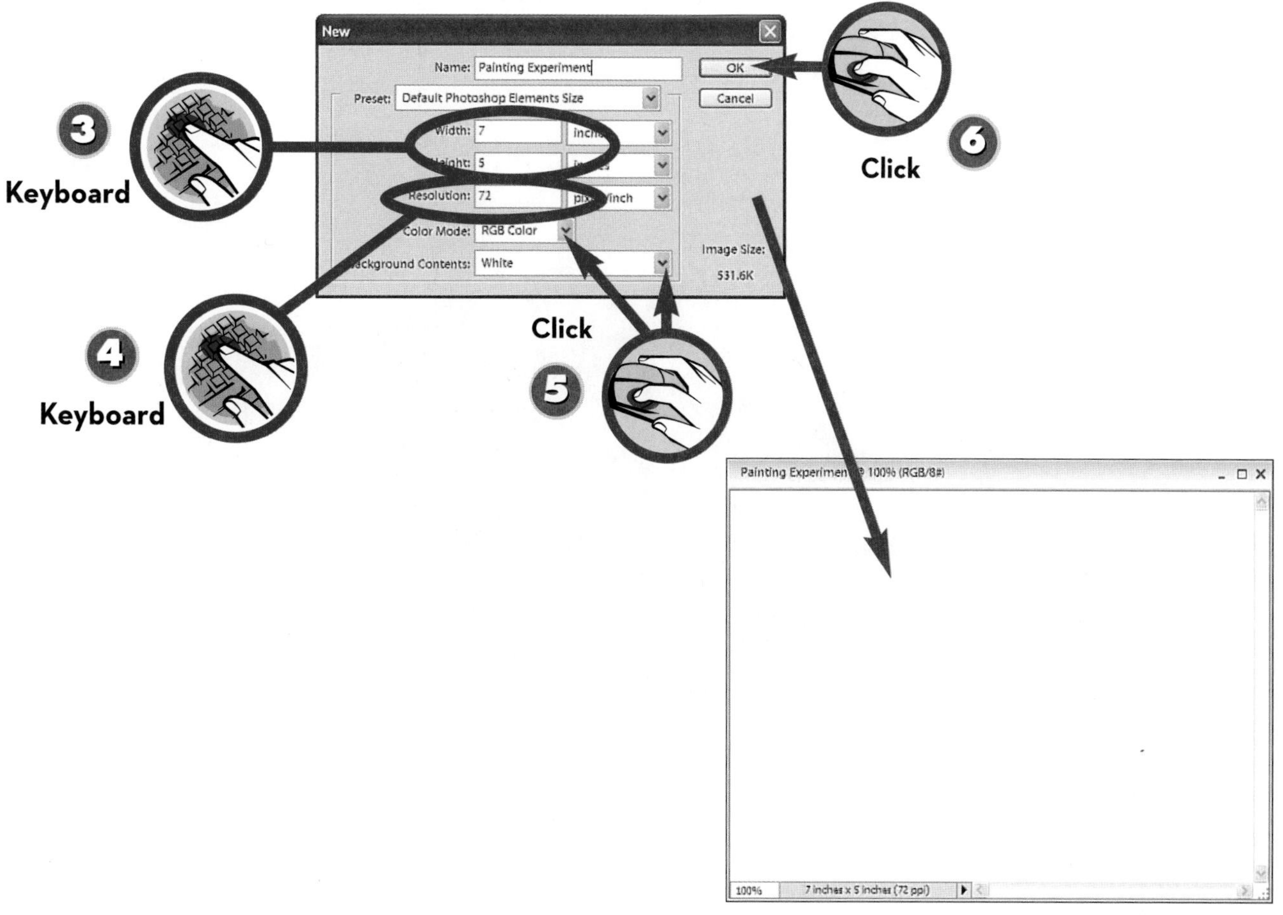

3. Enter **Width** and **Height** values for the new file.
4. Choose a **Resolution** value.
5. Set the **Color Mode** to RGB and choose an option from the Background Contents menu.
6. Click **OK** to create the new file. A blank image window opens.

End

TIP

Resolved: Choosing a Resolution

Resolution refers to how many pixels—tiny, square image elements—per inch there are in your image. Higher resolution values enable you to print an image at larger sizes without its becoming blocky. When you're creating a new image file, enter 72 ppi in the Resolution field for an image that you plan to display only on-screen, or a higher value such as 300 ppi for an image that you plan to print out.

CHANGING YOUR VIEW

When you have a picture file open for editing, you'll usually want to make it as large as possible onscreen. This gives you the clearest overall view, regardless of the actual image size. Then, you can use the Zoom tool (or the View, Zoom In command) to magnify small areas if you need to work in even finer detail.

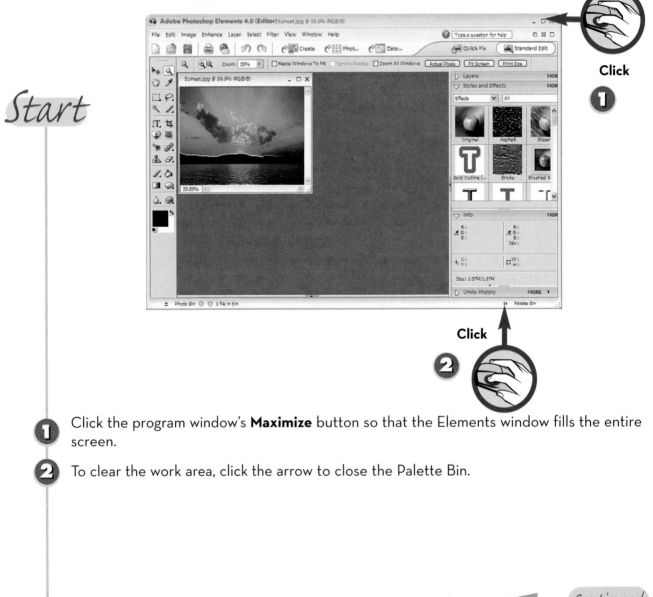

Start

1 Click the program window's **Maximize** button so that the Elements window fills the entire screen.

2 To clear the work area, click the arrow to close the Palette Bin.

Continued

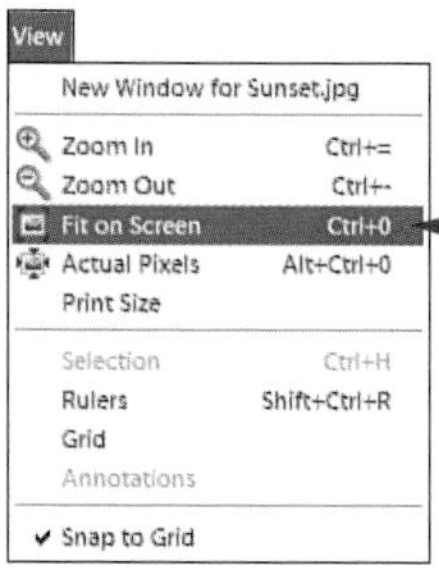

3 Click

4 Click and drag

3 From the menu bar, choose **View**, **Fit on Screen** or press **Ctrl+0** (zero). The active image window enlarges to fill the work area.

4 Click and drag the active image window's **title bar** to move the window around.

End

TIP

Open Windows

You can have several pictures open at the same time. Select one of them for editing (make it active) by clicking its title bar. (If you can't see all the title bars, choose **Window**, **Images**, **Cascade** to see them all.)

CHOOSING TOOLS FROM THE TOOLBOX

Tools in the toolbox help you work on portions of a picture in a variety of ways. An example is the Zoom tool, which enlarges your view of a picture. You can switch to the Zoom tool by clicking it in the toolbox or by pressing Z on the keyboard.

1. Hover and pause the pointer over the **Zoom** tool. Its name appears in a ToolTip, along with the letter of its shortcut key.
2. Click the **Zoom** tool or press **Z**. The pointer changes to a magnifying-glass symbol, and settings that affect the tool appear in the Options bar.
3. Click in the center of the area you want enlarged. A magnified view appears in the active image area.
4. Click again and again to enlarge the view in progressive steps. The magnification percentage appears in the title bar.

Continued

NOTE

Zoom In

Zooming doesn't make any changes to the picture itself, just to your view of it in Photoshop Elements so you can work on fine details.

TIP

Shortcut

When using the Zoom tool, right-click anywhere within the active image area and choose **Fit on Screen** to quickly view the entire image.

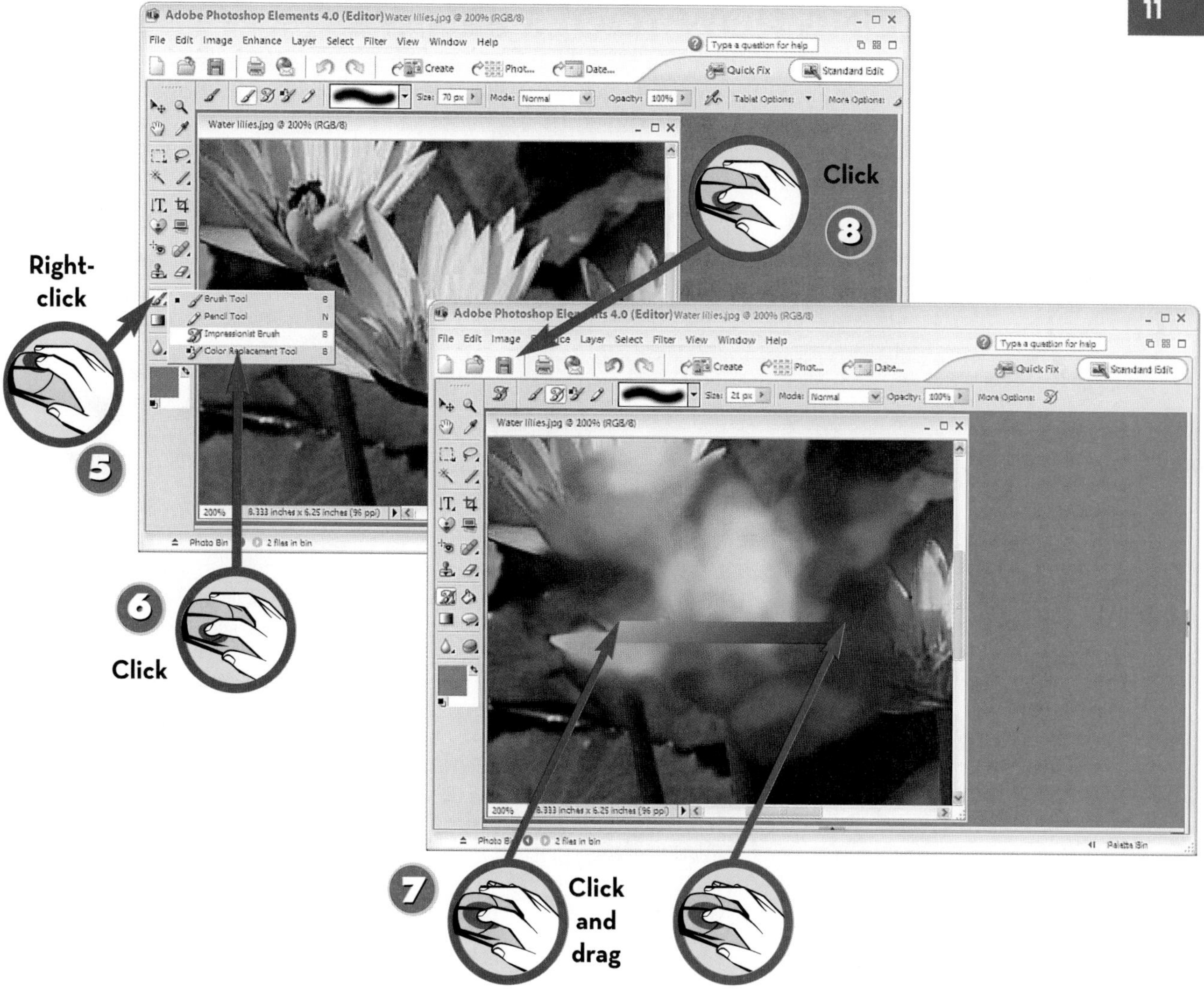

Right-click

5

6

Click

Click

8

7

Click and drag

5. Right-click the **Brush** tool.
6. Switch to the **Impressionist Brush** tool. The pointer changes to the brush tip, and settings for the tool appear in the Options bar.
7. Move the pointer to the area of the picture where you want to use the brush; then click and drag it around, as if painting, to apply the effect.
8. Because you made a change to the picture, click the **Save** shortcut in the Shortcuts bar to save your work.

End

TIP

Best-Quality Image

After you've made changes to a JPEG file, for best quality, you should use the **File, Save As** command to convert it to TIFF (**.tif**) format or save it as a Photoshop (**.psd**) file.

TIP

First Impressions

You can vary the effect of the Impressionist Brush by changing Options bar settings—Brush Size, Blending Mode, and Opacity, to name a few. To admire the result of your brushwork, choose **View, Fit on Screen** from the menu bar.

CONTROLLING HOW TOOLS BEHAVE

After you choose a tool from the toolbox, you can change settings in the Options bar that control its effect. Try it with the Horizontal Type tool.

Start

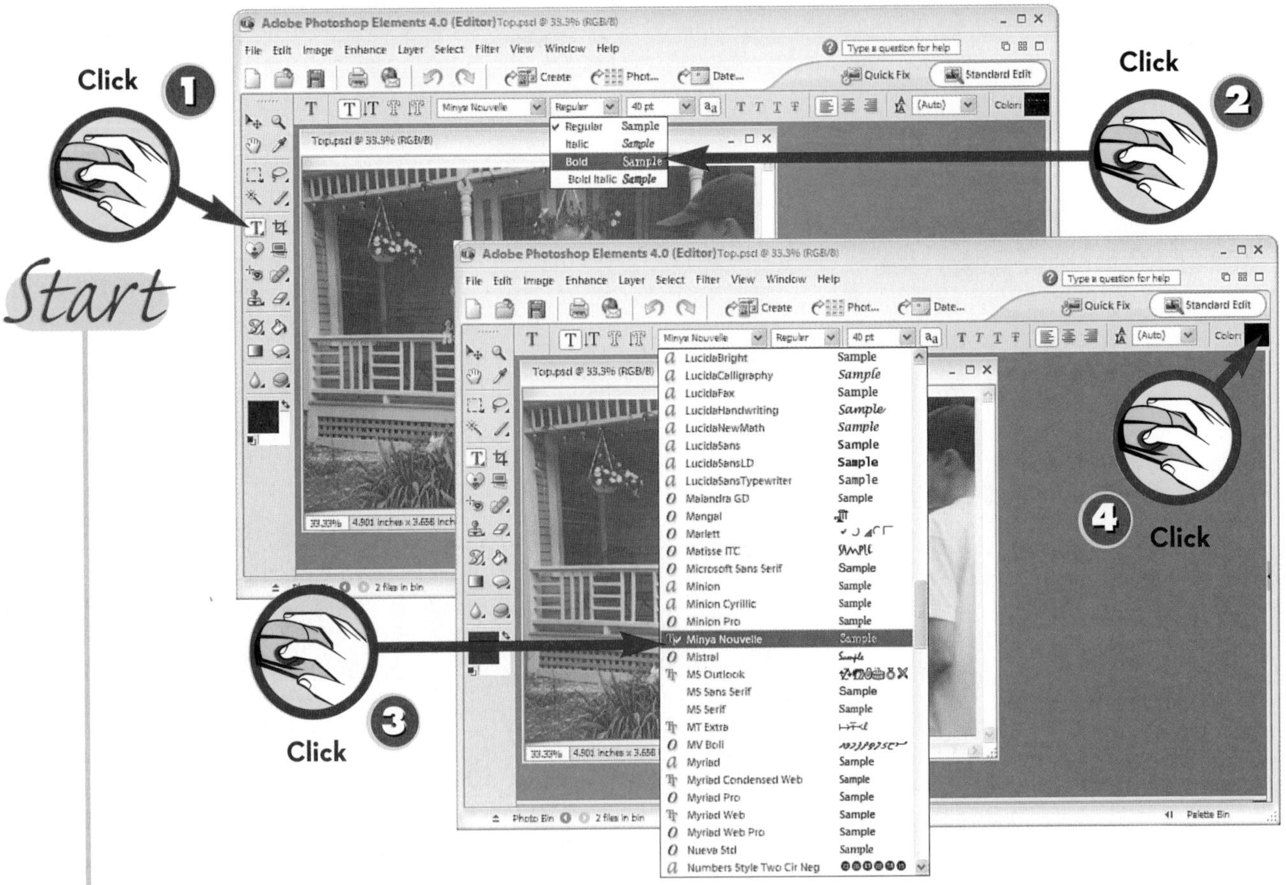

1. In the toolbox, click the **Horizontal Type** tool, or press **T**. Settings for the tool appear in the Options bar.
2. Choose a **Font Style** and **Font Size** from the pop-up menus in the Options bar.
3. Use the **Font** pop-up menu to choose a new font for your text, such as **Minya Nouvelle**.
4. Click the **Text Color** box; the Color Picker window opens.

Continued

TIP

I'm So Confused!

If the settings in the Options bar don't seem to be what you're looking for, check to make sure you haven't switched tools accidentally. Remember, each tool has different settings in the Options bar.

TIP

Hit Reset

The very first button on the Options bar has the same icon as whatever tool you're using. Click it to see a pop-up menu you can use to reset the options for the current tool or for all tools.

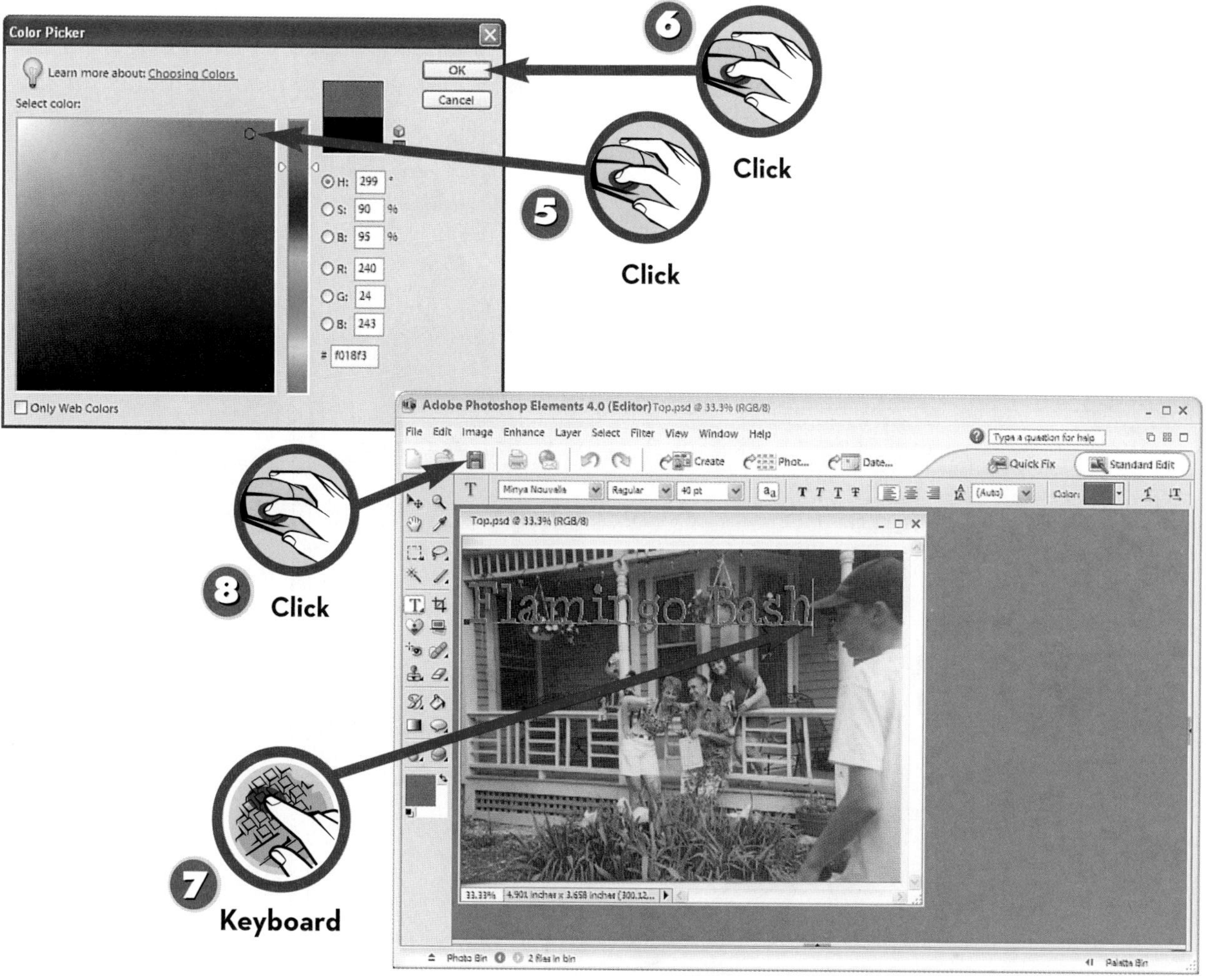

5. In the Color Picker, click in the color space to choose a color.
6. Click **OK**.
7. Type some text, such as **Flamingo Bash**.
8. Click the **Save** button to save your work.

End

NOTE

Settings Retained

Settings you make in the Options bar remain in effect for a particular tool until you change them again, even if you quit and then restart the program.

USING PALETTES

Palettes, floating windows that contain help and commands grouped by category, are a truly handy feature. For example, the Info palette shows color values and measurements for the current image or selected area.

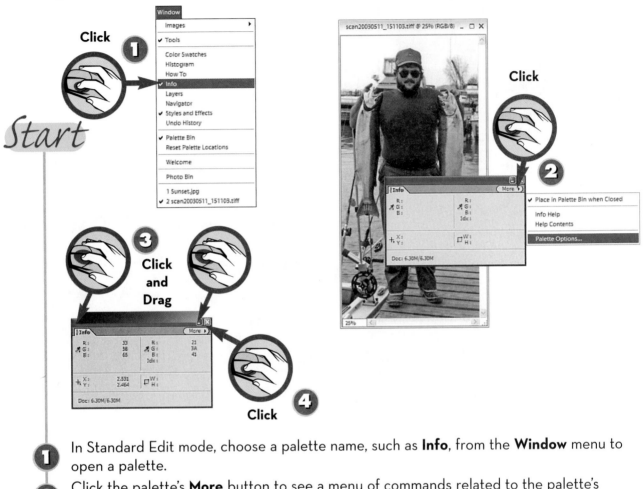

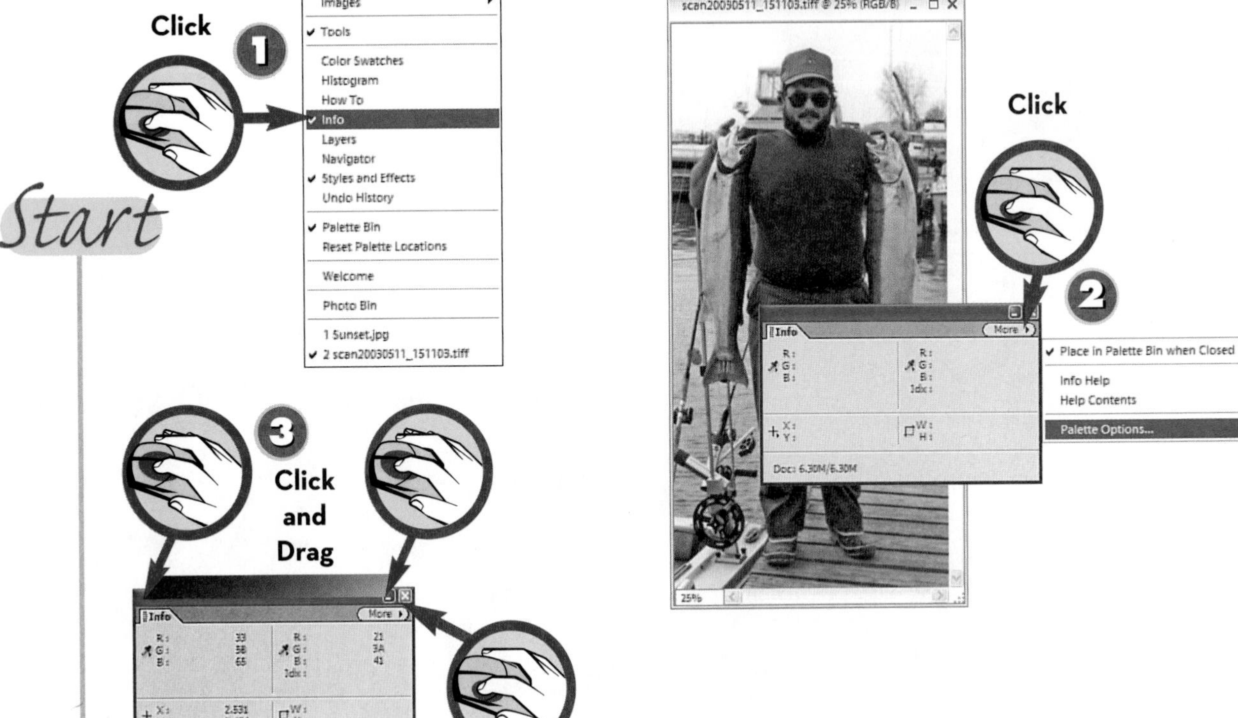

1. In Standard Edit mode, choose a palette name, such as **Info**, from the **Window** menu to open a palette.
2. Click the palette's **More** button to see a menu of commands related to the palette's function.
3. Drag the palette's title bar to move it around the screen.
4. Click the palette's close box to dismiss the palette.

NOTE

Getting More

The options in the More menu are different for each palette.

TIP

Layer Info

Especially as you begin to combine images or create artwork from them, get in the habit of leaving the Layers palette open. As you add text, graphics, painting, or images, you'll quickly see why keeping track of layers is important.

STORING PALETTES

Floating palettes are great, but they take up a lot of space on your screen. The Palette Bin on the right side of your screen is a handy place to stash palettes so they don't obscure your view of the image you're working on.

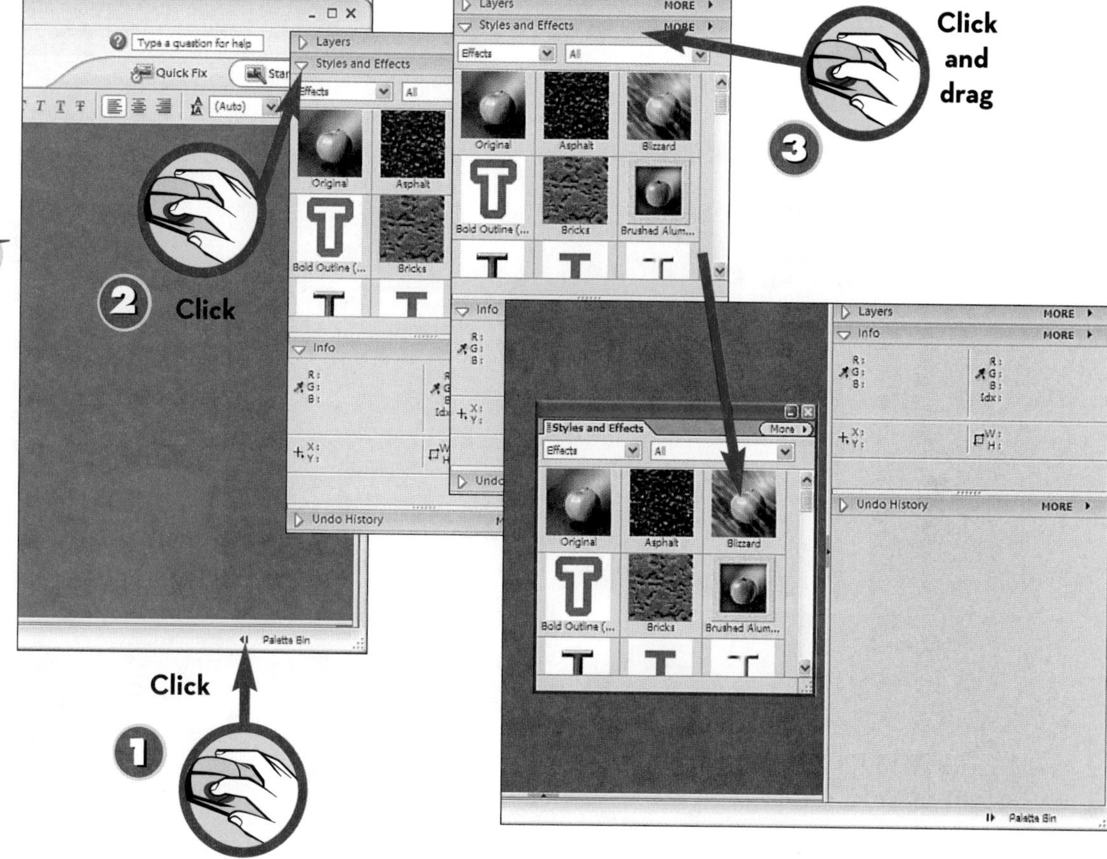

1. In Standard Edit mode, click the arrow labeled **Palette Bin** to open the bin.
2. Click the disclosure triangle in the title bar of a palette in the Palette Bin to expand or shrink the palette.
3. Drag a palette's title bar to remove it from the Palette Bin.

End

NOTE

Viewing Palettes

To use the Palette Bin effectively, set your screen resolution to at least 1024 × 768. If you work at 640 × 480 or 800 × 600, you might run out of room to expand palettes in the bin.

TIP

Adding to the Bin

To replace a palette in the Palette Bin, make sure a check mark is next to the Place in Palette Bin option in the palette's More menu; then click its close button.

USING CONTEXTUAL MENUS

Contextual menus pop up at the tip of your mouse cursor when you right-click in the image window. They're contextual because their contents change depending on which tool you're using, so the commands are always appropriate to their context.

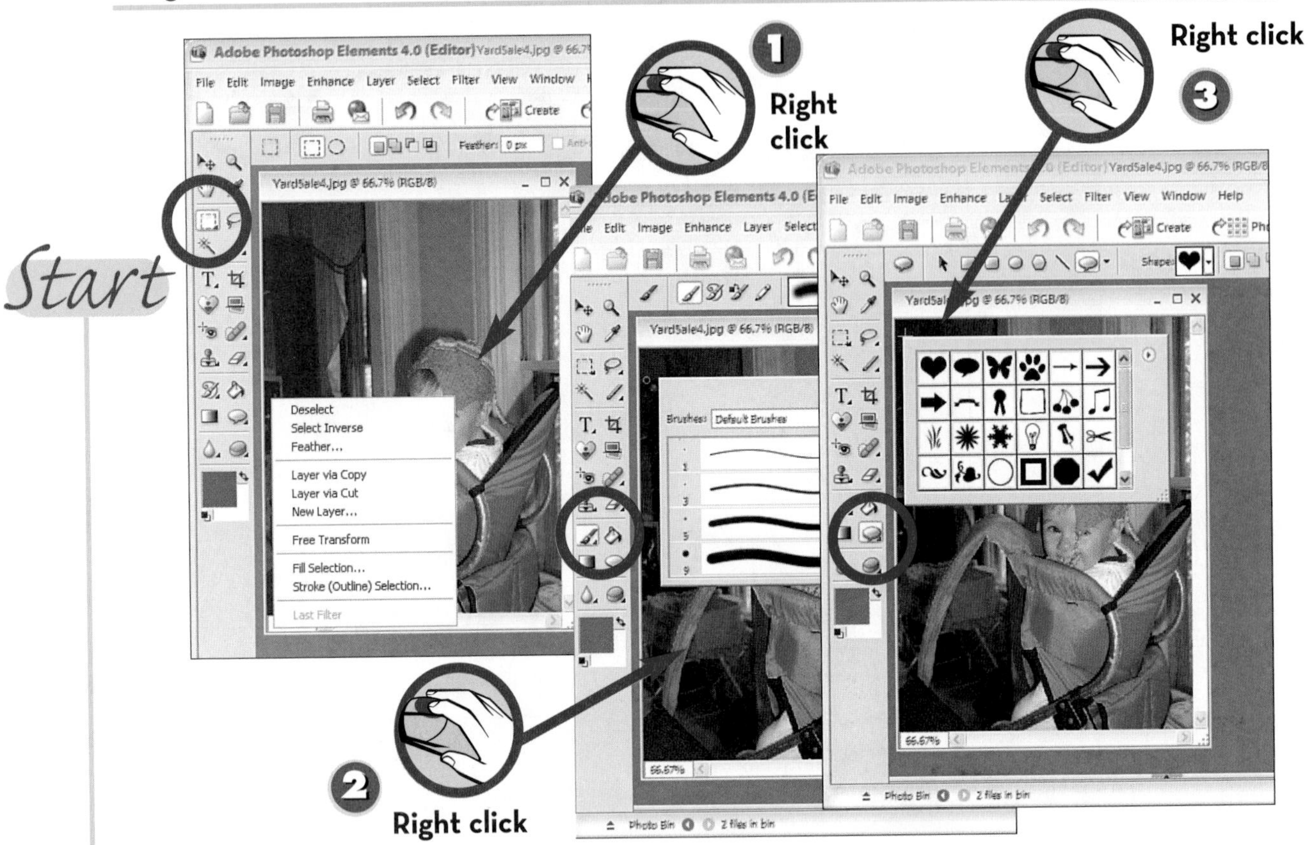

1. With a selection tool active, right-click in the image area to see a menu of selection commands.
2. With a painting tool active, right-click in the image area to see a menu of brush shapes.
3. With a shape tool active, right-click in the image area to see a menu of drawing shapes.

NOTE

Keeping Things in Context

Be sure to try right-clicking with each tool to see all the contextual menus Photoshop Elements has to offer. Using them is a real time-saver.

TIP

Layer by Layer

When you're building layered images (see Part 10, "Using Layers to Combine Photos and Artwork," **p. 168**.

SWITCHING BETWEEN QUICK FIX AND STANDARD EDIT MODES

Photoshop Elements has two working modes. In Standard Edit mode, all of Photoshop Elements's tools and palettes are available to you. In Quick Fix mode, the program's interface is stripped down to just the controls you need to apply fast, automated edits.

Start

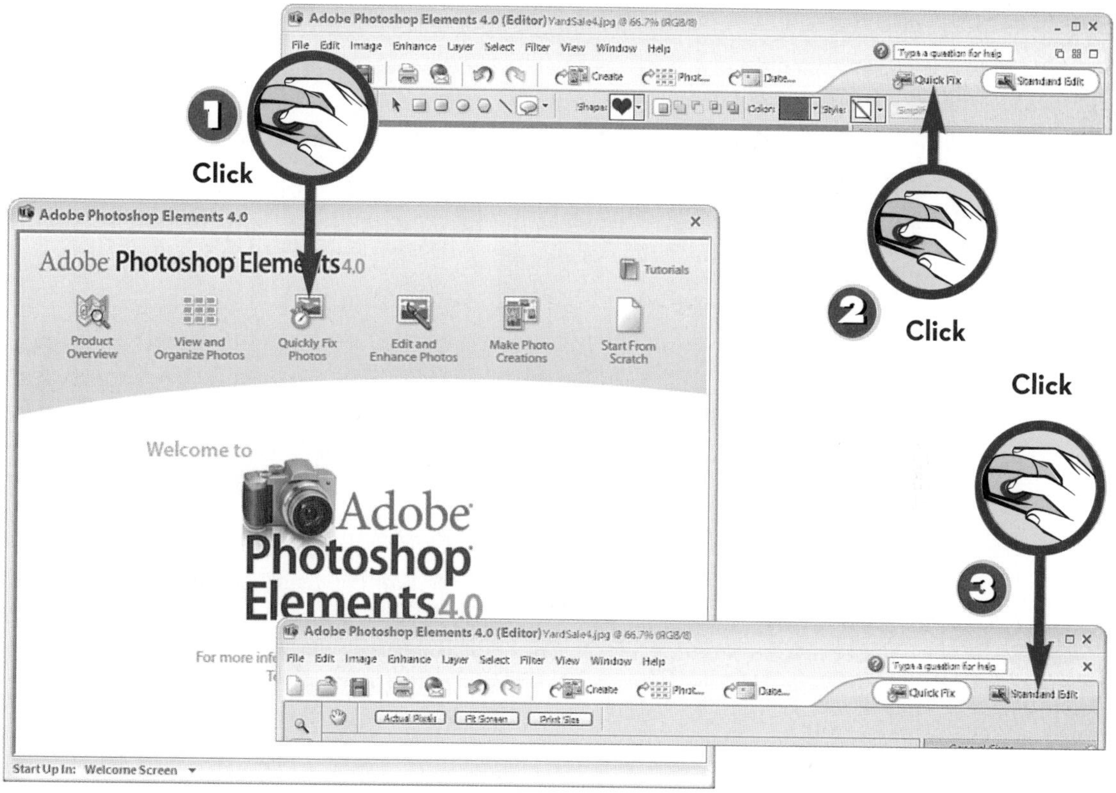

Click

Click

Click

End

1. Click the **Quickly Fix Photos** button on the welcome screen to get to Quick Fix mode, or click the **Edit and Enhance Photos** button to open in Standard Edit mode.
2. When you're in Standard Edit mode, click the **Quick Fix** button to switch to Quick Fix mode.
3. When you're in Quick Fix mode, click the **Standard Edit** button to switch to Standard Edit mode.

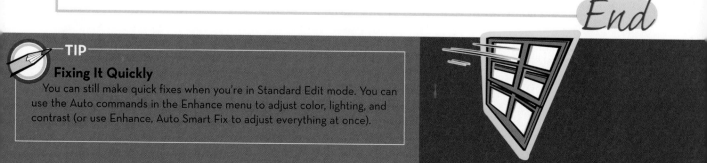

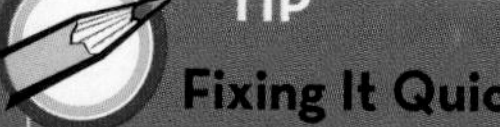

TIP

Fixing It Quickly

You can still make quick fixes when you're in Standard Edit mode. You can use the Auto commands in the Enhance menu to adjust color, lighting, and contrast (or use Enhance, Auto Smart Fix to adjust everything at once).

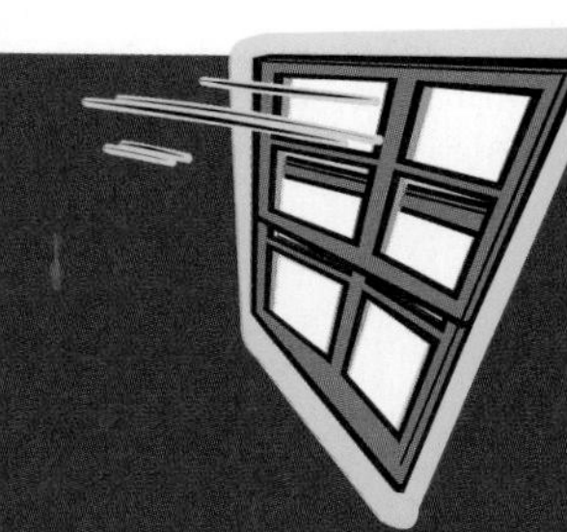

GETTING ADVICE FROM PHOTOSHOP ELEMENTS

Photoshop Elements has a lot of ways to give you suggestions when you can't remember the steps you need to take—or even where to begin. Here's one of the easiest: Just choose a topic from the How To palette and follow the easy instructions.

Start

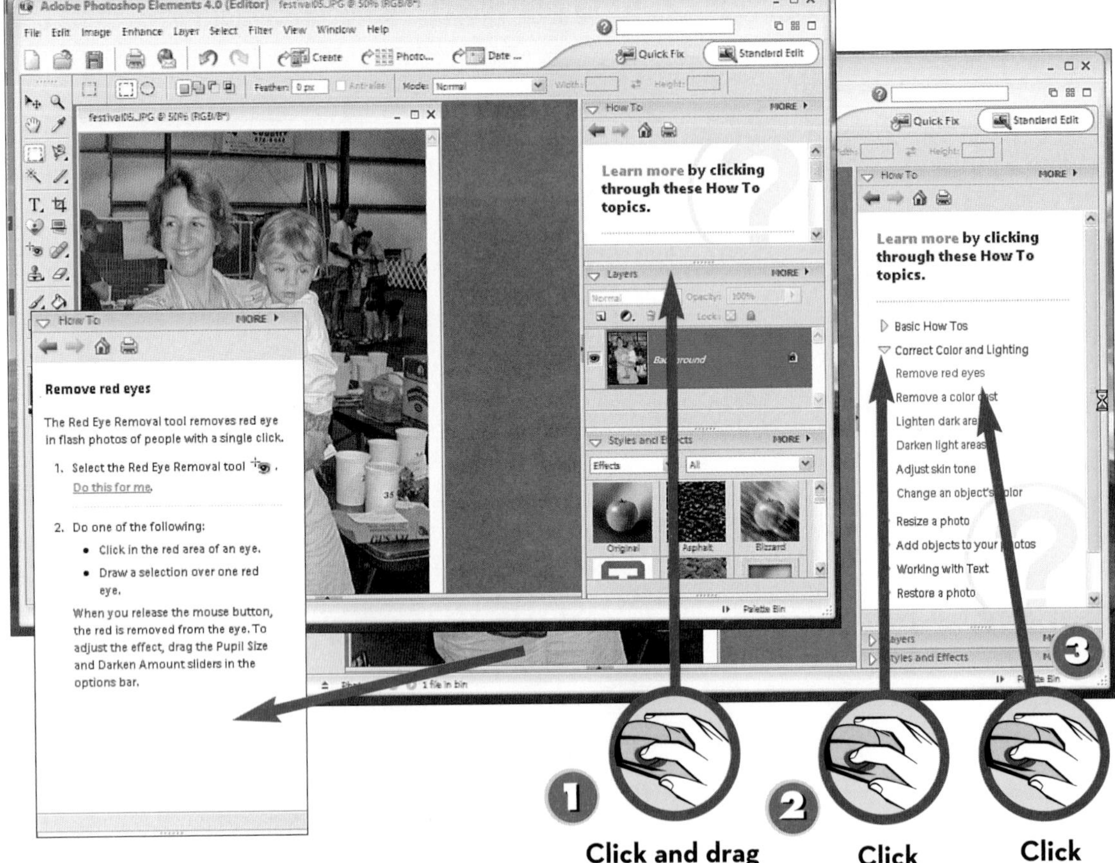

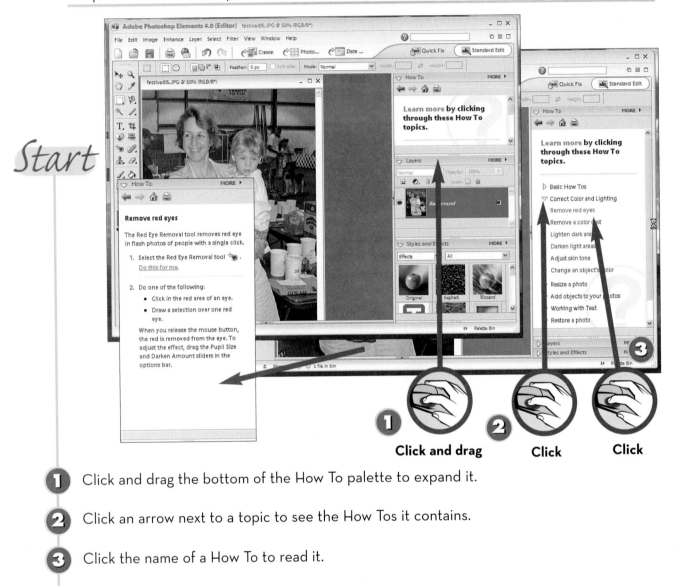

1. Click and drag the bottom of the How To palette to expand it.
2. Click an arrow next to a topic to see the How Tos it contains.
3. Click the name of a How To to read it.

End

NOTE

First Things First

Before you can follow the How To's steps, you must have a picture open in the active image area. Otherwise, you'll know what to do but lose the benefit of being able to apply the advice immediately.

TIP

Even Easier

When you see **Do this for me** in a How To, click it to have Photoshop Elements complete that step. For example, in the Remove Red Eyes How To, clicking **Do this for me** in Step 1 will switch to the Red Eye Removal tool.

TAKING A TUTORIAL

Photoshop Elements has online lessons for several of the program's basic concepts. Try working through these clear explanations of how to get photos into Elements and what to do with them once they're there.

Start

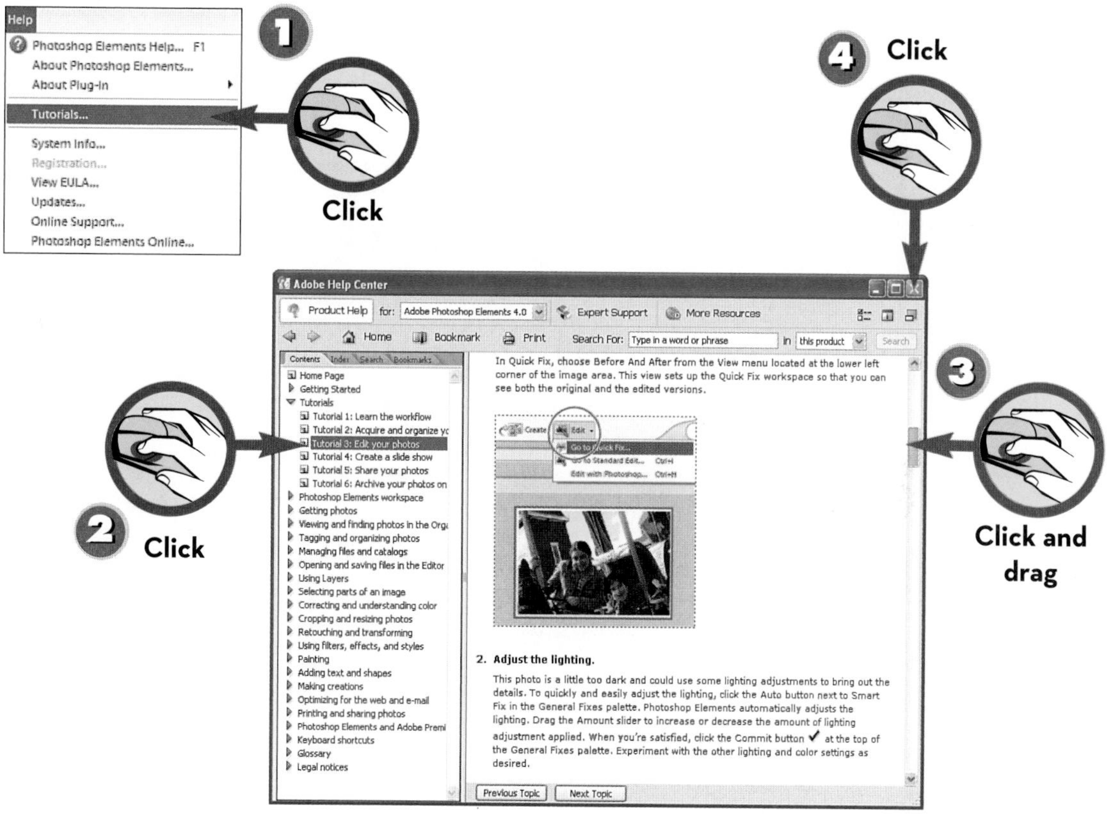

1. From the menu bar, choose **Help, Tutorials**.
2. In the Help window, click the title of the lesson you want.
3. Drag the **scrollbar** to read through the lesson.
4. When you're done, close the Help window to return to the program work area.

End

TIP

Choose from the Index

If you don't see a lesson on the topic you want, look in the How To palette, or choose **Help, Photoshop Elements Help**. Then click Index and choose a topic from the alphabetized list.

SETTING YOUR OWN PREFERENCES

These steps show you where to look if you want to customize how Photoshop Elements shows things in the work area, how it saves files, and other options. As just one of many options, these steps explain how to change the unit of measure in the work area from inches to centimeters.

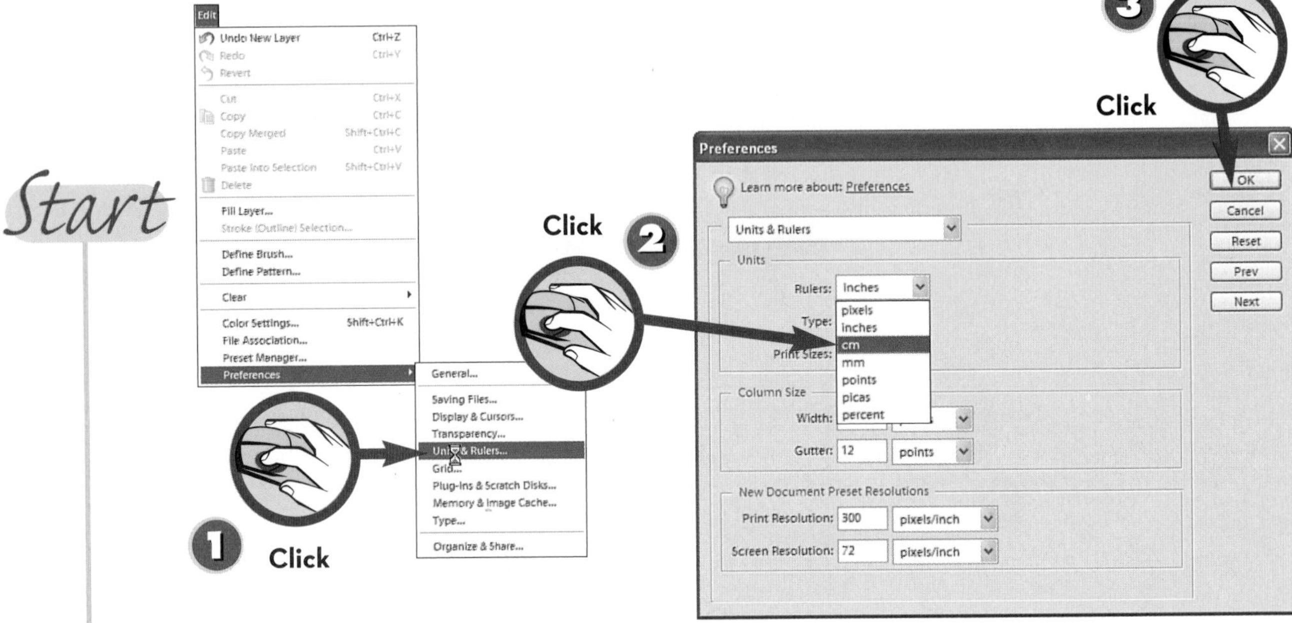

1. From the menu bar, choose **Edit**, **Preferences** and choose one of the commands from the submenu.
2. Set the options you want to change. For example, choose **cm** from the **Rulers** pop-up menu to change the unit of measure from inches to centimeters
3. Click **OK**.

End

NOTE

Default Settings

Default settings should work fine for most people. Experiment with the settings as you get more comfortable with the software. You might find you can improve your efficiency by changing a preference if you're always having to change a setting manually.

TIP

Restore Defaults

To restore default settings, restart the program and, as it's loading, press **Alt+Ctrl+Shift** and click an option in the opening screen. In the dialog box, click **Yes**.

SAVING YOUR WORK

All the work you do on a picture in Photoshop Elements will be lost unless you save the file to disk. If you are saving a file for the first time, you can simply click the **Save** button on the Shortcuts bar or press **Ctrl+S** on the keyboard. If you need to save a file to another location or under a new name, these steps show you how.

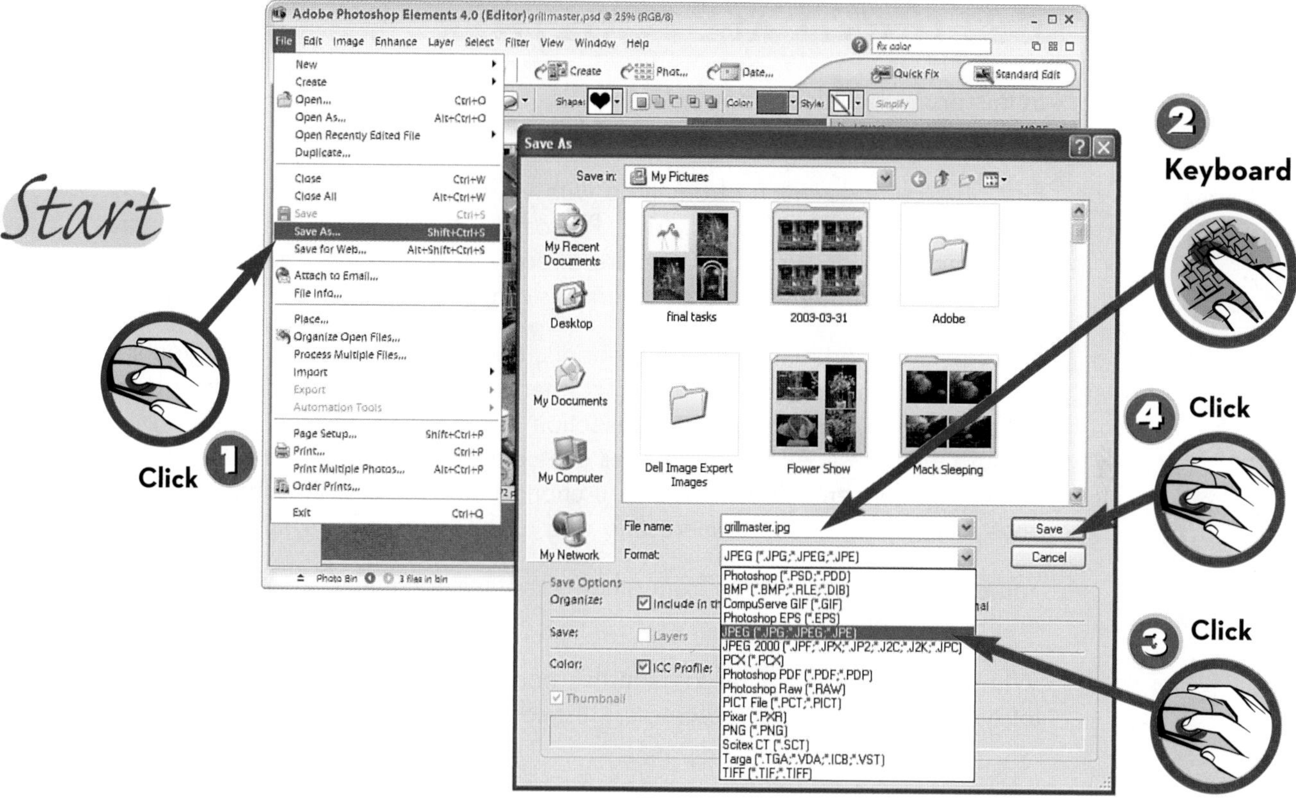

1. To save a file to a different drive or folder or with a different name, choose **File**, **Save As** from the menu bar or press **Shift+Ctrl+S**.
2. Type a name for the new file, such as **grillmaster**. (No need to type the extension, such as **.jpg**.)
3. Optionally, choose and option from the **Format** pop-up menu to change the file type.
4. Use the **Save In** pop-up menu to store the file in a different folder or on a different drive. Click **Save**.

End

NOTE

File Types

You can keep digital snapshots in the format the camera makes, usually JPEG (**.jpg**) files. But if you want more flexibility in editing them later and the best image quality, it's better to save them as Photoshop (**.psd**) files.

NOTE

Digital Negatives

If your computer can burn CDs, save your unedited camera originals to discs. These are your digital "negatives." That way, if you make changes to an image on your hard drive, you still have a copy of the untouched original.

part 2

GETTING IT ALL TOGETHER

In this part, you'll learn how to bring pictures into your computer so you can work with them in Photoshop Elements.

First, you can't do much of anything with your pictures until they exist as digital files on your computer's hard drive. Photos you take with your digital camera, DV camcorder, or camera phone are already stored as files, but you'll need to transfer them from the camera's internal storage to a disk in the computer.

You can also work with film shots—prints, negatives, and slides—but you'll have to *digitize* them first. That's what a scanner does. It scans a print with a beam of light, breaking the image into a collection of individual colored dots, or *pixels* (picture elements). All digital images are composed of pixels, and the main thing Photoshop Elements does is help you change the colors of thousands or even millions of pixels at once, in interesting and useful ways.

You can also grab pictures from other computer documents and from Web pages on the Internet.

Whether you use the other tasks in this book to work with your shots a little or a lot, you'll also learn how to create finished images as prints or contact sheets.

THE INS AND OUTS OF DIGITAL PHOTOGRAPHY

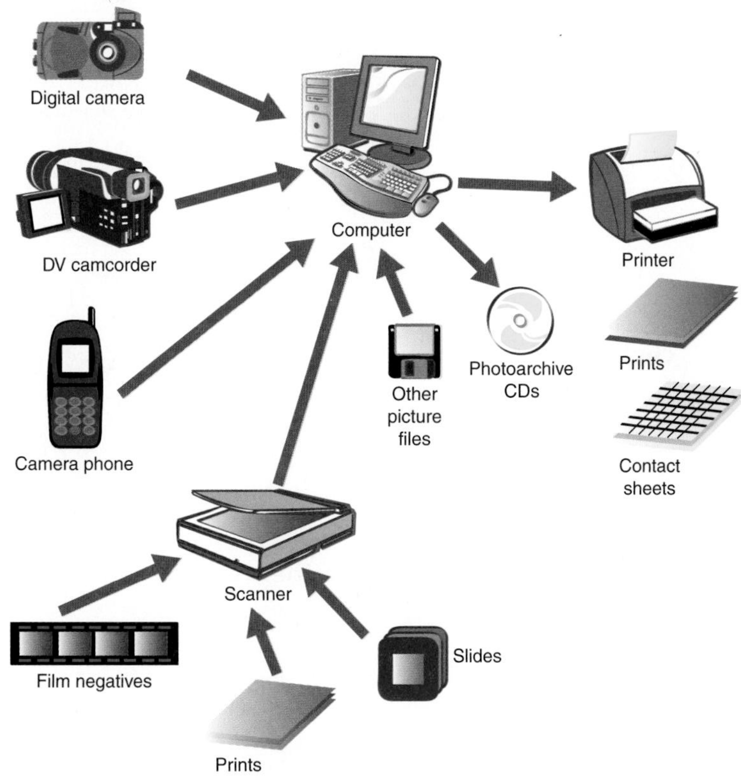

MOVING IMAGES FROM CAMERA TO YOUR COMPUTER

Most digital cameras and camera phones come with their own software for browsing image files and uploading them to your computer. However, you can use the steps described here to transfer files from most digital picture devices using the built-in functions of Photoshop Elements.

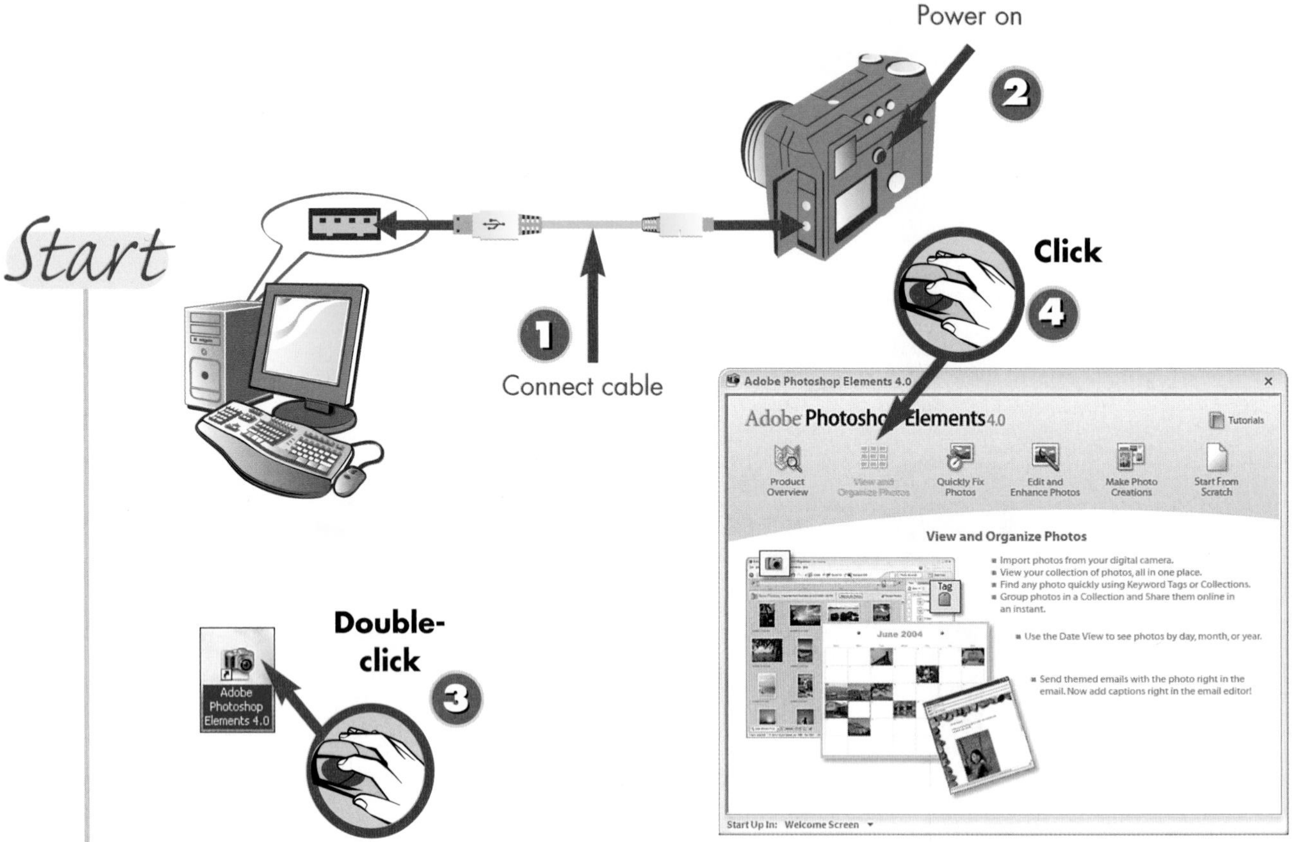

1. Connect the smaller end of the data cable to the camera, and the larger end to the USB port of your PC.
2. Turn the camera power on.
3. Double-click the program icon on the Windows Desktop to start Photoshop Elements.
4. In the Welcome screen, click **View and Organize Photos**.

Continued

TIP

Getting There from Here

If you're already working in Photoshop Elements when you want to import photos, click the **Photo Browser** button in the Editor's shortcuts bar.

TIP

What's in a Name?

Photoshop Elements automatically puts your images into a folder it names with the current date and time. You can specify a different name for the folder by clicking New Name and typing the name you want to use.

5. Choose **Camera** or **Card Reader** in the **Get Photos from** menu in the Shortcuts bar.
6. Choose your camera from the pop-up menu.
7. Click the boxes under the thumbnails to select the photos you want to import.
8. Click **Get Photos**.

End

TIP

Let Me See Your ID

If you use filenames to identify photos (such as when you're printing contact sheets), check the **Rename Files to** box and type a word or two in the text field. Elements renames the images with that text, plus a number.

TIP

Alphabet Soup

Cameras generate filenames automatically. For example: Pmdd0000.jpg, where P = still photo, m = single-digit month (1-9, A-C), dd = two-digit day, and an image number (0001-9999).

SCANNING IMAGES

Scanning and storing your old snapshots in your computer is not only a wonderful way to reduce clutter and organize those shoeboxes full of prints—but also Photoshop Elements has lots of ways to bring back faded color, touch up complexions, and even erase uninvited guests.

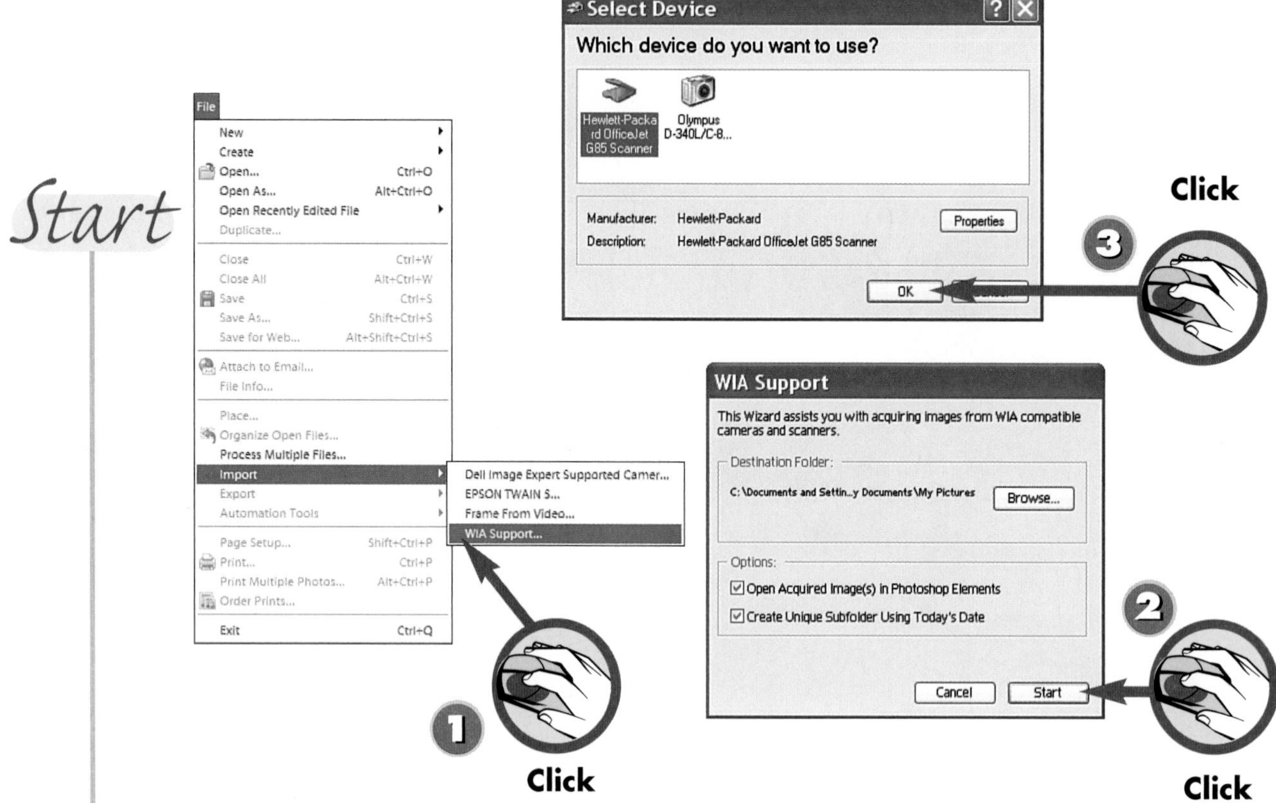

1. With the item to be scanned on the scanner glass and the lid closed, open Photoshop Elements and choose **File**, **Import**, **WIA Support** or the name of your scanner, if it's shown.
2. Click **Start**.
3. When using WIA Support, if you have more than one camera or scanner attached to your computer, choose the scanning device you want to use, and click **OK**.

Continued

NOTE

Final Destination

These steps create a file automatically. Specify the disk location in the Destination Folder field of the WIA Support dialog box. Be sure to resave the file if you edit the image.

TIP

Not My Type

The WIA (Windows Image Acquisition) Support feature scans a photo as a Windows bitmap (.bmp extension) by default. To change the file type, choose File, Save As and change the Format after the image has been imported.

Click

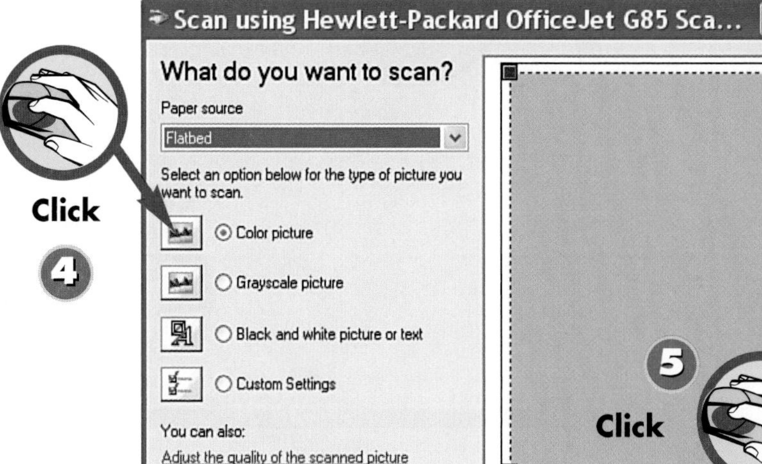

Click

1. Choose the type of picture, such as **Color Picture**.
2. Click **Scan**. The scanned print appears in the active image area, ready for editing.
3. After you edit the picture, click the Save button to save your work.

End

TIP

Scanning Secrets

The dialog box in step 5 might look different, depending on your scanner model. When adjusting quality, you can choose grayscale instead of black and white to capture shading. Use color instead of grayscale if a monochrome picture is sepia. For photos you might want to print later, set the resolution to 300 dpi.

GRABBING A VIDEO FRAME

Photoshop Elements can't capture still photos from uploaded DV files (.mov extension), but you can follow these steps to capture one or more stills as the camcorder plays back a tape, which achieves the same result.

DV

Start

Switch to Playback 2

1 Connect cable

File
New
Create
Open... Ctrl+O
Open As... Alt+Ctrl+O
Open Recently Edited File
Duplicate...
Close Ctrl+W
Close All Alt+Ctrl+W
Save Ctrl+S
Save As... Shift+Ctrl+S
Save for Web... Alt+Shift+Ctrl+S
Attach to Email...
File Info...
Place...
Organize Open Files...
Process Multiple Files...
Import
Export
Automation Tools
Page Setup... Shift+Ctrl+P
Print... Ctrl+P
Print Multiple Photos... Alt+Ctrl+P
Order Prints...
Exit Ctrl+Q

Dell Image Expert Supported Ca[illegible]er...
WIA-Canon DV Camcorder...
EPSON TWAIN 5...
Frame From Video...
WIA Support...

Click 3

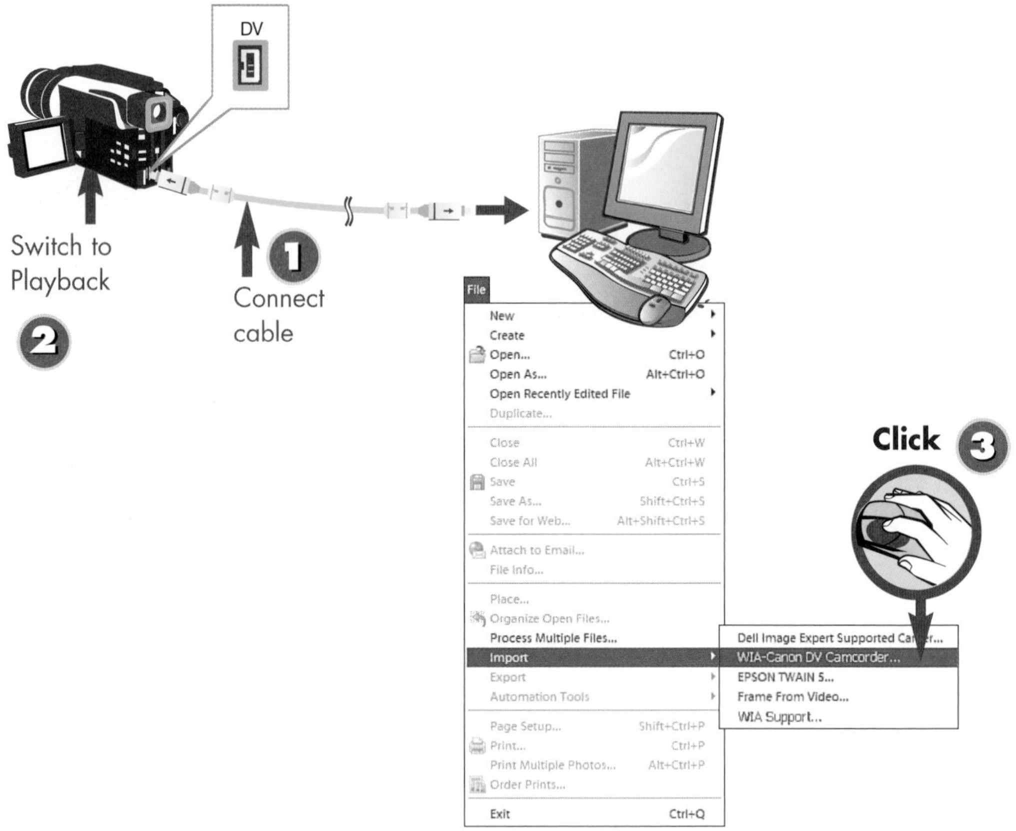

1. Connect the smaller end of the data cable to the camcorder, and the larger end to the FireWire port of your PC.
2. Switch the camcorder to **Playback** (or VCR) mode.
3. From the Photoshop Elements menu bar, choose **File**, **Import**, **WIA <camera name>**. Press **Play** on the camcorder to roll the tape.

Continued

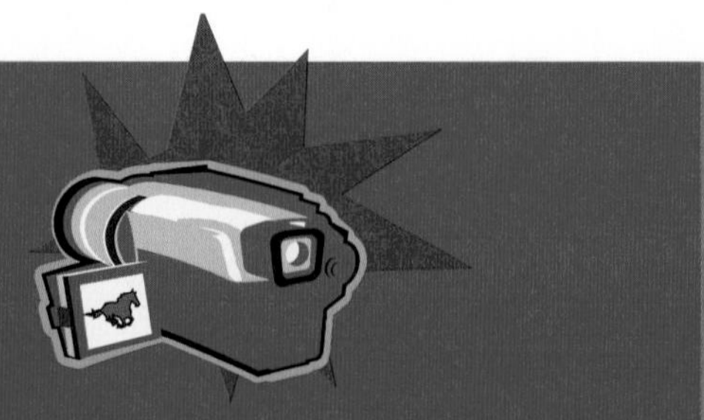

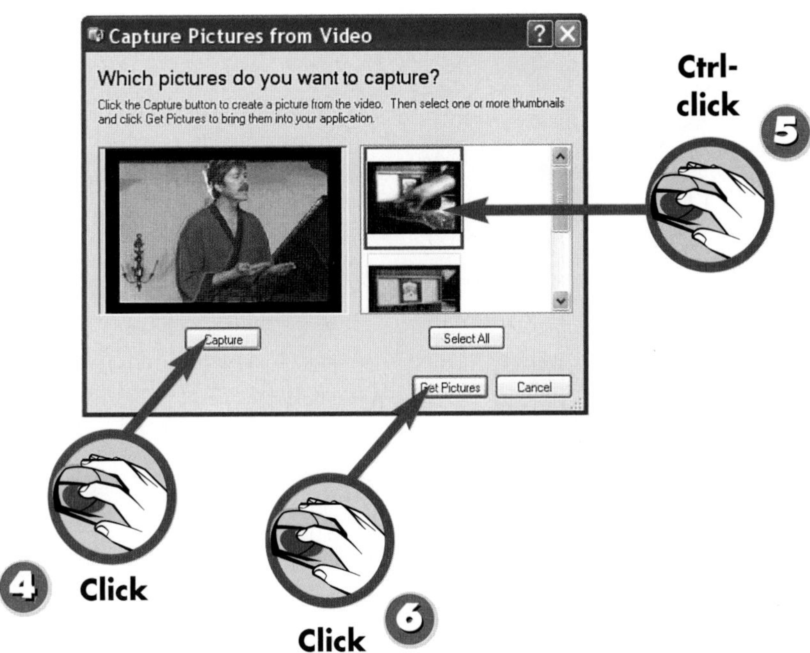

4 Video plays in the preview area on the left. When you see the frame you want, click **Capture**. (Repeat if you want multiple frames.)

5 Press **Ctrl** while you click each thumbnail you want (or click **Select All** to get all of them).

6 Click **Get Pictures**. The video stills open for editing in separate windows in the work area.

End

TIP

Other Options

For these steps to work with your camcorder, it must be a WIA device. If you have an older DV camcorder, upload the clips as video files, use a video editor such as Pinnacle Studio to save as a Windows movie (.wmv), and then choose File, Import, Frame from Video instead.

NOTE

You Must Remember This

Don't forget to click to select all of the images you want to bring into Photoshop Elements in the Capture Pictures dialog box. The ones you don't click will be deleted.

OPENING A PICTURE FROM THE CLIPBOARD

The Windows *Clipboard* is a reserved area of your computer's memory designed specifically for exchanging data—such as photos, drawings, or text—among applications. For example, you can open a document in Microsoft Word, select one of the pictures in it, and copy the image into Photoshop Elements.

Start

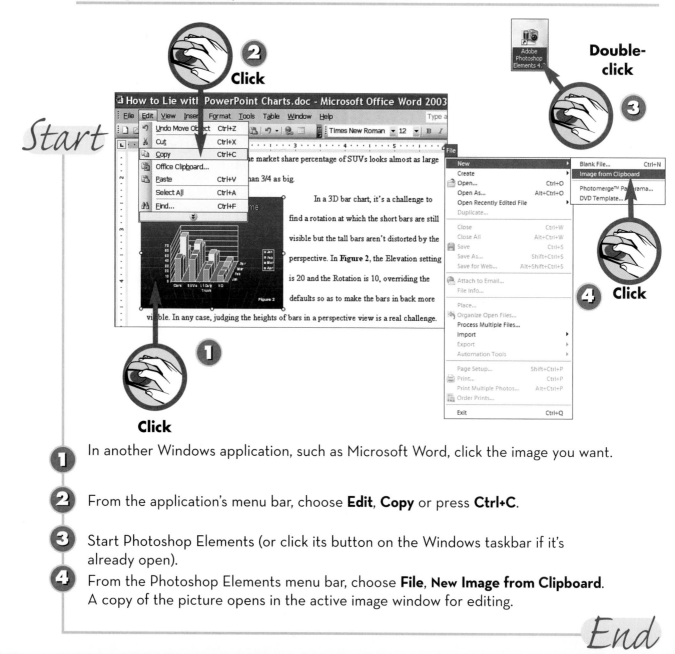

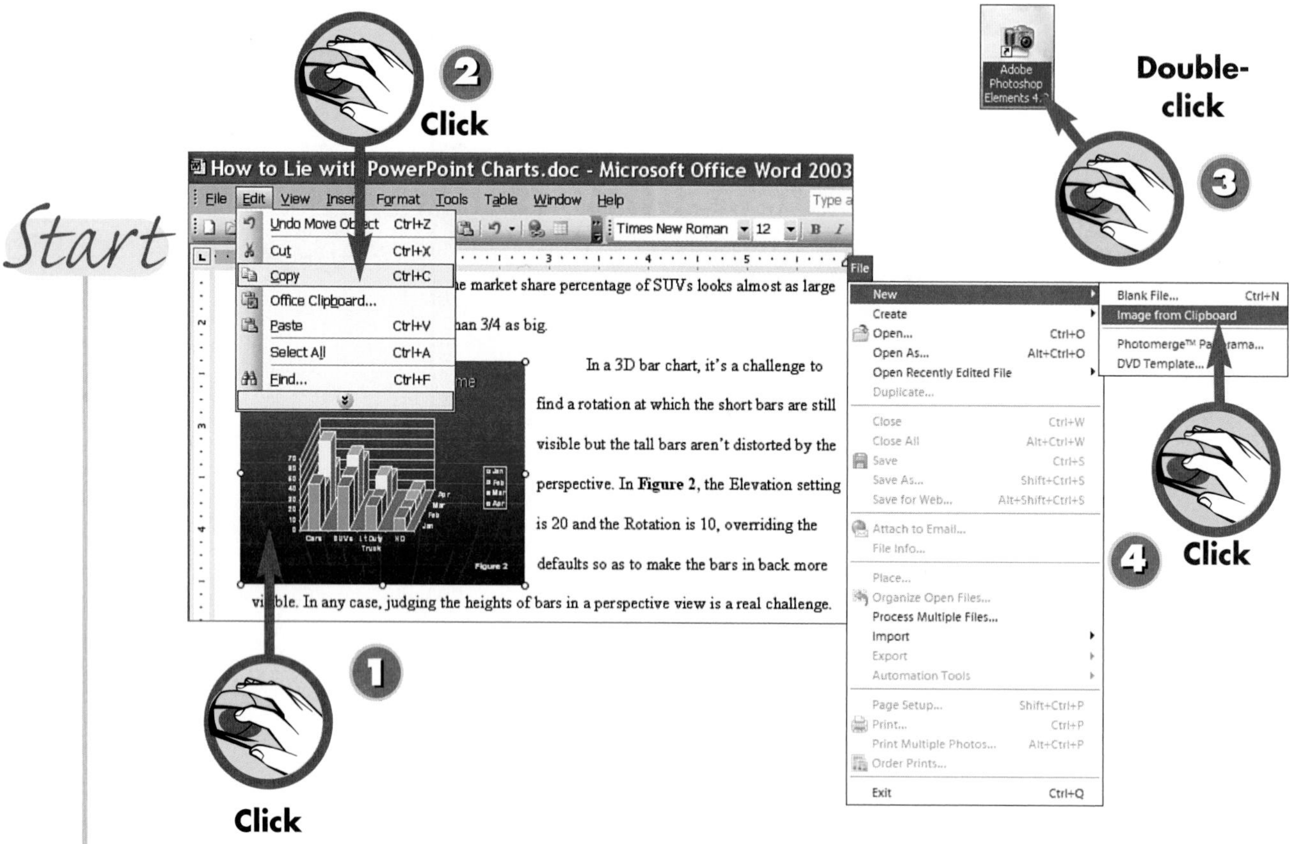

1. In another Windows application, such as Microsoft Word, click the image you want.
2. From the application's menu bar, choose **Edit**, **Copy** or press **Ctrl+C**.
3. Start Photoshop Elements (or click its button on the Windows taskbar if it's already open).
4. From the Photoshop Elements menu bar, choose **File**, **New Image from Clipboard**. A copy of the picture opens in the active image window for editing.

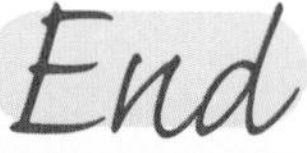

TIP

Native Files

The copied image comes into Photoshop Elements in whatever format it was in the original document, but if you edit it and then try to save, the program will prompt you to save it as a native Photoshop (**.psd**) file. Saving a copy of your image as a **.psd** file is a good idea, as it enables you to continue making edits to the file. If you save as another format, such as **.jpg** or **.gif**, the changes you make are incorporated into the file, and you can no longer undo them.

COPYING A PICTURE FROM A WEB PAGE

Think of the Internet as a global photo library at your fingertips. For example, if you need a photo of the Brooklyn Bridge to illustrate a report, surf to **www.google.com**, click the **Images** tab, and you're sure to find several choices. Then use the steps here to load the image into Photoshop Elements.

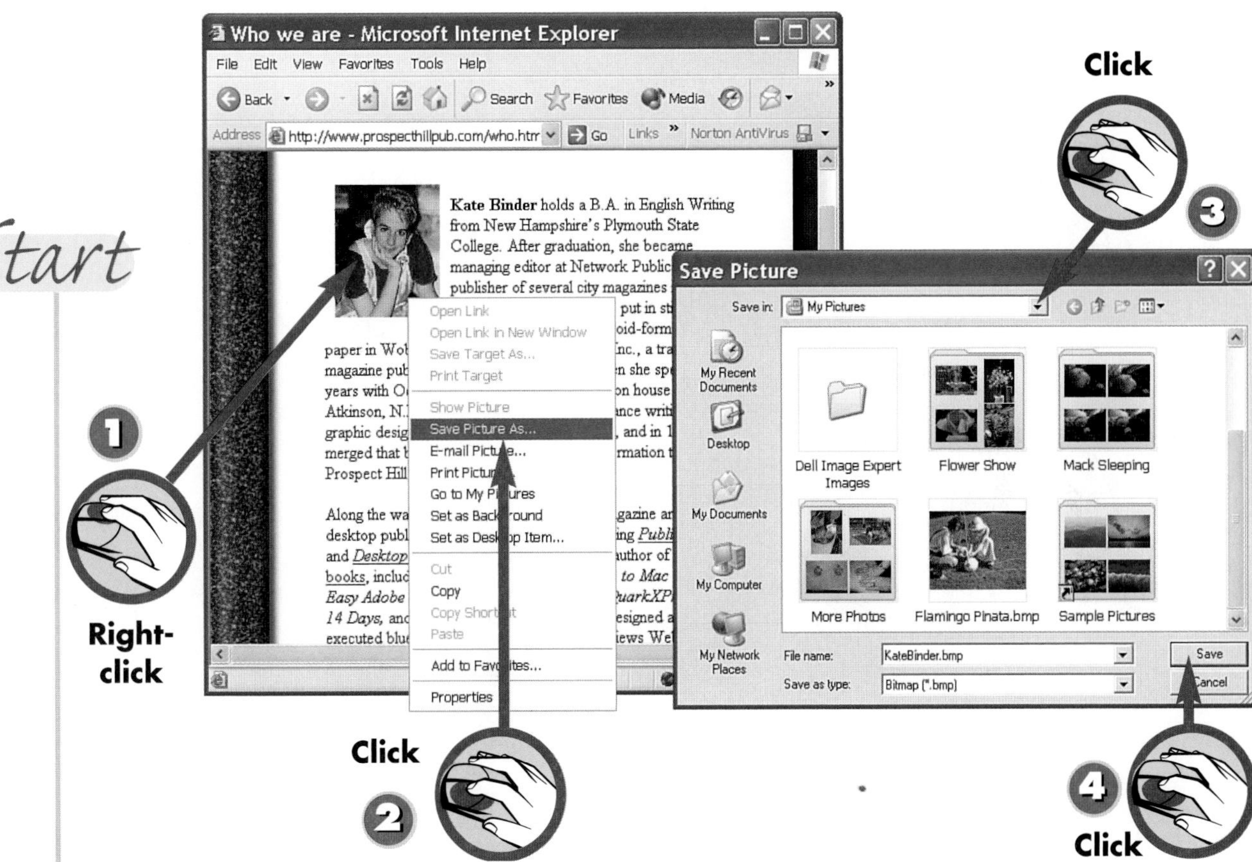

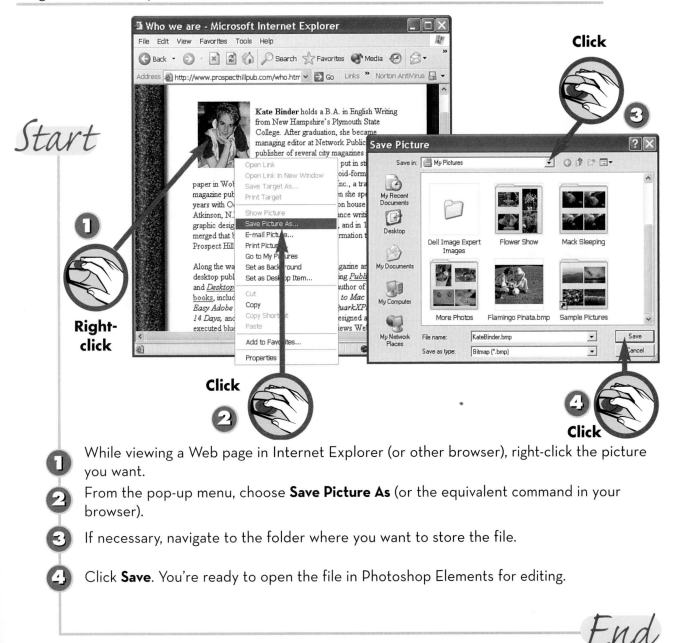

1. While viewing a Web page in Internet Explorer (or other browser), right-click the picture you want.
2. From the pop-up menu, choose **Save Picture As** (or the equivalent command in your browser).
3. If necessary, navigate to the folder where you want to store the file.
4. Click **Save**. You're ready to open the file in Photoshop Elements for editing.

NOTE

Know Your Rights

Photos and artwork on the Web are subject to copyright. Obtain permission from the rights holder before incorporating them in your Web sites, slide-shows, or newsletters.

TIP

A New Name

You can type a new name for the file in the **File Name** box before you choose **Save**. Don't type the extension part or try to change it.

SCANNING A SLIDE

You can scan your old slides much as you do prints. Many scanners have special transparency adapters you can buy, which provide backlight for a brighter, sharper picture. However, you can get good results with these steps, even if you don't have one of these attachments.

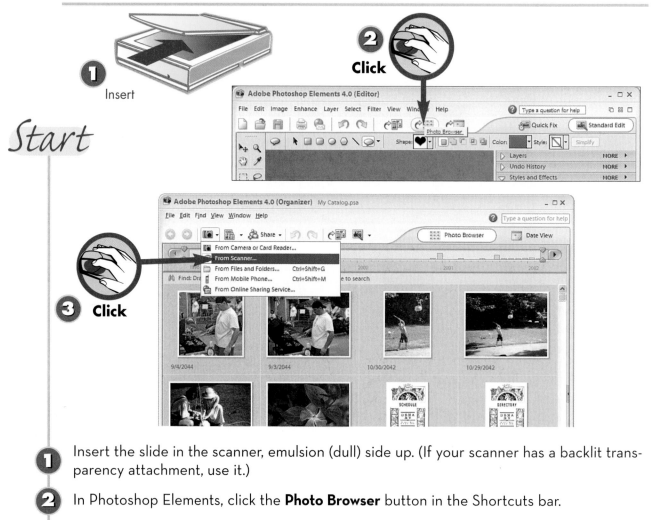

Start

1. Insert the slide in the scanner, emulsion (dull) side up. (If your scanner has a backlit transparency attachment, use it.)
2. In Photoshop Elements, click the **Photo Browser** button in the Shortcuts bar.
3. In the Organizer, click the **Get Photos** button and choose From Scanner in the pop-up menu. Elements automatically detects your scanner and starts up the scanner software.

Continued

NOTE

Clean Glass

Start by cleaning the scanner glass. Take color slides out of their paper or plastic mounts so they lie flat. For tips on scanning negatives, look at the next task, "Making a Positive from a Negative."

TIP

Another Route

You can also do the steps described here with the menu commands File, Import, WIA Support or File, Import, WIA-<scanner name>.

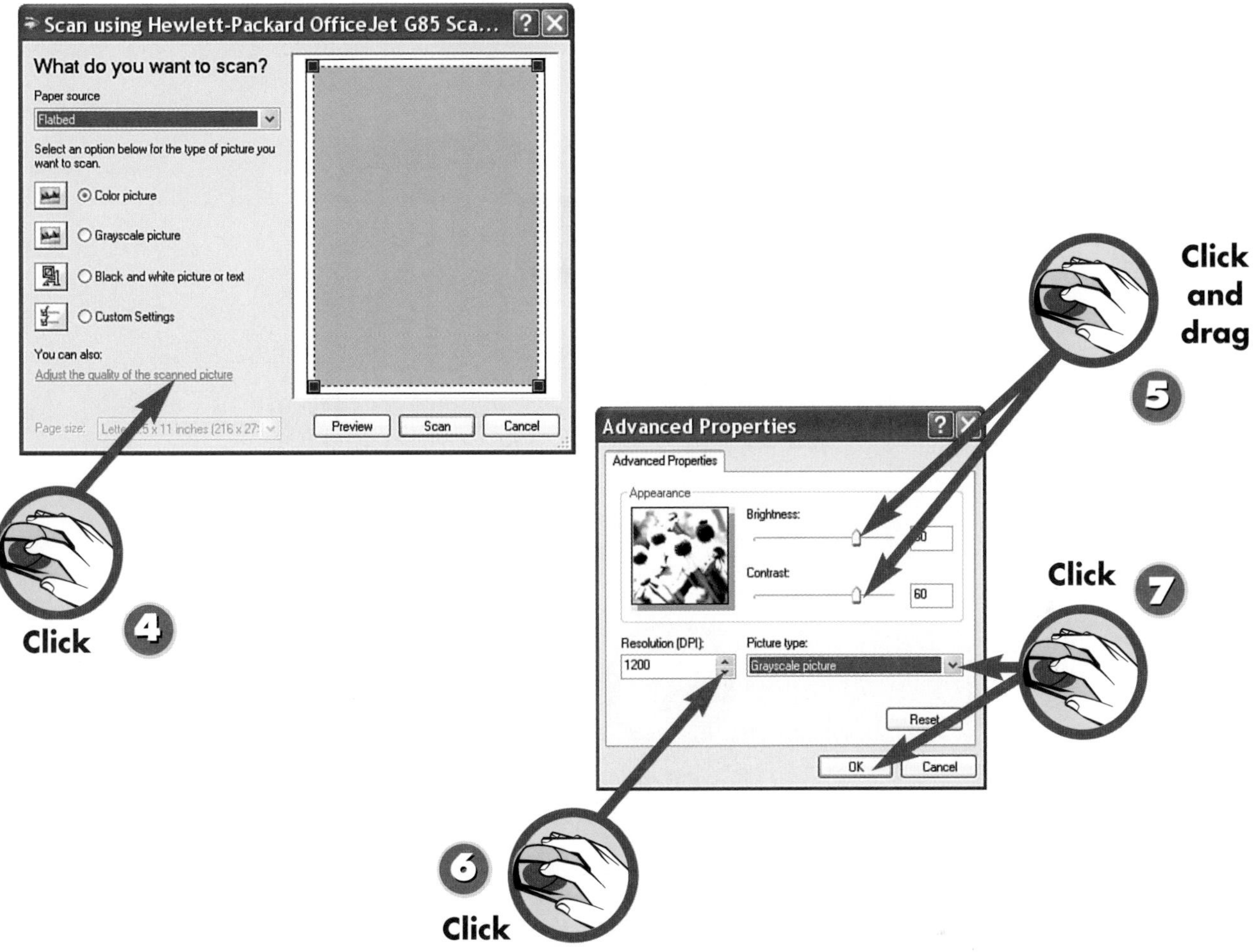

4. Click **Adjust the Quality of the Scanned Picture** (or its equivalent; the dialog box for your scanner might look different).
5. Increase the values of **Brightness** and **Contrast**, especially if you don't have a transparency attachment.
6. Increase the **Resolution** to at least **300 dpi** or more.
7. In the **Picture Type** pop-up menu, choose **Grayscale Picture** for black-and-white originals with shading, or **Color**, and click OK.

Continued

NOTE

It's Not All Black and White

In step 7, avoid the Black and White setting. The only time you'd use it would be for scanning line art, drawings, and text that have no shading.

TIP

Setting the DPI

In step 6, the smaller the transparency, the higher the dpi setting should be. For 35mm color slides, set the Resolution as high as it will go—1200 dpi on this scanner.

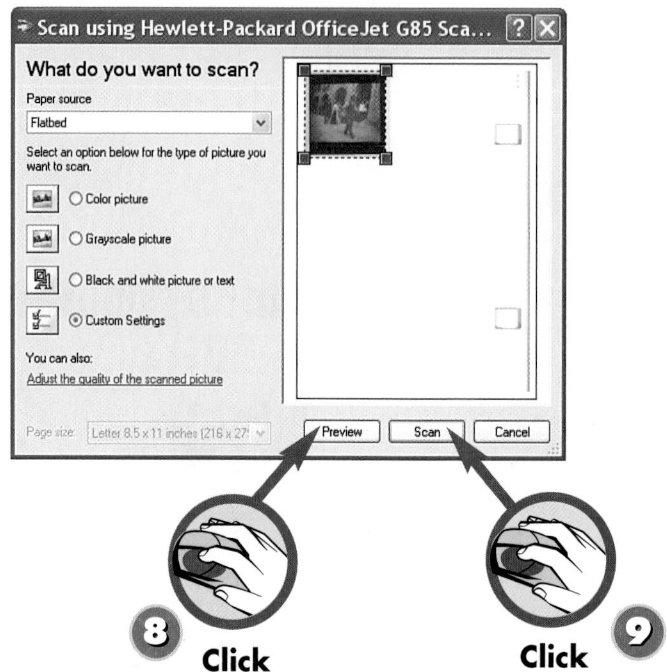

8. Click **Preview** (repeat steps 5–7 and adjust until the preview image looks right).

9. Click **Scan**. The scanned picture appears in the active image window.

End

NOTE

Making Adjustments

Adjusting brightness and contrast can help compensate for not having an adapter to backlight the transparency. Get the best image you can in step 9, and then you can make further adjustments after the picture is in Photoshop Elements.

NOTE

Outside Help

If you have a lot of slides, you might consider having your local photo lab convert them all to a photo CD. It'll save you the time and hassle of scanning them individually, and you'll have high-quality digital files.

RESIZING AND PRINTING AN IMAGE

Photoshop Elements reports the current print size of the image in the lower-left corner of the work area. With these few steps, you can resize the image to fit exactly on the printed page. This method uses the default paper size currently set for the printer.

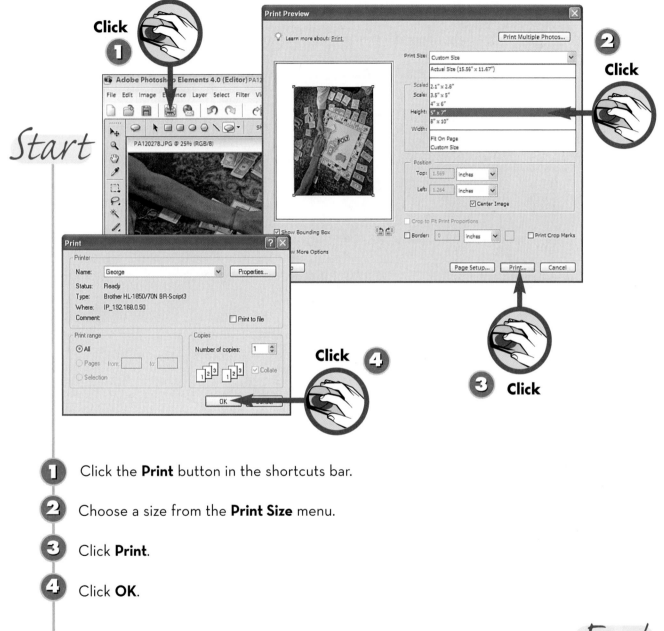

1. Click the **Print** button in the shortcuts bar.
2. Choose a size from the **Print Size** menu.
3. Click **Print**.
4. Click **OK**.

End

TIP

Switch Orientations

The default printer orientation is Portrait (long side vertical). To switch to Landscape (long side horizontal), after step 2, click the **Page Setup** button, choose **Landscape**, click **OK**, and then go to step 3.

NOTE

Glossy Prints

For the best-quality prints on a color inkjet printer, use glossy photo paper. Remove the plain paper and feed just one sheet at a time, because the glossy surface can stick to other sheets and cause jams.

ADDING A WHITE BORDER TO YOUR PRINTS

A good way to add a white border to your prints, even when you're using a borderless printer, involves resizing the image to be smaller than the canvas (paper) size by the amount of the margin you want, and centering the image on the canvas.

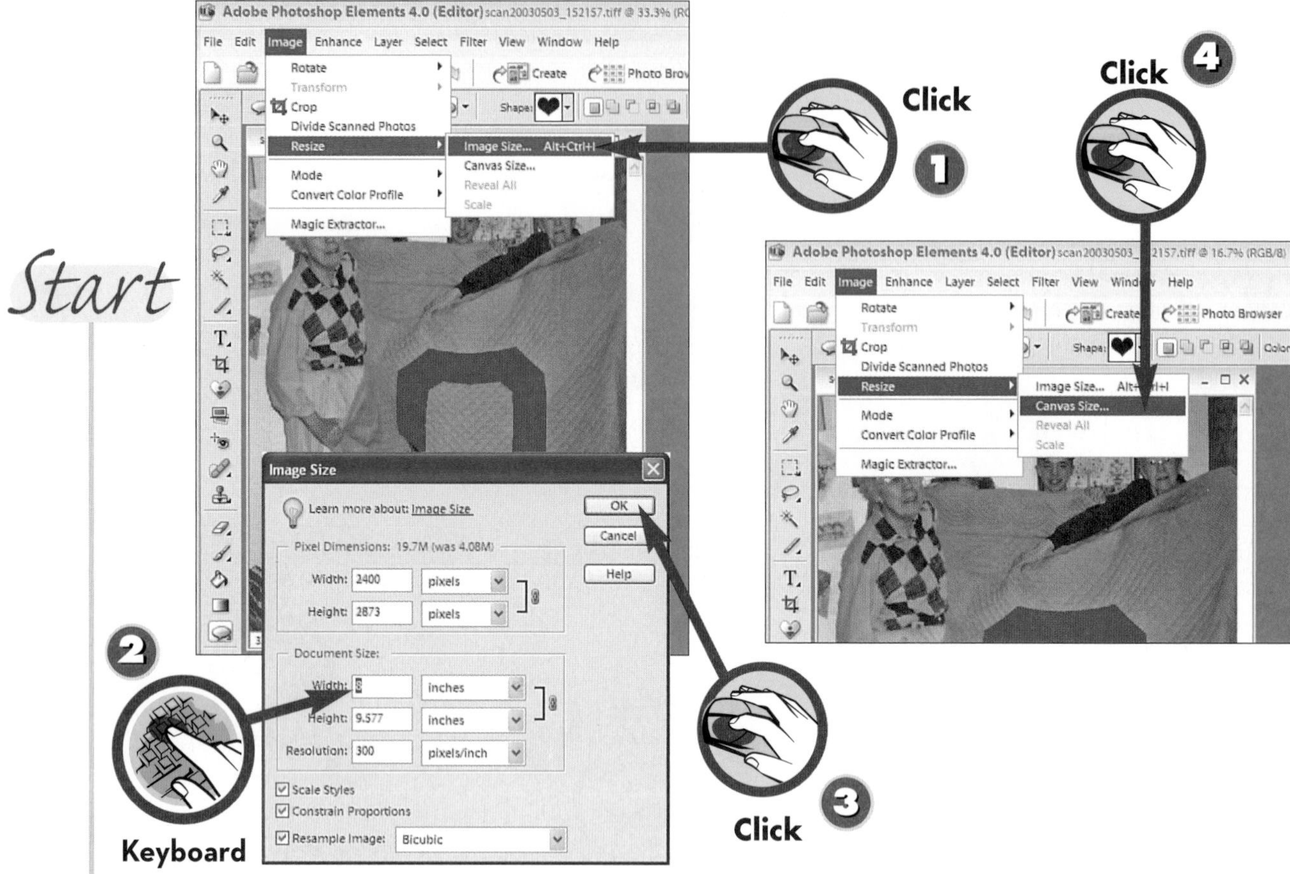

1. With a picture in the active image area, choose **Image**, **Resize**, **Image Size**.
2. Type the new image width, such as **8** inches.
3. Click **OK**.
4. Choose **Image**, **Resize**, **Canvas Size**.

Continued

TIP

When to Resample

In step 2, check **Resample Image** and increase the resolution if the number in the Resolution field is less than 150. To avoid distorting the image, let the program calculate the height.

TIP

Yet Another Way

To add a white border without resizing the canvas, choose **File**, **Print Preview**. Check the **Show More Options** check box; then click the **Border** button. You can specify the width of the border in inches, millimeters, or points.

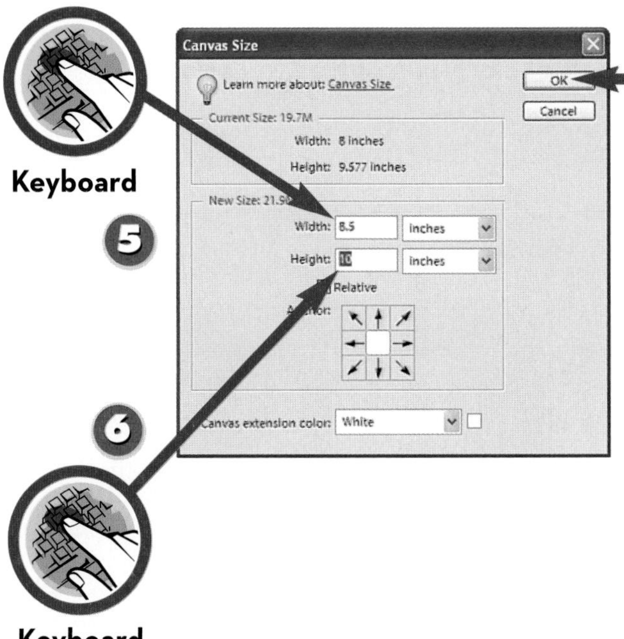

5 In the **Width** box, type the width of the print paper—larger than the image width—such as **8.5** inches.

6 In the **Height** box, type the height of the paper, such as **10.5** inches.

7 Click **OK**.

8 Load the printer with photo paper and click **Print**.

End

NOTE

Note the Printable Area

The border becomes part of the image file, so you shouldn't have to adjust print margins as long as the *printable area* of your paper matches the canvas size. Use these steps to add borders to the pictures you print with Picture Package, which uses standard print sizes.

NOTE

What's the Anchor Point?

The *anchor point* indicates the position of the image relative to the canvas edges. The default is centered.

PRINTING CONTACT SHEETS

Professional photographers routinely make contact sheets by printing negatives laid directly on photosensitive paper. Photoshop Elements will generate contact sheets that automatically show thumbnails with labels of any group of files you select.

Start

1. Click the **Photo Browser** button to switch to Organizer.
2. Select the photos you want to include in the contact sheet.
3. Choose Print or press **Ctrl+P**.

Continued

NOTE

Get the Contact

Print and store contact sheets with each of your photo archive CDs. It's a handy way of browsing the images when they're no longer on your hard drive.

TIP

Preview First

Save paper by using the preview area in the Print Selected Photos dialog box to see how many photos appear on the last page of your contact sheets. If there's just one or two, consider reducing the number of columns.

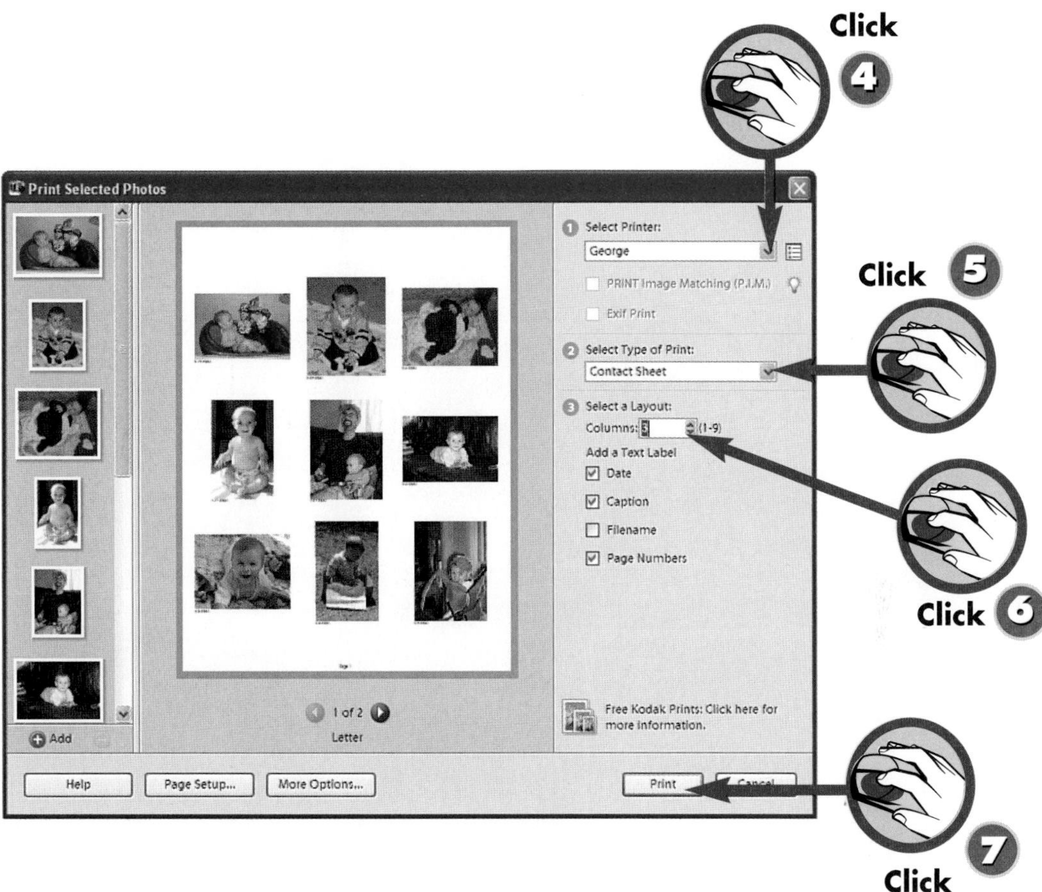

4. Choose a printer.
5. Choose **Contact Sheet** from the **Select Type of Print** menu.
6. Choose a layout, based on the size you want the photos to be on the contact sheet.
7. Load your printer with photo paper and click **Print**.

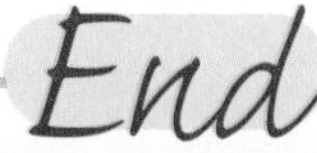

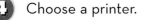

NOTE

Useful Captions

For more descriptive captions, rename camera files in Windows Explorer or in the browser before you generate the sheets.

NOTE

Out of a Jam

The thumbnails of the selected files won't necessarily fit on a single contact sheet. If they don't, Photoshop Elements will print multiple sheets. Remember, to avoid printer jams, load photo paper manually, one sheet at a time.

PRINTING A PICTURE PACKAGE

Professional photographers who shoot annual school photos, weddings, and social events offer their subjects *picture packages*, prints ranging from wallet size to 8×10s for framing. Photoshop Elements will print a variety of assorted sizes for you on a sheet of photo paper. It's sure to please your "customers."

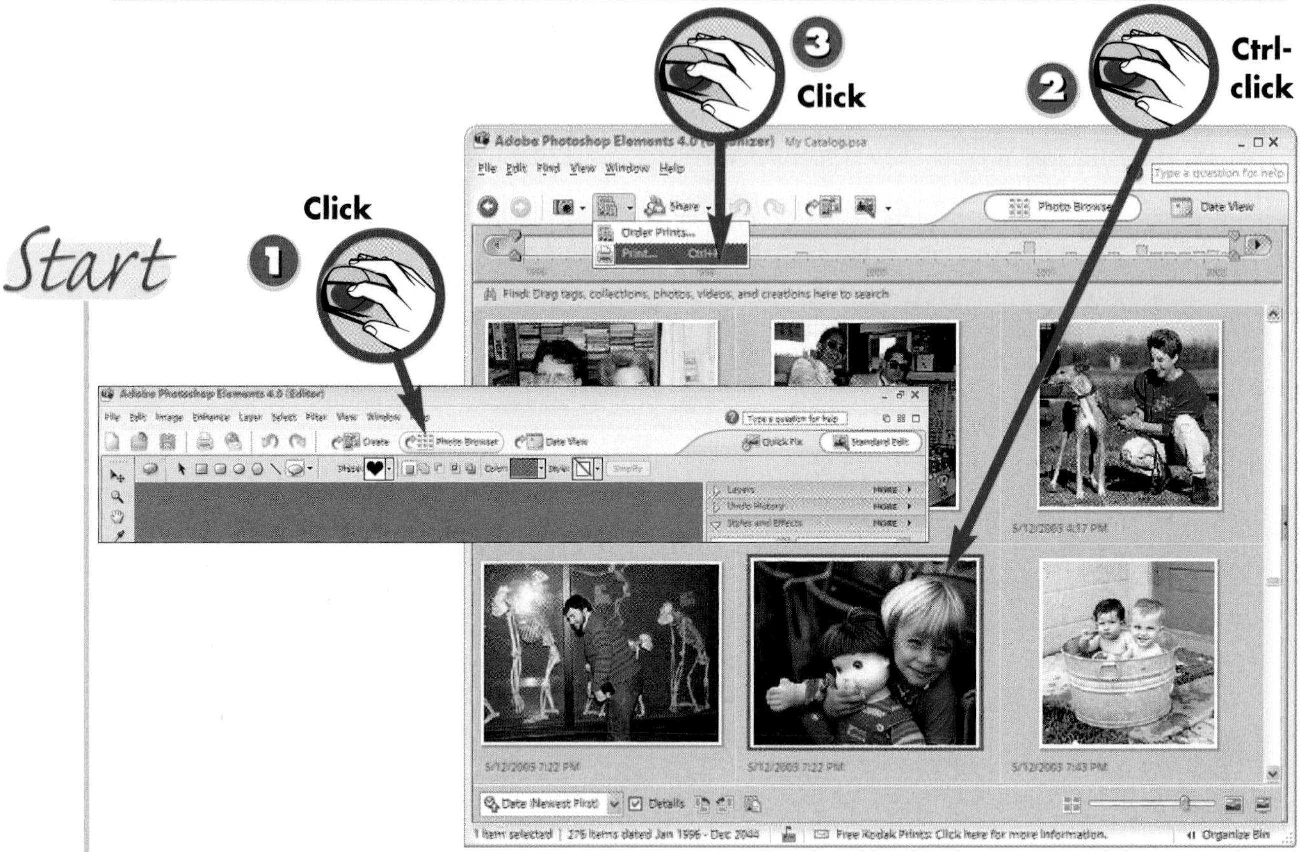

Start

1 Click

2 Ctrl-click

3 Click

1. Click the **Photo Browser** button to switch to Organizer.
2. Select one or more photos to include in the picture package.
3. Click **Print** or press **Ctrl+P**.

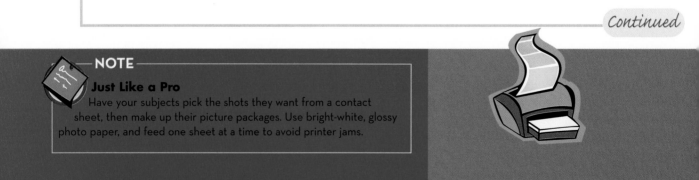

Continued

NOTE

Just Like a Pro

Have your subjects pick the shots they want from a contact sheet, then make up their picture packages. Use bright-white, glossy photo paper, and feed one sheet at a time to avoid printer jams.

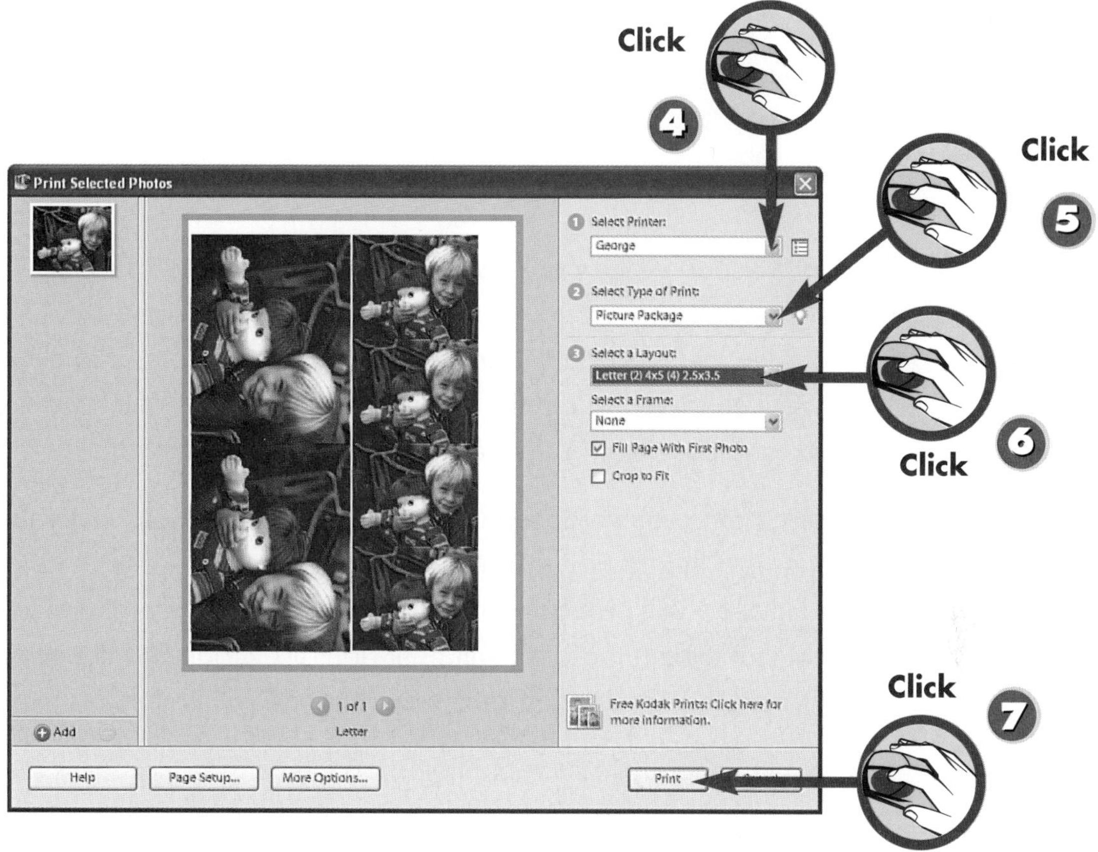

4. Choose a printer.
5. Choose **Picture Package** from the **Select Type of Print** menu.
6. Choose a layout. If you're printing just one photo, check the box marked **Fill Page with First Photo**.
7. Load your printer with photo paper and click **Print**.

TIP

Choose Your Size

If you're printing more than one photo, drag the photos in the preview area to change which photo is used for each size the layout includes.

TIP

Getting Framed

Don't forget to try the frame options available for picture package layouts. They range from actual frames (such as Country) to sophisticated edge treatments (such as Painted Edge).

part 3

BASIC PHOTO FIXING

Think of this part of the book as a comfy family restaurant where you could go for your daily bread and never be bored with the same meal twice. It's just not slick, or complicated, or arty. (Oh, we'll go there, too, eventually.) You'd be well served to return here again and again—but these steps are so quick and easy that to do them once is to know them cold.

Up to this point, you've opened files and printed them out, but you haven't changed how they look very much. If you need to fix a photo, come here first. Your quest will probably end here, and you'll be more than satisfied. The shot that looked too dark will perk right up, crooked will become straight, and that unflattering pallor on her face will become a rosy glow.

A particularly handy feature of Photoshop Elements is the Quick Fix workspace, which gives you single-click access to a variety of commonly needed repairs—with automatic corrections. The first two tasks in this part demonstrate its use.

So, if you have time to do only a few of the tasks in this book, choose some of these. You'll be hooked, and you'll recover a lot of shots you thought were duds.

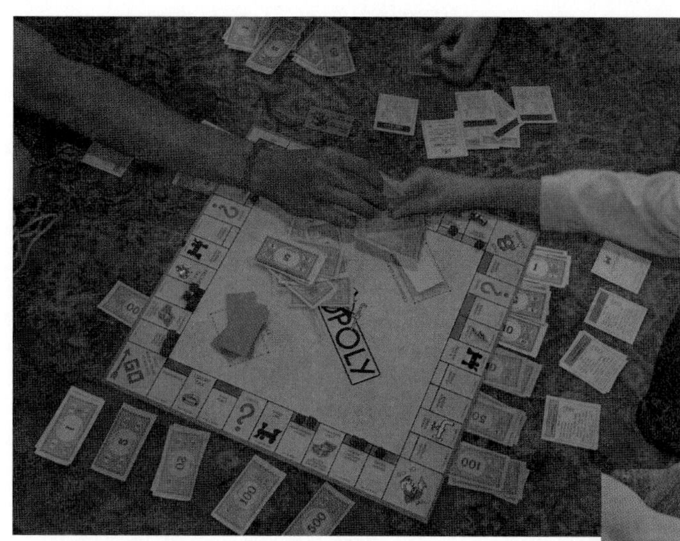

Before

After

MAKING A QUICK FIX

You can use Photoshop Elements's Quick Fix mode as one-stop-shopping for all the commands in the Enhance menu. Get there by clicking the **Quick Fix** button on the shortcuts bar, or by clicking **Quickly Fix Photos** in the Welcome screen.

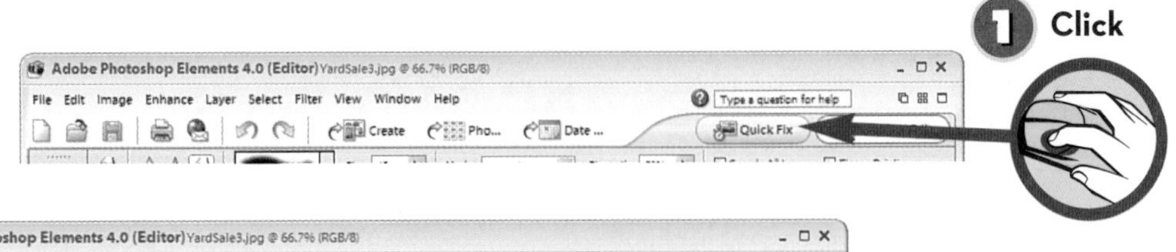

Start

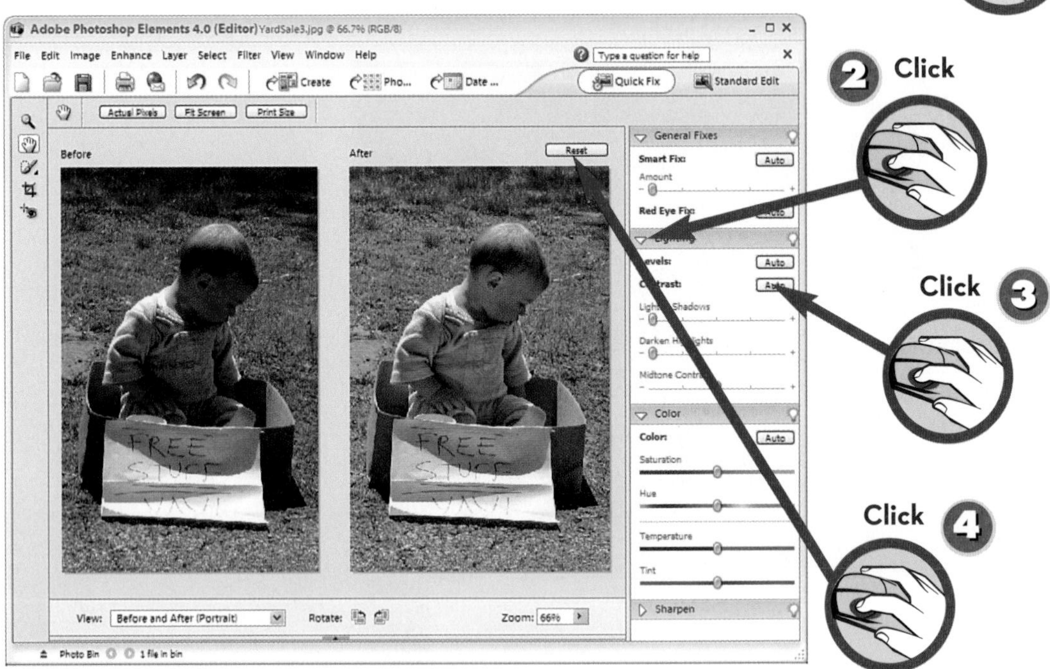

1. With the picture you want to fix in the active image area, click the **Quick Fix** button on the shortcuts bar.
2. Click the disclosure triangle for the section you want to use (such as **Lighting**).
3. Click an **Auto** button (such as **Levels**) to adjust the image; Levels adjusts the picture's balance of dark and light areas.
4. If you don't like the changes Elements makes, click **Reset** to restore the image to its original state.

End

NOTE

Auto and Semi-Auto Fixes

Each Auto adjustment requires just a single click. For more control over the changes being made to your image, use the sliders to determine the amount of modification made to lighting and color and the amount of sharpening (see the next task).

TIP

Don't Like *After?*

Your Quick Fix changes are cumulative, so you can do one, such as Auto Lighting, and then do another, such as a custom amount of sharpening applied with the slider—until the After image is just right.

MAKING A QUICK FIX WITH A SLIDER ADJUSTMENT

Elements's Auto functions are pretty good—but they're not perfect because the program doesn't really know what each image is supposed to look like. Only you know that, which is why you often get better results by adjusting a picture's color, lighting, and sharpness yourself.

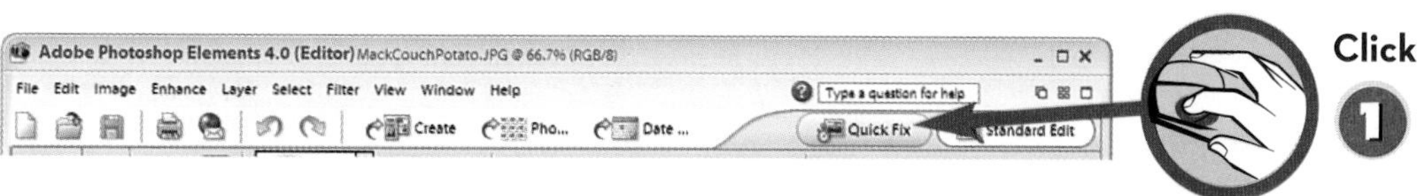

Start

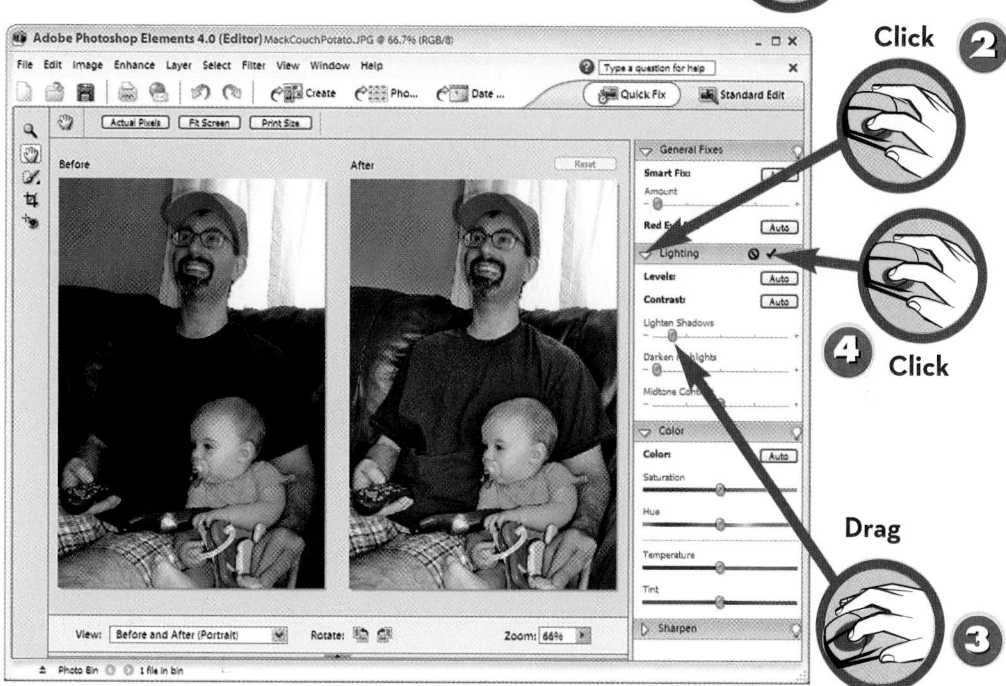

1. With the picture you want to fix in the active image area, click the **Quick Fix** button on the shortcuts bar.
2. Click the disclosure triangle to open the Quick Fix section you want to use.
3. Drag a slider to adjust the image.
4. Click the **Commit** button (✓) when you like the way the After image looks.

End

TIP

Cancel That

Next to the Accept button is a **Cancel** button; click it to remove the effects of the most recent change you made to the picture without reverting completely.

NOTE

The Color of Light

Temperature and Tint sliders can fix bad lighting. For yellowish photos taken under incandescent light, drag the Temperature slider toward Cool; for pictures taken under fluorescent light, Tweak the Tint slider toward the magenta end.

FIXING EVERYTHING

The Smart Fix feature adjusts every aspect of the image, based on Photoshop Elements's idea of what the ideal picture should look like. It's a great way to get an idea of how much improvement you'll be able to make in a photo, even if you opt to use the Reset button and make each adjustment manually for greater control.

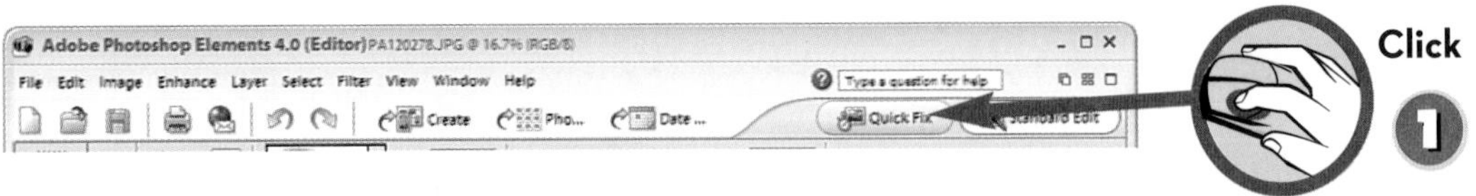

Click 1

Start

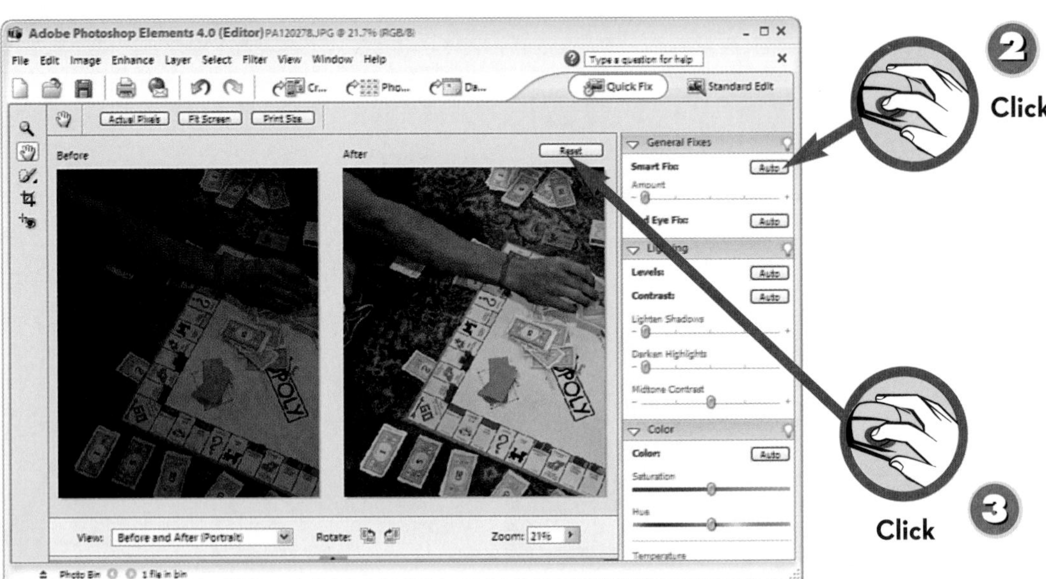

2 Click

Click 3

1. With the picture you want to fix in the active image area, click the **Quick Fix** button on the shortcuts bar.
2. Click the **Auto** button in the General Fixes section to adjust the image's color, lighting, and sharpness all at once.
3. If you don't like the changes Elements makes, click **Reset** to restore the image to its original state.

End

NOTE

More Fun with Quick Fix

In addition to the quick fixes shown here, you can also crop pictures and remove red-eye in Quick Fix mode by using the Crop and Red Eye Removal tools at the left side of the work area.

NOTE

Getting a Good View

Use the Zoom and Hand tools at the left of the work area to zoom in and out and move the picture around. That way, you can get a good idea of how your changes are affecting different areas of the image.

UNDOING YOUR MISTAKES

Don't think of any photo-fixing decisions you make as mistakes, for two good reasons: You can always undo them, and experimenting is the only way to learn what works and what doesn't. So, click away—you have nothing to lose but playtime!

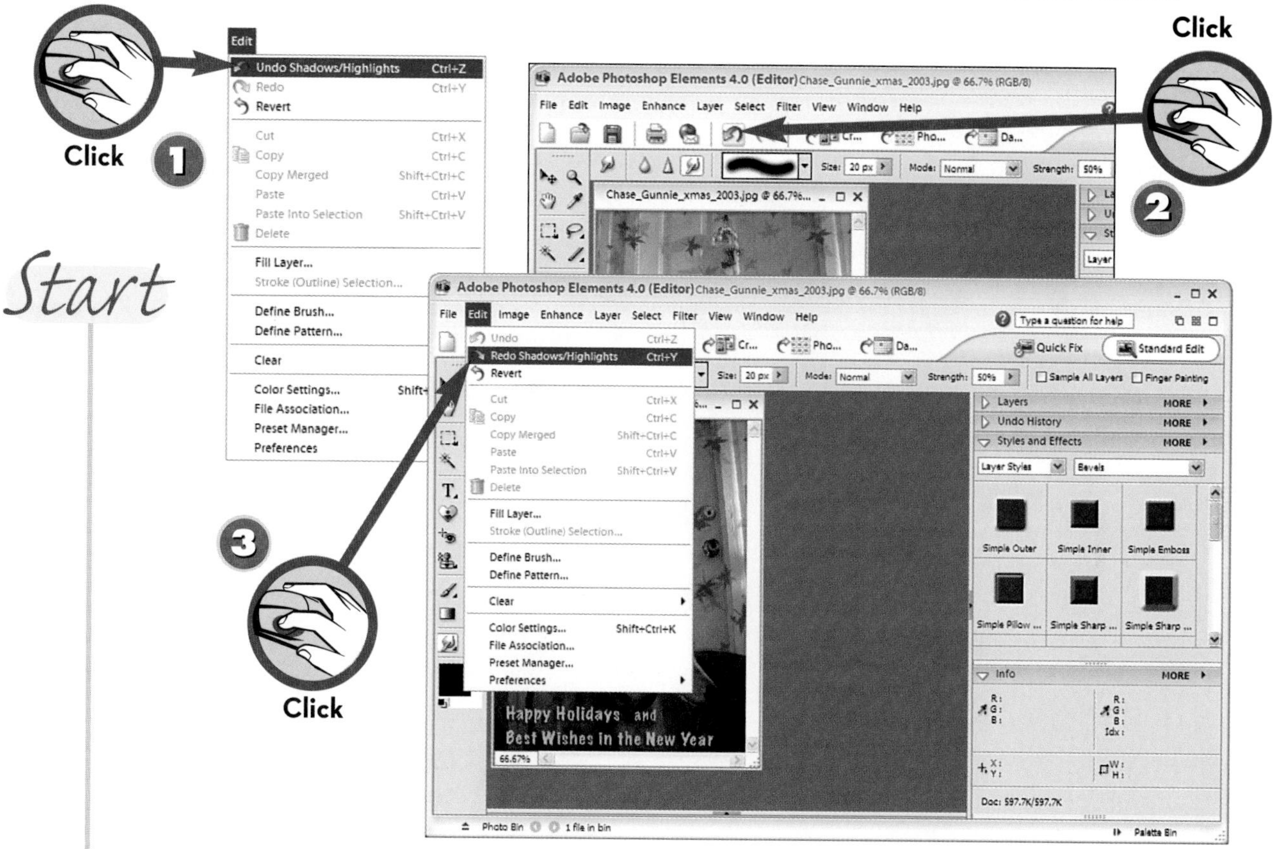

1. Immediately after making any change to the picture in the active image area, choose **Edit**, **Undo**, or press **Ctrl+Z**.
2. To undo the next-most-recent change, click the **Undo** shortcut (or press **Ctrl+Z)** again.
3. To reapply the last change you undid, choose **Edit**, **Redo**, or press **Y** before you do anything else.

TIP

Other Ways to Undo

If you want to see everything you've done to an image before you start undoing, you can use the Undo and Redo shortcuts, or open the Undo History palette. Right-click the step you want to undo, and choose **Delete** (subsequent steps are deleted, too).

TIP

Canceling All Changes

To undo all your changes during a session—before you save—choose **E, Revert**. The last saved version of the file appears in the active image area.

CROPPING A PICTURE

One hallmark of a skilled photographer is pleasing composition, or arrangement of the things you're shooting within the picture frame. You can't always take the time to get the composition just right. Cropping used to be one of the most common fixes made in the darkroom—now you can do it with the lights on.

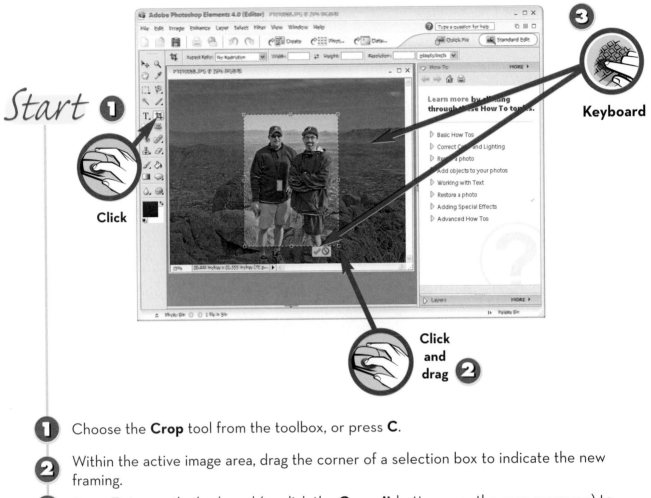

1. Choose the **Crop** tool from the toolbox, or press **C**.
2. Within the active image area, drag the corner of a selection box to indicate the new framing.
3. Press **Enter** on the keyboard (or click the **Commit** button near the crop marquee) to accept the change.

End

TIP

Adjusting Width and Height

After step 1, type a Width and Height in the Options bar to match the proportions (type **5** for Width and **7** for Height for a 5×7 print). Or, pressing **Shift** while dragging forces a perfectly square selection.

TIP

Canceling the Crop

In step 3, to cancel the cropping operation, click the **Cancel** button (just left of the Commit button) near the crop marquee or press **Esc**.

STRAIGHTENING A CROOKED PICTURE

This type of automatic straightening works best when the subject is just slightly out of alignment—a tower that appears to be leaning, for example. The program finds a strong vertical or horizontal line in the image and aligns it on the nearest 90° angle.

Start

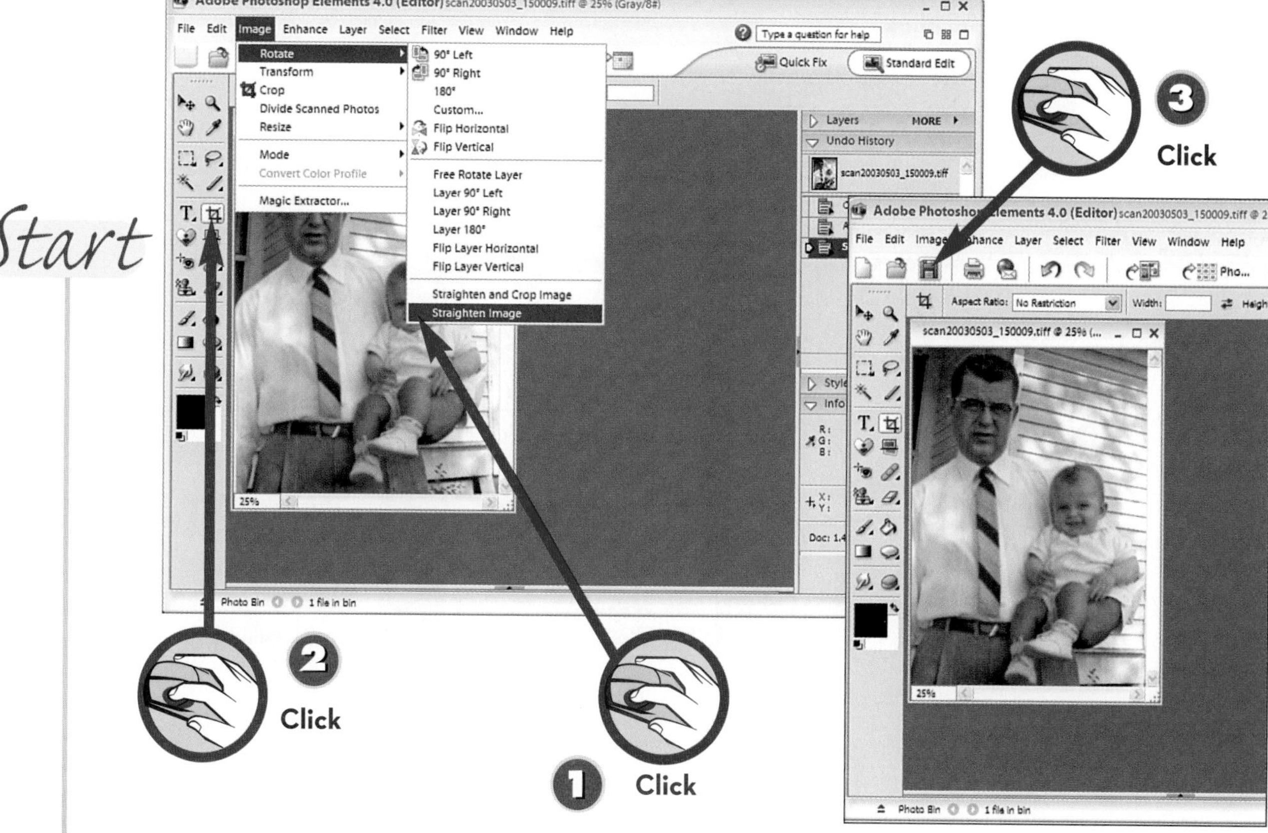

1. With the picture in the active image area, choose **Image**, **Rotate**, **Straighten Image**. The program aligns the image.
2. Crop the photo as desired.
3. Click the **Save** shortcut to save your changes.

End

> **TIP**
> **Severely Off-Angle?**
> If the subject is severely off angle, use one of the **Image**, **Rotate** or **Image**, **Transform** commands instead.

> **TIP**
> **Straighten *and* Crop**
> As an alternative, the program can both straighten *and* crop automatically (choose **Image**, **Rotate**, **Straighten and Crop Image**). But you'll be happier with the results if you crop it yourself.

ROTATING AN IMAGE ON OPENING

Like film cameras, digital cameras take all pictures in landscape orientation—with the long side of the frame horizontal. To take a portrait, you must physically rotate the camera. The most common reason to rotate an image in Photoshop Elements is so that you can view it correctly for editing and printing.

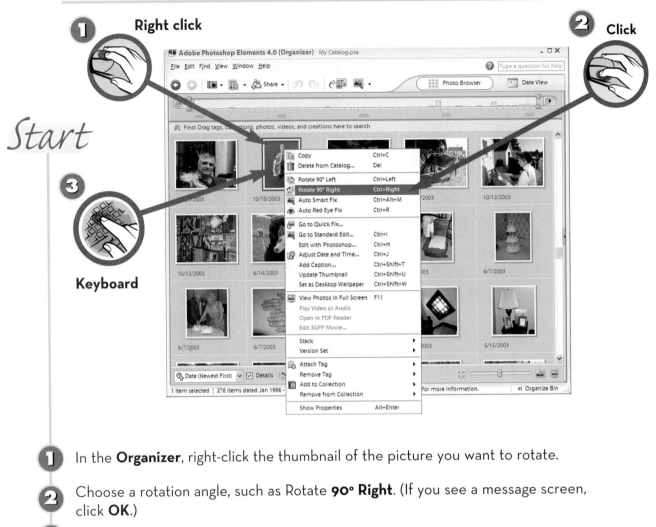

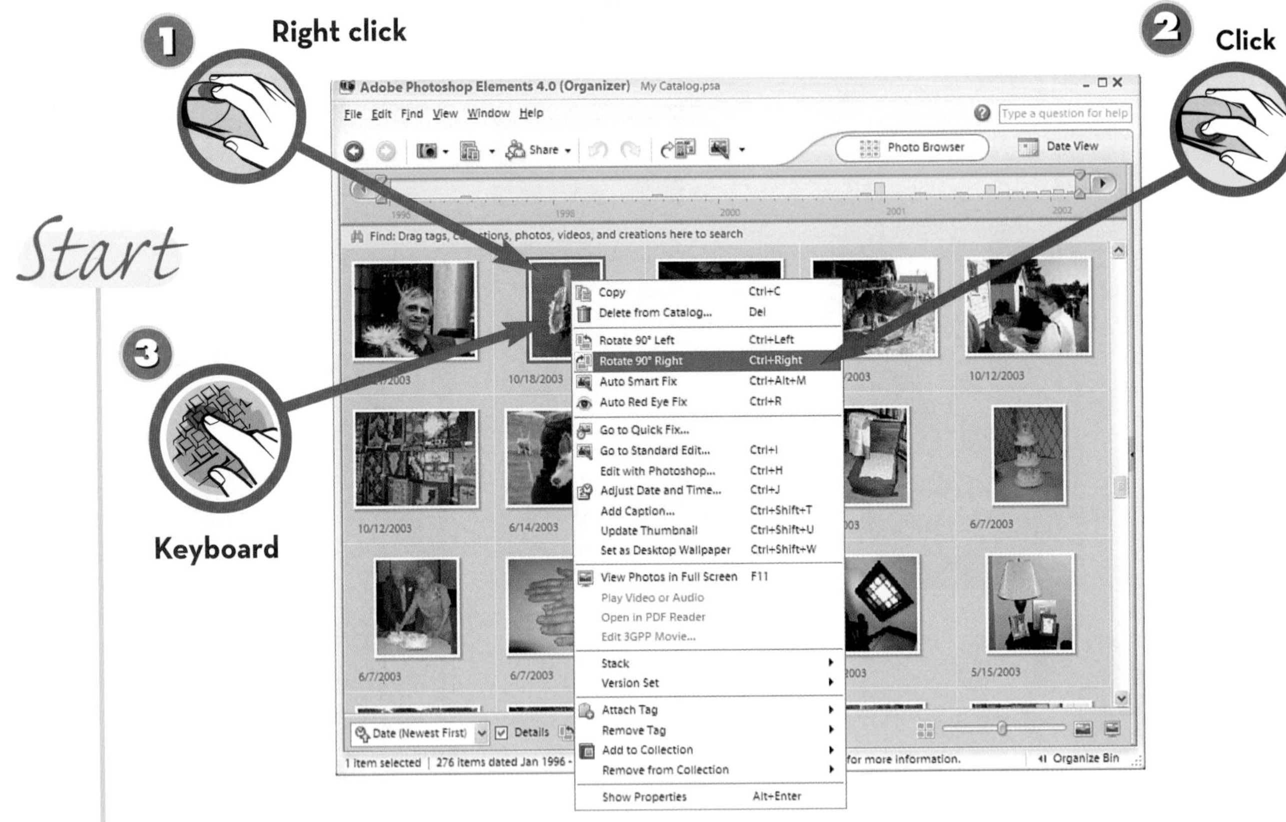

1. In the **Organizer**, right-click the thumbnail of the picture you want to rotate.
2. Choose a rotation angle, such as Rotate **90° Right**. (If you see a message screen, click **OK**.)
3. Press **Ctrl-I** to open the file for editing.

End

TIP

Quick and Easy Rotation

This method of rotating a picture has the same effect as choosing one of the **Image**, **Rotate** commands from the menu bar. But you'll find it's more convenient for quickly rotating all your portrait shots. If you Ctrl-click multiple thumbnails before you do step 1, you can apply the same rotation to multiple shots with a single command. But you must then open the files individually.

ROTATING AN IMAGE FOR ARTISTIC EFFECT

Graphic artists call this type of rotation a Dutch angle. Perhaps the most familiar example is the nightclub poster with rotated glamour portraits of the performers. It's a great technique for adding flair to greeting cards and family Web pages.

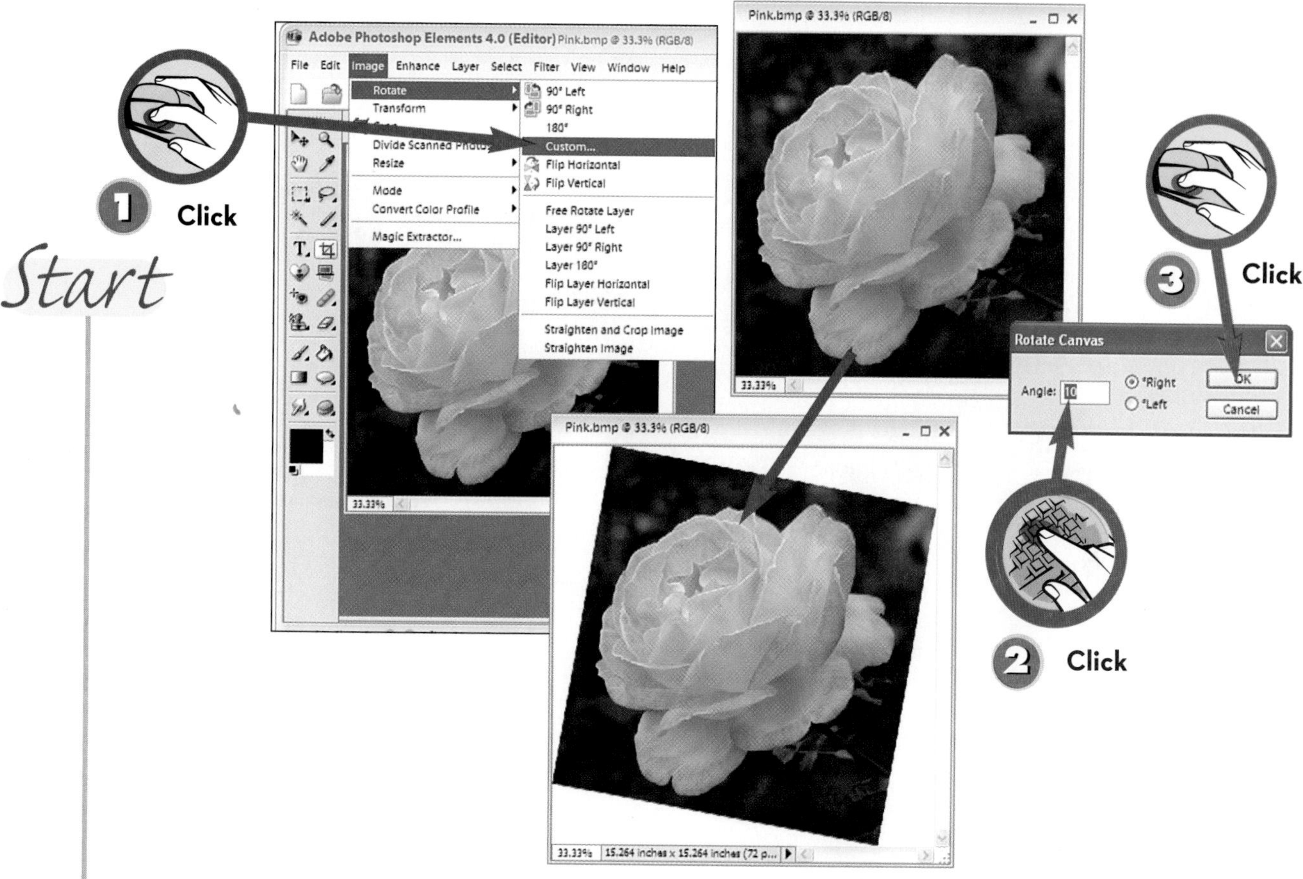

1. With the picture in the active image area, choose **Image**, **Rotate**, **Custom**.
2. In the Rotate Canvas box, type a rotation angle in degrees (clockwise from 12 o'clock; or, click **Left** for counterclockwise rotation).
3. Click **OK**.

End

TIP

Auto-Adjust Canvas Size

Photoshop Elements automatically increases the canvas size to create a frame large enough to hold the rotated picture without reducing the image size. The area outside the picture is the current background color.

TIP

Continuous Rotation

As an alternative, you can choose **Image**, **Rotate**, **Free Rotate Layer** and drag a corner to rotate the image continuously. However, this way does *not* increase the canvas size, and some cropping of the picture corners occurs.

RESIZING AND RESAMPLING AN IMAGE

Digital photos are composed of a finite number of pixels. Resizing and resampling often go hand in hand: If you increase the size of an image, the result can look coarse unless you resample it to increase the resolution at the same time. If you reduce the image size, it decreases the resolution, resulting in a smaller file size.

Start

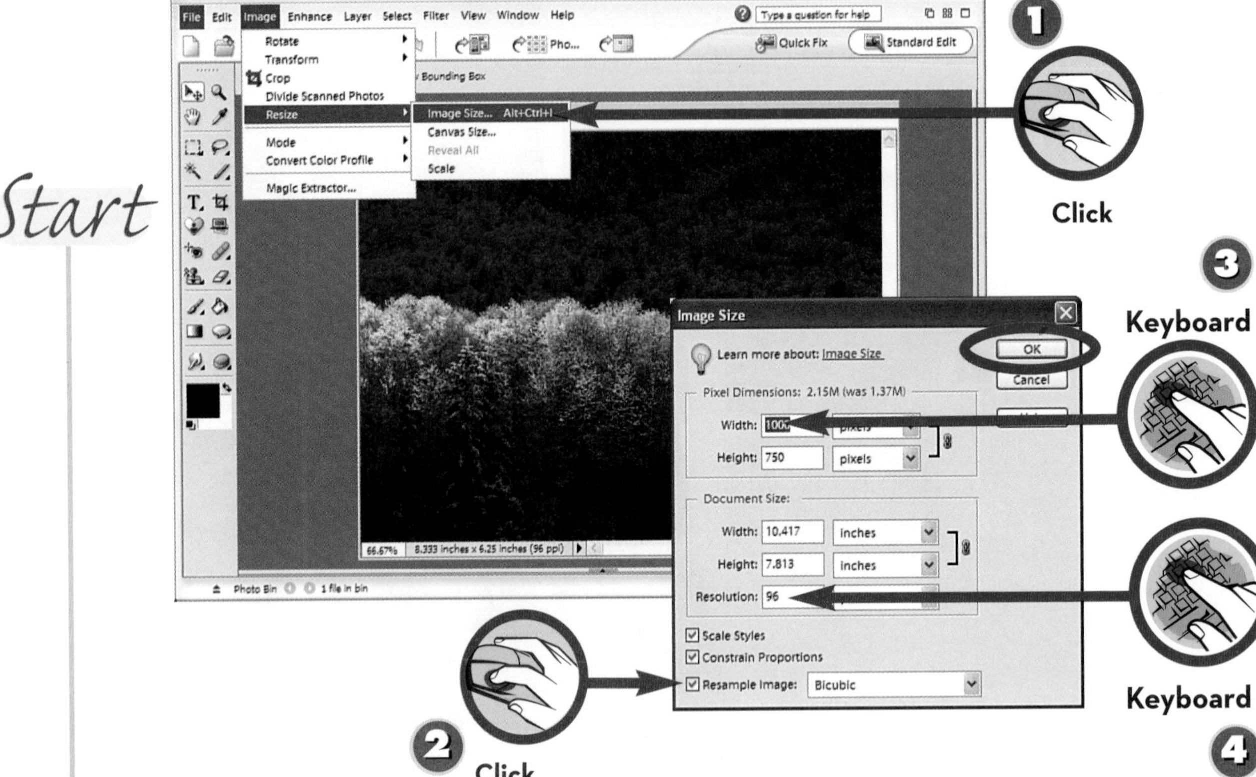

1. With a picture in the active image area, choose **Image**, **Resize**, **Image Size**.
2. Click **Resample Image**.
3. Type a new width in either **Width** field.
4. If desired, type a new value in the **Resolution** field. Click OK.

End

TIP

Enter Width *or* Height

In step 3, make sure Constrain Properties is checked, then enter Width or Height, but not both. If you enter one, the program calculates the other so that the image isn't distorted.

TIP

Bicubic Is Best

For all but the slowest computers or very large images, leave the Resample Image option set to Bicubic, which gives the highest-quality result. Bilinear, which takes less processing time, is the next-best choice.

REMOVING A SCRATCH FROM AN IMAGE

Damage to old photos is a fact of life—but fortunately, it's one that's easy for Photoshop Elements to deal with. If your scanned photo shows rips or scratches—in this case, something was stuck to the original print—you can restore the parts of the image that have been obscured. You just have to take it slow and easy.

Start

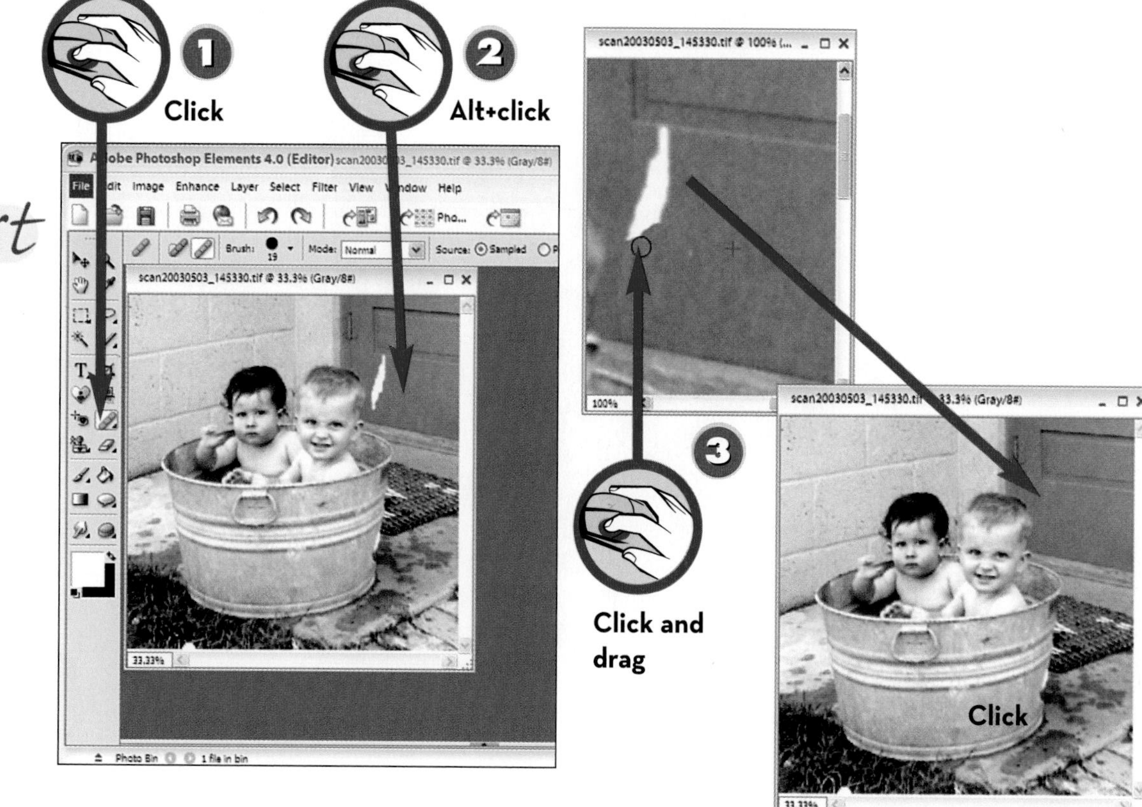

1. Click the **Healing Brush** tool in the toolbox.
2. Press **Alt** as you click a clear area that matches the background.
3. Click and drag over the object you want to remove from the image.

End

NOTE

Know Your Tools

The Healing Brush works well for areas of relatively similar color and texture, such as the door in this example. If you need to fill in a more varied area, try using the Clone Stap. Use several short strokes to blend the pixels in neatly.

NOTE

More Removal Magic

Turn to "Removing Blemishes," **p. 141** to learn more about using the Healing Brush and its sibling, the Spot Healing Brush.

REMOVING RED-EYE IN FLASH PHOTOS

The telltale red-eye effect happens when the flash is mounted on or built into the camera and the subject is looking directly into the lens. The retina of the eye bounces the light right back. Take these steps to dispel those smoldering looks.

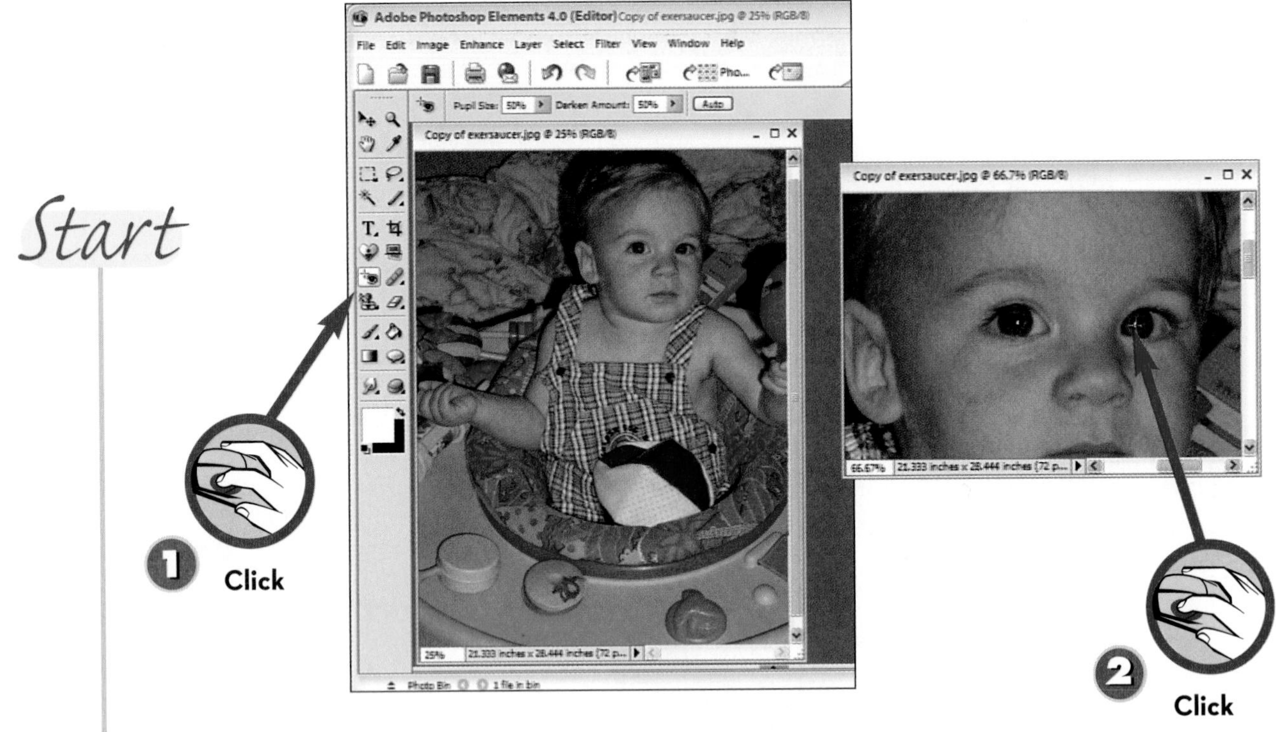

1. With the photo that needs fixing in the active image area, click the **Red Eye Removal** tool, or press **Y**.
2. Click the red area in the photo to choose the color you want to remove.

End

TIP

Zooming Will Help

This task is much easier if you *zoom* your view of the eye so that you can see the detail before you apply the brush. If the effect is tiny, you may be able to wash it out with a single click—no scrubbing.

TIP

Multicolored Reflections?

Remember that this command only replaces a single color. Red-eye reflections may actually be multicolored. Repeat these steps for each individual shade of red you need to remove.

REMOVING "GREEN EYE" IN ANIMAL PHOTOS

Fixing the animal kingdom's equivalent of red eye—usually green eye—is a bit more complicated, because Elements doesn't have a built-in tool to do the job. This method uses a special painting mode—Linear Burn—to enable you to change the eye color without eliminating the eyes' natural highlights and shadows.

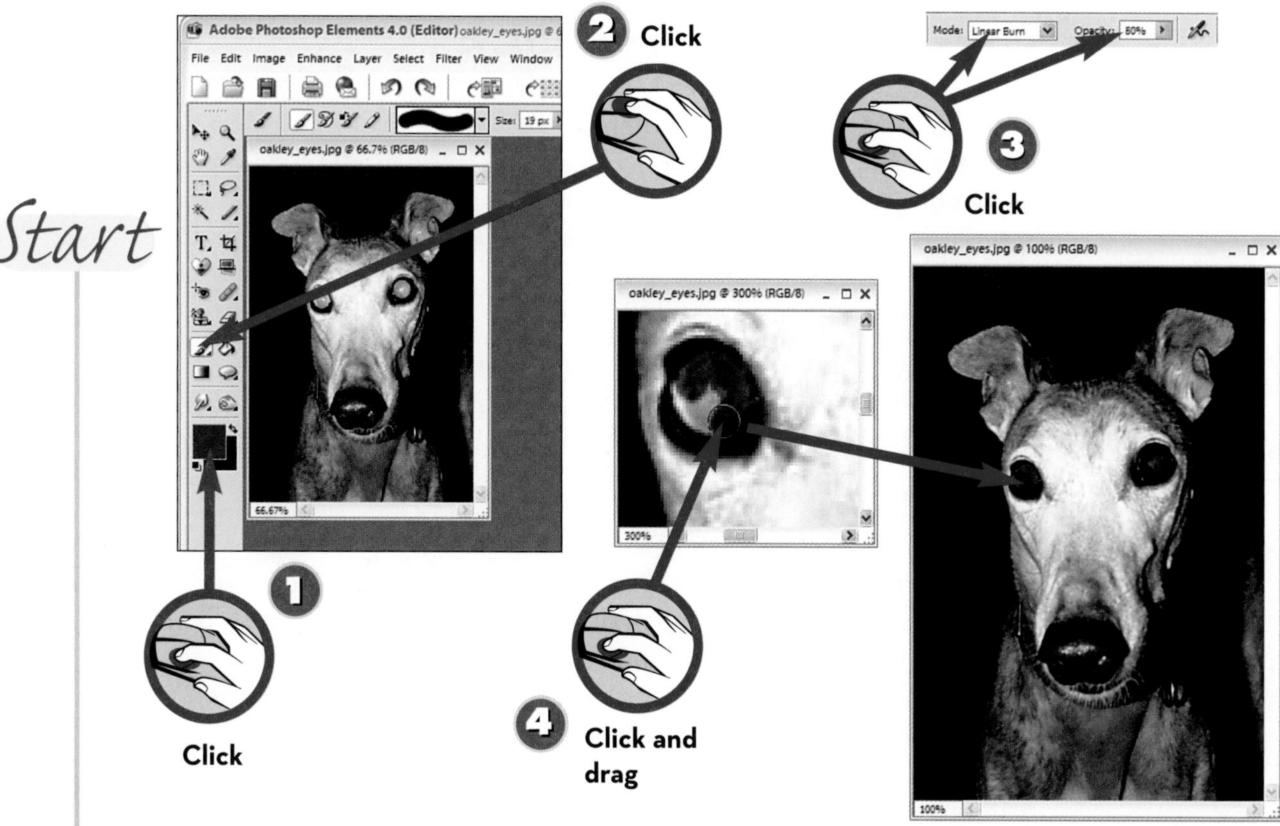

1. Choose a foreground color similar to the color the animal's eye should be, such as a dark brown for a dog.
2. Switch to the **Brush** tool.
3. In the Options bar, set the **Opacity** to 80% and the **Mode** to Linear Burn.
4. Paint carefully over the eyes.

End

TIP

Handle With Care

Be sure to paint only over the green portion of the eye; if you tend to "go outside the lines," turn to "Selecting Part of an Image" in Part 4 to learn how to mask off the portion of the photo that you don't want to paint.

TIP

A Better Way

The best way to fix green eye is not to have the problem in the first place. Try getting an accomplice to attract your subject's attention so that the animal isn't looking directly at you when you take your shot. That way the flash won't reflect from the beastie's eyes.

4

part

ADVANCED PHOTO FIXING

Are you ready to kick it up a notch? Here's where your photo editing gets a bit more extensive. In this part, you'll learn how to brighten up dark photos, clarify blurry ones, make skin tones look more natural, and even change the color of Grandma's shirt if you like. Want to delete Cousin Steve's ex from the family portrait? No problem—just keep reading and you'll learn how to do that, too.

The first thing to learn, however, is how to isolate just the part of the image you want to work on to make sure you don't alter the rest of the picture unintentionally. The first three tasks in this part show you different ways to *select* part of an image so you can work with it. Even if you skip the rest of the tasks in this part, don't skip these—creating selections is a skill you'll need over and over again.

As you learn these editing techniques, you'll realize why photographs are no longer considered proof of much of anything. Digital images are so easy to change that it's hard to know when you should stop. Try to use a light touch so that your photos still say the same things they did when you picked up your camera to shoot; the idea is just to make that message a bit clearer.

FOCUSING ON THE DETAILS

A dark, boring photo before...

...and a striking, colorful landscape after. You'll be amazed at what a few lighting and color adjustments and a bit of sharpening can accomplish.

SELECTING PART OF AN IMAGE

When you're painting the trim in your house, you use tape to mask off the parts of the wall where you don't want to get paint. That's what selections are all about in Photoshop Elements—with part of the image selected, any changes you make are applied to just that area, leaving the rest of the image untouched.

1. With a picture in the active image area, click the **Rectangular Marquee tool**.
2. Click and drag to select a rectangular portion of the image.
3. Shift-click and drag to add to the selection marquee.

Continued

TIP

Circles and Squares

When drawing selections using one of the Marquee tools—the Rectangular Marquee or the Elliptical Marquee—you can create squares or circles, respectively, by pressing **Shift** as you drag out the selection.

NOTE

Shift This, Shift That

When you want to add to an existing selection, be sure to press **Shift** *before* you click in the image again. If you click outside the selection without Shift or Alt held down, the selection will disappear.

Alt + Click and drag

Click

Click and drag

4 Alt-click and drag to remove part of the selection marquee.

5 Click the **Lasso tool**.

6 Click and drag around any part of the image to select an irregular area.

End

TIP

Mix It Up

You can use any combination of selection tools to create a selection that's just the shape you're looking for. For example, you might start out with a rectangular or circular selection, then use the **Lasso tool** to add and subtract smaller areas.

TIP

Selection Magnetism

Click and hold the **Lasso** tool to display the **Magnetic** Lasso. To create a selection, click in the image, then click again to indicate a corner point of the selection area. Close the selection by clicking the first point again.

SELECTING AREAS BASED ON COLOR

With the Magic Wand tool you can quickly select an irregular area that's all the same color, such as a flower, a T-shirt, or even the sky. By changing the Tolerance value, you can make the Magic Wand more or less picky about how closely a pixel must match your target pixel in order to be selected.

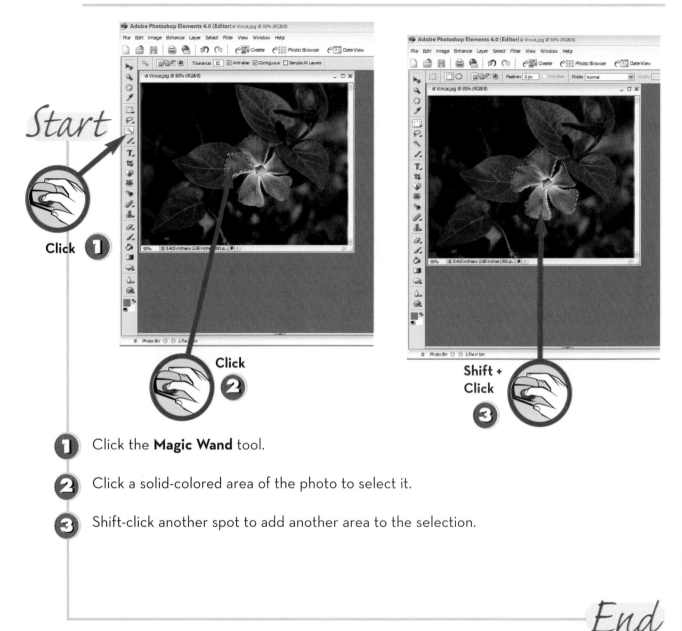

Start

Click 1

Click 2

Shift + Click 3

1. Click the **Magic Wand** tool.
2. Click a solid-colored area of the photo to select it.
3. Shift-click another spot to add another area to the selection.

End

TIP

All About Tolerance

Tolerance can range from 0 to 255, and it determines how close a pixel's color must be to the pixel you click on to be included in the selection. At 0, only pixels that match the original pixel exactly will be selected; at 255, the entire picture will be selected.

TIP

Right Next Door

When the **Contiguous** box on the Options bar is checked, the Magic Wand only selects pixels that are next to each other in the image. To select pixels of the same color throughout the image, uncheck **Contiguous**.

BRIGHTENING UP SHADOWED AREAS

If you're like many users of Photoshop Elements, the Shadows/Highlights command may turn out to be the one that you use on virtually every photo you open in the program. It's not considered a Quick Fix—yet its results are amazing and you'll love its ease of use.

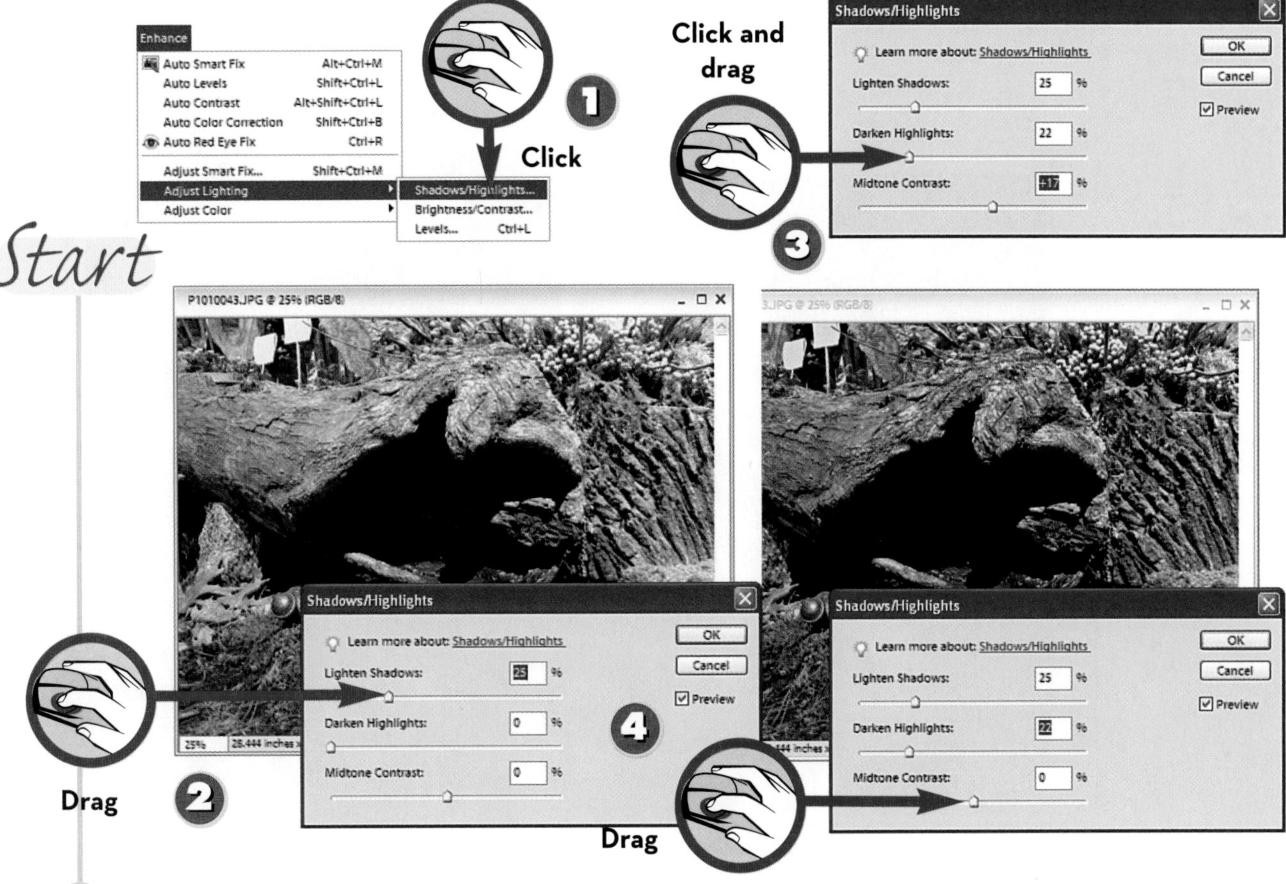

1. With an image open, choose **Enhance**, **Adjust Lighting**, **Shadows/Highlights**.
2. Drag the **Lighten Shadows** slider to the right to bring out shadow detail.
3. Drag the **Darken Highlights** slider to the right to tone down the image's bright areas.
4. Drag the **Midtone Contrast** slider to the right to make the image's colors stand out more against a dark background.

End

NOTE

Easy Does It

Be careful not to increase shadow lightness too much—it's fun to bring out the shadow details that you didn't even realize were there, but shadows that are too light don't contrast enough with the brighter areas.

NOTE

The Starting Point

Elements always starts you out with a 25% increase in shadow lightness. For most images taken with a point-and-shoot camera, especially indoor shots, that provides an amazing improvement.

MAKING SELECTIONS MAGICALLY

You may have thought the Magic Wand was enough magic for one program—but you haven't seen the Magic Selection Brush yet! With this funky new tool, you scribble across the area you want to select, and Elements figures out what you want selected.

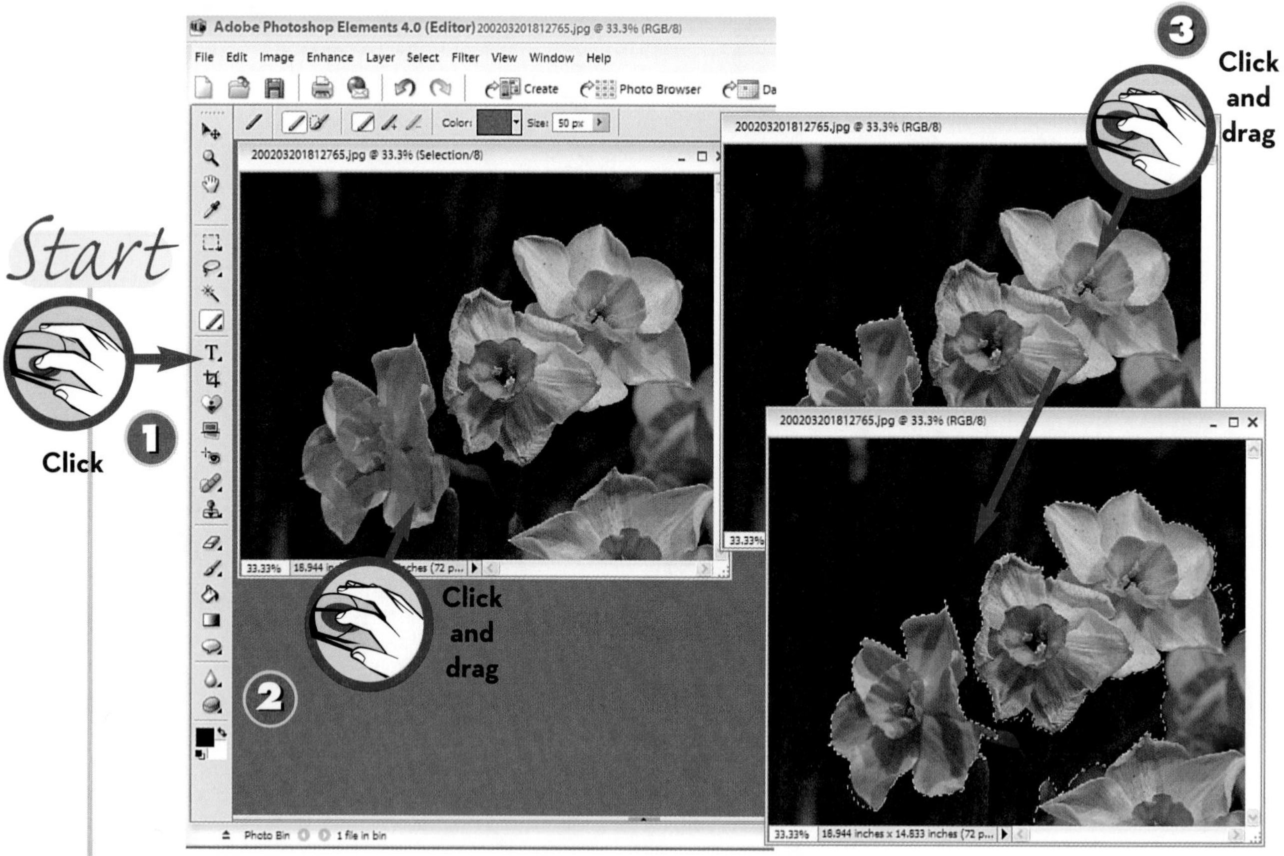

Start

Click

Click and drag

Click and drag

1. Click the **Magic Selection Brush** tool in the toolbox.
2. With the **Magic Selection Brush** tool, click and drag to roughly cover the area you want to select.
3. Click and drag again to add to your selection.

Continued

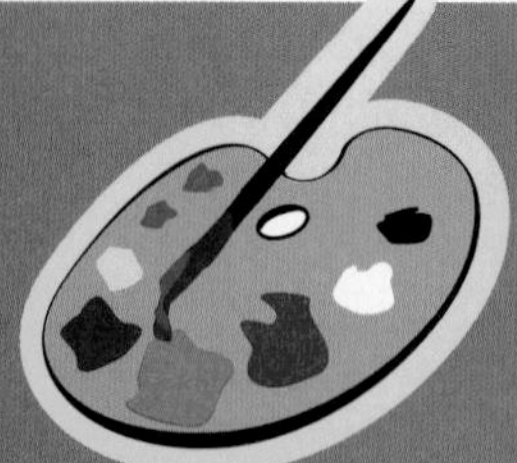

4. Click the **Indicate Background** button on the Options bar.

5. Click and drag to remove areas from your selection.

End

TIP

The Magic Modes

Three buttons on the Options bar control the behavior of the Magic Selection Brush. You always start out in **New Selection** mode, and you can click this button at any time to start your selection over. Click **Indicate Foreground** when you want to paint over more colors that should be included in the selection—Elements automatically switches to this mode after you make your initial strokes with the tool. Finally, click **Indicate Background** when you want to paint over areas that should *not* be included in the selection.

CORRECTING A COLOR CAST

If a photo has an undesirable overall tint, then it's because the image's *white balance* is off. Daylight has a blue cast, light bulbs indoors make everything orange, and fluorescents can make faces a sickly green. This command compensates by rebalancing all the colors in the picture in relation to pure white.

Start

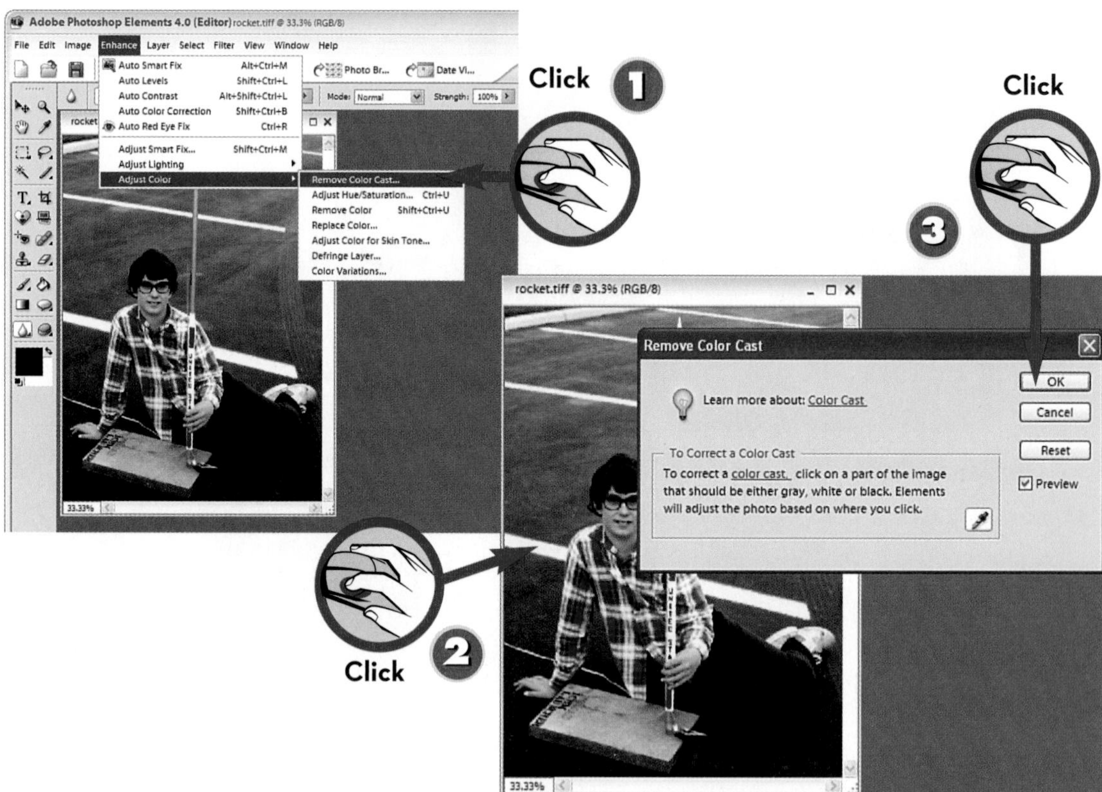

1. With a picture in the active image area, choose **Enhance**, **Adjust Color**, **Remove Color Cast**.
2. Click an area of the image that should be white.
3. Click **OK**.

End

NOTE

Pick Pure White

In step 2, pick an area such as teeth, white of the eye, or a white tablecloth or shirt collar. Any blown-out (overexposed) area usually gives the best result. If there's no white anywhere in the picture, click a neutral area (gray or black).

ADJUSTING SKIN TONES

New to Photoshop Elements 4 is a handy command designed specifically to fix "off" skin tones in photos of people. You can compensate for poor lighting by lightening or darkening skin tones and changing the picture's yellow/pink balance, and you can also adjust overall lighting of the scene.

Start

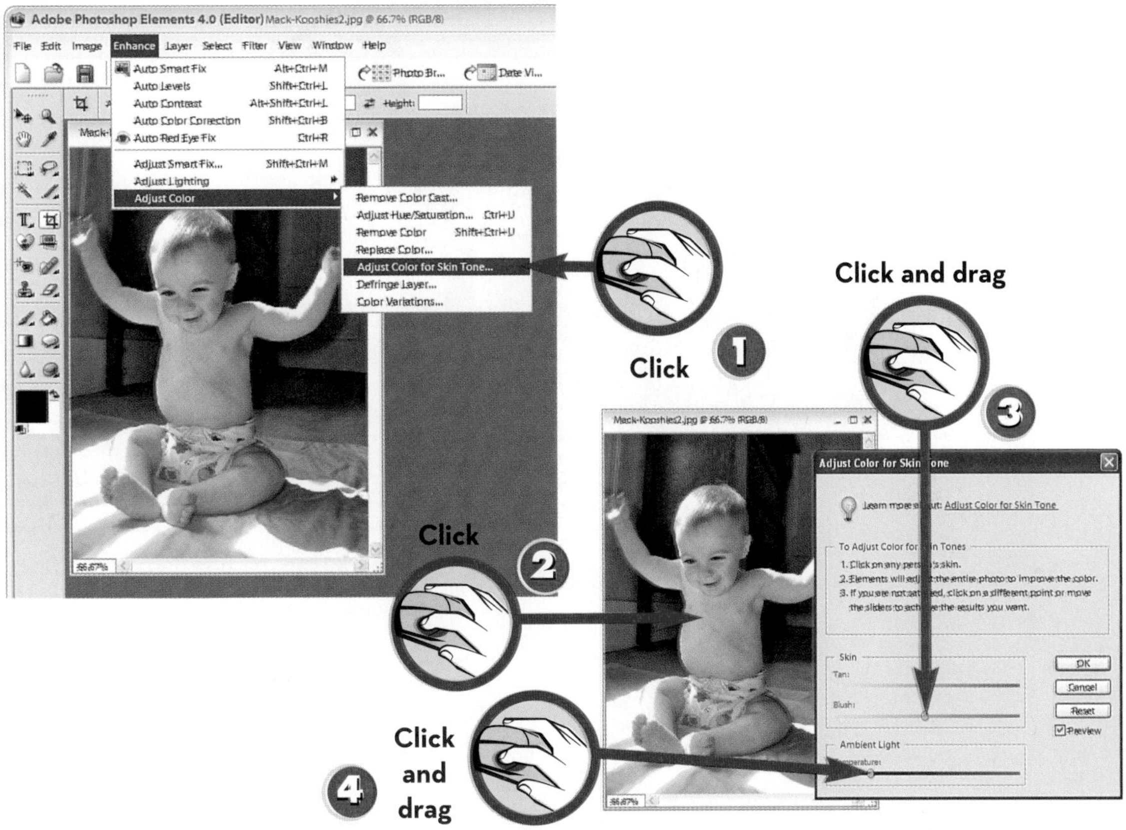

1. With a picture in the active image area, choose **Enhance**, **Adjust Color**, **Adjust Color for Skin Tone**.
2. Click on a patch of skin in the image. Elements adjusts all the skin tones in that range within the picture.
3. To refine the skin tones, click and drag the **Tan** and **Blush** sliders.
4. Click and drag the **Temperature** slider to make the entire image look warmer or cooler.

End

NOTE

Tone Deaf

Elements looks at the color of the area you click to determine what colors in a photo qualify as skin tones. If people in your photo have widely varying skin colors, you may not find this command as useful as it is when the subjects' skin colors are similar.

SELECTING COLOR VARIATIONS

Perhaps it's not that the colors in the picture are wrong, you'd just like to see them different. For example, an interior decorator might want to view a room in a different light or with the decor a different shade. Experiment with color variations, which can be more dramatic than just correcting the overall cast.

Start

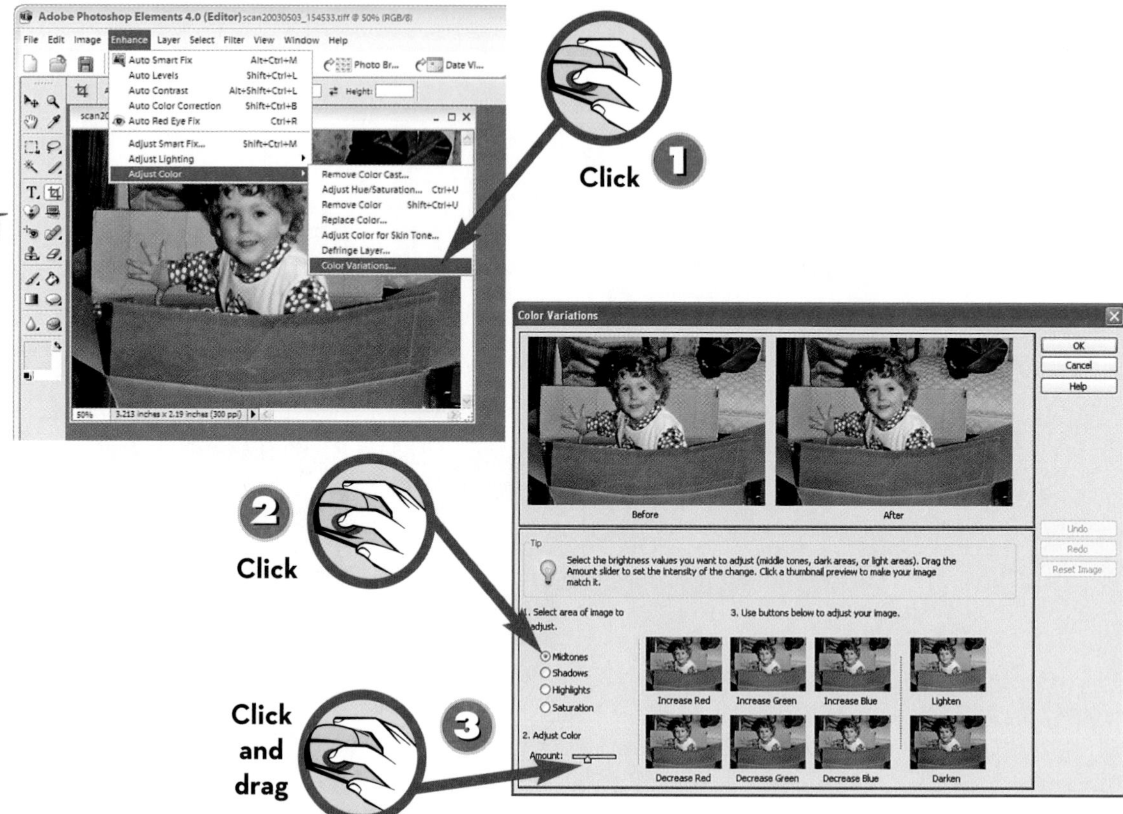

1. With a picture in the active image area, choose **Enhance**, **Adjust Color**, **Color Variations**.
2. Click a radio button to choose what part of the image you want to adjust.
3. Drag the **Amount** slider to make the differences between the Variation thumbnails greater or less.

Continued

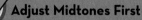

NOTE

Adjust Midtones First

Of the selections Midtones, Shadows, Highlights, and Saturation, Midtones (values ranging between shadows and highlights) usually give you the most noticeable results. To change the magnitude of an effect, drag the **Adjust Color Intensity** slider before you apply it.

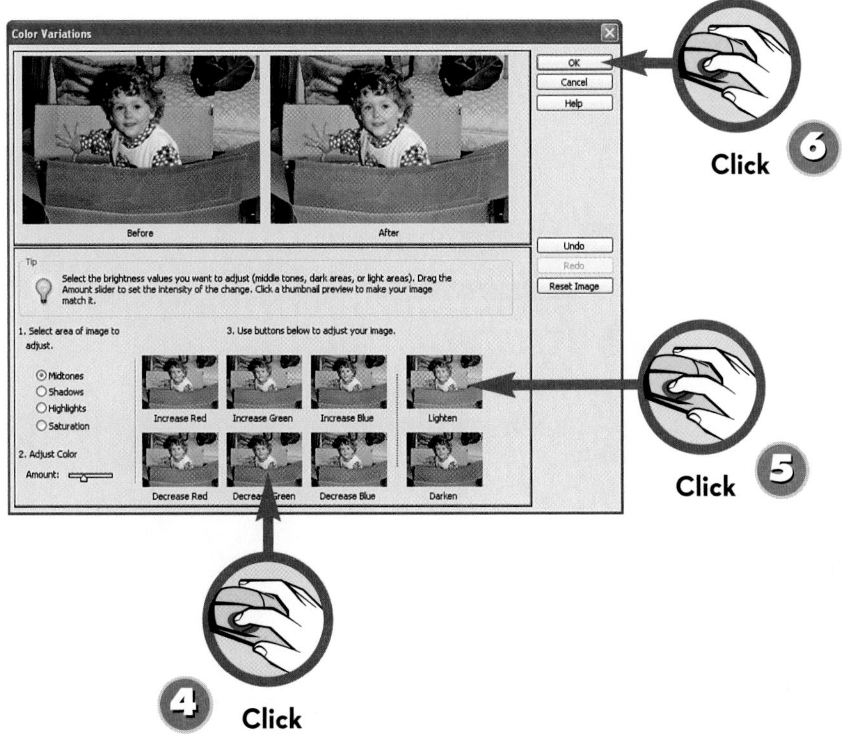

4. Click a thumbnail, such as **Decrease Green**, to change color or brightness in the shot.
5. Click the same thumbnail again to increase its effect, or click another thumbnail to adjust a different color or the image's brightness.
6. When the After image looks right, click **OK**.

End

TIP

Take Baby Steps

Don't overlook the **Amount** slider; be sure to adjust it before clicking the Variation thumbnails. The default setting is usually a bit too coarse, meaning that it changes the image too much with each click. It's better to click multiple times on a thumbnail to build up the effect gradually than to click once and end up with too much change.

REPLACING A SPECIFIC COLOR

Don't like the color of that dress? Does the sofa clash with the drapes? Want to make the sky pink or the river run green? You can make it so at no extra charge—with your choices limited only by your fashion sense.

Start

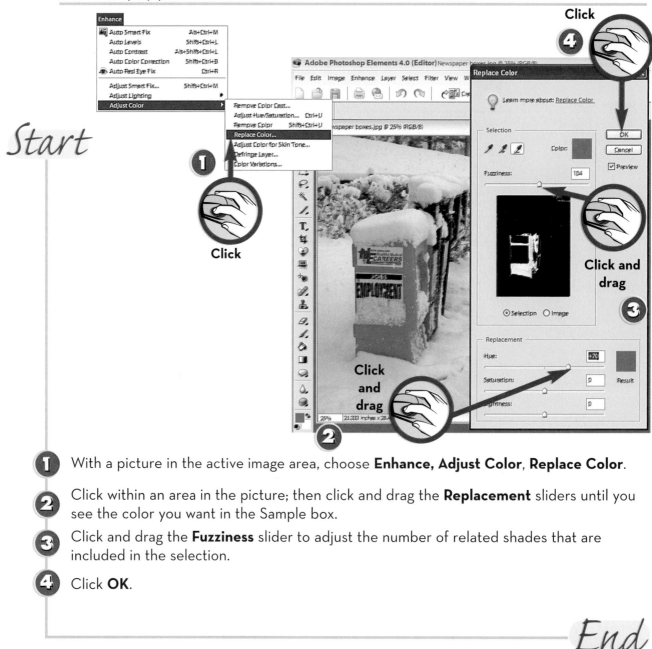

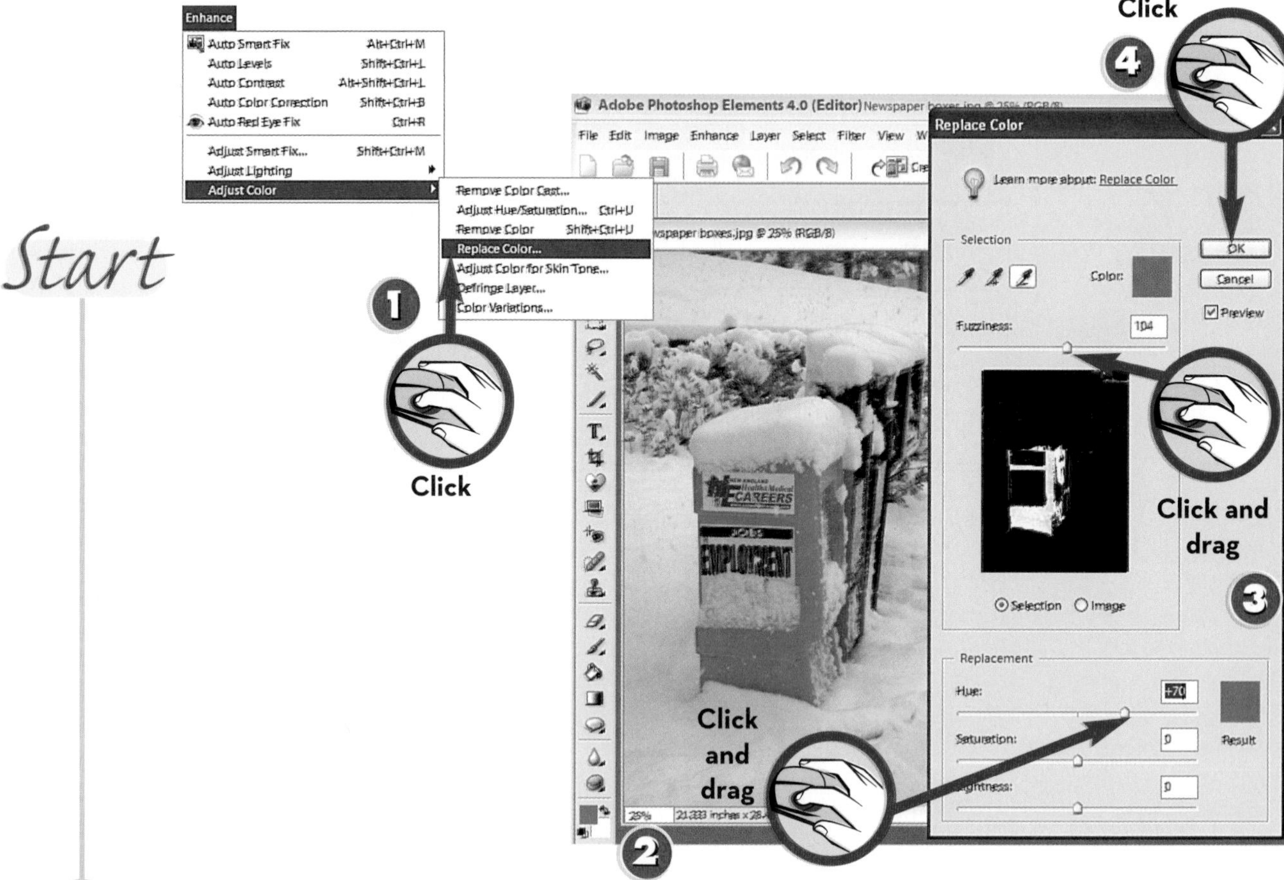

1. With a picture in the active image area, choose **Enhance, Adjust Color**, **Replace Color**.
2. Click within an area in the picture; then click and drag the **Replacement** sliders until you see the color you want in the Sample box.
3. Click and drag the **Fuzziness** slider to adjust the number of related shades that are included in the selection.
4. Click **OK**.

End

TIP

Add or Subtract

Click the **Add to Sample** or **Subtract from Sample** eyedroppers (marked with + and -) and click the area in the picture to add or remove it. Then, dragging the **Replacement** sliders applies the color change to the entire selection.

NOTE

What Changes?

These steps change all instances of the same color anywhere in the image, not just on the area you select in step 2.

ADJUSTING BRIGHTNESS AND CONTRAST

Sometimes a Quick Fix like Auto Contrast just doesn't do the trick—especially if the image has bright highlights, deep shadows, or both. These steps give you more control so that you can make continuous adjustments while previewing the result.

Start

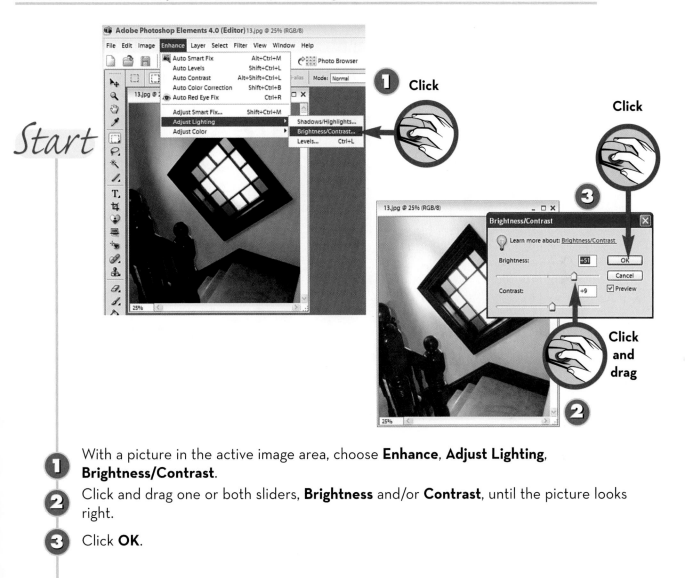

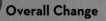

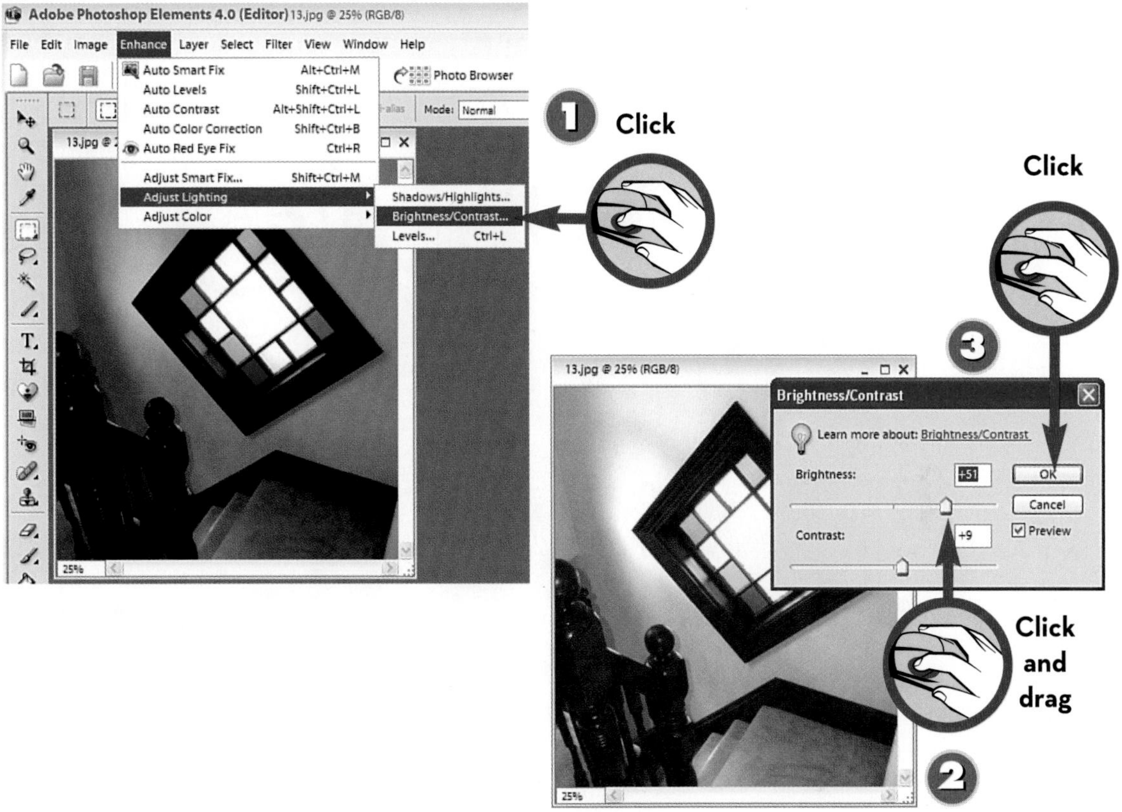

1. With a picture in the active image area, choose **Enhance**, **Adjust Lighting**, **Brightness/Contrast**.
2. Click and drag one or both sliders, **Brightness** and/or **Contrast**, until the picture looks right.
3. Click **OK**.

End

TIP

Overall Change

Changing brightness and contrast affects the entire image unless you select a particular area first. Some of the available selection tools are Rectangular Marquee (for rectangular areas), Lasso (for irregular areas), and Magic Wand (for intricate shapes).

NOTE

Subject in the Dark?

If your subject is too dark overall (underexposed), try the Fill Flash fix first. It boosts brightness only in the darker areas, leaving the lighter areas—usually, the background—alone.

CHANGING A COLOR PHOTO TO BLACK AND WHITE

You'll occasionally need black-and-white pictures for newsletters that will be printed one-color—or perhaps when you're in a vintage-movie kind of mood. You can easily convert your color shots to B&W, but remember to finish by adjusting the contrast to make them suitably snappy.

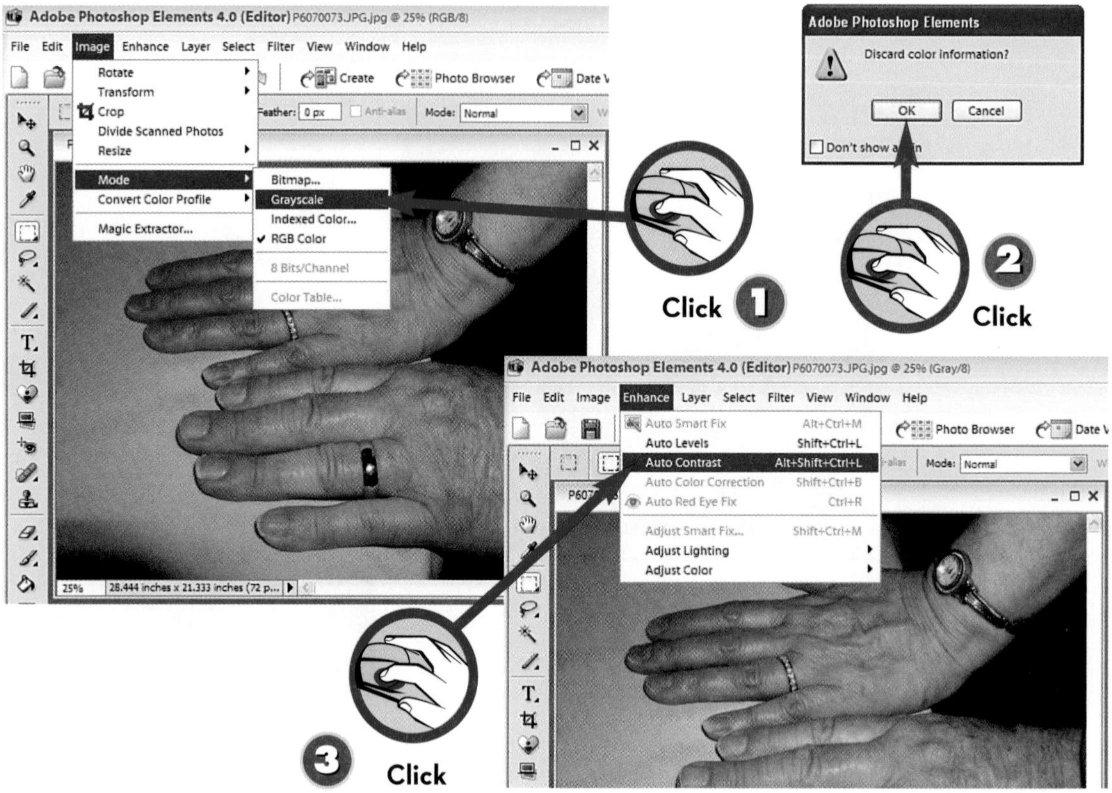

1. With a color picture in the active image area, choose **Image**, **Mode**, **Grayscale**.
2. Click **OK**.
3. Choose **Enhance**, **Auto Contrast**.

TIP

Sepia (a brownish monochrome) is actually a color effect. After converting to B&W and adjusting contrast, repeat the **Image**, **Mode** command and choose **RGB Color**; then apply one or more **Color Variations**.

REMOVING OBJECTS FROM AN IMAGE

To take a great photo, you have to catch both the subject and the setting at just the right time. If another object intrudes into the scene at the crucial second, Photoshop Elements makes it easy to remove that little "extra" at a later date.

Start

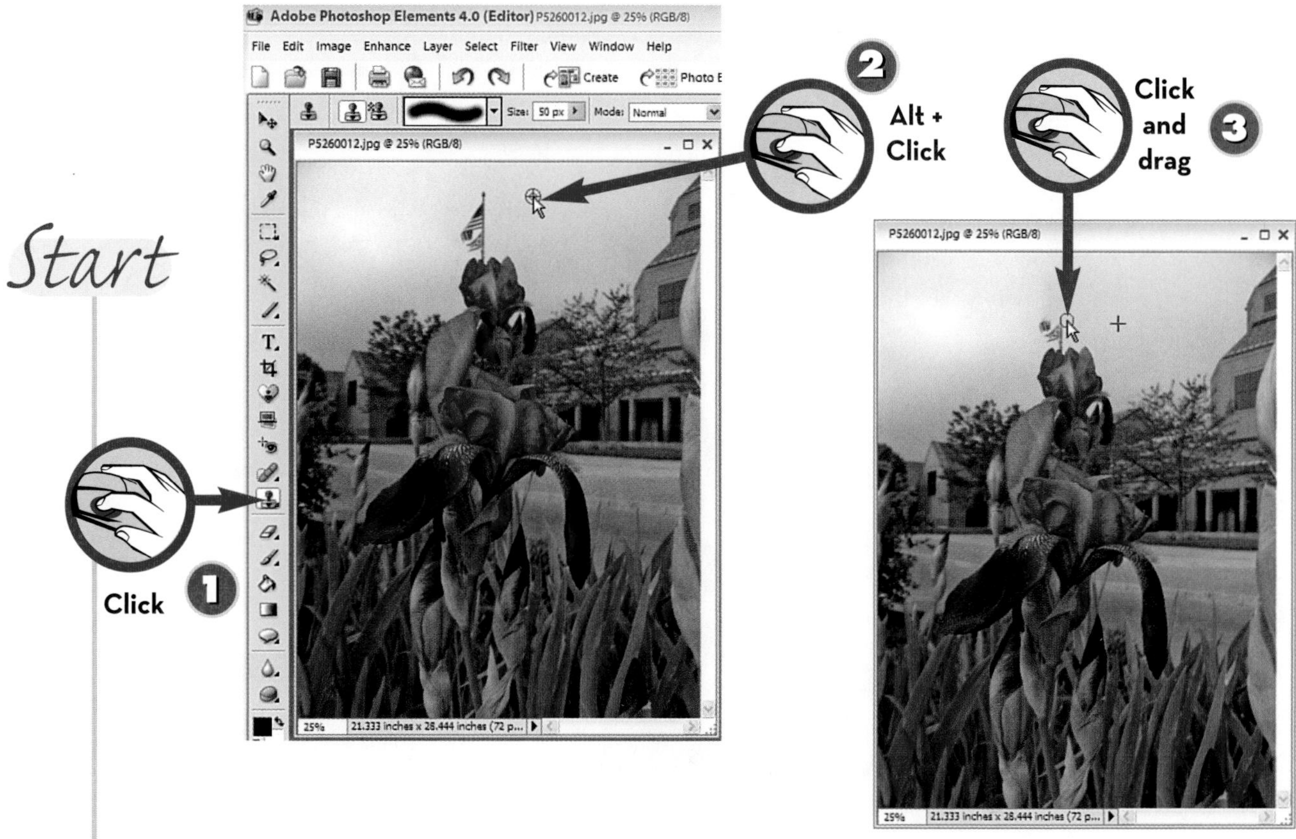

1. Click the **Clone Stamp** tool in the toolbox, or press **S**.
2. Press **Alt** as you click a clear area that matches the background.
3. Click and drag over the object you want to remove from the image.

End

NOTE

Take Your Time

You might need to apply the Clone Stamp multiple times, using short strokes, to blend the new pixels in with the existing background.

NOTE

Object Removal Magic

The Clone Stamp tool is a good choice for removing objects on irregular backgrounds, and for larger objects. For small objects, Elements includes special "healing" tools. Turn to "Removing Blemishes," **p. 141**, to learn more.

TRANSFORMING IMAGE PERSPECTIVE

The Image, Transform submenu actually has three other commands besides Perspective: Free Transform, Skew, and Distort. But you apply them all the same way—by dragging picture corners. Try each of them using these steps to see how their effects differ.

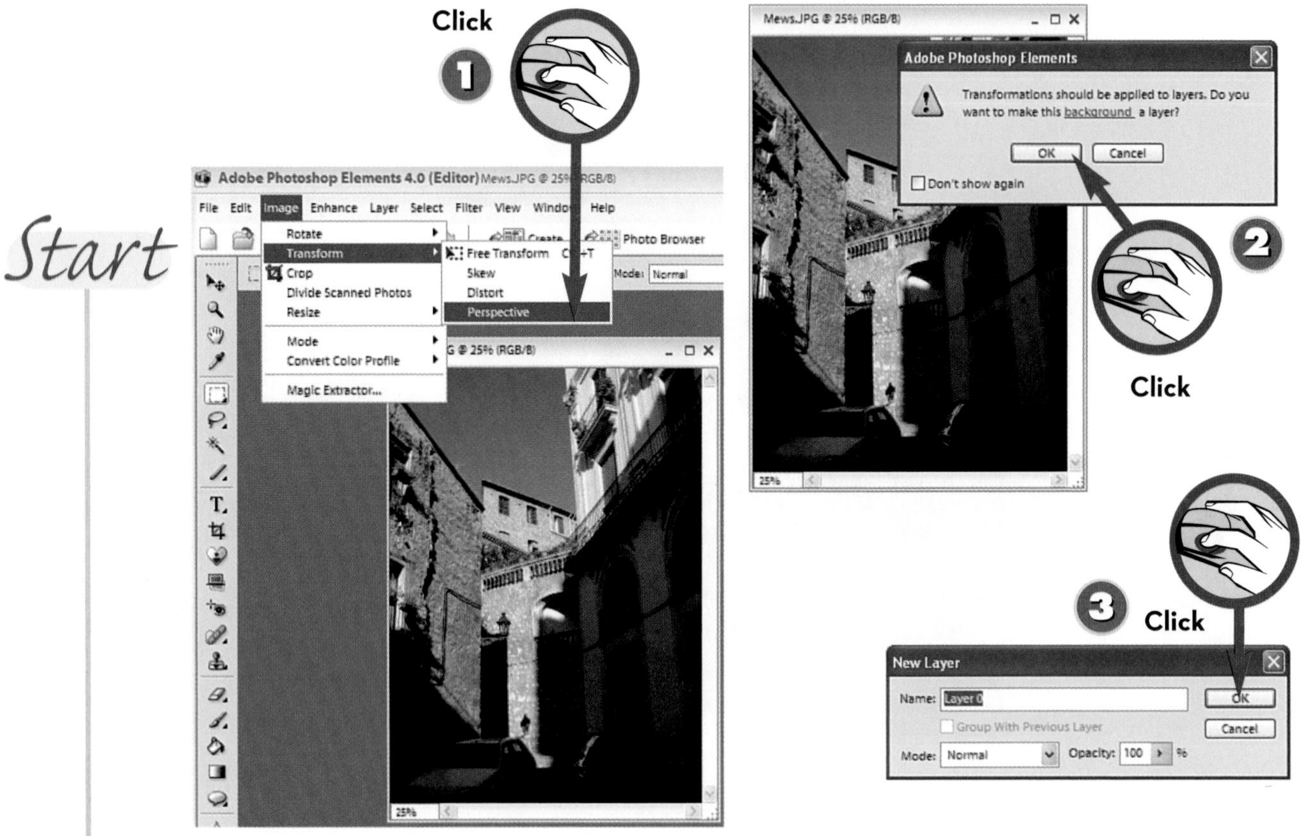

Start

Click

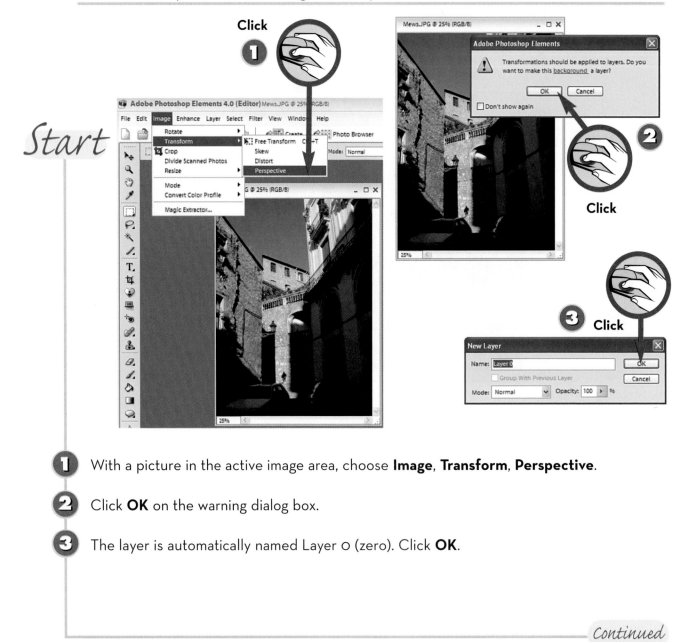

Click

Click

1. With a picture in the active image area, choose **Image**, **Transform**, **Perspective**.
2. Click **OK** on the warning dialog box.
3. The layer is automatically named Layer 0 (zero). Click **OK**.

Continued

TIP

Severe Distortion?

Severe distortion on subjects such as tall buildings results not only from perspective but also from an effect of optical lenses called barrel distortion—which adds curvature.

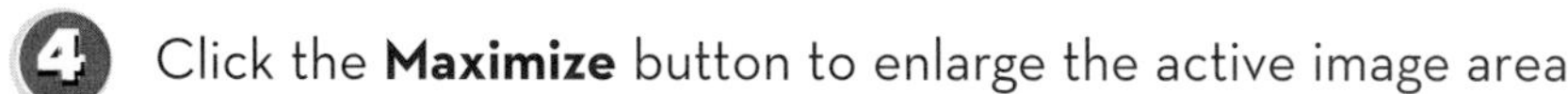

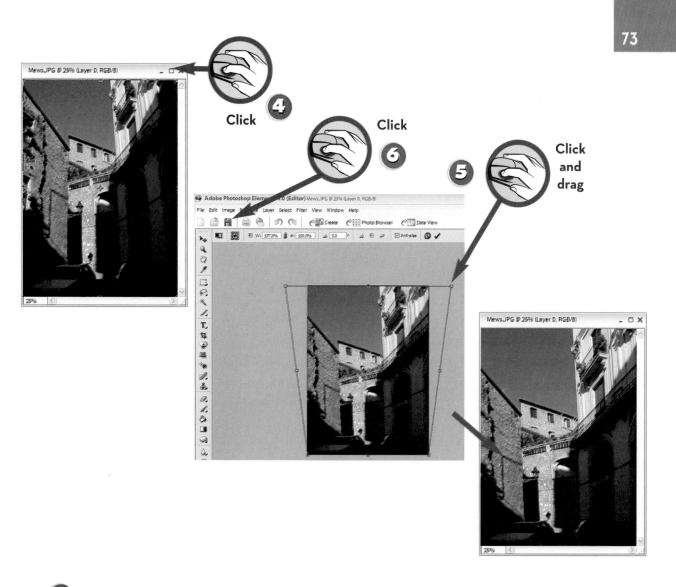

4 Click the **Maximize** button to enlarge the active image area.

5 Click and drag a corner to adjust the perspective and press enter.

6 **Save** the transformed image.

End

NOTE

Watch for Keystoning

Keystoning, another type of distortion, results from aiming the camera either up or down at a severe angle. To compensate for keystoning, drag the corner in step 5 that's nearest the pinched end of the subject outward.

NOTE

Don't Squish Your Folks

Be careful that in removing distortion from one part of a picture, such as the slope of a building, you don't add distortion in another part—squishing cars or, worse, the faces of your loved ones.

SHARPENING A BLURRY PHOTO

Digital cameras have an *auto-focus* feature, which attempts to make the edges of the subject in the center of the frame as sharp as possible. It doesn't always work. For more consistent results, learn how to focus manually. But you can always try this simple step to sharpen shots that are slightly blurred.

Start

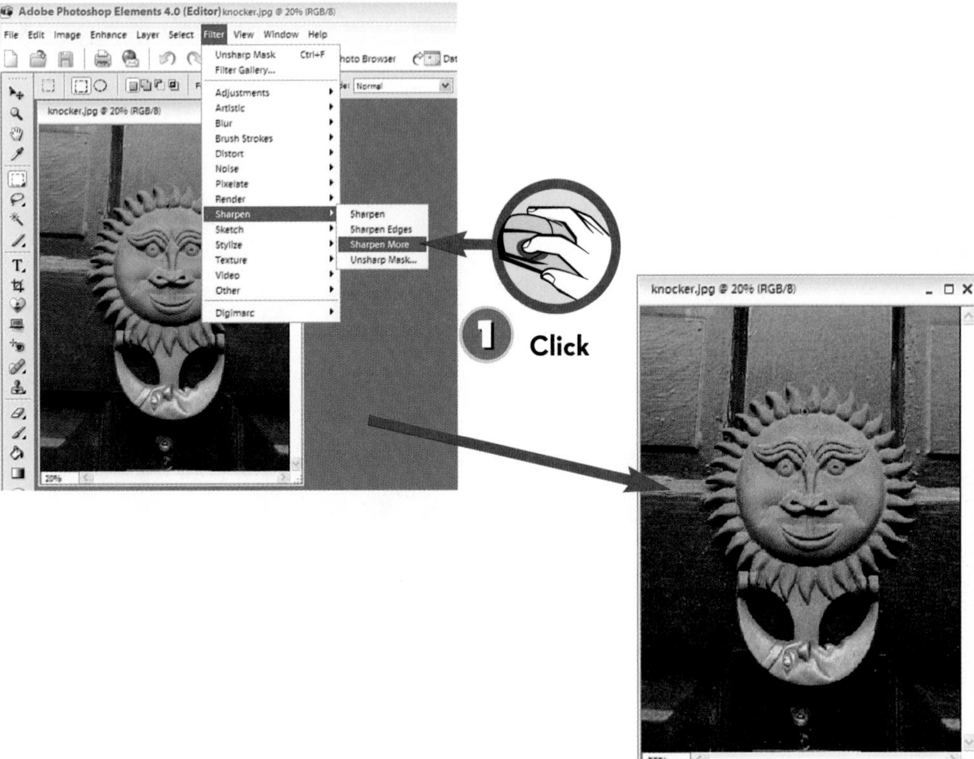

1. With a picture in the active image area, choose **Filter**, **Sharpen**, **Sharpen More**.

End

NOTE

Focus Manually

The Sharpen command can improve the look of a blurred shot somewhat, but it's no substitute for proper manual focusing. That's particularly true when you're doing *closeups*—with the subject less than four feet away.

TIP

Don't Overdo It

This task uses **Sharpen More** because you might not see much of a difference from the original when you use the Sharpen submenu command. And Sharpen Edges can overdo it.

MAKING EDGES SOFTER

There are at least two good reasons to soften focus: It can make a portrait look more flattering, blending out lines, pores, and small blemishes; and it can save a shot that's only slightly out of focus—making the softness look more deliberate.

Start

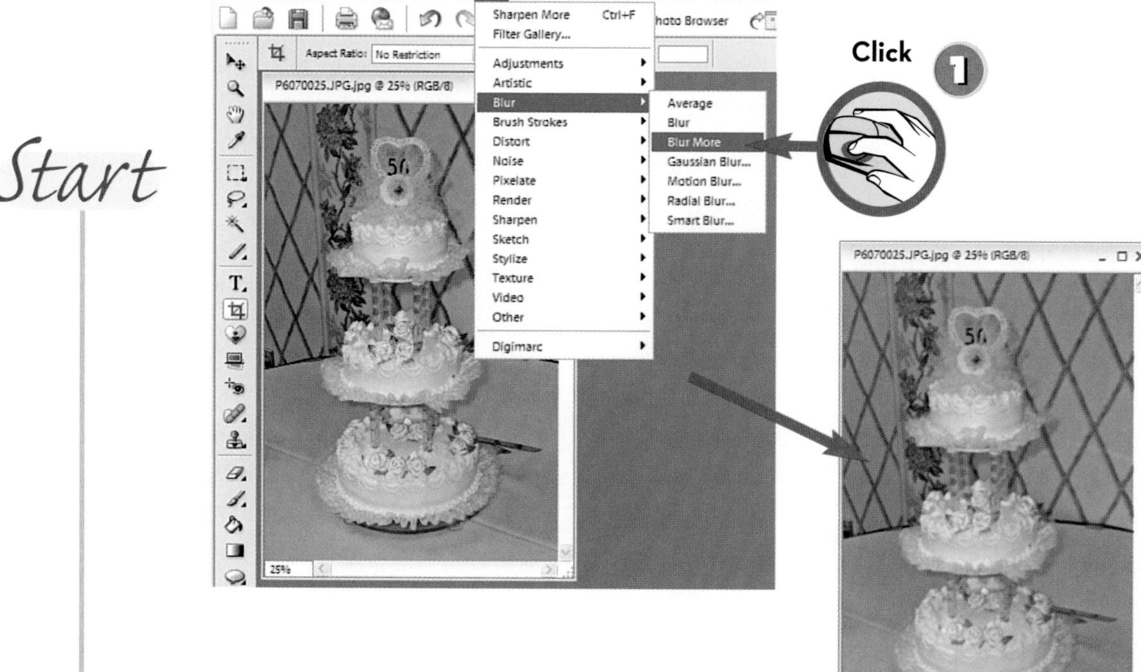

1. With a picture in the active image area, choose **Filter**, **Blur**, **Blur More**.

End

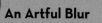

TIP

An Artful Blur

This task uses **Blur More** because the result of the Blur command in the submenu can be hard to see. The other Blur commands in the submenu are for when you're feeling arty.

part 5

ADDING TITLES AND TEXT

Being able to print text on your photos can turn your digital snaps into greeting cards, invitations, postcards, or posters.

An interesting photo with a caption can be a news item for a community newsletter or family Web site.

And even if you don't aspire to craft your own greetings or write your own news, including captions in your picture files is a much better way of identifying and describing your photos than writing on the back of the prints with a ballpoint pen.

As you gain skill working with text, you'll want the flexibility of keeping different pieces of text on separate *layers*, which work like clear sheets of acetate you can draw on. Layers permit you to add text and artwork without making any permanent changes to the underlying image. So be sure to take a look at the tasks in Part 10, "Using Layers to Combine Photos and Artwork."

And don't worry. None of this is complicated. Photoshop Element's built-in features help you create professional-looking output, whether it be for a Web site or picture postcard, without having to sweat the technical details.

SAY IT WITH PICTURES AND WORDS

Don's new Kawasaki motorcycle is much redder
than his previous Yamaha model.

Adding a caption can give a photo "news value."

Why not think of your life as a game—and you're the star!

ADDING AND PRINTING PHOTO CAPTIONS

This method of adding a caption to a photo stores the text information with the image file. When you check the Caption check box in the Print Preview dialog box, your photo prints with the caption outside the image area, centered beneath it.

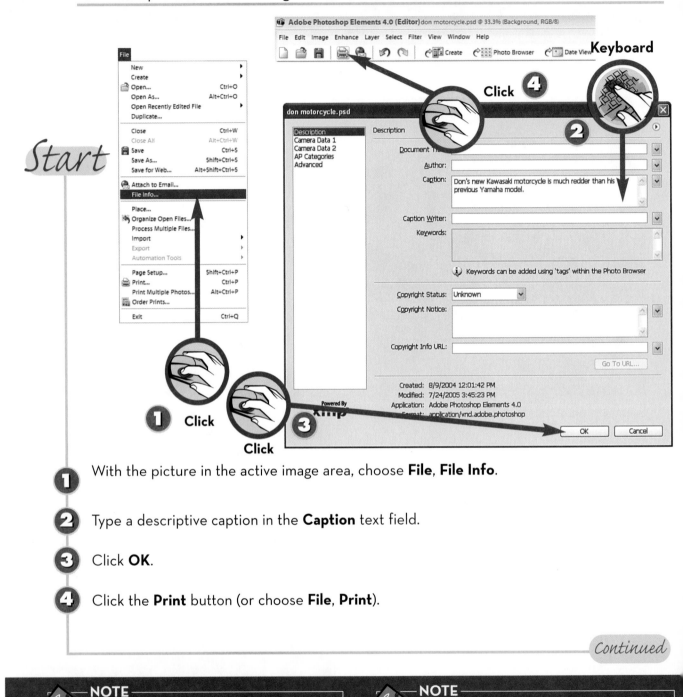

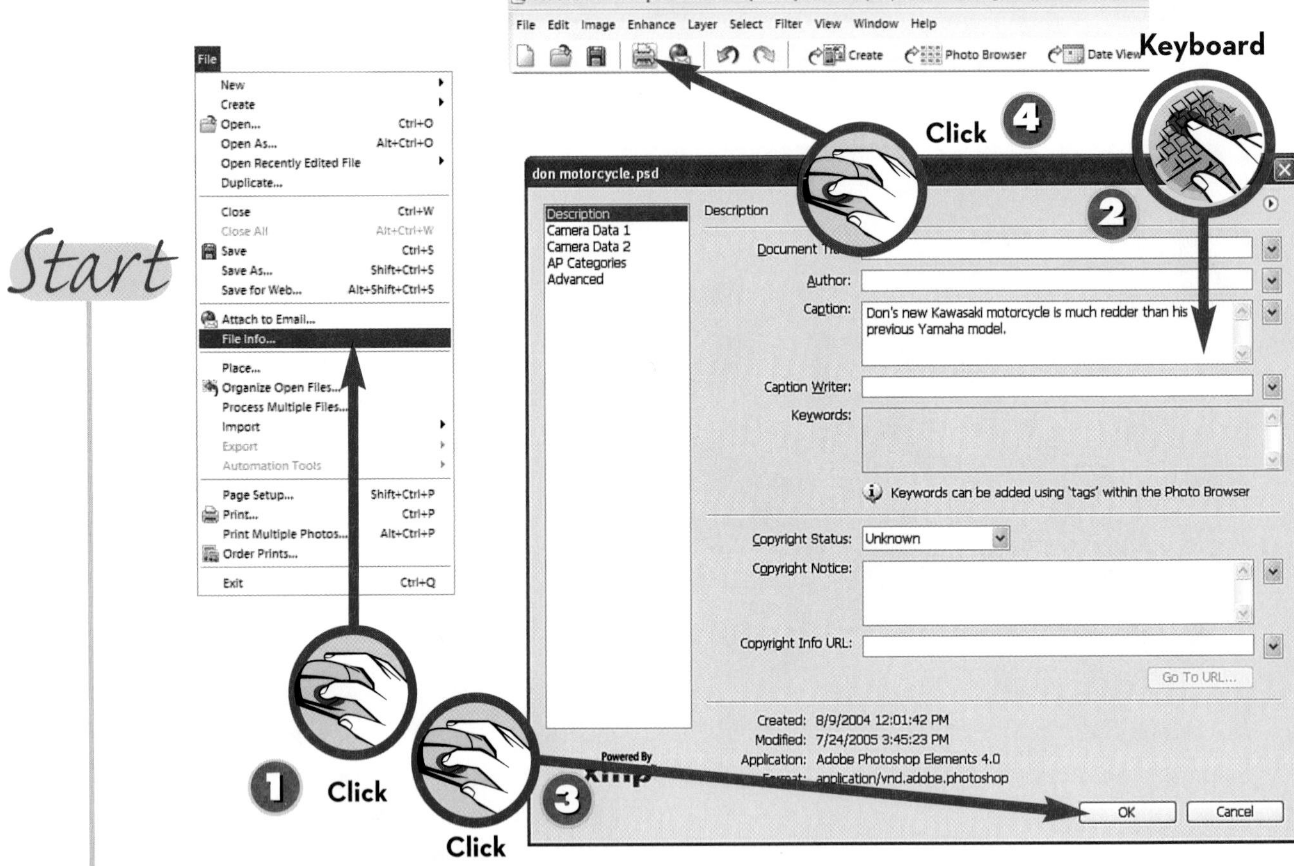

1. With the picture in the active image area, choose **File**, **File Info**.
2. Type a descriptive caption in the **Caption** text field.
3. Click **OK**.
4. Click the **Print** button (or choose **File**, **Print**).

Continued

NOTE

Dear Diary...

In step 2, the Caption text field can hold about 25 double-spaced pages. That's enough to paste a whole text document from the Clipboard. You could use it to hold your journal entries from a trip, for example.

NOTE

Title and Author Boxes

You can also type entries into the Document Title and Author boxes seen on the File Info dialog. However, only the Caption field is printed by this procedure.

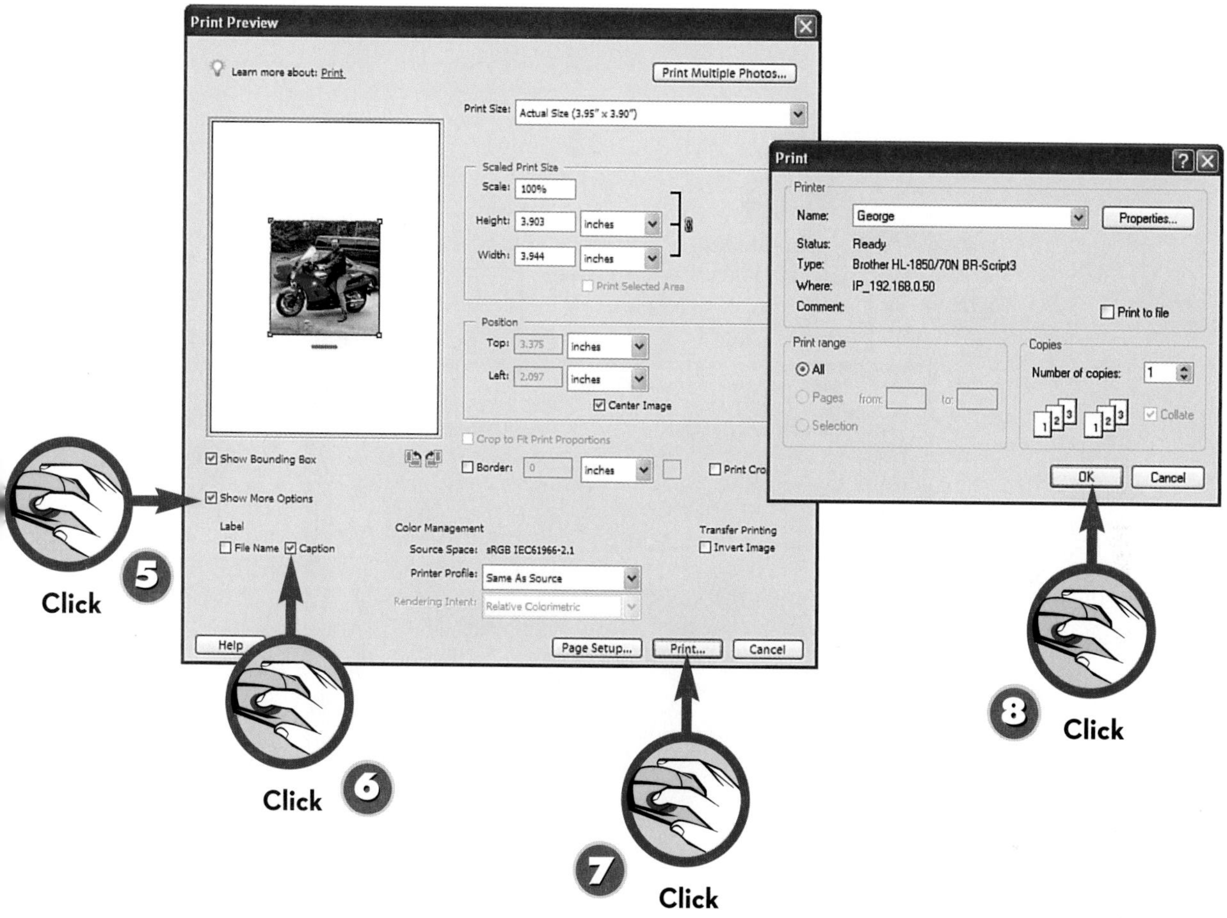

Click 5

Click 6

Click 7

Click 8

1. Check the **Show More Options** check box.
2. Check the **Caption** check box.
3. Click **Print**.
4. Click **OK** in the Print dialog box.

End

TIP

Fitting on the Page

If you haven't sized the image to fit the canvas and the canvas to the paper size, choose **Fit on Page** from the Print Size pop-up menu in the Print Preview dialog box, and Photoshop Elements fits to the paper size chosen for the printer.

OVERLAYING TYPE ON AN IMAGE

Here's the direct approach—just type over an image anywhere you want. You can press Enter between typing multiple lines in the same block of text, or you can click Commit and then repeat these steps to create a separate block that you can move and work with independently.

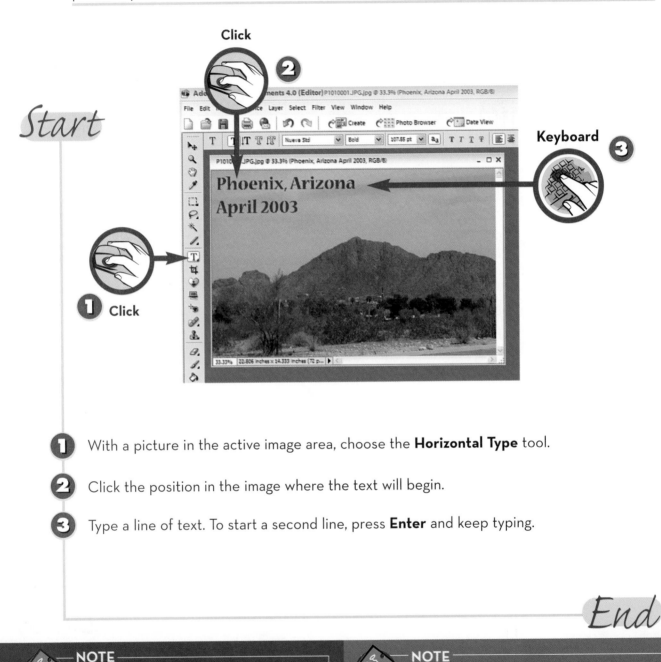

1. With a picture in the active image area, choose the **Horizontal Type** tool.
2. Click the position in the image where the text will begin.
3. Type a line of text. To start a second line, press **Enter** and keep typing.

End

NOTE

Alignment Options

The starting point for the text line in step 2 depends on the current Alignment setting in the Options bar (Left Align, Centered, or Right Align).

NOTE

New Text Layer

These steps create a new text layer automatically. Think of a layer as a clear sheet you can write or draw on without changing the image underneath.

ADDING PARAGRAPH TYPE

Photoshop Elements 4 adds a new feature to its collection: the ability to create paragraph text. This text stays within the bounding box you specify, wrapping to the next line whenever it hits the right margin. In every other way, paragraph text is just like regular text, and you can edit it the same way.

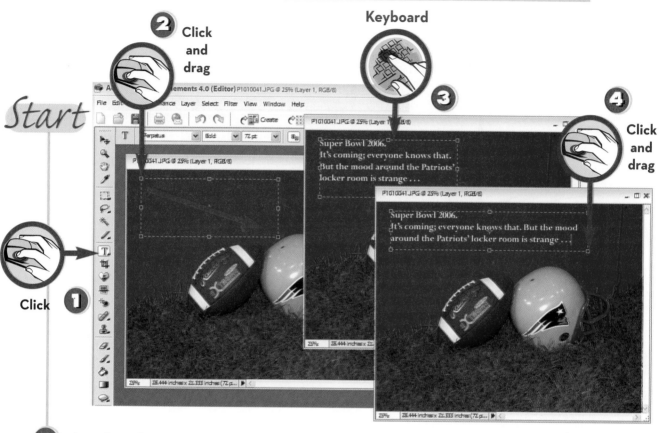

1. Switch to the **Horizontal Type** tool.
2. Click and drag in the photo to define the area you want the type to occupy.
3. Enter your text.
4. With the **Type** tool still active, click and drag a corner handle to reshape the type's bounding box.

End

TIP

When and Why

Use paragraph text when you're adding more than just a few words of text and when the precise place where each new line begins isn't important to you.

TIP

Selective Selecting

When you're editing text, double-click to select a whole word. Triple-click to select an entire line, and quadruple-click to select a paragraph. Finally, quintuple-click (wow!) to select the entire contents of a text block.

SELECTING AND EDITING TYPE

A handy way to remember how to edit text is "swipe and type" because you must first highlight the letters you want to replace.

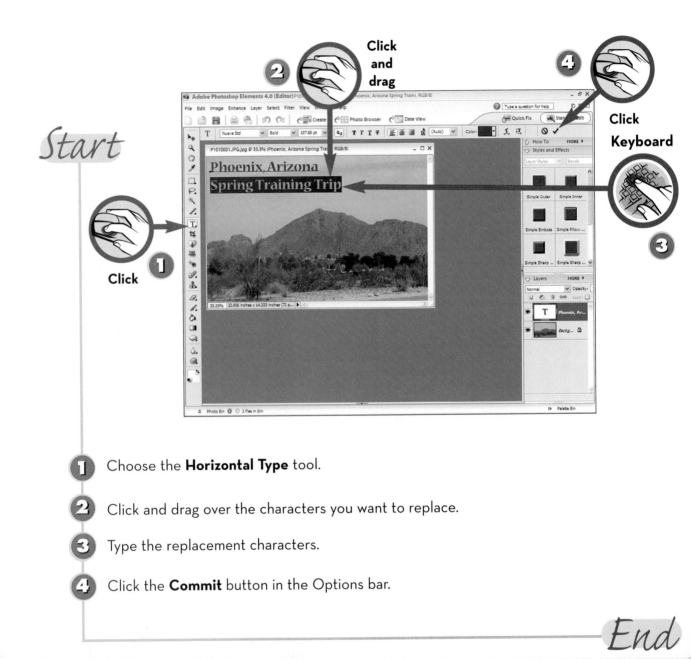

Start

1. Choose the **Horizontal Type** tool.
2. Click and drag over the characters you want to replace.
3. Type the replacement characters.
4. Click the **Commit** button in the Options bar.

End

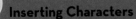

TIP

Inserting Characters

To insert one or more characters rather than replace some, just click at the insertion point in step 2 and then type.

NOTE

Keep Text Editable

You can't edit text after the text layers have been merged with the image (as in a JPEG file, for example). To keep text editable, save your work as a native Photoshop file.

CHANGING FONTS AND TYPE PROPERTIES

Words or even individual characters can have different properties, such as color or font, than adjacent characters in the same block.

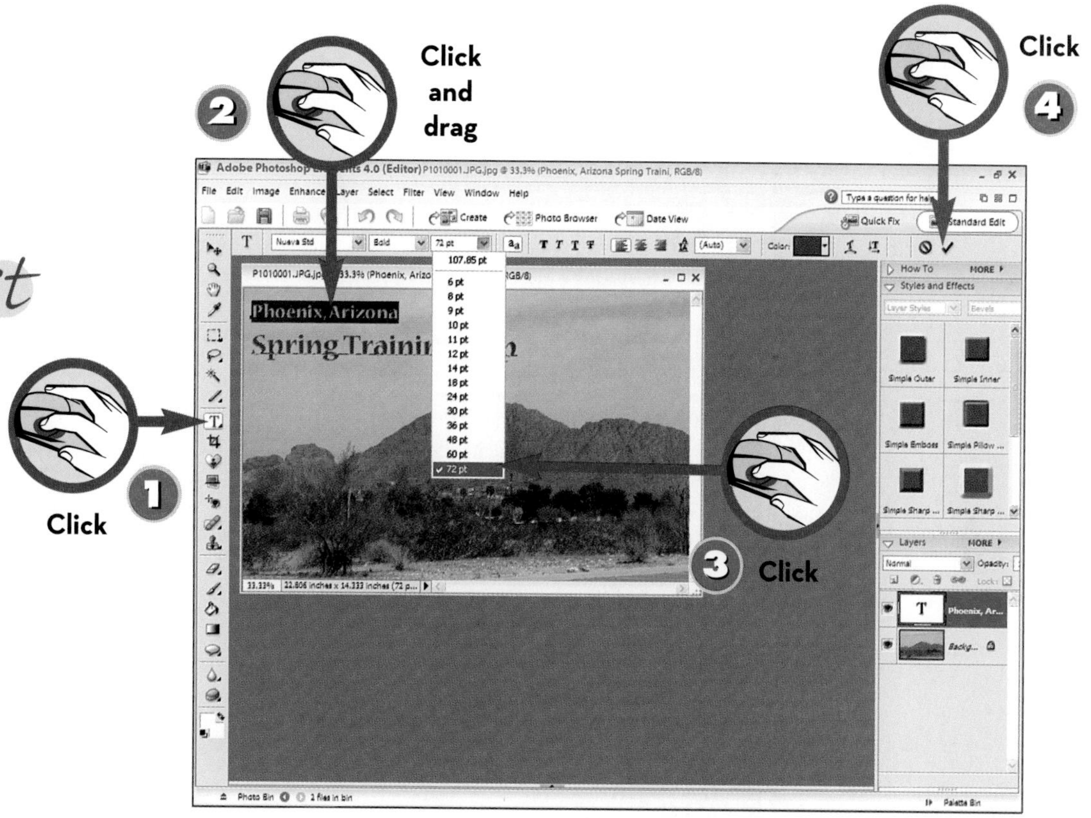

Start

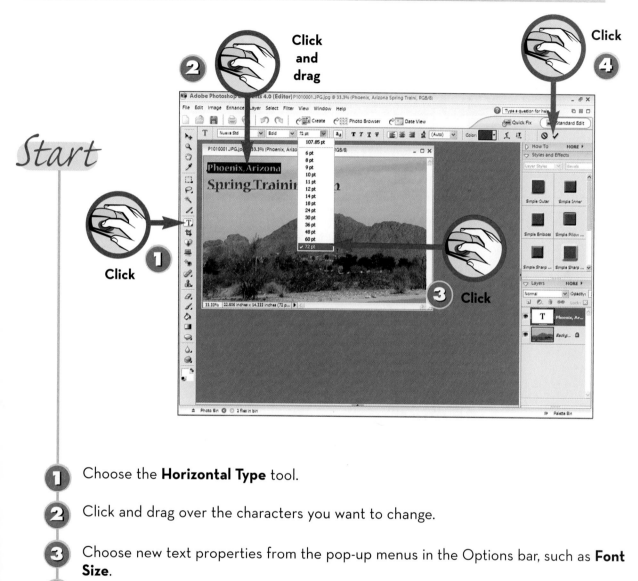

1. Choose the **Horizontal Type** tool.
2. Click and drag over the characters you want to change.
3. Choose new text properties from the pop-up menus in the Options bar, such as **Font Size**.
4. Click the **Commit** button in the Options bar.

End

TIP

Lines and Blocks of Text

Create the text in a single text block rather than individual ones when you want Photoshop Elements to take care of alignment and spacing between lines.

NOTE

Text Properties

Settings for all text properties become available in the Options bar when a text object is selected in the active image area.

RESIZING TYPE

This procedure works just like a move, but you drag a handle (corner) rather than the center of the object. It works best for condensing or extending, shrinking or enlarging text by small amounts.

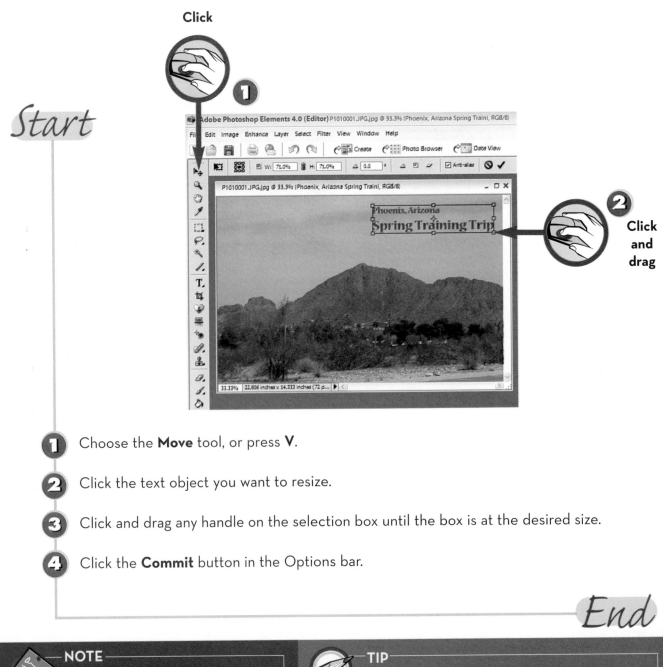

Click

Start

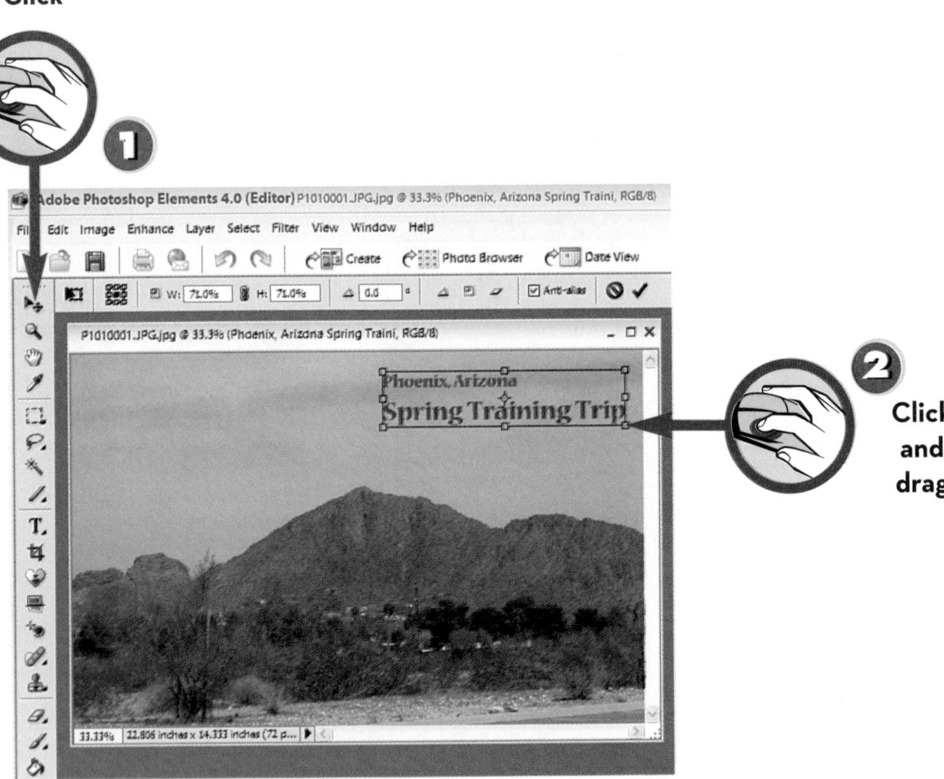

1. Choose the **Move** tool, or press **V**.
2. Click the text object you want to resize.
3. Click and drag any handle on the selection box until the box is at the desired size.
4. Click the **Commit** button in the Options bar.

End

NOTE

Auto Select Layer

For step 2 to work, the Auto Select Layer box must be checked in the Options bar (the usual setting). If it's not checked, you must switch to the corresponding text layer using the Layers palette.

TIP

Best Resizing Results

To enlarge and distort text so that its edges stay smooth, first use the Type tool to change the **Font Size** in the Options bar and then adjust slightly by dragging object handles. Or, distort with the **Image**, **Transform**, **Free Transform** command instead.

CREATING VERTICAL TYPE

Vertical text can be difficult to read, but there are times when it's the best fit in a tight space. Text created this way reads from the top downward.

Right click

Keyboard

Click

Start

Click

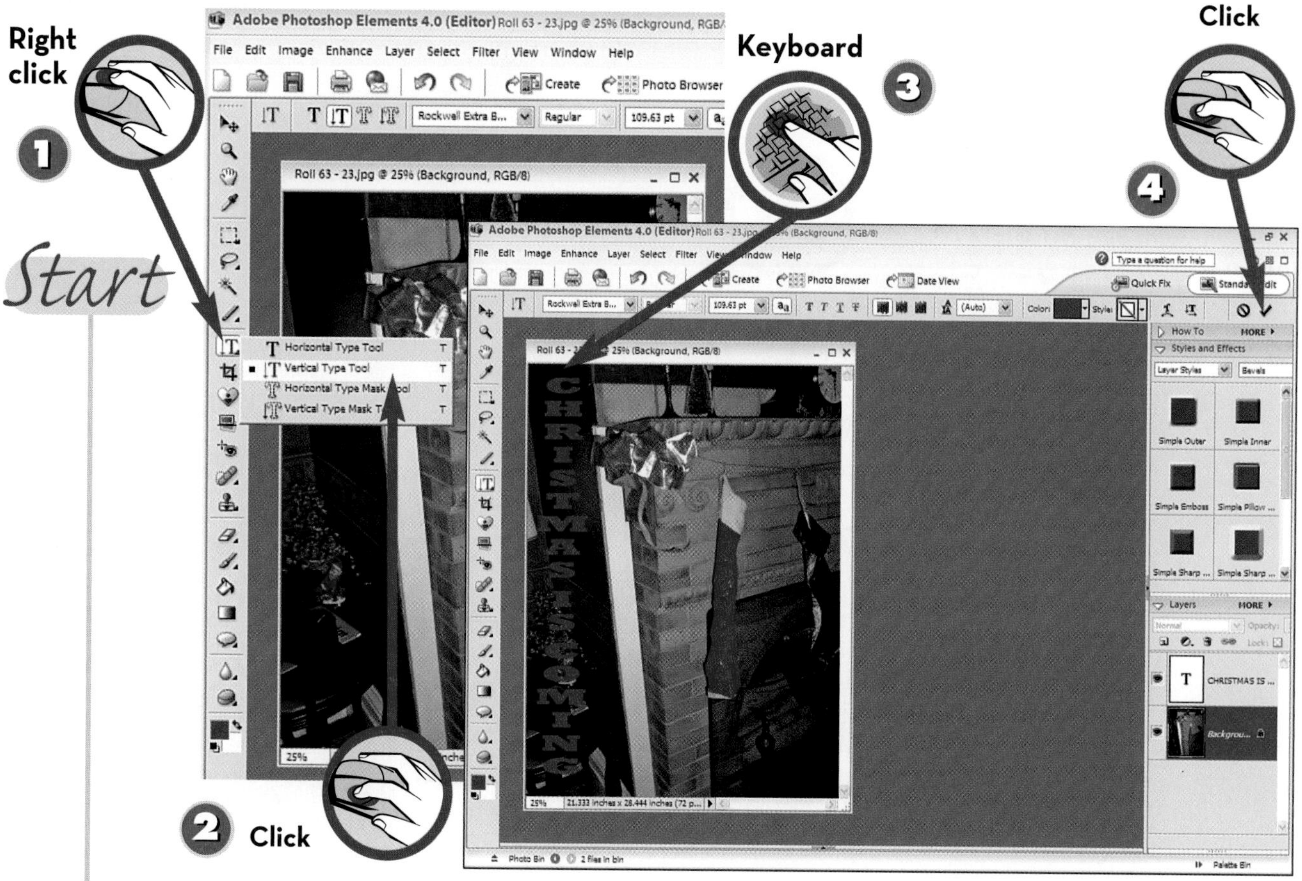

1. Right-click the **Type** tool.
2. Choose **Vertical Type Tool** from the submenu.
3. Click the starting point in the image and type some text.
4. Click the **Commit** button in the Options bar.

End

TIP

Adding More Text Lines

Press Enter after step 3 to add more vertical lines of text to the same block. But for some odd reason, the lines read from right to left. (Enter the second line first if you want them to read from left to right.)

TIP

Vertical Alignment Options

Selections for vertical alignment of text in the Options bar are Top Align, Center, and Bottom Align. But in all cases, text reads from the top downward.

ROTATING TYPE

You might want to rotate text to achieve a smarter design or to fit it to an object in the image. Just remember that it might become difficult to read if the angle is too severe.

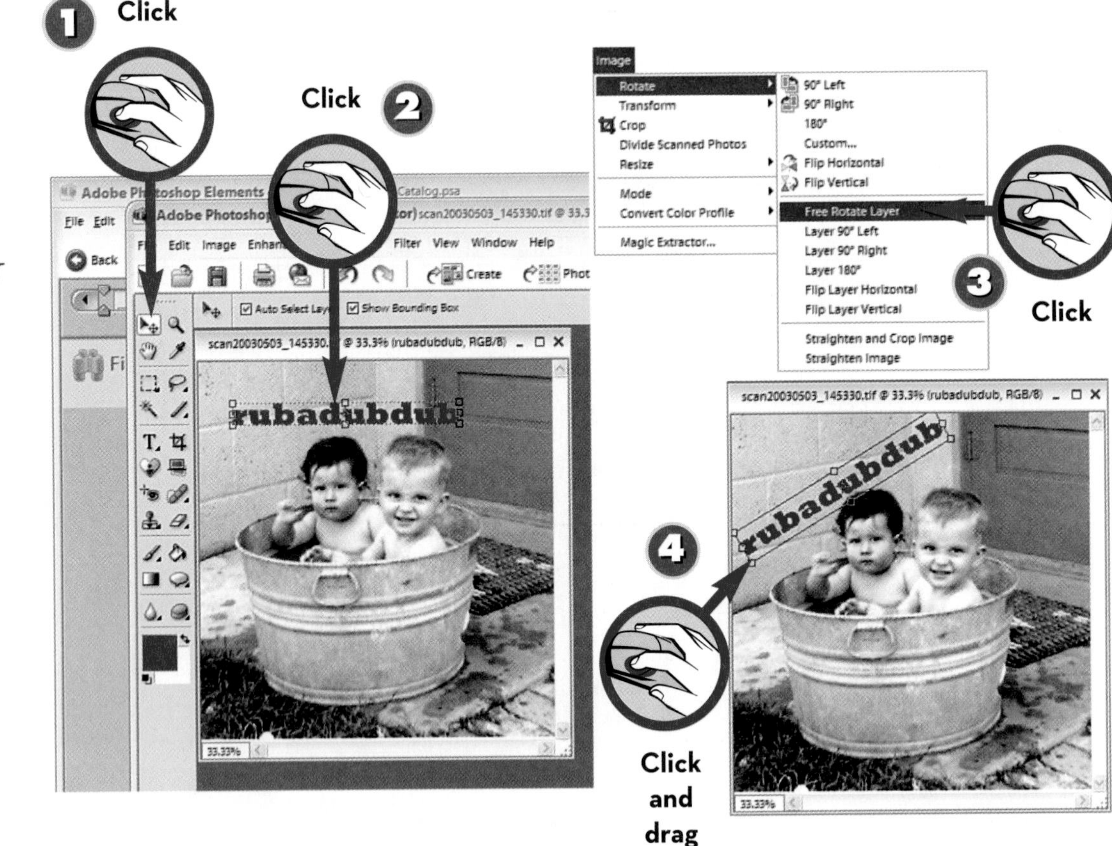

Start

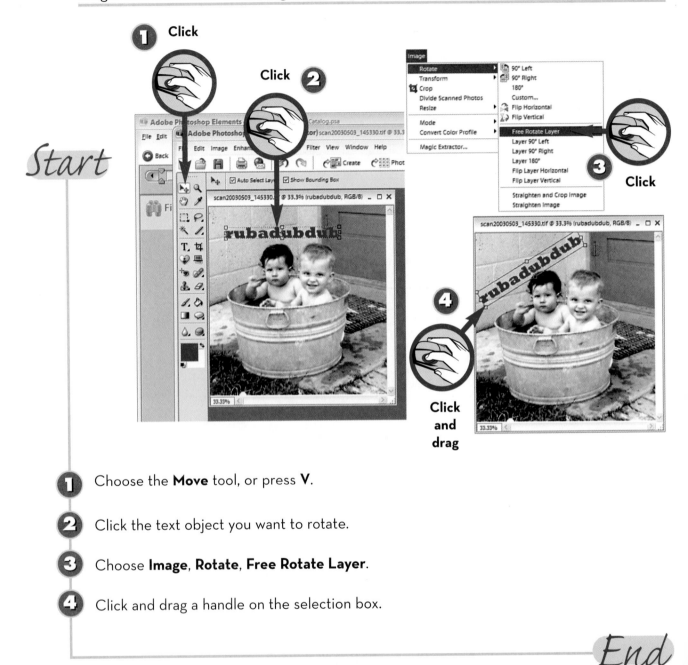

1. Choose the **Move** tool, or press **V**.
2. Click the text object you want to rotate.
3. Choose **Image**, **Rotate**, **Free Rotate Layer**.
4. Click and drag a handle on the selection box.

End

TIP

Flipping Text

Flipping (creating a mirror-image of) text can be done by choosing **Image**, **Rotate**, **Flip Layer Horizontal** or **Flip Layer Vertical**. (Submenu commands that don't include "Layer" affect the entire image.)

NOTE

Auto Select Layer

For step 2 to work, the Auto Select Layer box must be checked in the Options bar (the usual setting). If it's not checked, you must switch to the corresponding text layer using the Layers palette.

TRANSFORMING AND SKEWING TYPE

Skewing text can give it either an italic or backslanted effect, or make it appear to run up- or downhill. You can also distort it in the process if you want. Free Transform is a similar command, by which you can stretch and squish text in any direction.

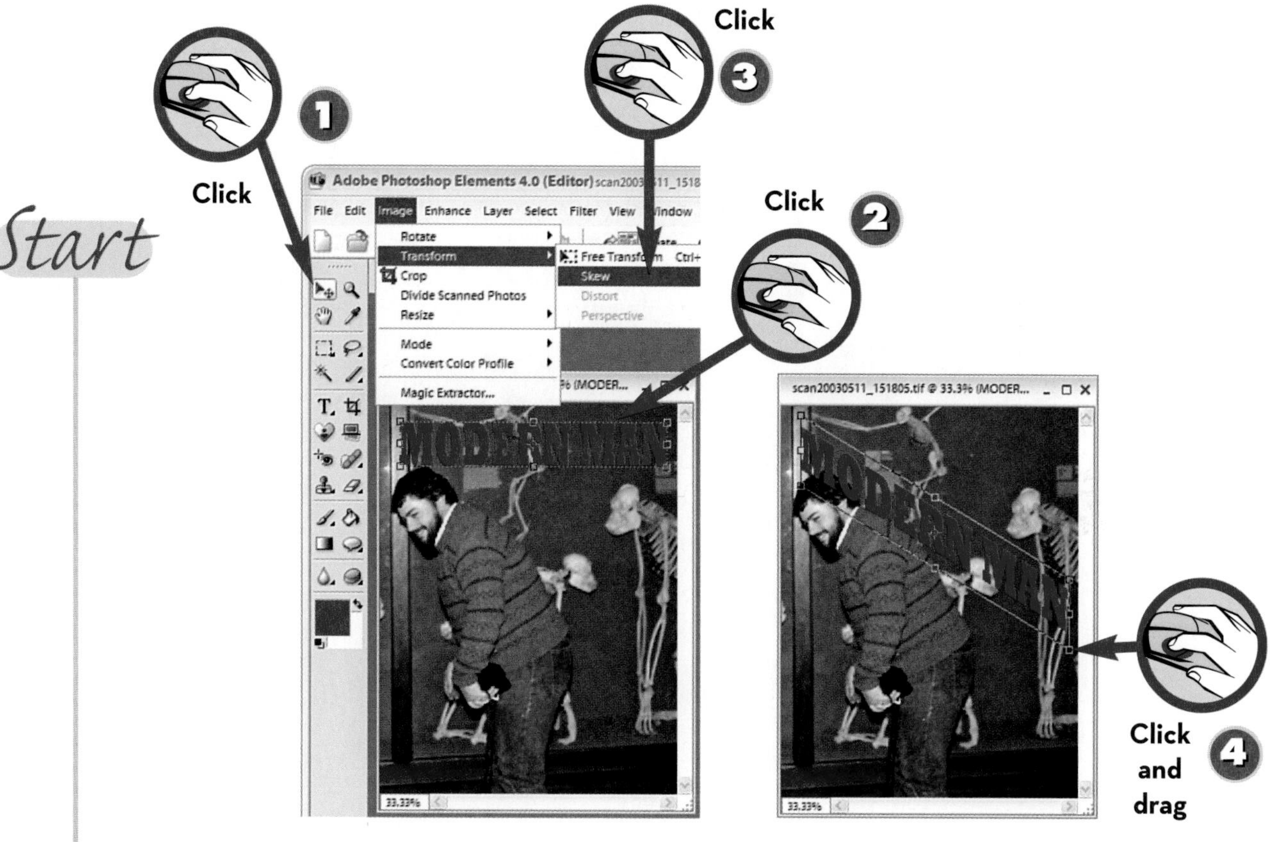

1. Choose the **Move** tool, or press **V**.
2. Click the text object you want to transform.
3. Choose **Image**, **Transform**, **Skew**.
4. Click and drag a handle of the selection box to resize and/or distort the text.

End

NOTE

Auto Select Layer

For step 2 to work, the Auto Select Layer box must be checked in the Options bar (the usual setting). If it's not checked, you must switch to the corresponding text layer using the Layers palette.

TIP

Grow or Distort Text

You can grow or distort text using the same procedure, except choose **Image**, **Transform**, **Free Transform** (or press **Ctrl+T**) in step 3. Try it and notice how this type of transformation differs from Skew.

WARPING TYPE

You can apply all kinds of fancy effects to text by this method, which is great for adding dramatic or comic touches to titles of albums and slideshows.

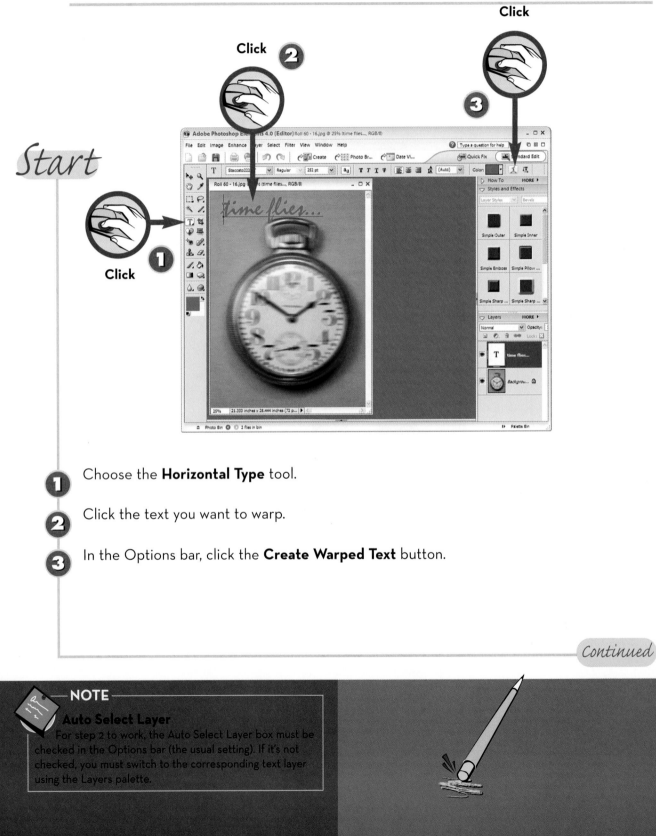

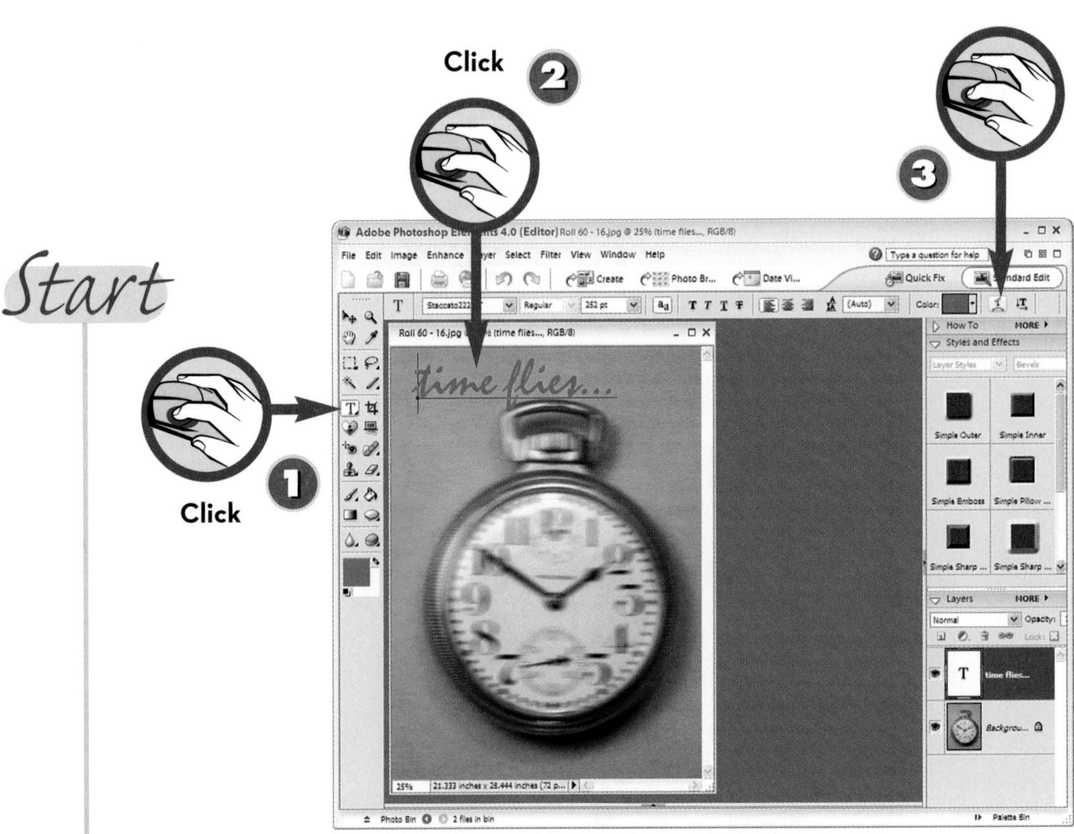

1. Choose the **Horizontal Type** tool.
2. Click the text you want to warp.
3. In the Options bar, click the **Create Warped Text** button.

Continued

NOTE

Auto Select Layer

For step 2 to work, the Auto Select Layer box must be checked in the Options bar (the usual setting). If it's not checked, you must switch to the corresponding text layer using the Layers palette.

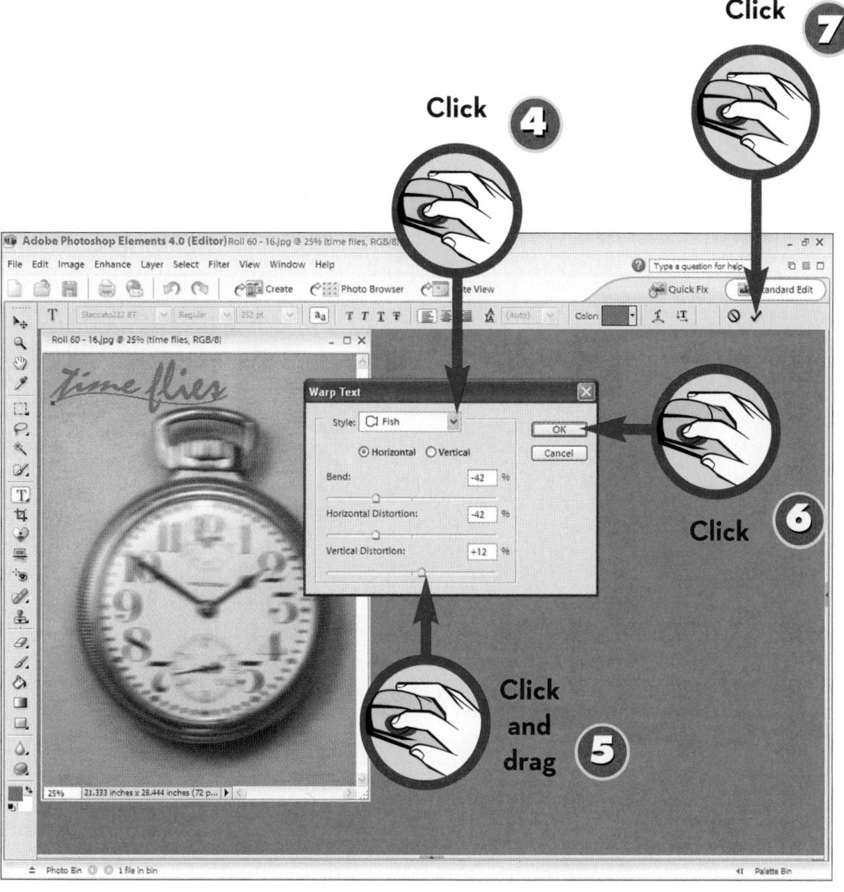

4. Choose a style from the pop-up menu, such as **Fish**.
5. Click and drag one or more sliders to adjust the degree of the effect.
6. Click **OK**.
7. Click the **Commit** button in the Options bar.

End

NOTE

Warped, Not Crazy

Warping text is usually done for comic effect. For best results, choose a font with fat letters. Some fonts don't warp well. For example, Old English and cursive fonts can become downright unreadable.

TIP

Another Way to Warp

Here's an alternative method for warping your words: Right-click the text and choose **Warp Text** from the pop-up menu.

ADDING A TALK BUBBLE

Oh, those wacky relatives and the wild things they say! A *talk bubble* can add a whimsical touch to your greeting cards and Webmail. It's actually just one of many shapes that Photoshop Elements can draw so that you don't have to create them freehand.

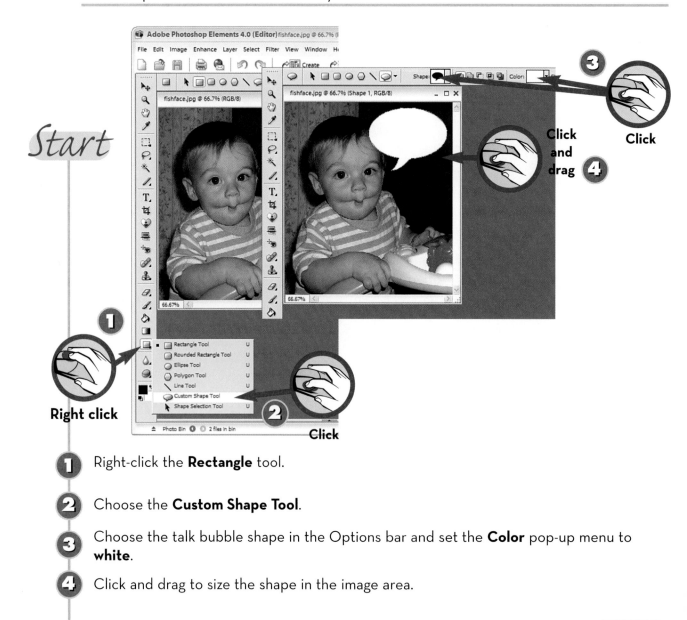

Start

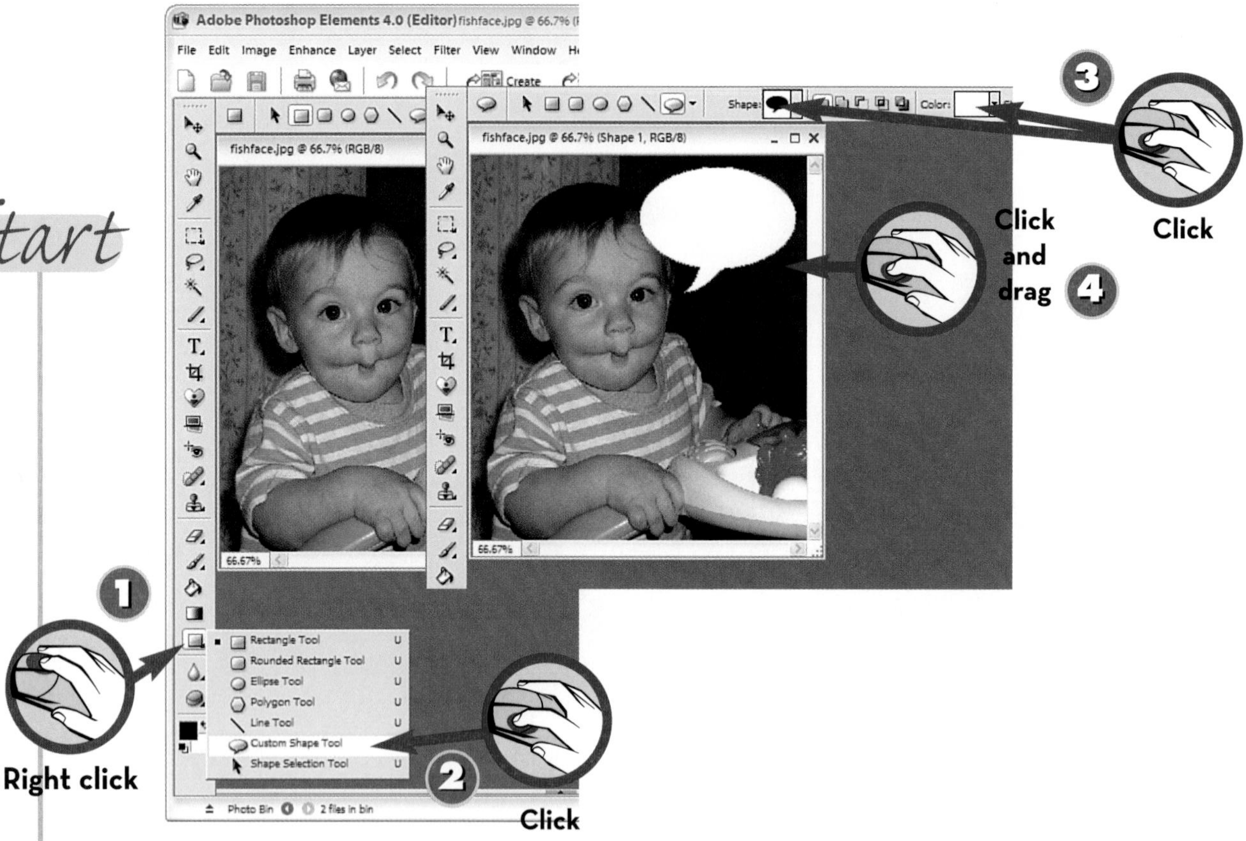

Right click

Click

Click

Click and drag

1. Right-click the **Rectangle** tool.
2. Choose the **Custom Shape Tool**.
3. Choose the talk bubble shape in the Options bar and set the **Color** pop-up menu to **white**.
4. Click and drag to size the shape in the image area.

Continued

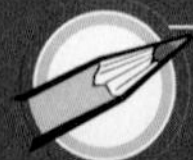

TIP

Hearts and Flowers

The talk bubble--or *speech balloon*--is just one of an assortment of custom shapes. To pick one, after choosing the Custom Shape tool, choose the **Shape** pop-up menu in the Options bar.

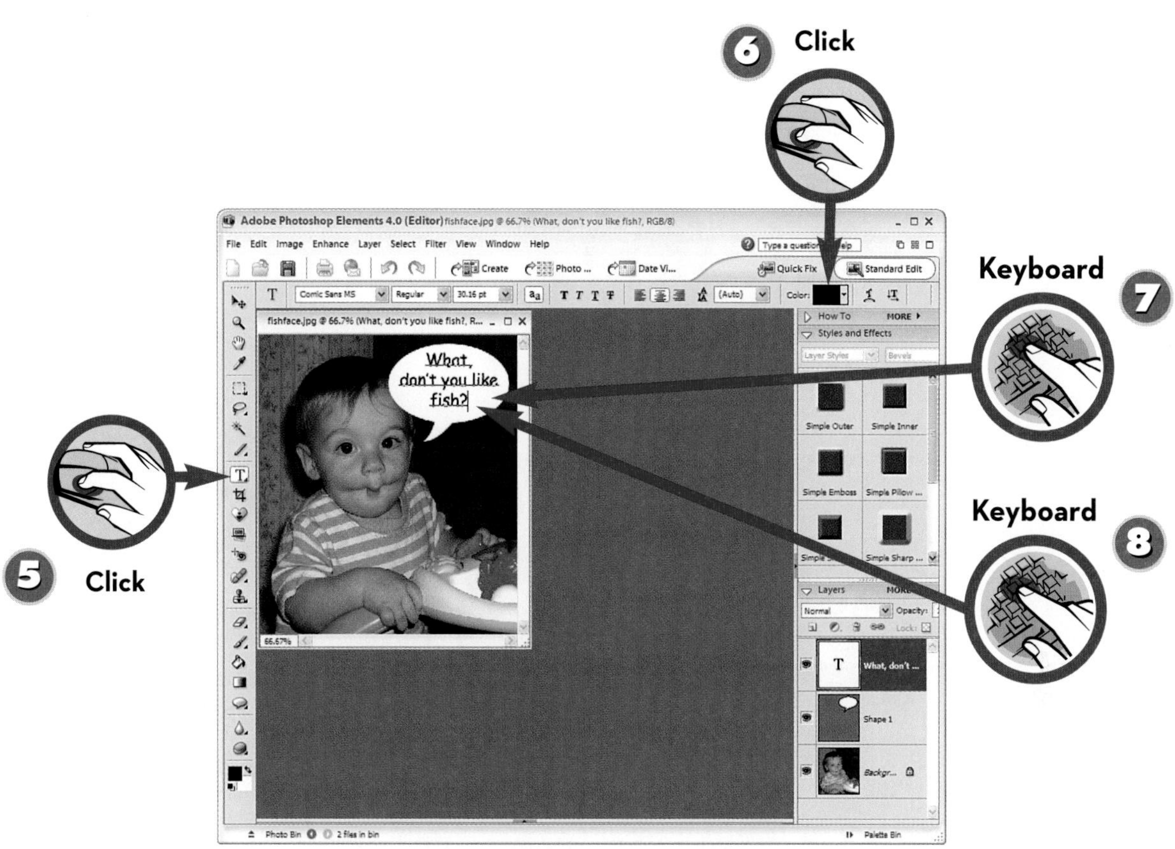

6 Click

Keyboard 7

Keyboard 8

5 Click

5 Choose the **Horizontal Type** tool.

6 Choose **black** from the **Color** pop-up menu in the Options bar.

7 Click inside the talk bubble and type some text.

8 Press **Enter** on the numeric keypad when finished typing the text.

End

TIP

Don't See a Talk Bubble?

The toolbar shows the Custom Shape tool you used last. If the Talk Bubble isn't there, choose the Custom Shape tool and choose the shape you want from the Shape box in the Options bar.

NOTE

Other Shape Tools

Besides custom shapes, other tools in the Shape submenu in the toolbar are Rectangle, Rounded Rectangle, Ellipse, Polygon, and Line.

APPLYING A TYPE EFFECT

Thumbnails in the Effects palette marked T are text effects, which you can apply to selected text with a click. If Photoshop Elements didn't include these "canned" effects, you'd have to be a skilled graphic artist, and it would take a lot more work to reproduce them.

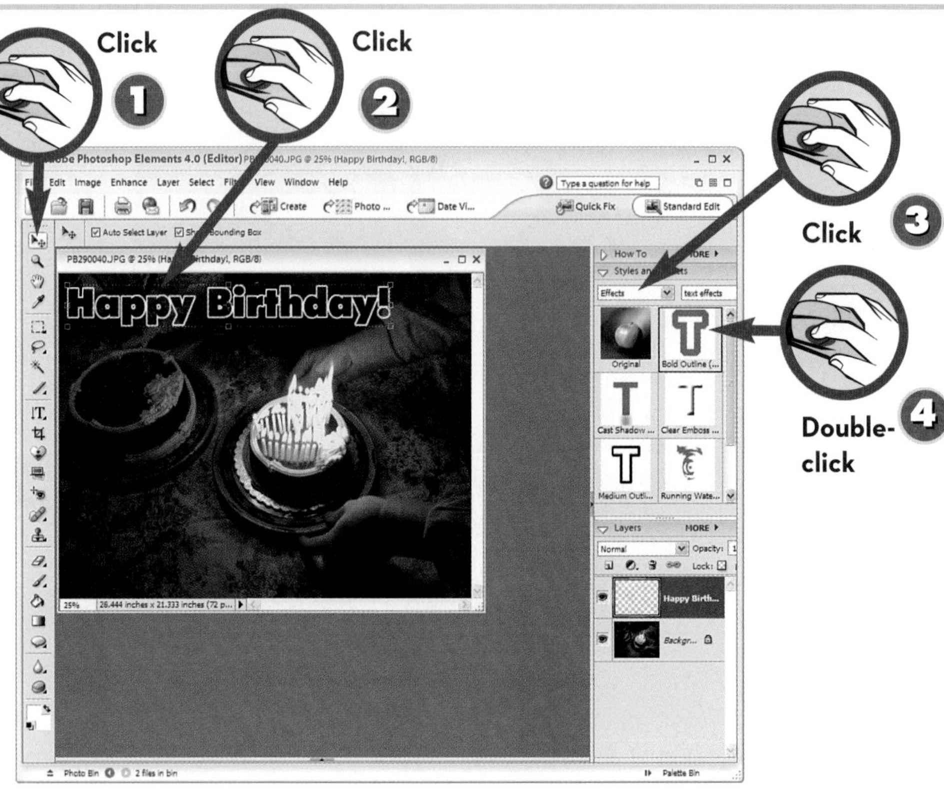

1. Choose the **Move** tool, or press **V**.
2. Click the text that needs the effect (**Auto Select Layer** must be checked).
3. In the Effects pallete, choose **Effects** from the lefthand pop-up menu, then **Text Effects** from the righthand menu.
4. Double-click the effect you want, such as **Bold Outline**.

End

TIP

Effects Palette Open?

To clear your work area, you may want to close or dock the Effects palette when you're finished. If it's not in the palette well, you can always get it back by choosing **Window, Styles and Effects**.

NOTE

Applying Text Effects

Use only effects marked T. The others will affect the entire image, not just text. You can also apply text effects by dragging an effect from the palette and dropping it on the text.

ADDING A DROP SHADOW TO TYPE

Place a drop shadow behind text to make it appear to "pop" out from the background so that it's more readable. This is particularly handy when the background has both light and dark areas and you can't find a solid area to serve as a background for the text that gives enough contrast.

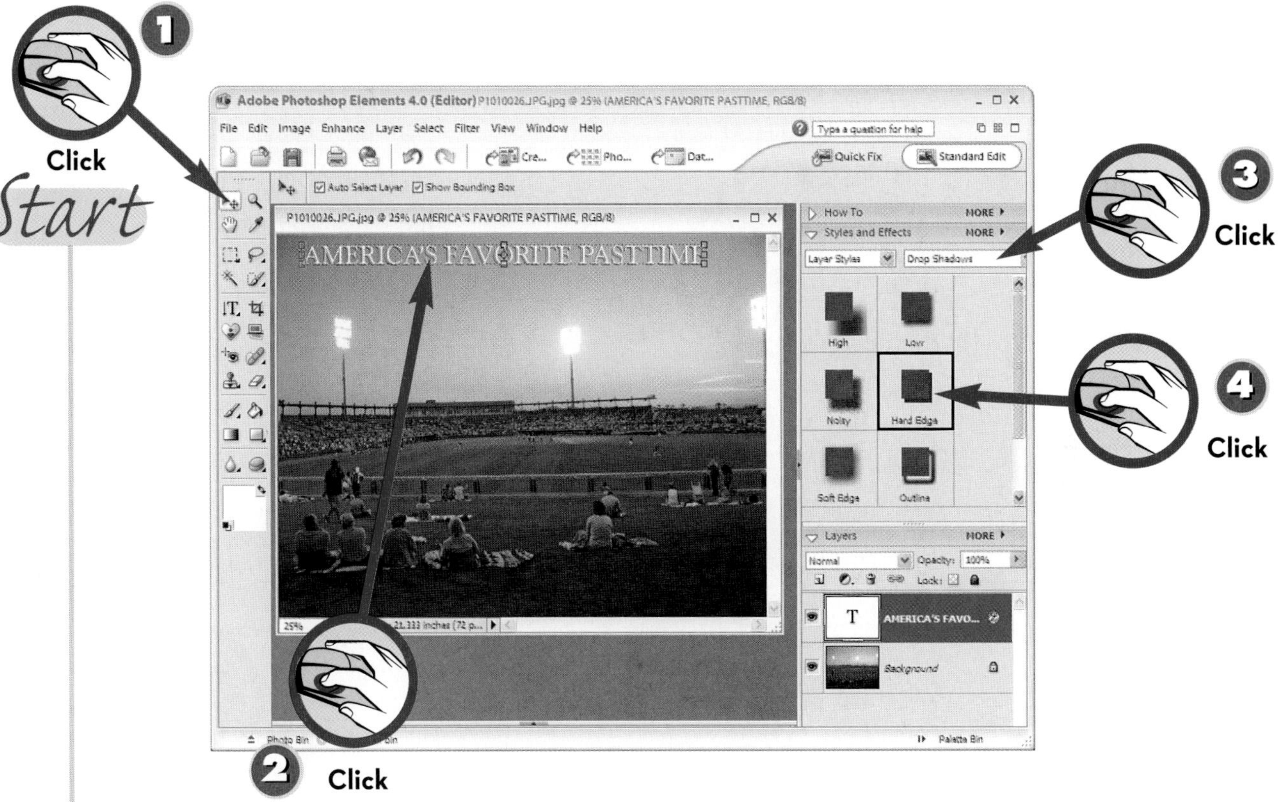

Start

1 Click

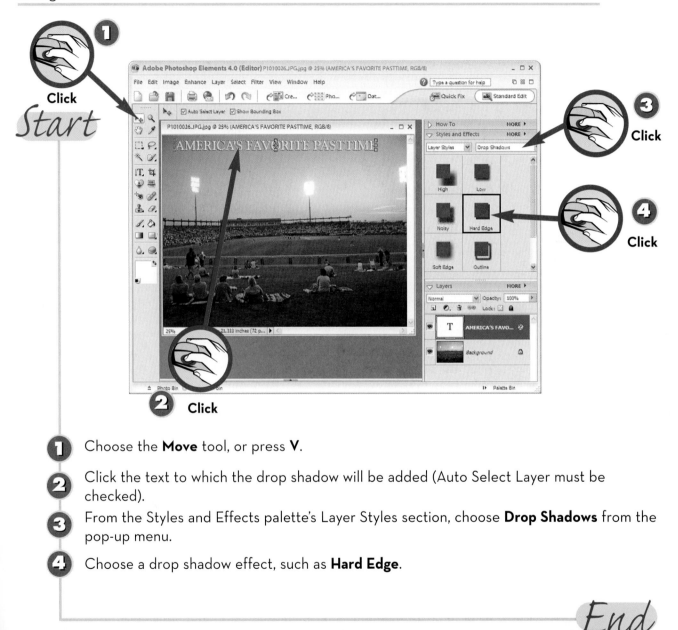

2 Click

3 Click

4 Click

1. Choose the **Move** tool, or press **V**.
2. Click the text to which the drop shadow will be added (Auto Select Layer must be checked).
3. From the Styles and Effects palette's Layer Styles section, choose **Drop Shadows** from the pop-up menu.
4. Choose a drop shadow effect, such as **Hard Edge**.

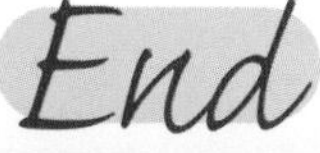

NOTE

Auto Select Layer

For step 2 to work, the Auto Select Layer box must be checked in the Options bar (the usual setting). If it's not checked, you must switch to the corresponding text layer using the Layers palette.

NOTE

Make Your Own?

You can experiment with creating your own drop shadow effects if you know this: A drop shadow is actually a duplicate of the text object, in a contrasting color, positioned behind it and offset slightly.

CREATING "HOLLOW" TYPE

A type mask is a selection—just like one you'd make with the Lasso, Marquee, or Magic Wand tool—but it's shaped like type. You can use it to fill type with pieces of the image (or another image).

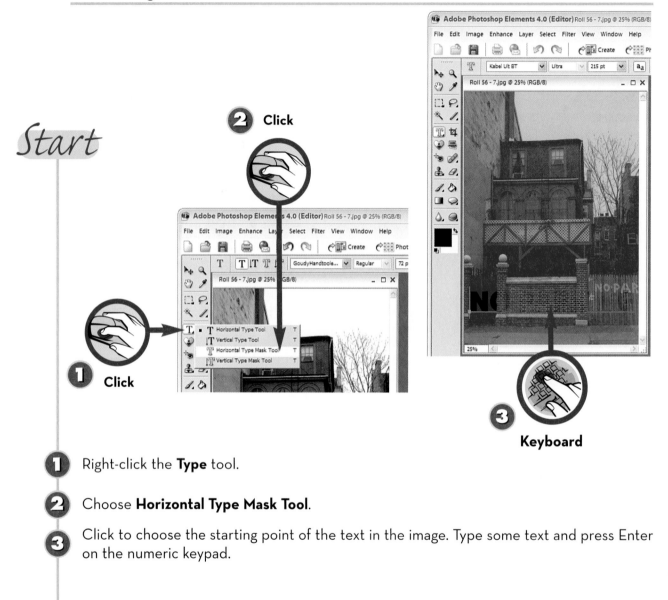

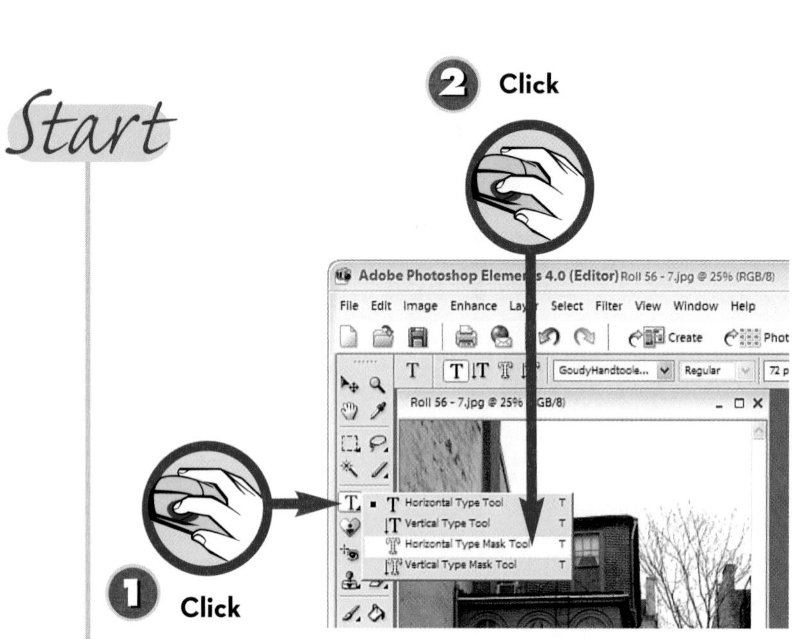

1. Right-click the **Type** tool.
2. Choose **Horizontal Type Mask Tool**.
3. Click to choose the starting point of the text in the image. Type some text and press Enter on the numeric keypad.

Continued

TIP

Use Fat Letters

A type mask works best with big, fat letters. Use it on titles for a decorative effect. If you apply it to smaller text or to a block of words, the result probably won't be readable.

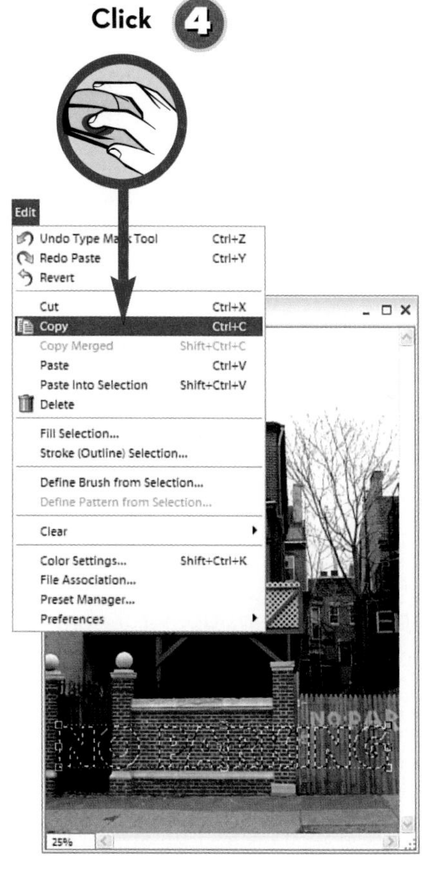

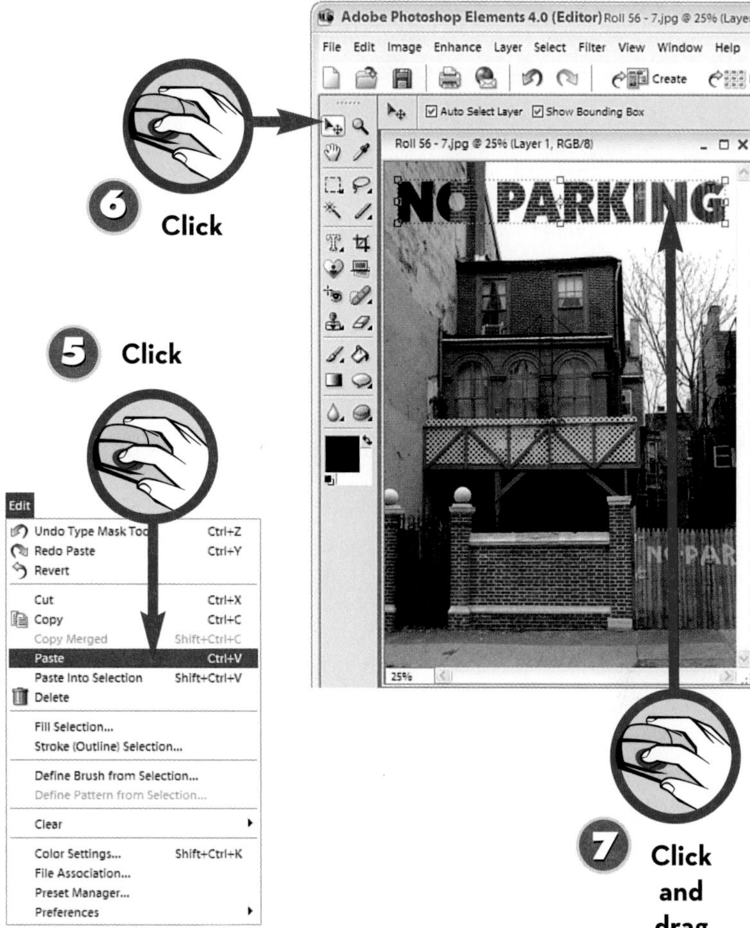

4. Choose **Edit**, **Copy**, or press **Ctrl+C**.
5. Choose **Edit**, **Paste**, or press **Ctrl+V**.
6. Choose the **Move** tool, or press **V**.
7. Click and drag the copy of the text to reposition it in the image. The background from the original position shows through the "hollow" text.

End

NOTE

Use a Variegated Background

This effect works best on variegated backgrounds, cutting and pasting from a lighter to a darker area, or vice versa. If the background is too uniform, the effect won't be obvious.

NOTE

Take It Easy

Because they're selections, rather than actual objects, type masks aren't editable after you create them. Be careful to get their font, size, position, and (of course) spelling just the way you want it because you can't go back and fix it later.

6 part

CREATING SNAZZY EFFECTS

With the invention of the electronic calculator, schoolchildren are the only ones who fret over doing arithmetic by hand. Similarly, you might be surprised at how many commercial artists don't draw from scratch anymore. Many of them earn their daily bread using computer graphics software like Photoshop Elements to make photos look like fine art.

When you've worked through the tasks in this part, you'll know many of their secrets. You can make greeting cards and party invitations look as if they were hand-drawn by a skilled sketch artist, create photo-realistic illustrations for flyers and newsletters, and add expensive-looking graphics that will give a professional touch to your personal Web site.

Photoshop Elements helps you achieve artistic effects by way of *filters* that can transform an image with a click, but in complex ways. The program comes with a wide variety of filters, and you can download even more of them (called plug-ins) from **www.adobe.com** and other vendors' Web sites. There are far too many filters to cover them all here, but you'll see enough to show you how easy they are to apply--and to start you thinking about all the creative possibilities.

HOW DID YOU DO *THAT?*

Before It helps to start with a photo that has an interesting composition, and some bright colors and contrasts.

After Here's some "fine art" that too less than a minute to make. It's the result of adding both the Palette Knife artistic filter and a Sandstone texture, and finally adjusting Hue for brighter greenery.

ADDING A DECORATIVE BORDER

A frame is just one example of the wide variety of custom, prebuilt shapes available in Photoshop Elements. To make the frame even fancier, this example applies a Craquelure filter to give the frame a rich, dimensional look.

Start

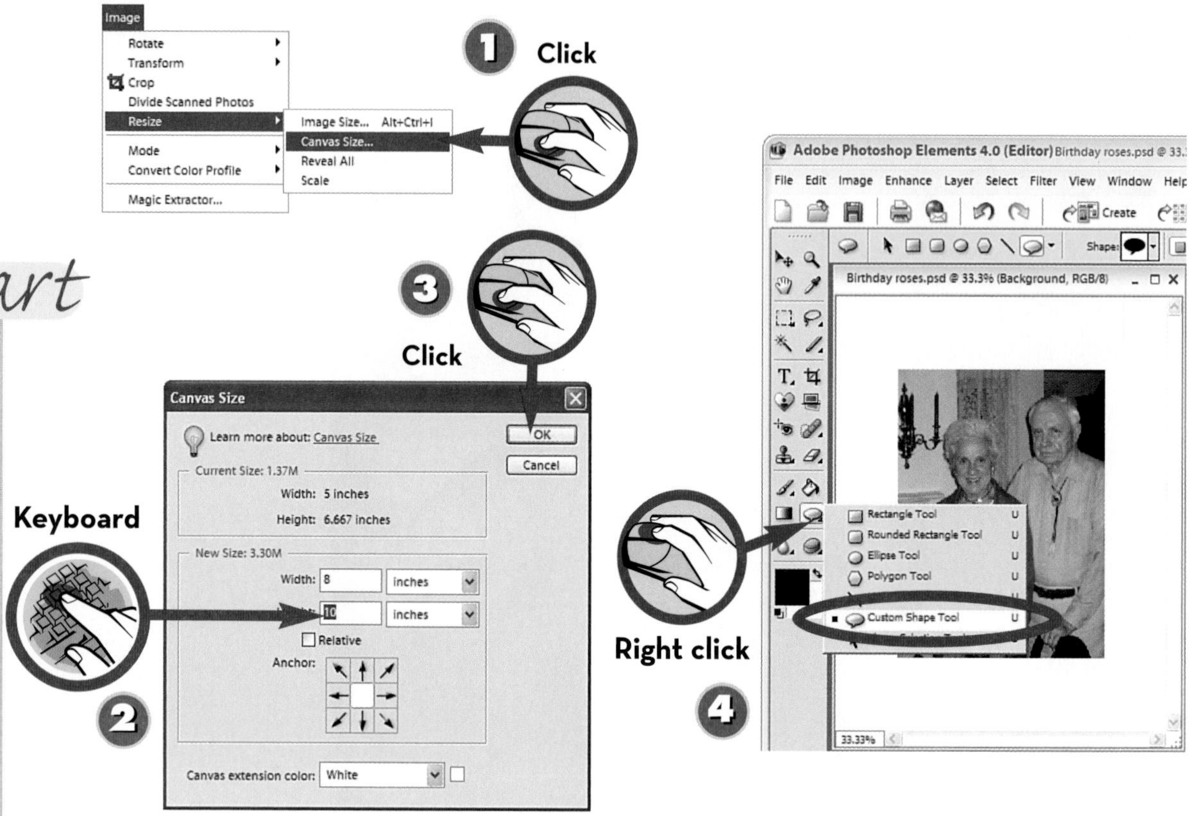

1. With a picture in the active image area, choose **Image**, **Resize**, **Canvas Size**.
2. Type a Width the same as the print size and about 2 inches wider than the current image size. Do the same for Height.
3. Click **OK**.
4. Right-click the **Shape** tool in the toolbar and choose **Custom Shape Tool**.

Continued

NOTE

Know the Image Size

In this example, the image size of the photo is about 5×7 inches. Placing it on an 8×10 canvas adds just the right amount of border for the decorative frame.

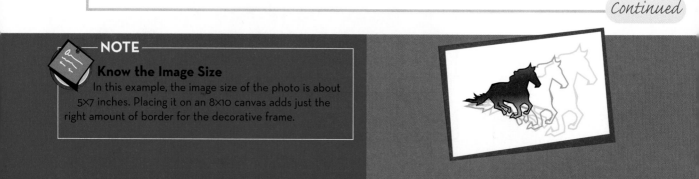

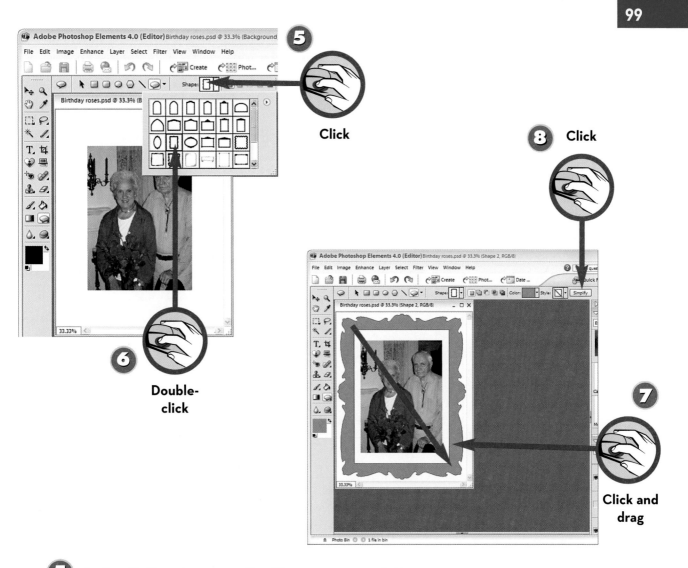

5 In the Options bar, open the **Shape** pop-up palette.

6 Double-click any **Frame** shape.

7 With the foreground color set to the color you want the frame to be, click and drag in the image to surround the photo with the frame.

8 Click the **Simplify** button.

Continued

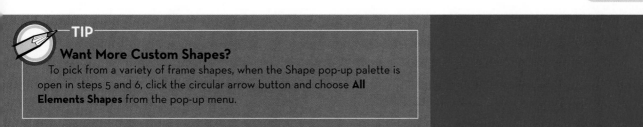

TIP

Want More Custom Shapes?

To pick from a variety of frame shapes, when the Shape pop-up palette is open in steps 5 and 6, click the circular arrow button and choose **All Elements Shapes** from the pop-up menu.

The frame used here is just one of many Custom Shapes, which are ready-made so you don't have to do any freehand drawing. Categories include Animals, Arrows, Banners and Awards, Characters, Default, Frames, Fruit, Music, Nature, Objects, Ornaments, Shapes, Signs, Symbols, Talk Bubbles, and Tiles.

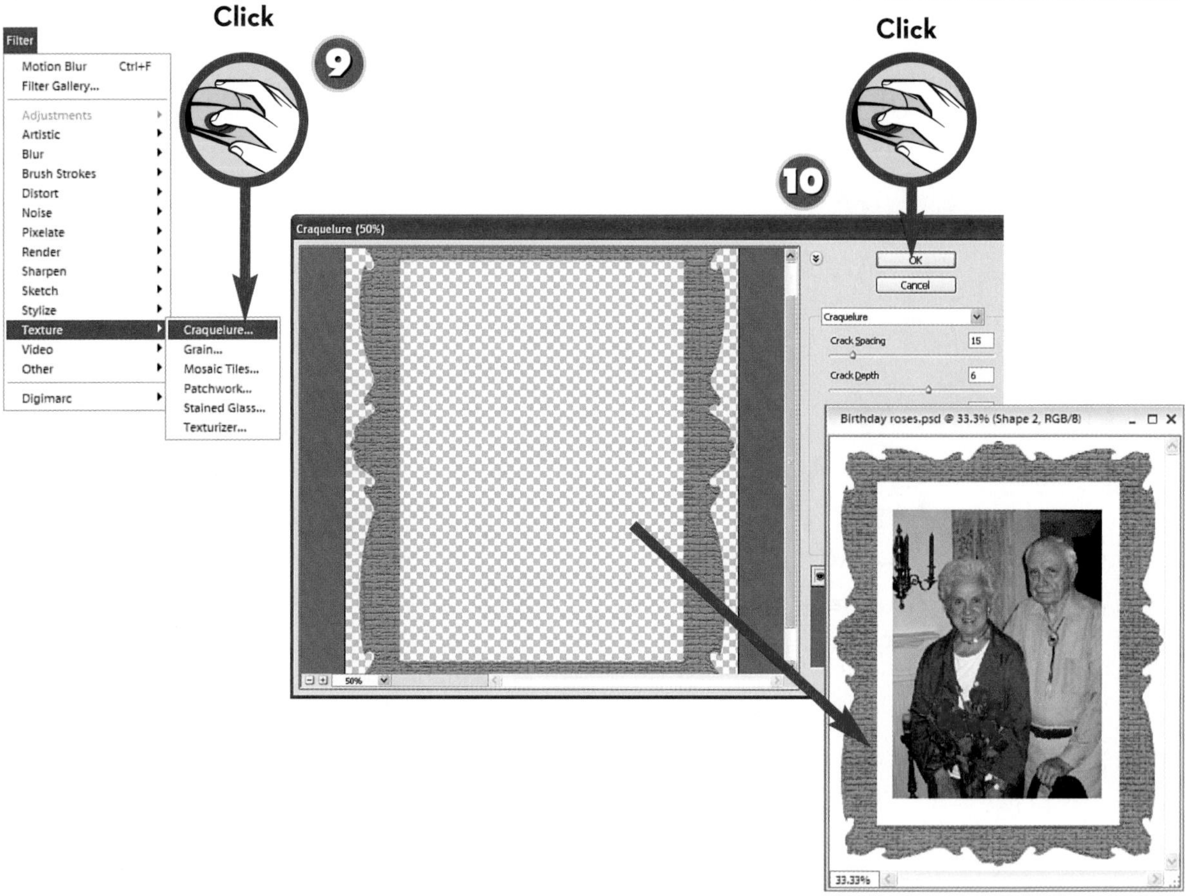

9. Choose **Filter**, **Texture**, **Craquelure**.

10. Click **OK** again.

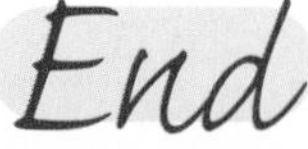

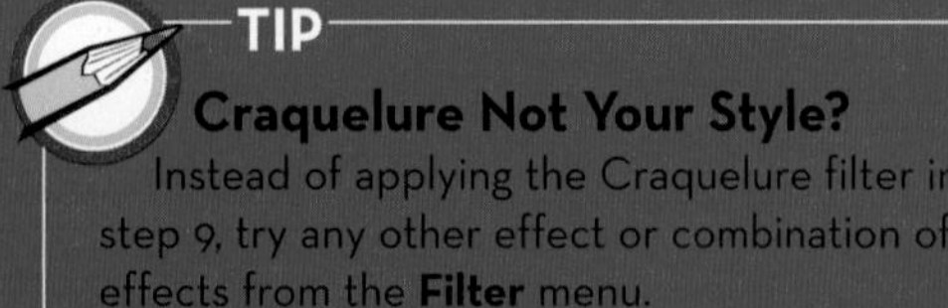

TIP

Craquelure Not Your Style?

Instead of applying the Craquelure filter in step 9, try any other effect or combination of effects from the **Filter** menu.

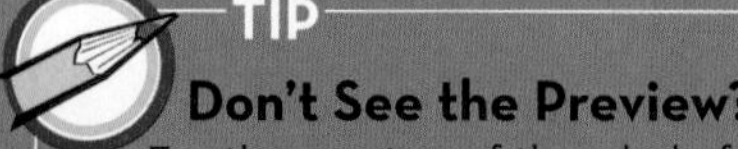

TIP

Don't See the Preview?

For the preview of the whole frame to be visible in the Craquelure dialog box in step 10, click the – button several times to reduce the view percentage from 100 to 14 percent.

CREATING A GRADIENT FILL

A *gradient fill* is a blended transition—usually between two colors—within a selected area. In this example, the gradient is applied to the entire background, but it could also be used to fill any object you select, even hollow text.

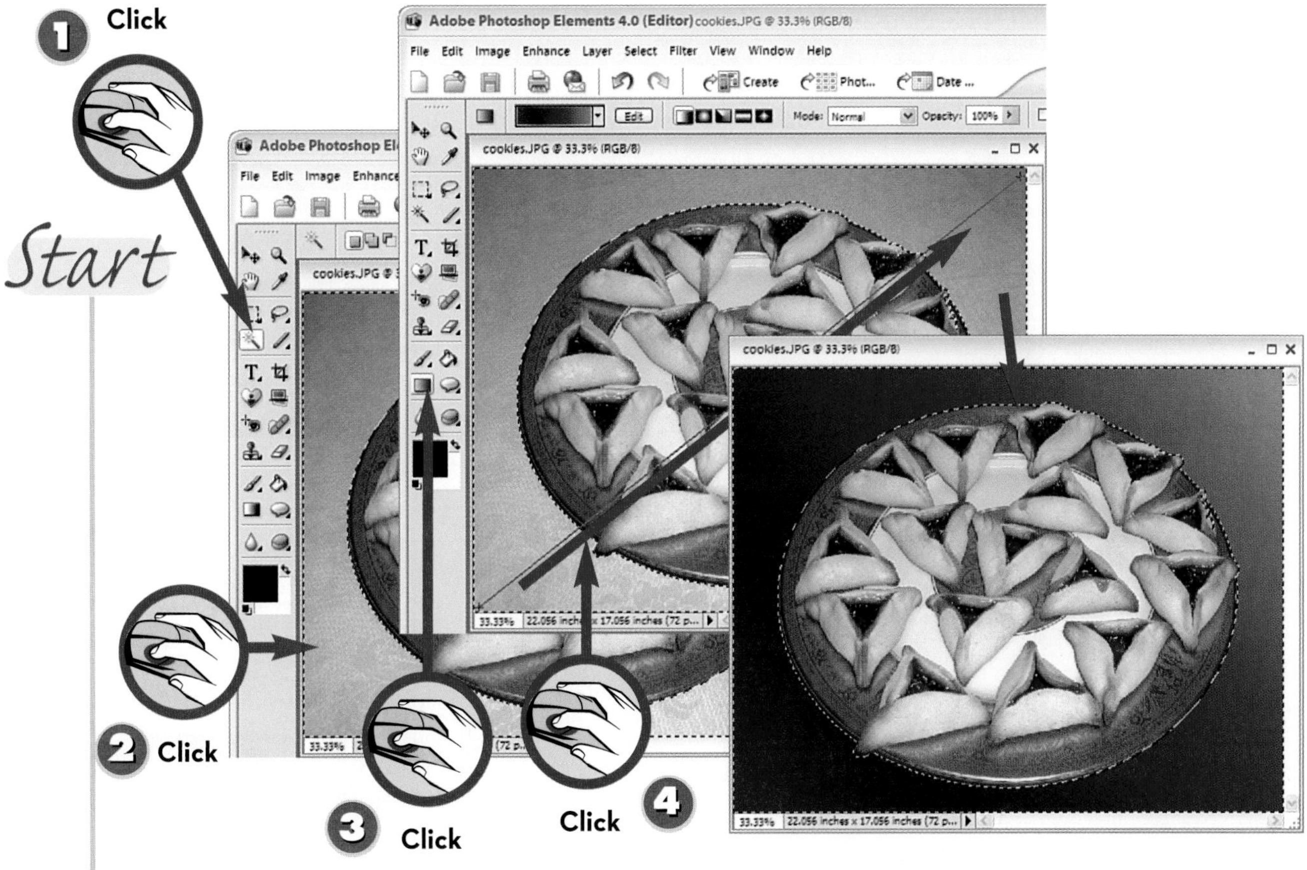

Start

1. With the picture in the active image area, choose the **Magic Wand** tool, or press **W**.
2. Click to select the area in the image to which the effect will be applied.
3. Choose the **Gradient** tool, or press **G**.
4. Click and drag across the area to be filled in the direction you want the color gradation to take. (Press **Ctrl+D** to release the selection.)

End

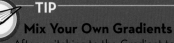

TIP

Making Your Selection

Use any combination of selection tools in step 1 (Magic Wand, Lassos, or Marquees). Press **Shift** as you select with a tool to add an area to the current selection, **Alt** to subtract.

TIP

Mix Your Own Gradients

After switching to the Gradient tool, clicking the **Edit** button in the Options bar opens the Gradient Editor, which contains options for creating custom gradients.

MOUNTING A PHOTO ON A FANCY BACKGROUND

Putting a cherished family photo in an expensive frame is a fine idea, but the price of a custom matte is a needless expense. Create your own fancy background, and it won't cost you any more than a little extra printer ink. And yours will probably be prettier than any you can buy.

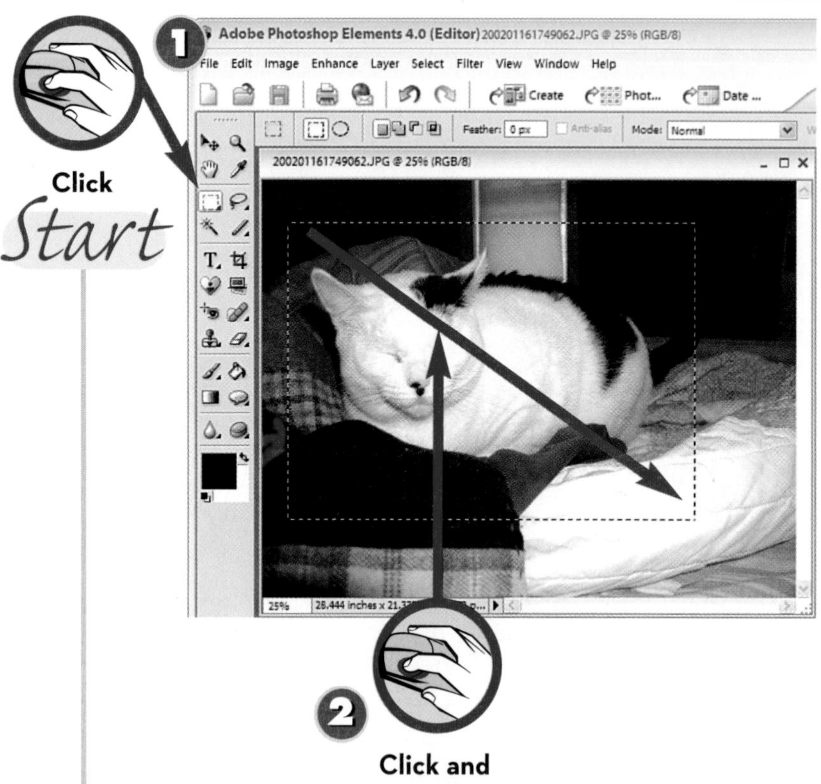

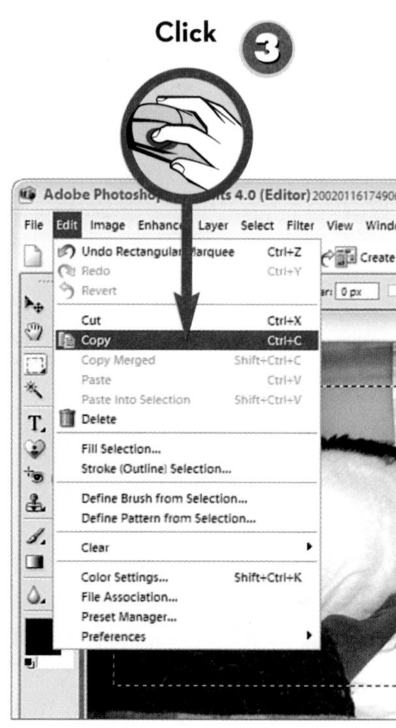

1. With the photo in the active image area, choose the **Rectangular Marquee** tool, or press **M**.
2. Click and drag to frame the image.
3. Choose **Edit**, **Copy**, or press **Ctrl+C**.

Continued

NOTE

Crop, While You're at It

You don't need to crop your photo first, because selecting the area to copy has the same result. But if the selection is too small in relation to the fancy background image, resample the image first to increase resolution.

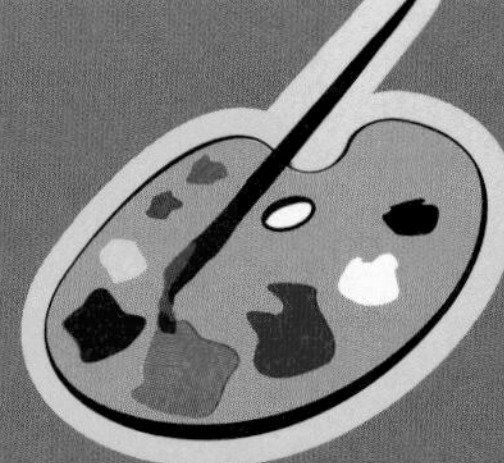

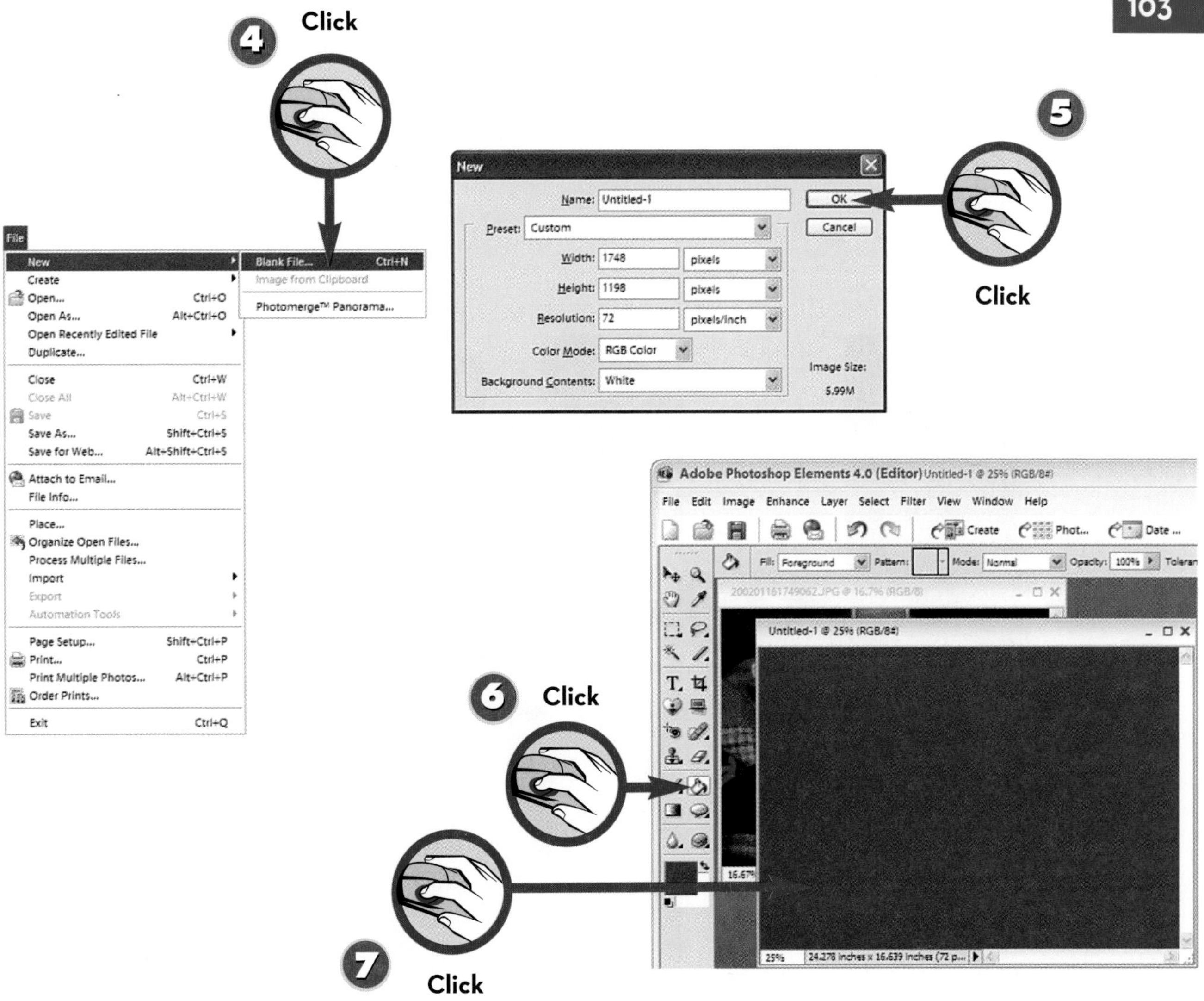

Choose **File**, **New**, **Blank File** or press **Ctrl+N**.

Increase the Width and Height measurements by about 20%; then click **OK**.

Choose the **Paint Bucket** tool, or press **K**.

Click in the new image area to fill it with color.

Continued

TIP

What Color Do You Prefer?

The Paint Bucket tool deposits the current foreground color. To make a different choice, click the topmost color patch at the bottom of the toolbar, and choose a new color from the Color Picker.

TIP

You're Not Stuck

In step 6, for a different look, after switching to the **Paint Bucket** tool, choose **Pattern** in the Fill box in the Options bar, choose a pattern, and click inside the image area to fill the background with the pattern.

By adding a frame using Photoshop Elements, you can begin to think of every photo you shoot as just the starting point for a piece of attractive, personalized artwork. Traditionally, film photographers didn't get involved in such artistic cutting and pasting, but in today's digital realm, it's just so easy.

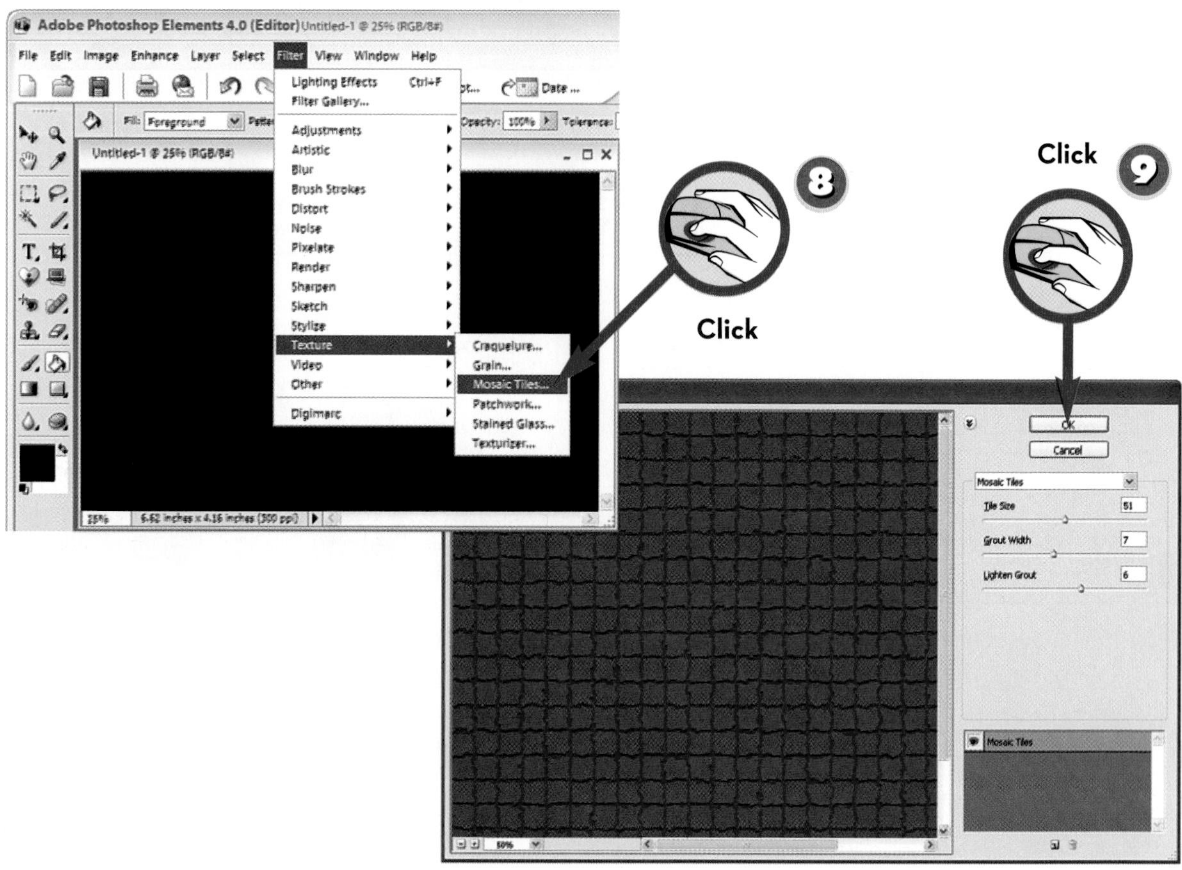

8 Choose **Filter**, **Texture**, **Mosaic Tiles**.

9 Click **OK**.

Continued

NOTE

Varying Textures

Like the Craquelure filter shown previously, you can vary Mosaic Tiles by adjusting sliders after step 8. Other available textures are Grain, Patchwork, Stained Glass, and Texturizer (for surface effects such as Canvas and Burlap).

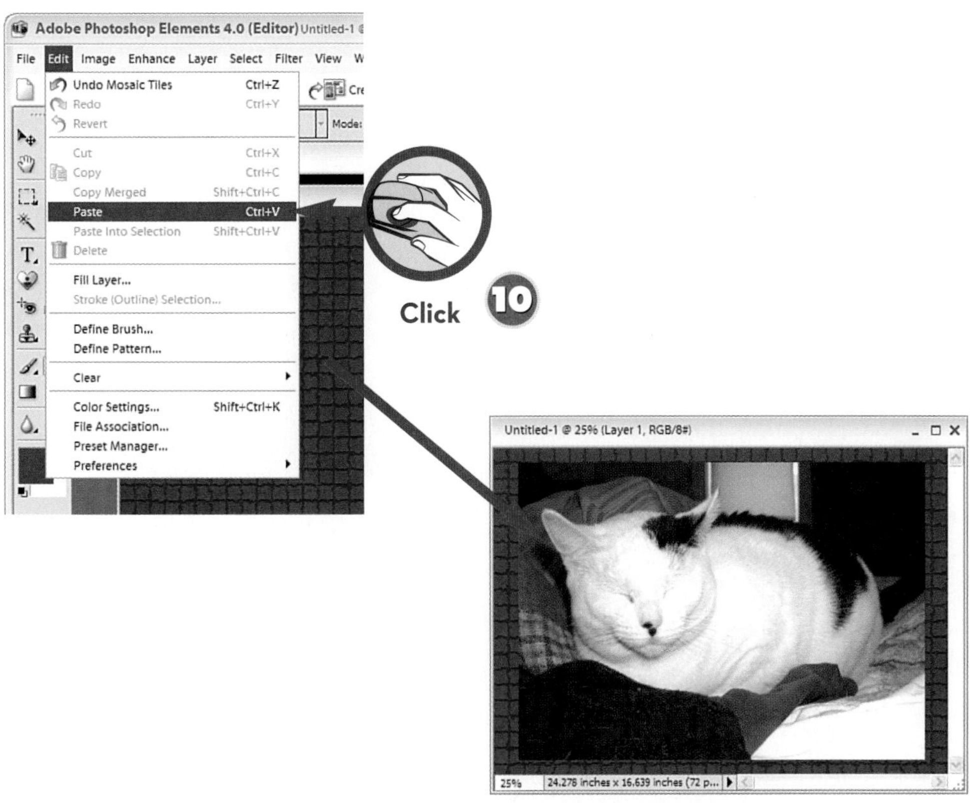

10 Choose **Edit**, **Paste**, or press **Ctrl+V**.

End

NOTE

Metal or Paper?

Applying a gradient effect to the background instead of the grainy texture can give the impression of a metallic picture frame.

TIP

Didn't Work as Advertised?

The size of the pasted photo in the new window depends on the relative image sizes of the two pictures. If the photo size needs adjustment, choose the **Move** tool after step 9 and reposition/resize it.

ADDING A VIGNETTE TO A PORTRAIT

Somehow, putting a soft edge around the subject of a portrait just seems to make the image more special. It's a traditional darkroom technique that's incredibly easy to emulate with Photoshop Elements.

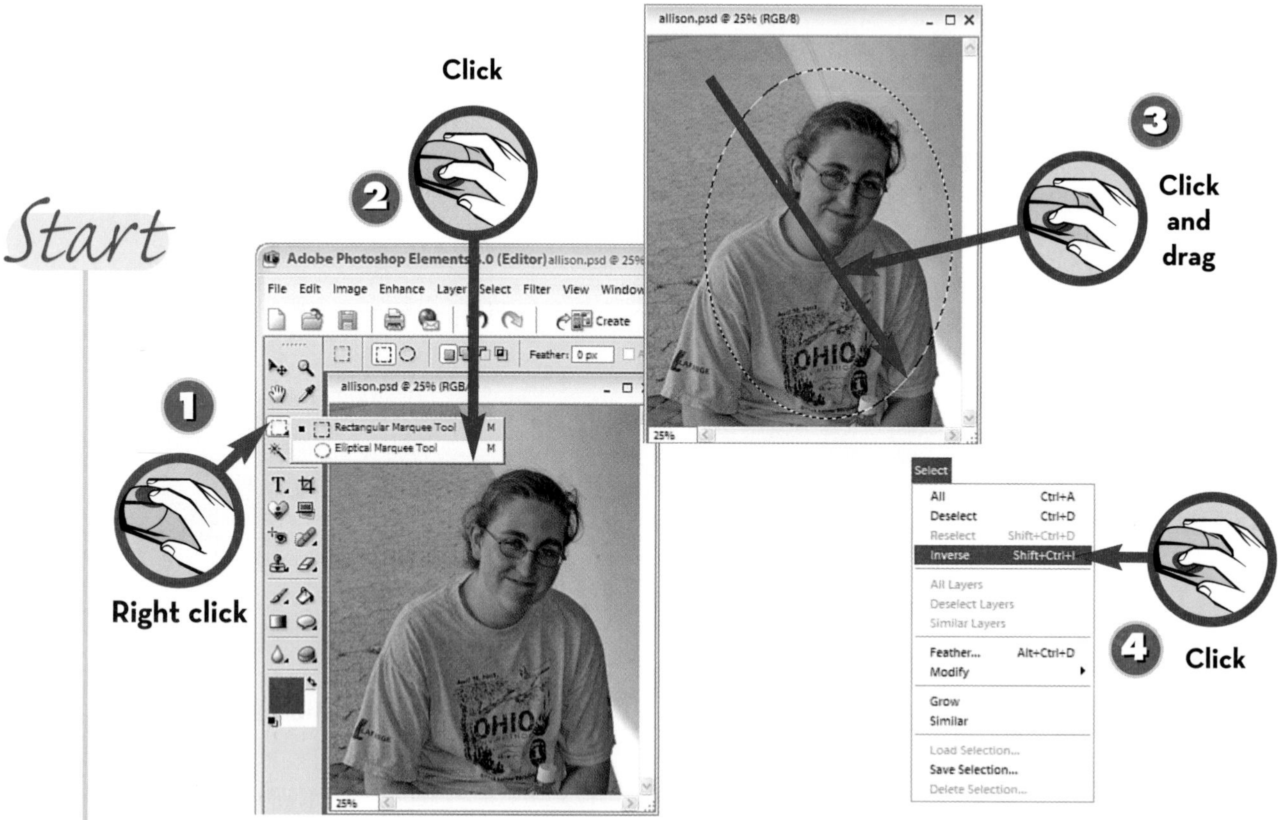

Start

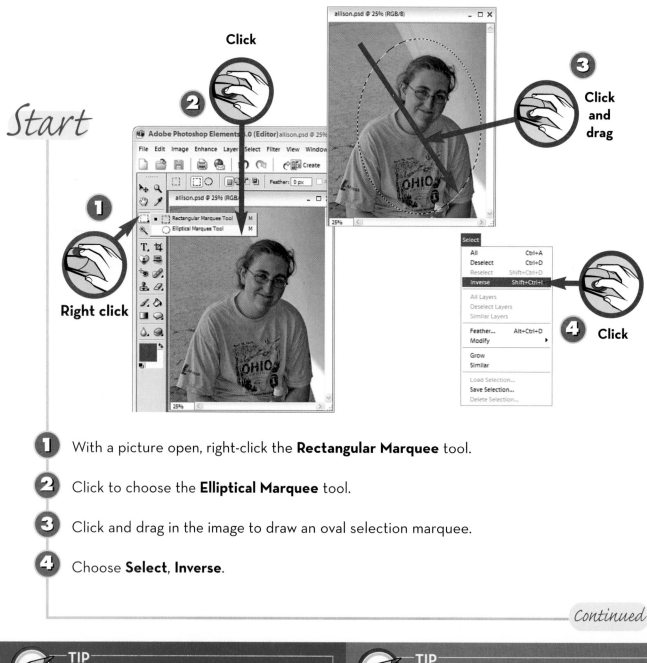

Right click

Click

Click and drag

Click

1. With a picture open, right-click the **Rectangular Marquee** tool.
2. Click to choose the **Elliptical Marquee** tool.
3. Click and drag in the image to draw an oval selection marquee.
4. Choose **Select**, **Inverse**.

Continued

TIP

Keep Trying

The amount of feathering you add depends on the resolution and size of the image; you may have to try a few different settings before you're satisfied. Don't forget that you can use the **Undo History** palette to back up and try again.

TIP

Getting in Shape

Don't feel that you have to stick to creating an oval vignette—that's just the most traditional shape. Experiment with other shapes, including using the **Lasso** tool to draw a freeform selection.

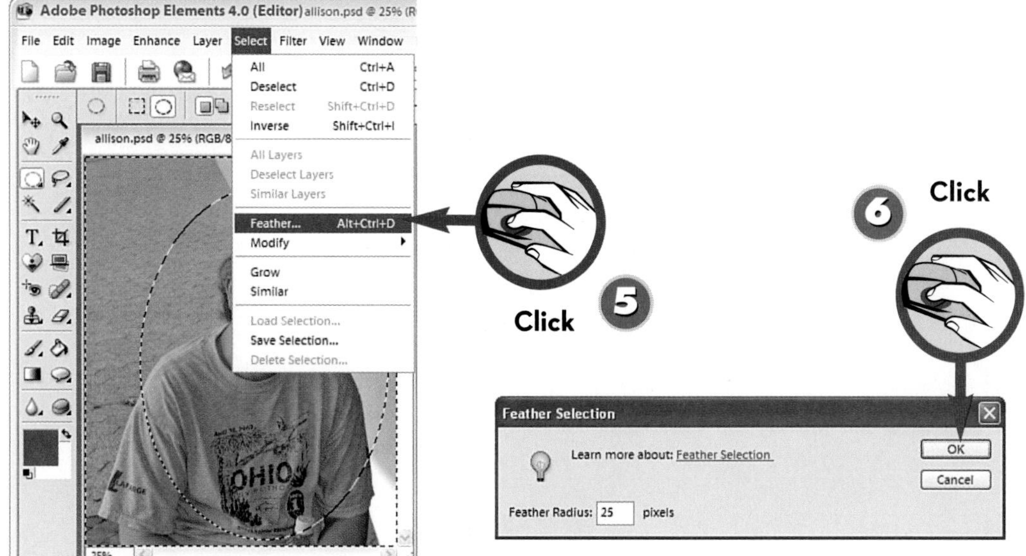

5 Choose **Select**, **Feather**.

6 Enter a number of pixels in the **Feather Radius** field and click **OK**.

7 Press **Delete** to remove the background.

End

NOTE

Going Way, Way Back

For a really old-fashioned feel, combine this vignette effect with a sepia tone effect. Check out the tip on **p. 70** for instructions.

TIP

Tidying Up

To center the vignetted photo in the image, invert the selection after step 7 and choose **Image**, **Crop**. That gets rid of the photo's asymmetrical white border.

ADDING A BEAUTIFUL SKY

Replacing the sky is a particularly neat trick, permitting you to scoff at overcast days, not to mention getting rid of power lines and intrusive foliage. Add a gorgeous sunset and forget it was raining that day.

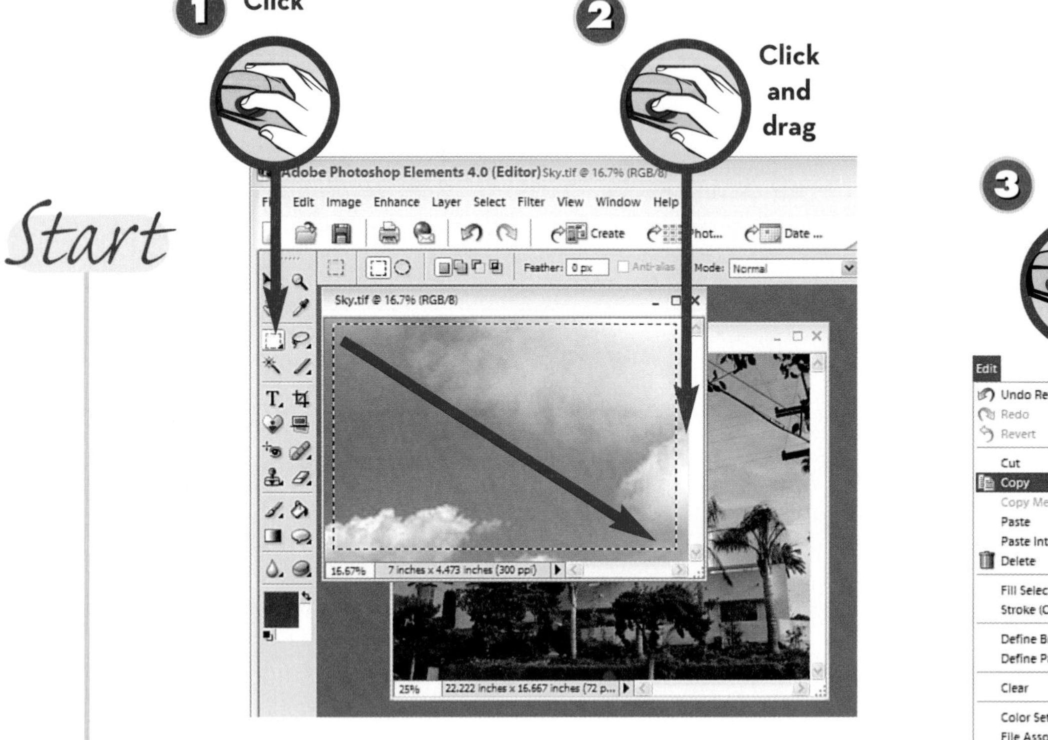

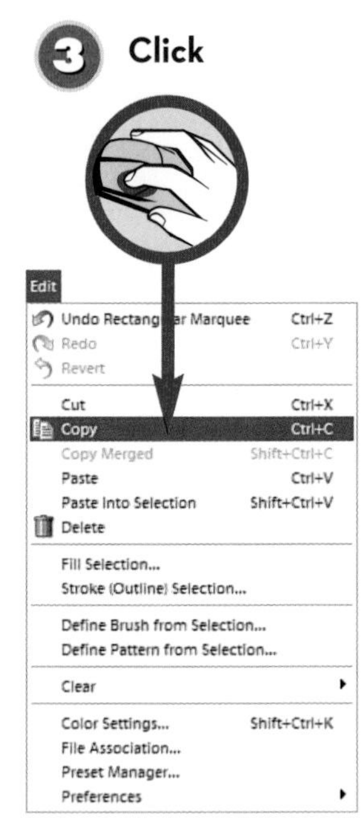

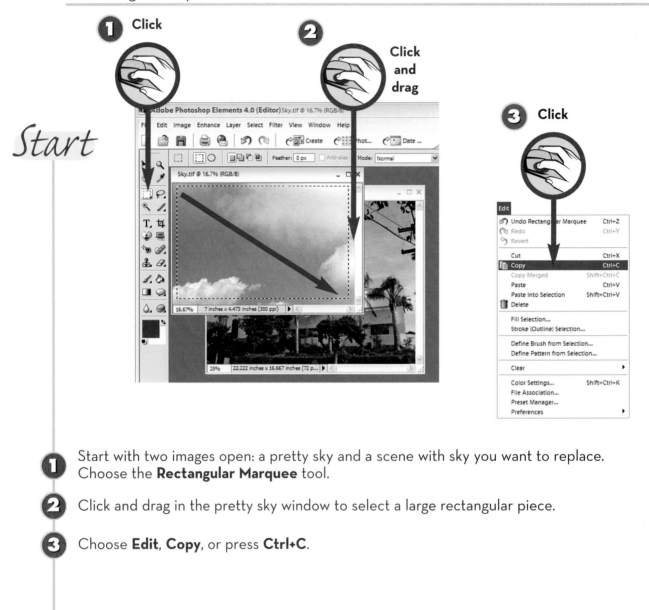

1. Start with two images open: a pretty sky and a scene with sky you want to replace. Choose the **Rectangular Marquee** tool.
2. Click and drag in the pretty sky window to select a large rectangular piece.
3. Choose **Edit**, **Copy**, or press **Ctrl+C**.

Continued

TIP

Be Sure to Grab It All

In step 2, use any combination of selection tools. The Lasso tool is particularly handy for irregular areas, followed by several Shift-clicks with **Magic Wand** to get the rest.

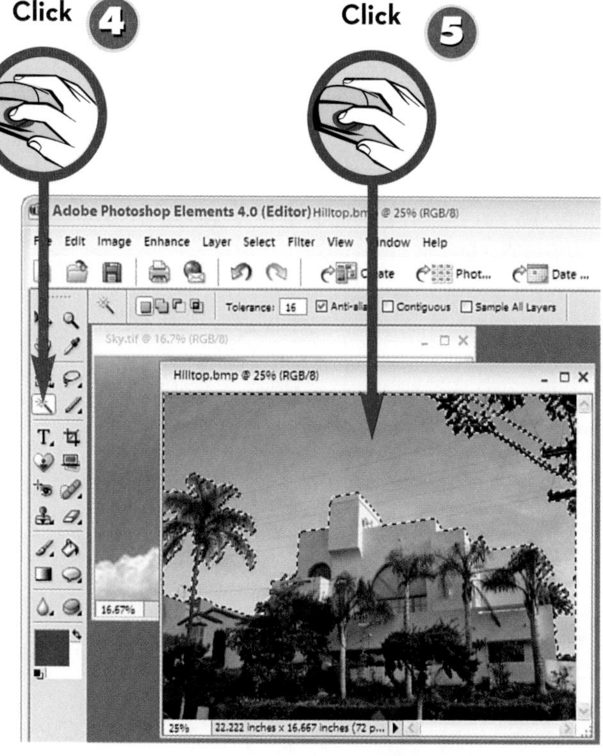

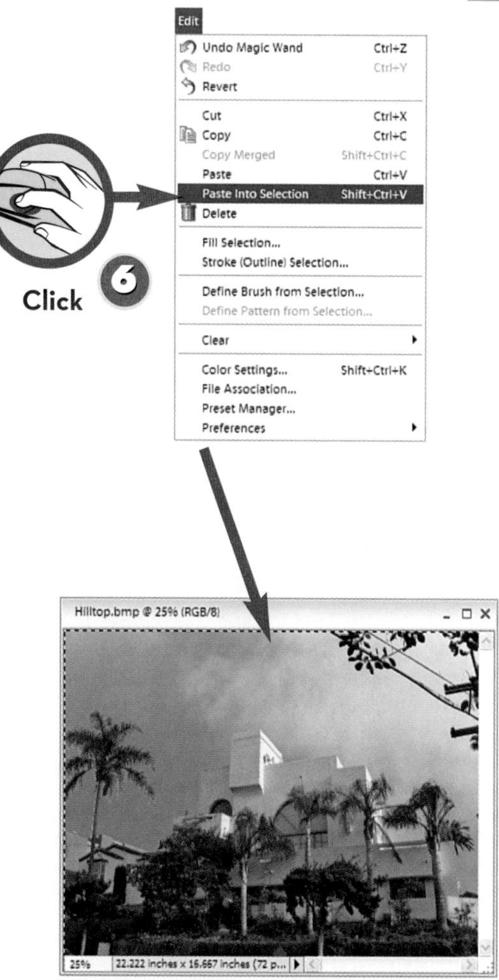

4. Choose the **Magic Wand** tool, or press **W**.
5. In the scene window, click to select the sky that needs replacing. (Shift+click to add other areas to the selection.)
6. Choose **Edit**, **Paste into Selection**, or press **Shift+Ctrl+V**.

End

TIP

Release and Let's Go

When you're finished with this task, to release the selection and continue working, choose **Select**, **Deselect**, or press **Ctrl+D**.

NOTE

But Don't Leave Home

You can try the same technique used here for replacing sky to replace the background of any photo with any other shot. Keep your subjects in place and take them to some exotic locale--at no expense!

CREATING A HIGH-CONTRAST BLACK-AND-WHITE PICTURE

Back in the ancient days of film, high-contrast (hi-con) transparencies were called *Kodaliths*, the name of a Kodak product for mastering printing plates. You can create some dramatic artistic effects doing the same thing digitally—by converting a photo to black-and-white, with no shading.

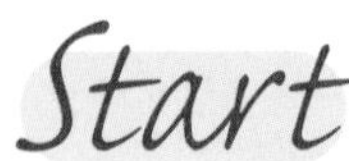

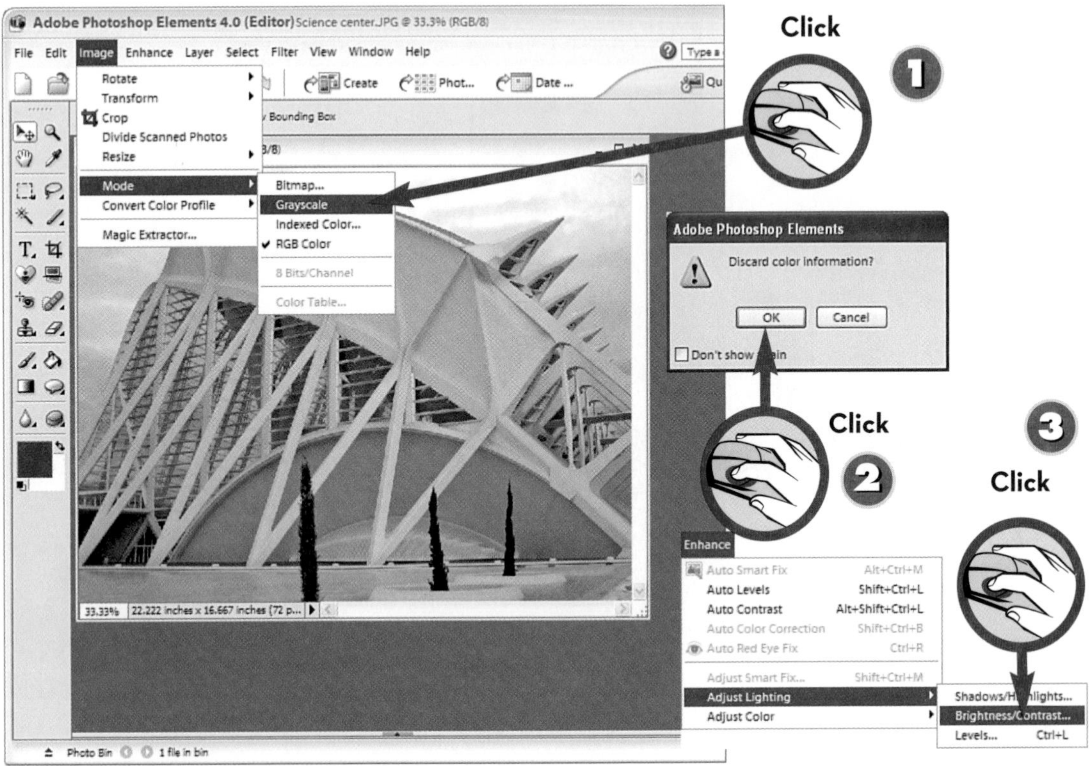

1. With a picture in the active image area, choose **Image**, **Mode**, **Grayscale**.
2. Click **OK**.
3. Choose **Enhance**, **Adjust Lighting**, **Brightness/Contrast**.

Continued

NOTE

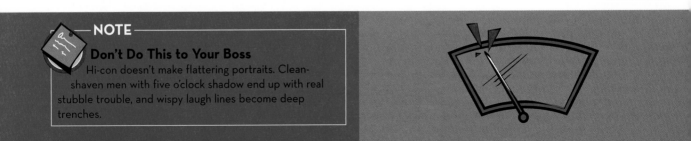

Don't Do This to Your Boss

Hi-con doesn't make flattering portraits. Clean-shaven men with five o'clock shadow end up with real stubble trouble, and wispy laugh lines become deep trenches.

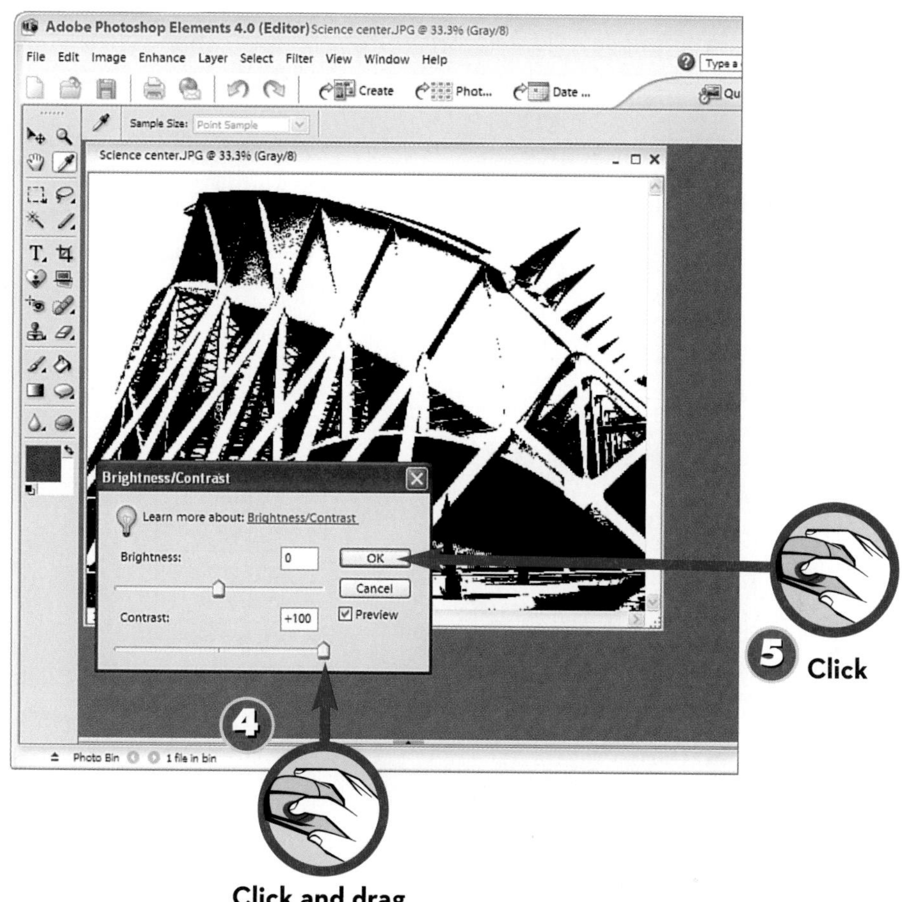

4 Adjust the **Contrast** slider to **100**.

5 Click **OK**.

End

NOTE

Adjust Brightness

In step 4, after increasing Contrast, it may also be necessary to adjust the Brightness slider a bit, as done here.

NOTE

Consider the Source

Hi-con effects work best on images with smooth surfaces and sharp edges, such as architectural views. If the source photo has shaded areas, keep the Contrast setting below 80 percent to preserve some grayscale.

FADING OUT COLOR

You'll often see this effect used in advertising—it's a neat way to convey the idea of an object moving from the past to the present, or from a humdrum world into an exciting one. One side of the image is black and white, and the other side is full color, with a smooth transition between the two modes in the middle.

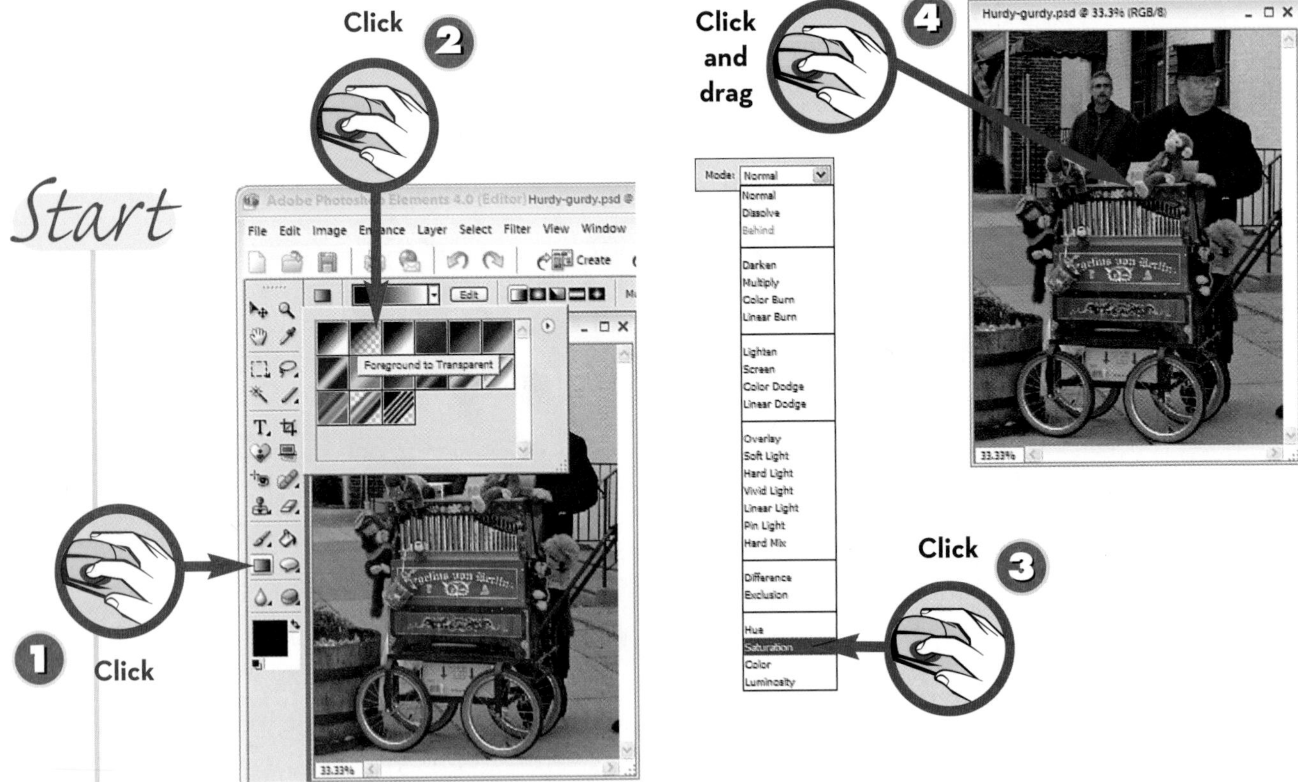

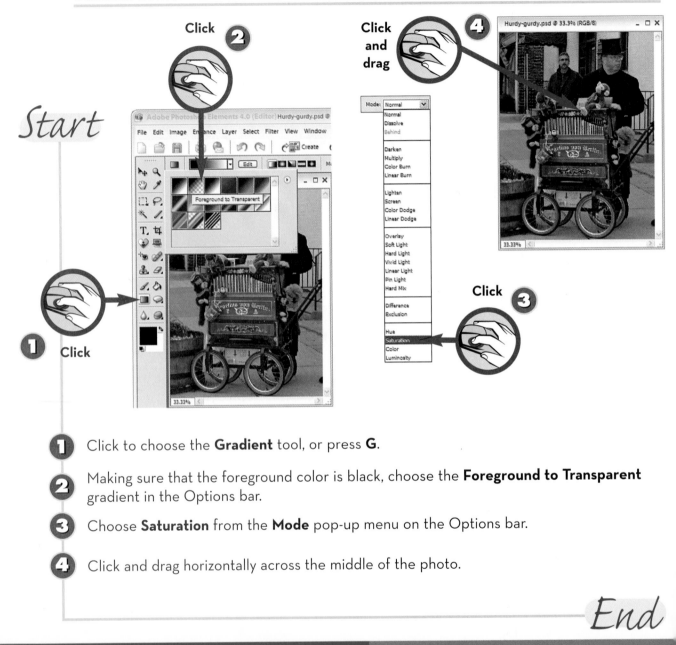

1. Click to choose the **Gradient** tool, or press **G**.
2. Making sure that the foreground color is black, choose the **Foreground to Transparent** gradient in the Options bar.
3. Choose **Saturation** from the **Mode** pop-up menu on the Options bar.
4. Click and drag horizontally across the middle of the photo.

End

NOTE

Messing Around

Feel free to experiment! Try different Mode settings and different gradients. You can also set the Gradient tool to generate one of the four other gradient shapes, such as radial.

COLORING A SINGLE OBJECT

Remember the striking image of the little girl's pink coat in the black and white movie *Schindler's List*? One color object really stands out against a black and white background. Here's how to achieve that effect in your own photos.

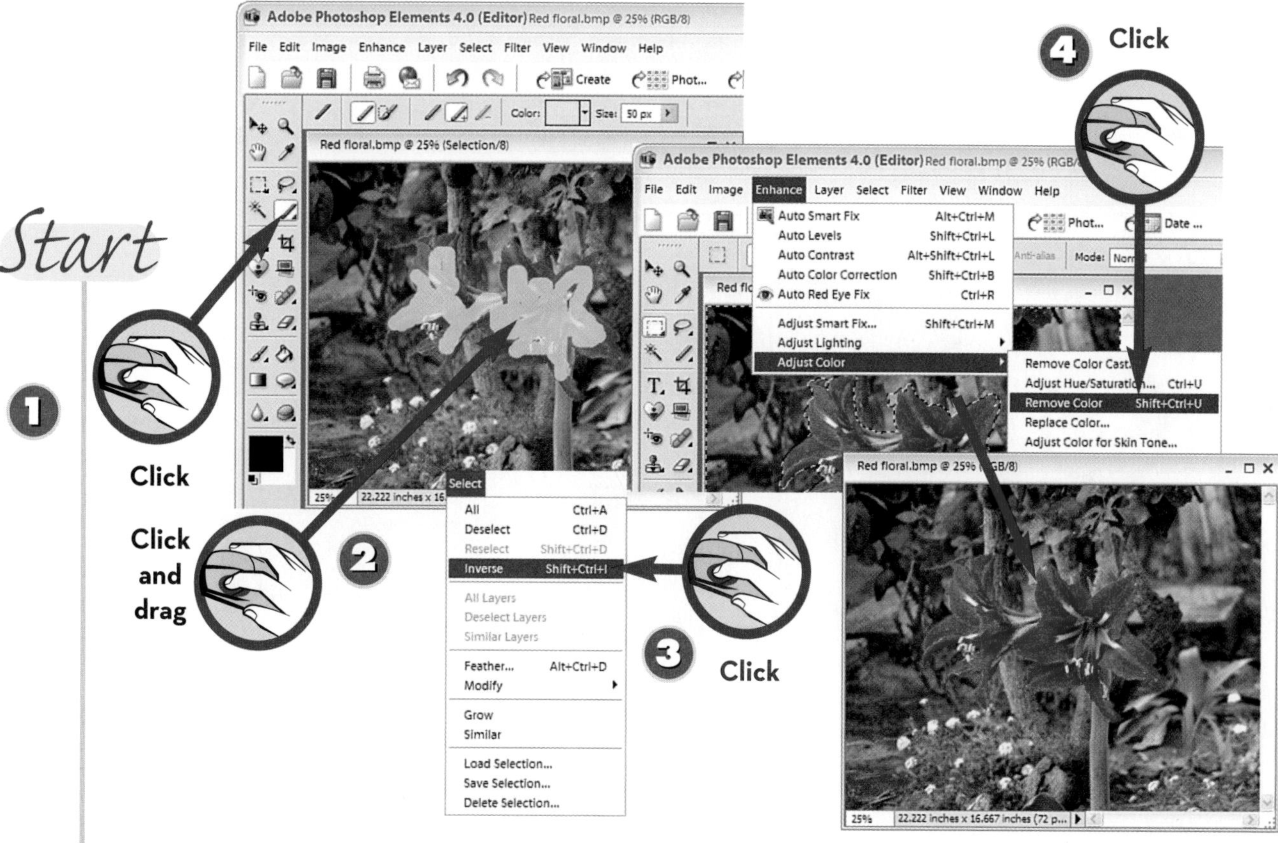

1. Click to choose the **Selection Brush**.
2. With the **Selection Brush**, paint over the object you want to leave in color.
3. After the selection is made, choose **Select**, **Inverse**.
4. Choose **Enhance**, **Adjust Color**, **Remove Color**.

End

TIP

Bonus Points

For an extra color boost, choose **Enhance**, **Adjust Color**, **Adjust Hue/Saturation** after step 2. Drag the **Saturation** slider to the right to make the one colored object even more vivid.

NOTE

It's All About You

You can use any tool to create the selection in step 1; the Magic Selection Brush, the Lasso, or the Magic Wand are all good choices. Use whichever tool you're most comfortable with.

DELETING THE BACKGROUND

Backgrounds can be useful, but they can also be distracting. When you want to pull an object out of its environment by removing its background, turn to Photoshop Elements 4's new command, the Magic Extractor.

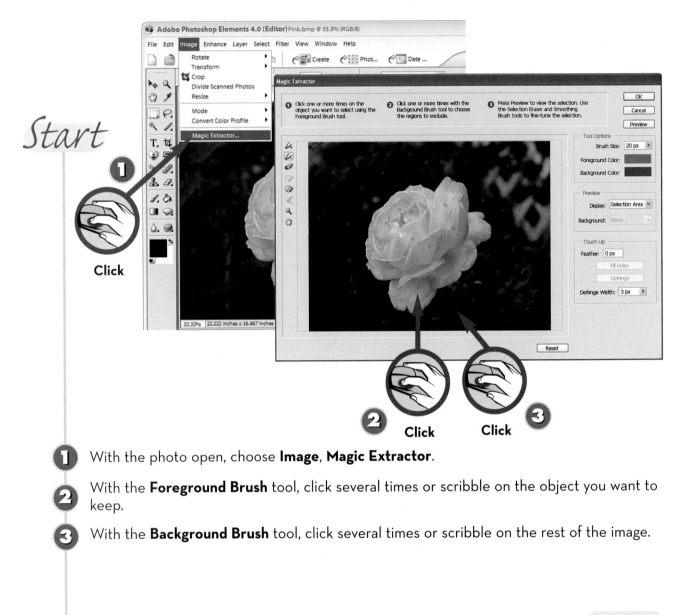

Start

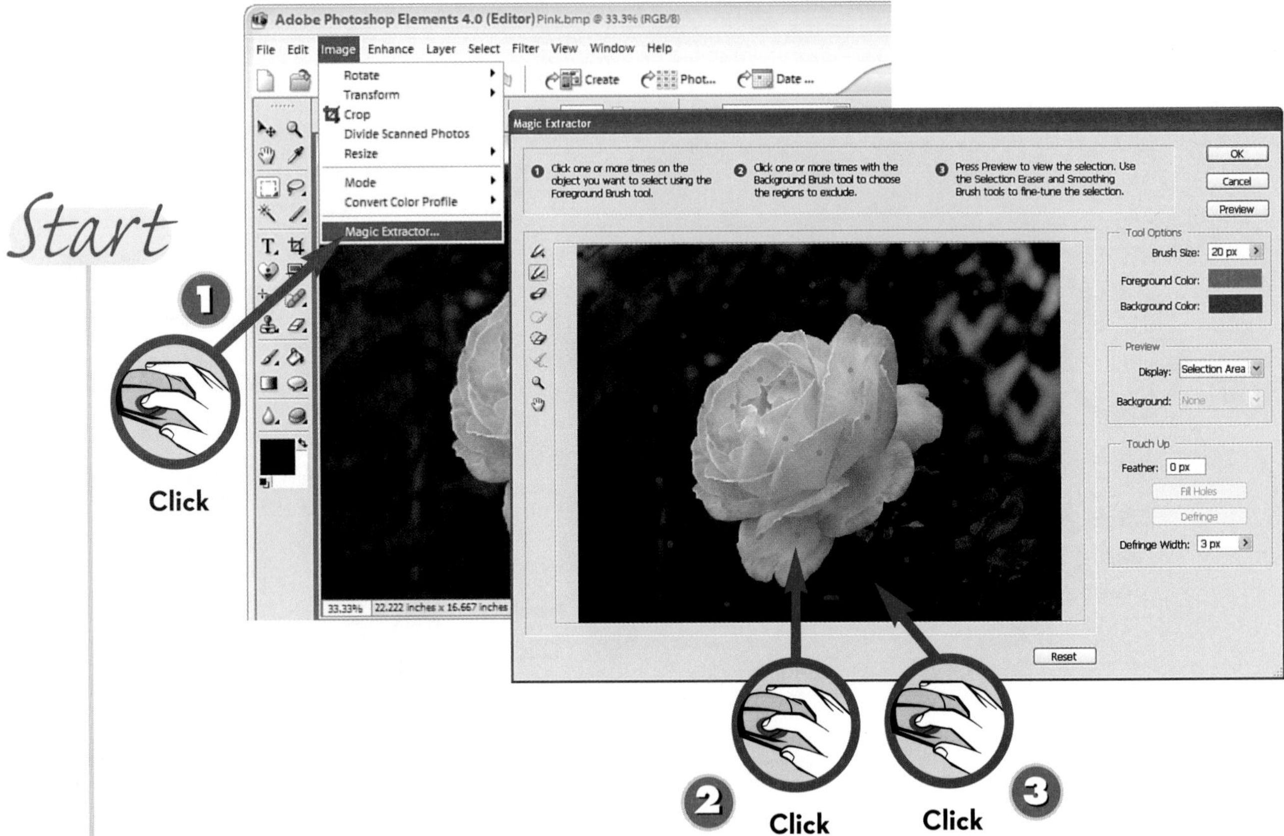

1. With the photo open, choose **Image**, **Magic Extractor**.
2. With the **Foreground Brush** tool, click several times or scribble on the object you want to keep.
3. With the **Background Brush** tool, click several times or scribble on the rest of the image.

Continued

NOTE

Almost the Same

This technique works similarly to the Magic Selection Brush. The dialog box's instructions say to click on the areas you want to indicate as background and foreground, but scribbling works just as well.

NOTE

Best Bets

You'll achieve the best results when you use an image that has a distinct foreground object that's very different in color or in lightness from the background.

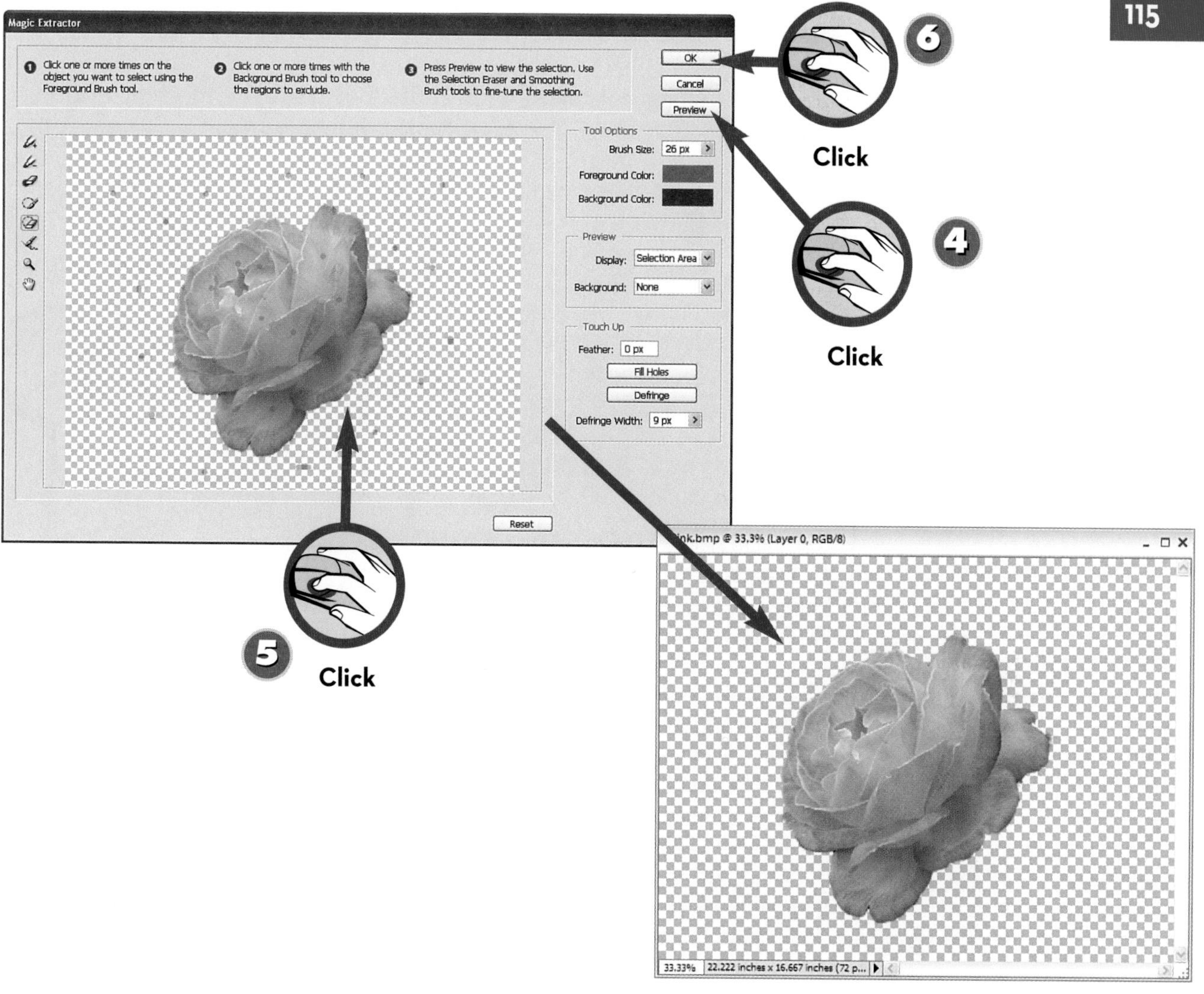

4 Click **Preview** to see how the object looks with the background removed.

5 Use the **Selection Eraser** and the **Smoothing Brush** tools to delete leftover background areas or restore missing foreground areas.

6 Click **OK** to finalize the background removal.

End

NOTE

Go Back, Go Back

Take as long as you need to complete step 5; this is where the quick-and-dirty jobs are separated from the truly professional-looking ones.

TIP

Background Notes

Once you've removed the photo's background, you can choose **Layer**, **Flatten Image** to replace the transparent pixels with the background color. Or, if you prefer, you can drag the image into another photo to give it a new background.

MAKING A PHOTO LOOK LIKE AN OIL PAINTING

No one's proposing you start cranking out fake Rembrandts, but there's something about brushstrokes on canvas that says high class. Try this with the family portrait and pretend you sat for a Dutch master.

Start

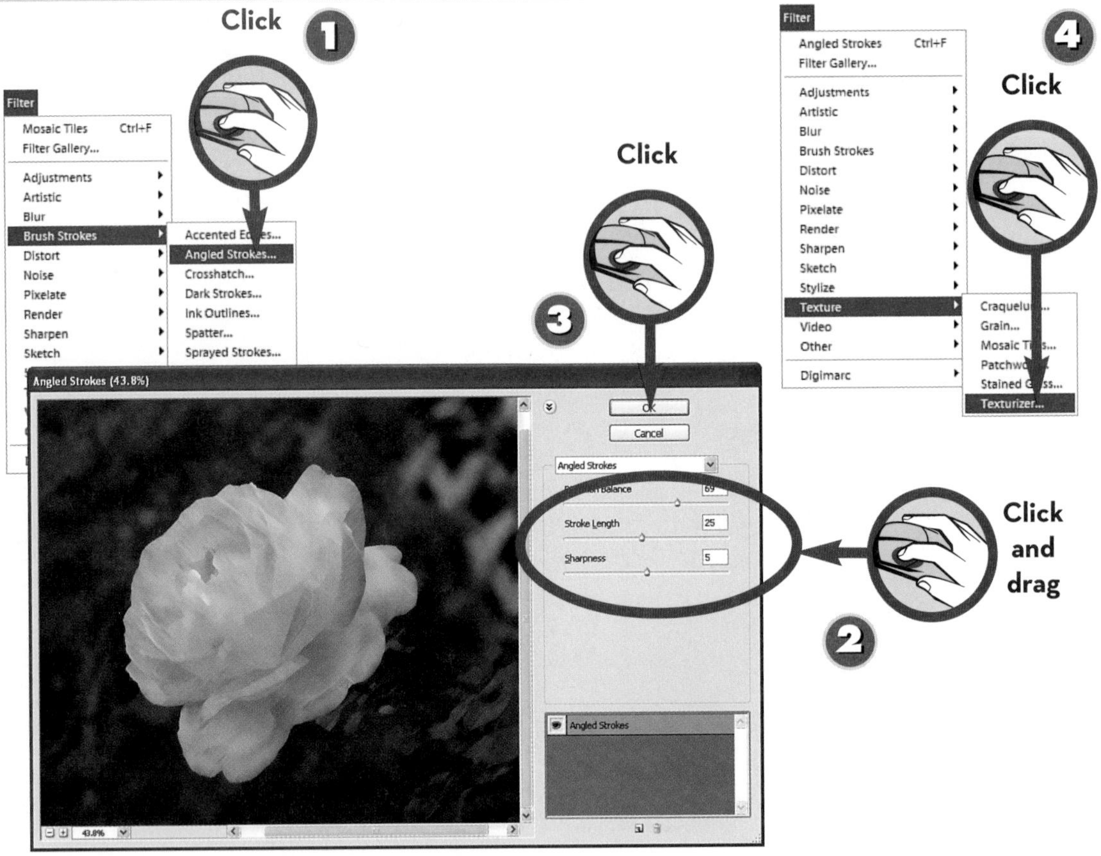

Click

Click

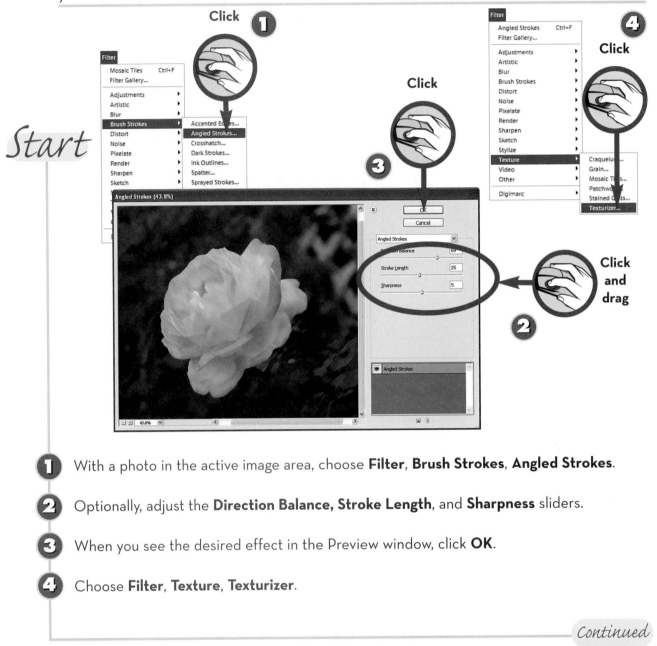

Click

Click and drag

1. With a photo in the active image area, choose **Filter**, **Brush Strokes**, **Angled Strokes**.
2. Optionally, adjust the **Direction Balance, Stroke Length**, and **Sharpness** sliders.
3. When you see the desired effect in the Preview window, click **OK**.
4. Choose **Filter**, **Texture**, **Texturizer**.

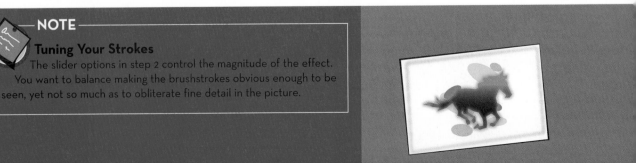

Continued

NOTE

Tuning Your Strokes

The slider options in step 2 control the magnitude of the effect. You want to balance making the brushstrokes obvious enough to be seen, yet not so much as to obliterate fine detail in the picture.

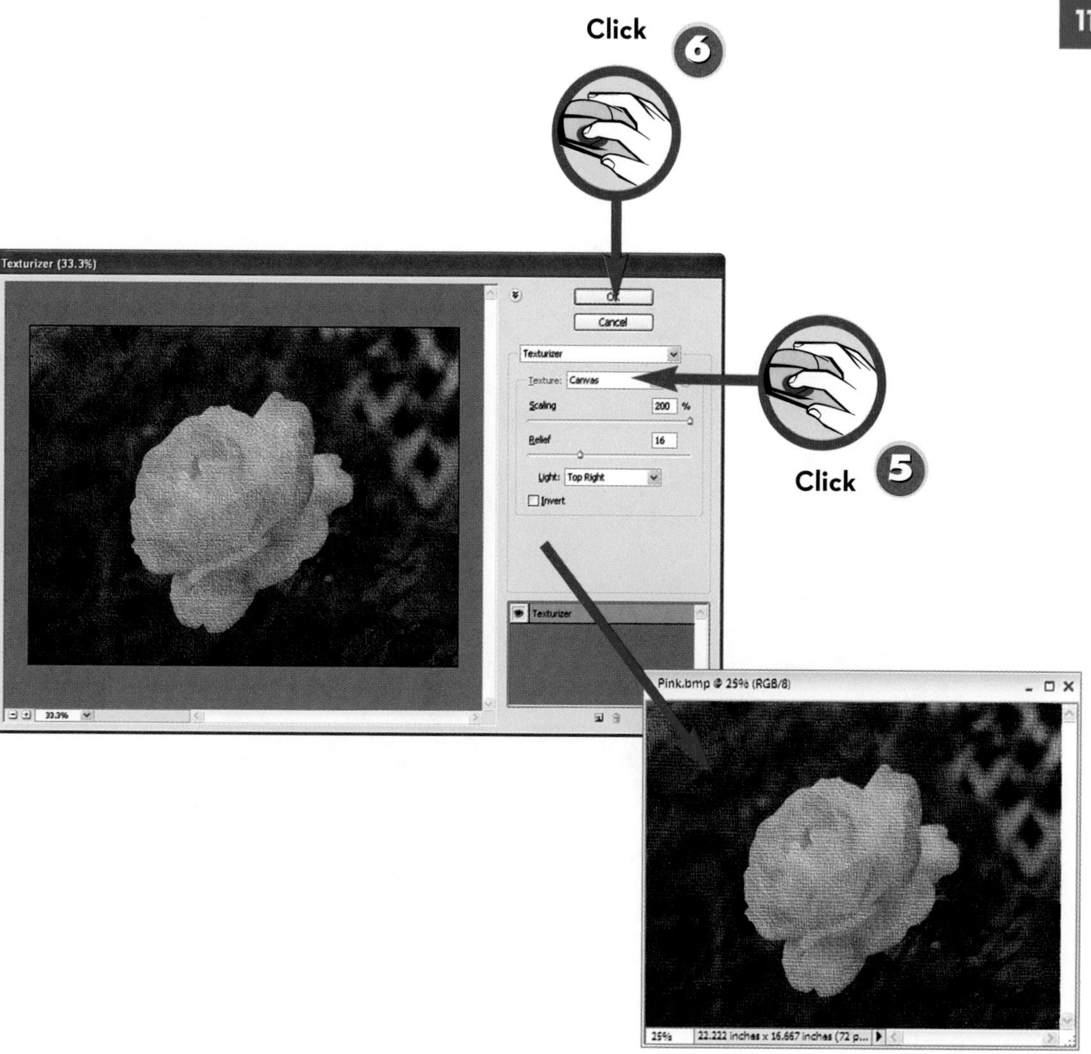

5 From the Texture pop-up menu, choose **Canvas**.

6 Click **OK**.

End

NOTE

How Rough Is Your Canvas?

As with brushstrokes, you can adjust Texturizer options to control roughness and lighting on the canvas: Scaling, Relief, and Light Direction. The Invert option reverses light and dark effects.

TIP

No Rules

There are no rules for applying artistic effects. Be guided by your own taste. For example, instead of a Canvas texture, try Burlap or Sandstone. And remember, results vary depending on the source material.

POSTERIZING A PICTURE

Posterization became popular in the psychedelic movement of the 1960s as a way of making images seem more intense. Photoshop Elements includes a filter called Poster Edges to create this effect.

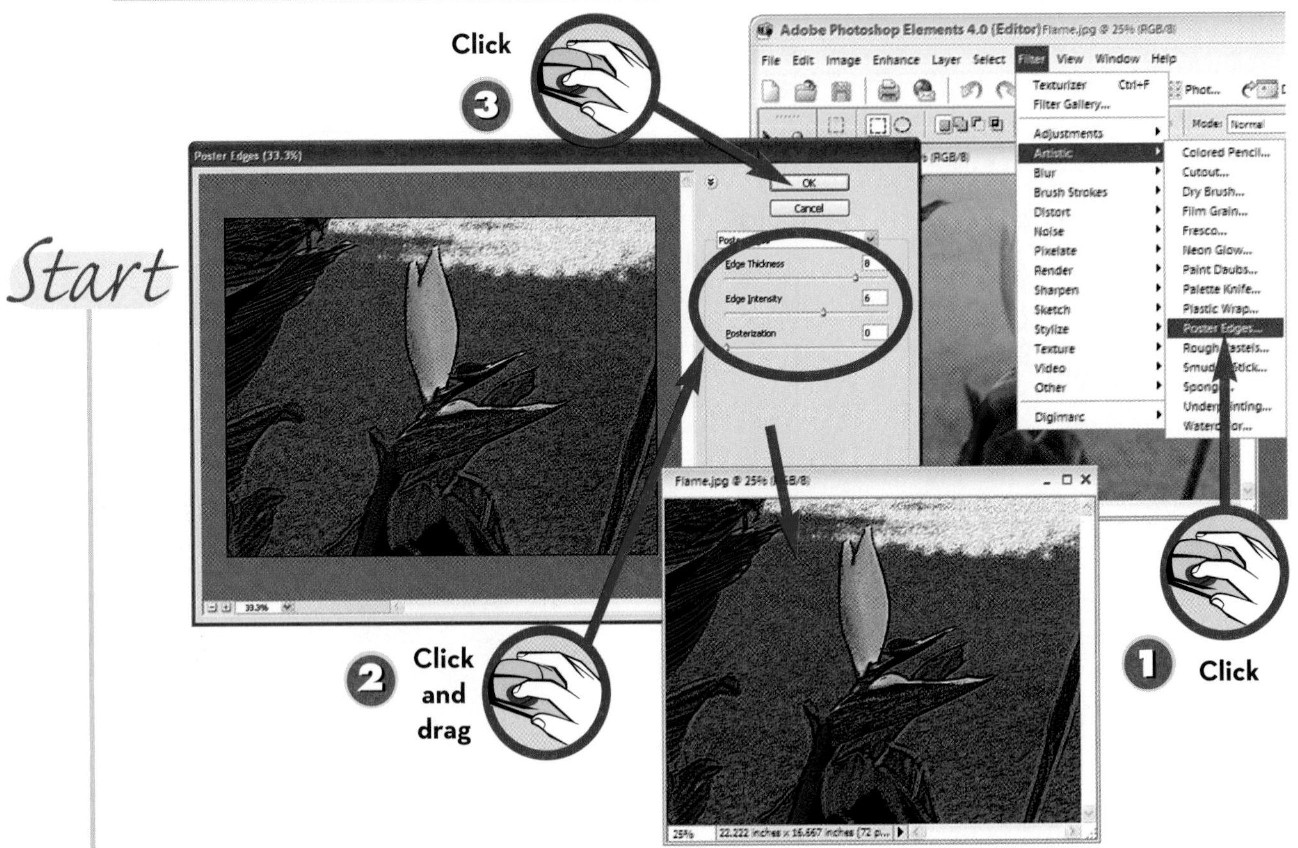

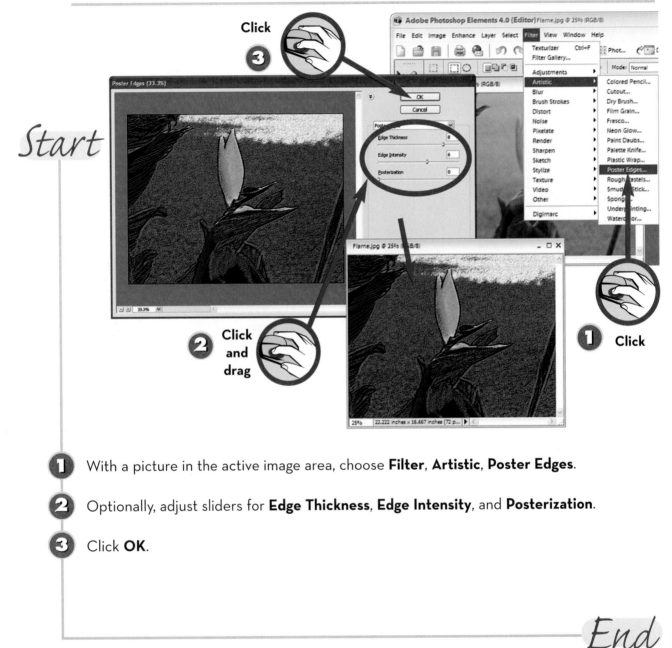

1. With a picture in the active image area, choose **Filter**, **Artistic**, **Poster Edges**.
2. Optionally, adjust sliders for **Edge Thickness**, **Edge Intensity**, and **Posterization**.
3. Click **OK**.

End

NOTE

Ideas for Greeting Cards?

Applying the Poster Edges effect to a photo can make it look like a fine watercolor and ink drawing, or an elaborate illustration in a children's book.

MAKING A PHOTO LOOK LIKE A SKETCH

Whether your drawings look like stick figures or you're just in too big a hurry to sit down with your sketchpad, Photoshop Elements can make any photo look hand-drawn. For example, take a photo of the curbside view of your home, convert it to a sketch, and use it to illustrate personalized party invitations or stationery.

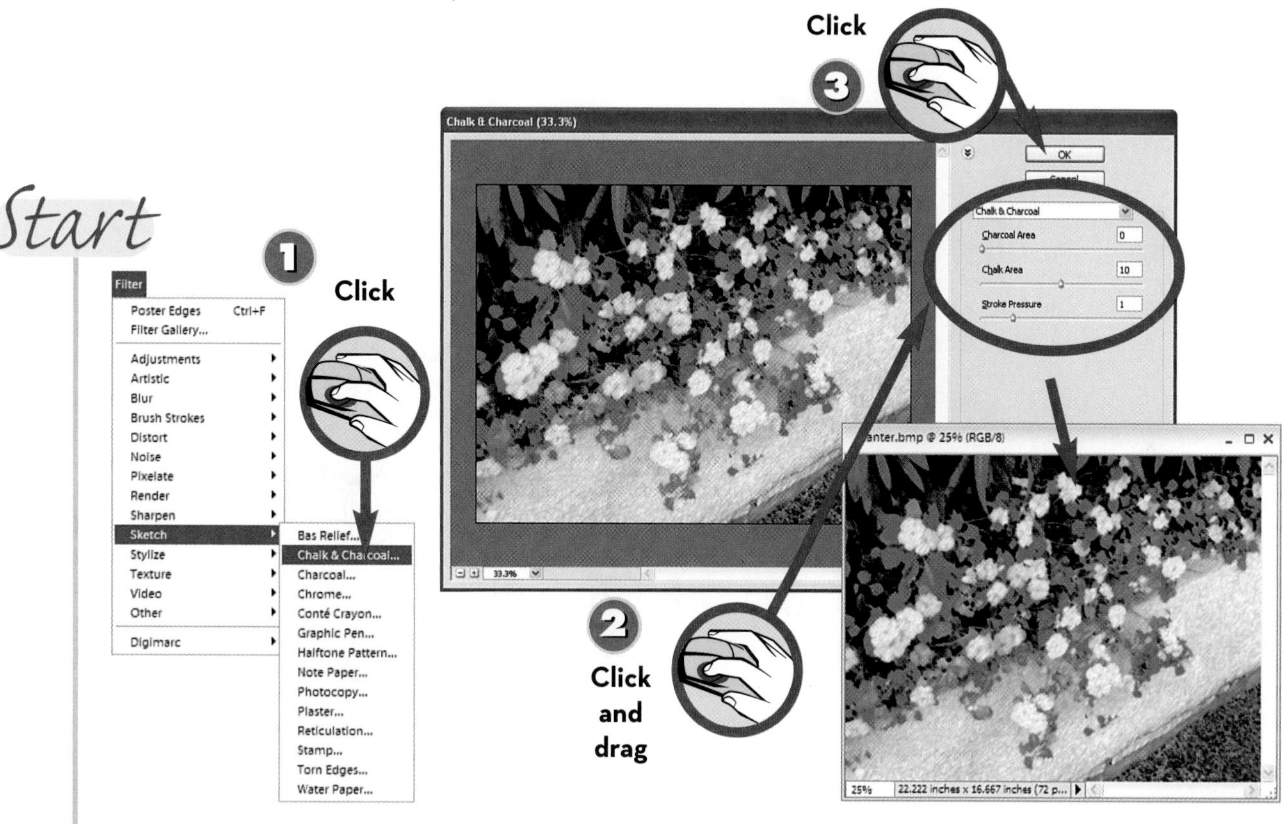

1. With a photo in the active image area, choose **Filter**, **Sketch**, **Chalk & Charcoal**.
2. Optionally, adjust sliders for **Charcoal Area**, **Chalk Area**, and **Stroke Pressure**.
3. Click **OK**.

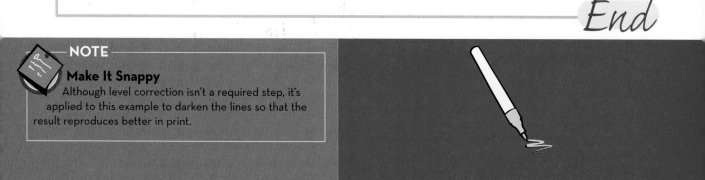

End

NOTE

Make It Snappy

Although level correction isn't a required step, it's applied to this example to darken the lines so that the result reproduces better in print.

APPLYING THE POINTILLIZE FILTER

Pointillism is a technique pioneered by French Impressionist painter Georges Seurat more than a century ago. His paintings are composed of thousands of tiny dots of bright colors—and the overall effect was apparent only when viewing the work from a distance. In a sense, he invented pixels, which are the building blocks of today's computerized, digital images.

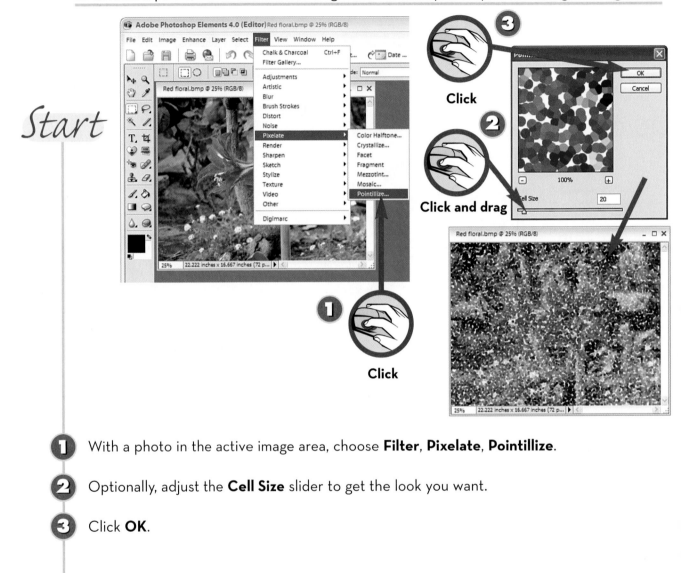

Start

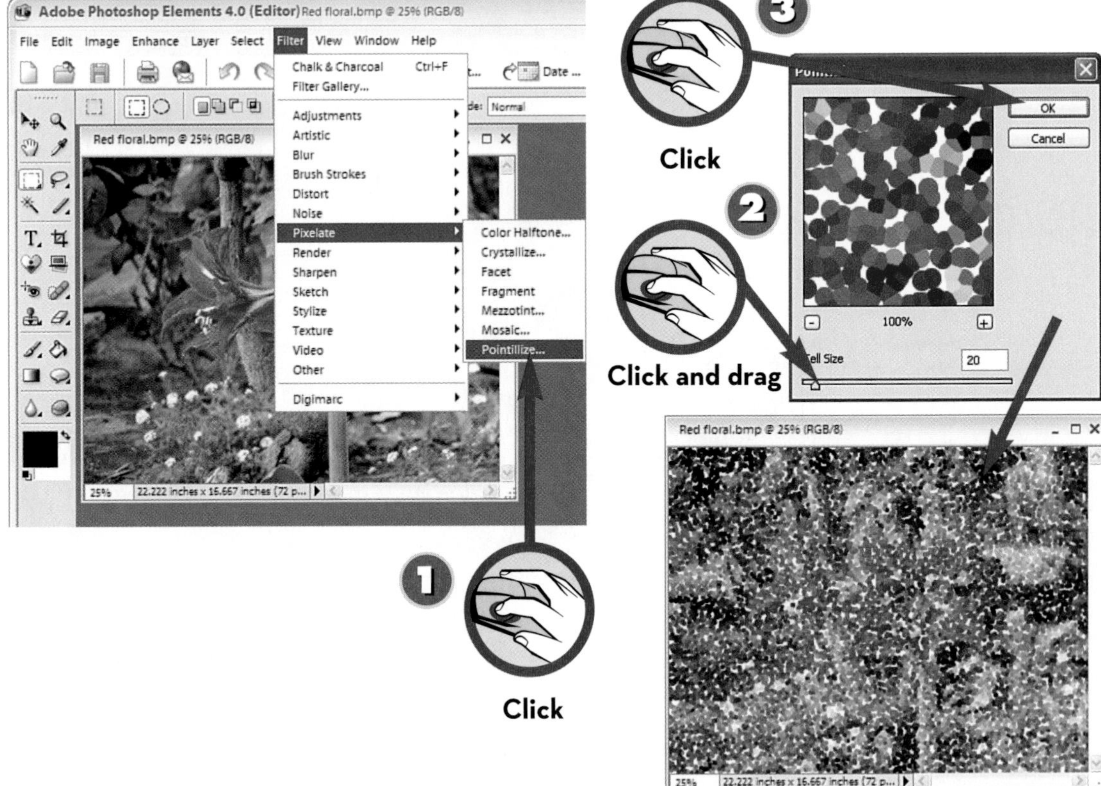

1. With a photo in the active image area, choose **Filter**, **Pixelate**, **Pointillize**.
2. Optionally, adjust the **Cell Size** slider to get the look you want.
3. Click **OK**.

End

TIP

How Big Is a Cell?

Cell size in step 2 controls the size of the picture dots and the magnitude of the effect. You want it large enough to make the effect visible, small enough to preserve important picture details.

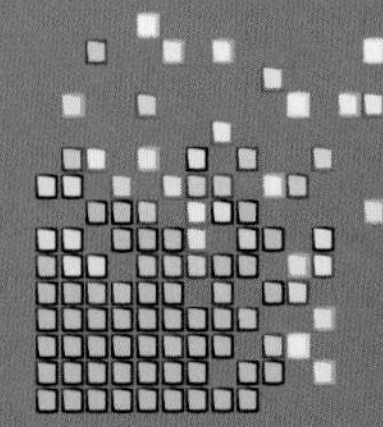

ADDING A MOTION BLUR

Many of the artistic filters in Photoshop Elements might well be applied to the whole picture. Blurring is an example of a filter you'd normally apply only to a selected portion of an image, such as there normally speedy greyhouds.

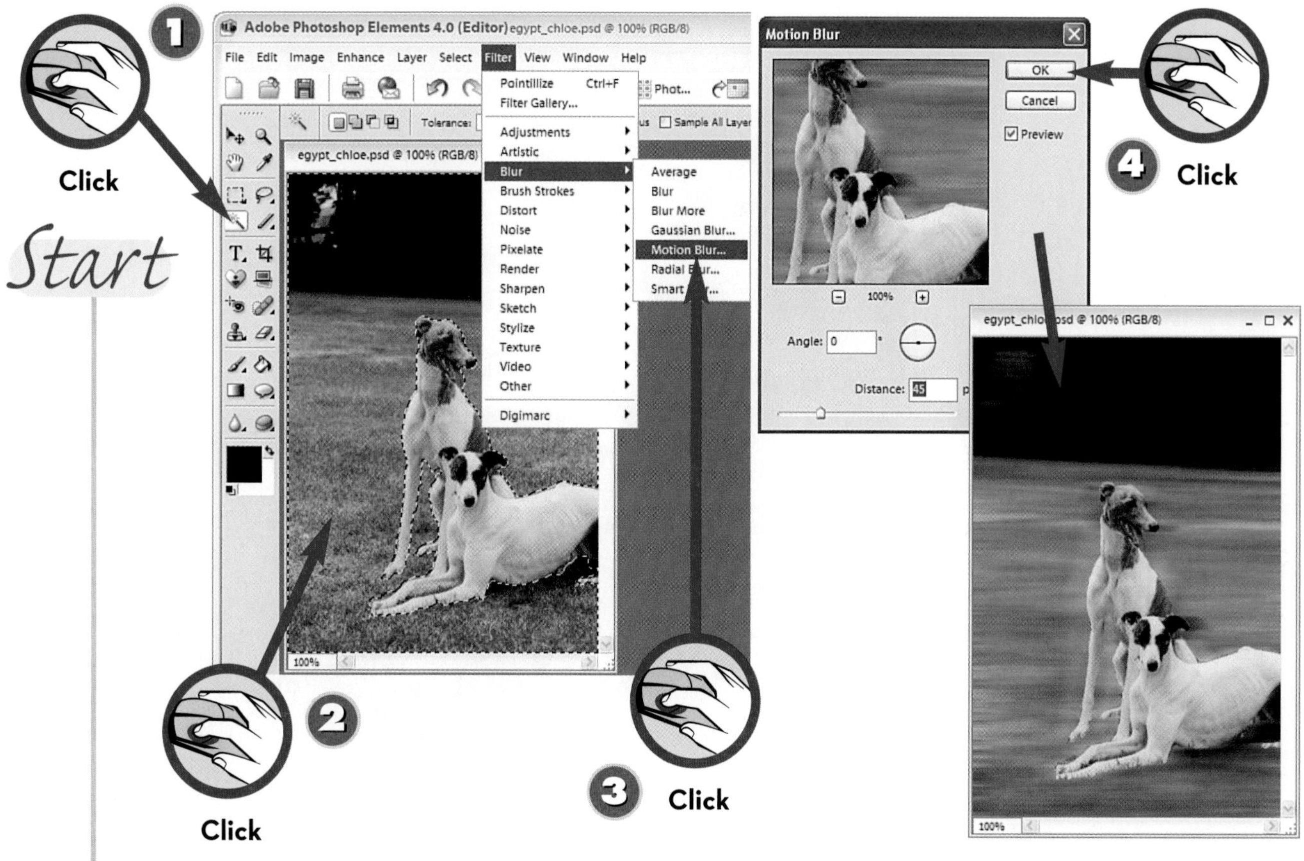

1. With a photo in the active image area, click a selection tool, such as **Magic Wand**.
2. Click to select the area in the image to which you want the blurring effect applied.
3. Choose **Filter**, **Blur**, **Motion Blur**.
4. Click **OK**. (To keep working on the photo, press **Ctrl+D** to release your selection.)

TIP

Giving Directions

Change the angle of the blur to change the direction of the perceived motion. This horizontal blur brings to mind the cross-country speed of greyhounds, but a vertical or steeply angled blur might imply the dogs were taking off into space.

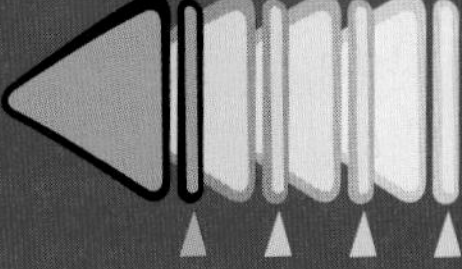

PUTTING A PHOTO BEHIND GLASS

Use the Glass filter to give a photo a little *trompe-l'oeil* flair; somehow, adding a layer of glass in front of the picture makes it look that much more real—as though the printed page or monitor screen is actually a window.

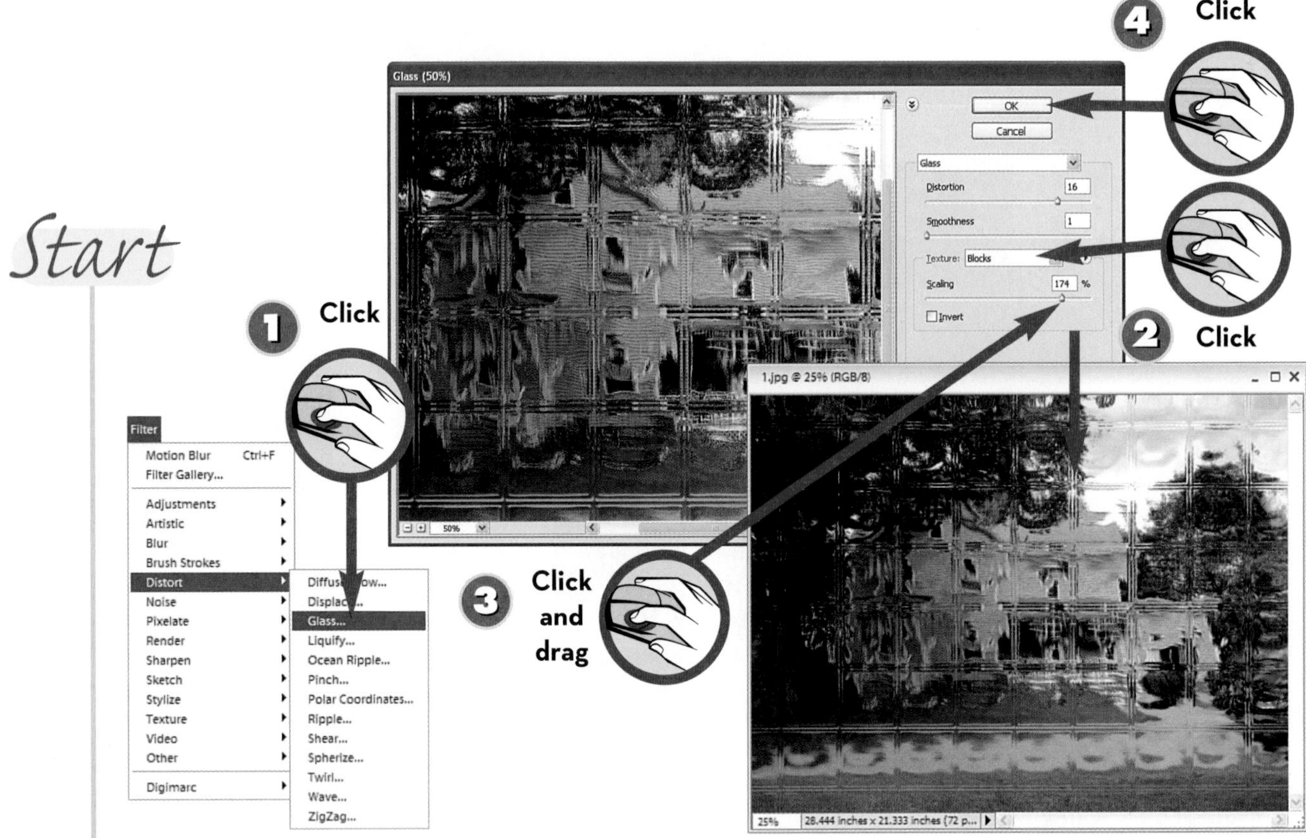

1. With a photo in the active image area, choose **Filter**, **Distort**, **Glass**.
2. Choose a glass texture, such as **Blocks**.
3. Optionally, drag the **Scaling** slider to change the size of the blocks.
4. Click **OK**.

End

NOTE

It'll Really Frost You

If you're looking for an arty, painted appearance and haven't gotten the results you want using other filters, try a careful application of the Glass filter using the Frosted glass texture. You'll be surprised at the organic effects you get.

TIP

Honey, I Shrunk the Photo

A similar effect is Plastic Wrap (choose **Filter**, **Artistic**, **Plastic Wrap**). Using this filter, you can make the subject of your photo look as though it has been shrink-wrapped with a clear film.

TRIMMING A PHOTO INTO A CUSTOM SHAPE

Who says photographs have to be square or rectangular? The sky's the limit as far as Photoshop Elements's Cookie Cutter tool is concerned, so you can make the shape of the photo part of the message it communicates. Try them all!

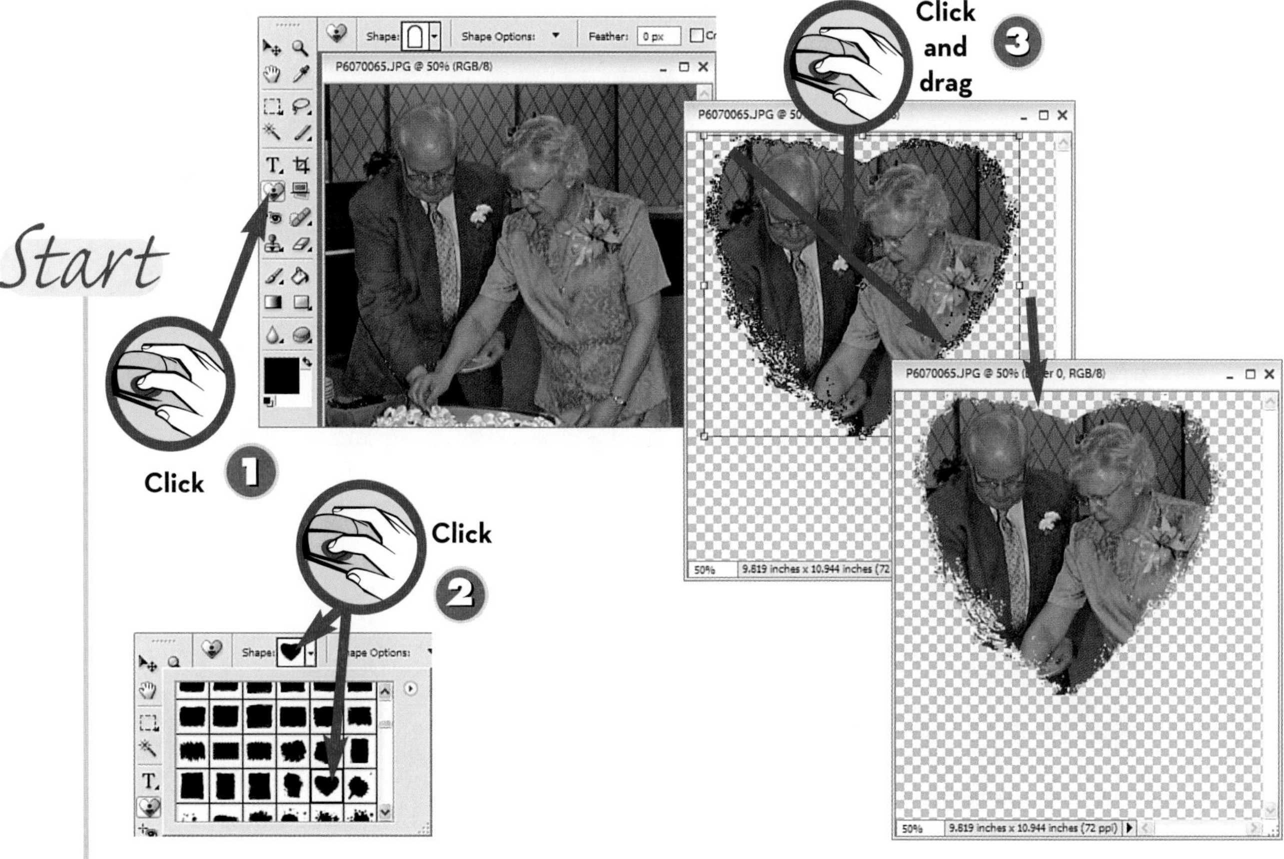

1. Choose the **Cookie Cutter** tool from the toolbox.
2. Click to open the **Shape** pop-up menu, and then select a shape.
3. Click and drag in the document window to create the shape.

End

NOTE

Cutting and Cropping

After you've applied the Cookie Cutter tool to your image, you might want to use the Crop tool to get rid of the extra empty space surrounding the new shape.

NOTE

There's Time to Get It Right

Until you press Enter, click the Commit button on the Options bar, or switch to another tool or layer, you can move and resize the shape as much as you want to perfectly frame your picture.

SHINING A SPOTLIGHT ON YOUR SUBJECT

The Lighting Effects filter comes in handy in many situations. Here, it can help hide the distracting objects around the edges of the photo and focus attention where it belongs—on this comedian's act.

Start

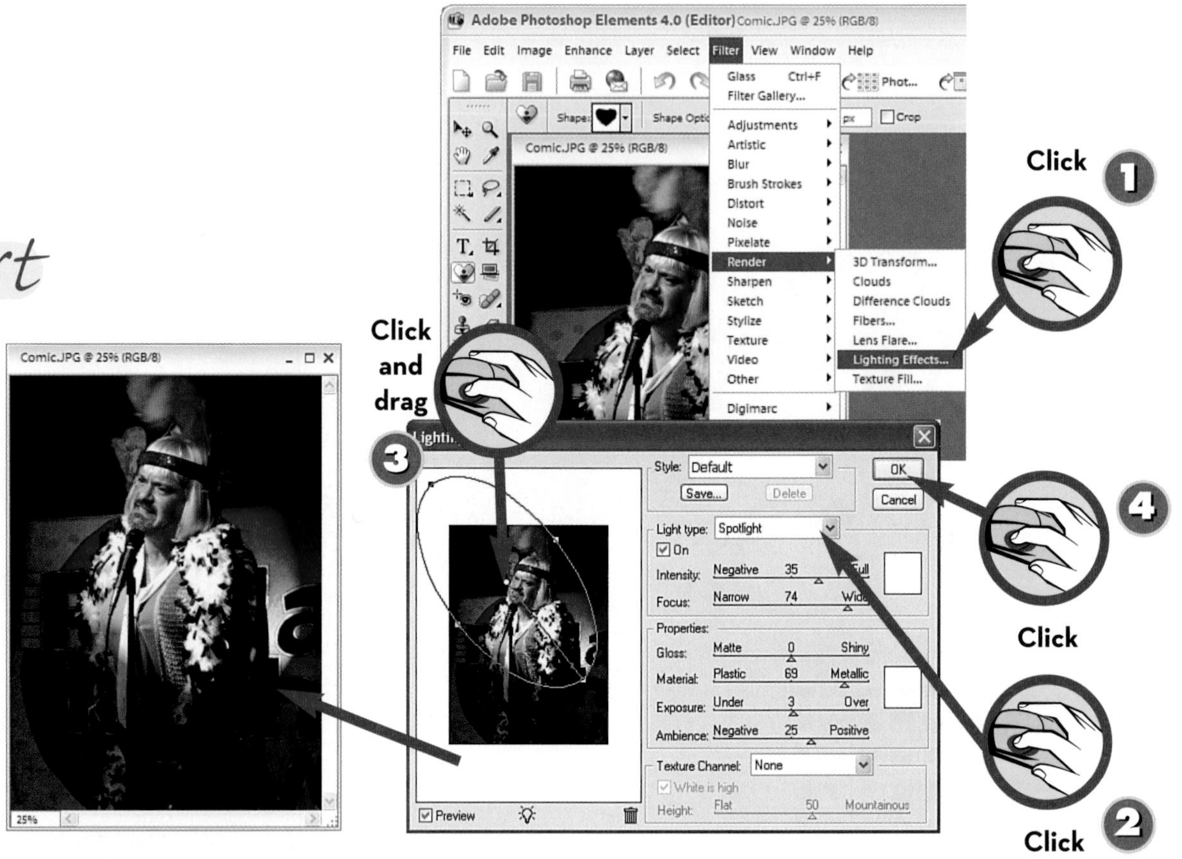

Click 1

Click and drag 3

Click 4

Click 2

1. With a photo in the active image area, choose **Filter**, **Render**, **Lighting Effects**.
2. Choose a **Light Type**, such as **Spotlight**.
3. Drag the light so that it shines on the subject of the photo.
4. Click **OK**.

End

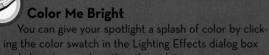

TIP

Color Me Bright

You can give your spotlight a splash of color by clicking the color swatch in the Lighting Effects dialog box and choosing a color other than white.

GIVING YOUR SUBJECT A HALO

Just for fun, why not try giving your little angel his or her own halo? Or maybe you'd prefer to add a spectral glow, or a colorful aura, to your favorite portrait. You can use this effect for still life photos, too—that's one way to make a basket of fruit really stand out from the crowd.

Start

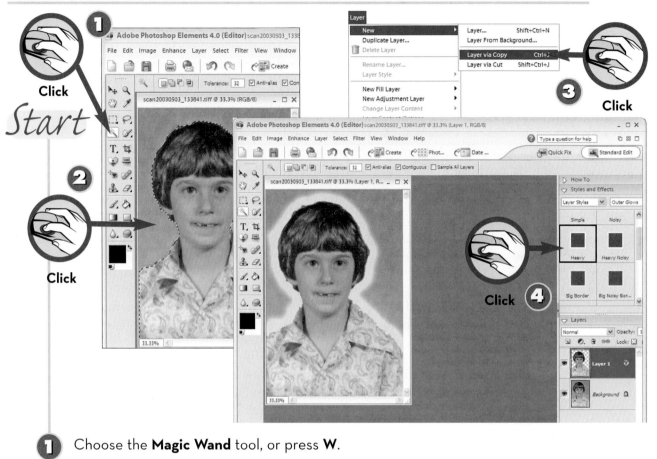

1. Choose the **Magic Wand** tool, or press **W**.
2. Click as many times as necessary to select the background.
3. Choose **Layer**, **New**, **Layer Via Copy**.
4. In the **Styles and Effects** palette's **Layer Styles** section, click any of the **Outer Glow** effects.

End

TIP

Halo Too Light?

If the halo isn't wide enough to suit you, choose **Layer**, **Layer Style**, **Scale Effects** and drag the **Scale** slider to the right until you like what you see, then click **OK**.

part 7

PAINTING AND DRAWING

Many people think of Photoshop Elements mainly as a digital photo lab, but it's also an art studio. So, welcome to your all-electronic work-and-play room—where you never have to wear a smock, clean a brush, or deal with that nasty turpentine.

Those of you who start with a photo as a background may have a more practical purpose in mind—such as making ads and brochures.

And along with adding text, combining your photos with your original artwork gives a wonderfully personal touch. Recipients of your greeting cards, party invitations, photo email, and newsletters will appreciate the care you took—even though none of this is nearly as hard as they might imagine!

Getting a bit more serious, you can also illustrate business presentations, school reports, and instructional materials with professional-looking diagrams and drawings. No more crude pencil sketches, and good-bye forever to stick figures!

But don't stop there. Set aside a rainy Saturday afternoon to discover the joy of digital painting and drawing. Vincent Van Gogh never had such a rich and varied set of tools!

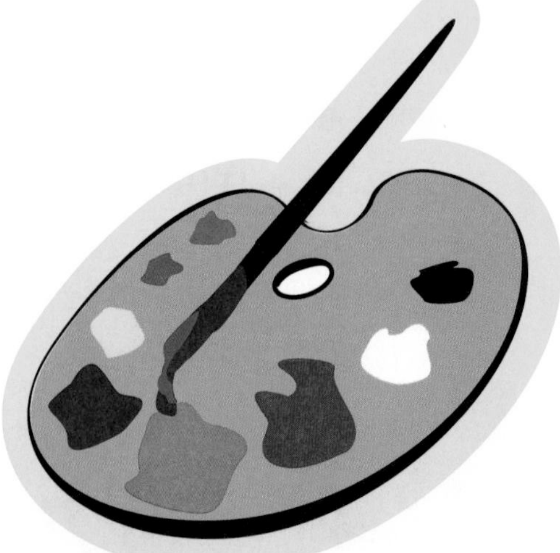

LOOK WHAT I MADE!

8th Annual
GREYHOUND
FESTIVAL
GREYHOUND PLACEMENT SERVICE
OF NEW HAMPSHIRE
VOTE GREYHOUND IN 2004!

This event logo was drawn and colored entirely in Photoshop Elements. Who needs paper and paints when you have pixels?

CREATING A SHAPE

Photoshop Elements generates a variety of geometric shapes for you. Here we show drawing over an image. You can also start by choosing **File**, **New** to draw on a blank canvas.

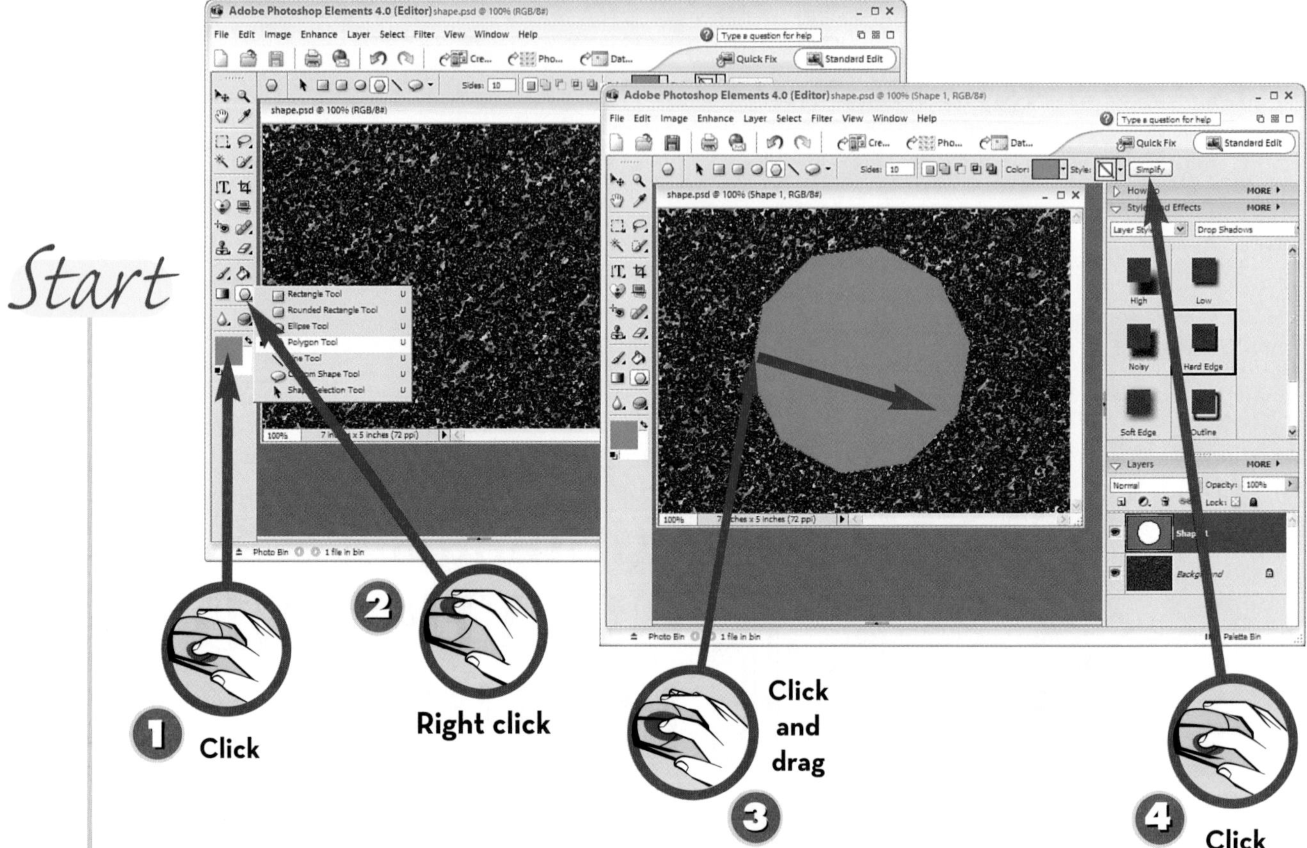

1. Click to choose a foreground color.
2. Right-click the **Shape tool** and choose the shape tool you want, such as **Polygon Tool**.
3. Click and drag in the image area to adjust the size and proportions of the shape.
4. To make the pixels of the shape editable, click the **Simplify** button.

End

TIP

Shift to Get Regular

Hold down the **Shift** key after you've started drawing to make Rectangles square, Ellipses circular. Lines follow the closest 45° angle.

NOTE

Moving and Resizing

To move or resize a shape before it's simplified, use the Shape Selection tool. When simplified, use the Move tool instead. For best-quality shapes, always try to resize before you simplify.

ADDING A BEVEL TO A SHAPE

New shapes can look plain and flat. Adding a bevel gives the shape a dimensional quality that can also make it stand out from the background. Photoshop Elements provides a nice selection of bevel styles that can give your object a bold, dimensional look. Just click the one you like, and it's applied automatically.

Start

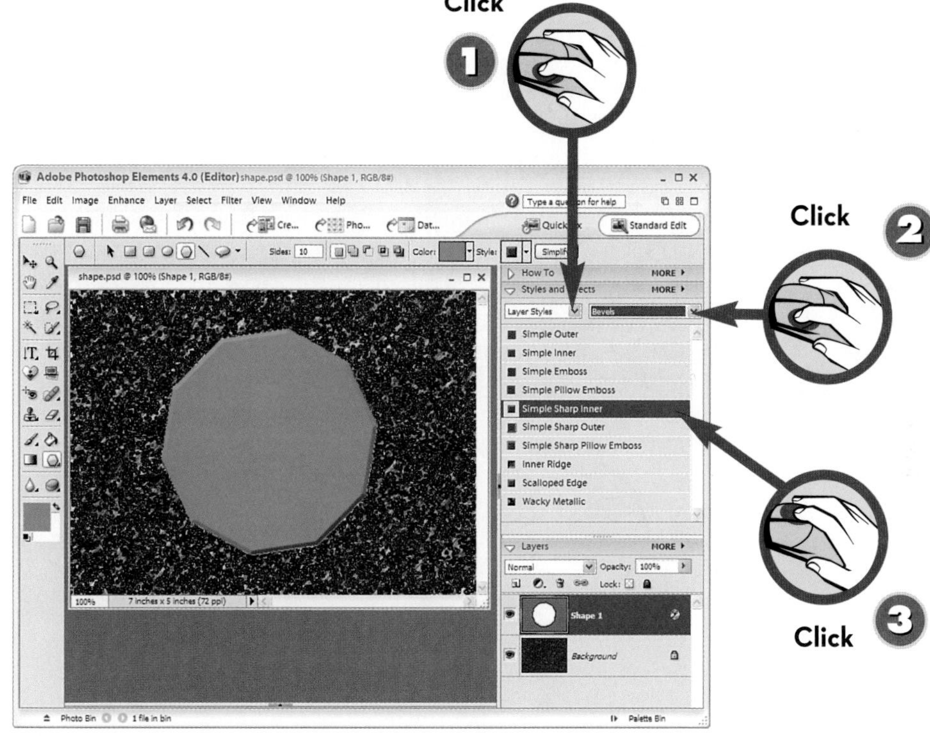

1. With a shape selected, choose **Layer Styles** from the **Styles and Effects** palette's pop-up menu.
2. Choose **Bevels** in the Style Libraries pop-up menu.
3. Click the bevel style you want to apply.

End

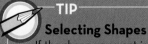

TIP

Free Samples

If you don't like the bevel style you apply, just click another thumbnail to apply a different style—you don't have to remove the first bevel before changing it.

TIP

Selecting Shapes

If the shape you want isn't the most recent one you created, select it with the Move tool before you do step 1 (Auto Select Layer must be checked). If the shape is one of many on a layer, use the Shape Selection tool instead.

FILLING A SHAPE WITH COLOR

If you've worked through the tasks to this point, this won't be the first time you've used the Paint Bucket tool. But notice how quickly and easily you can recolor a shape. Always remember that the Paint Bucket—like other painting tools—uses whatever you've set as the current foreground color.

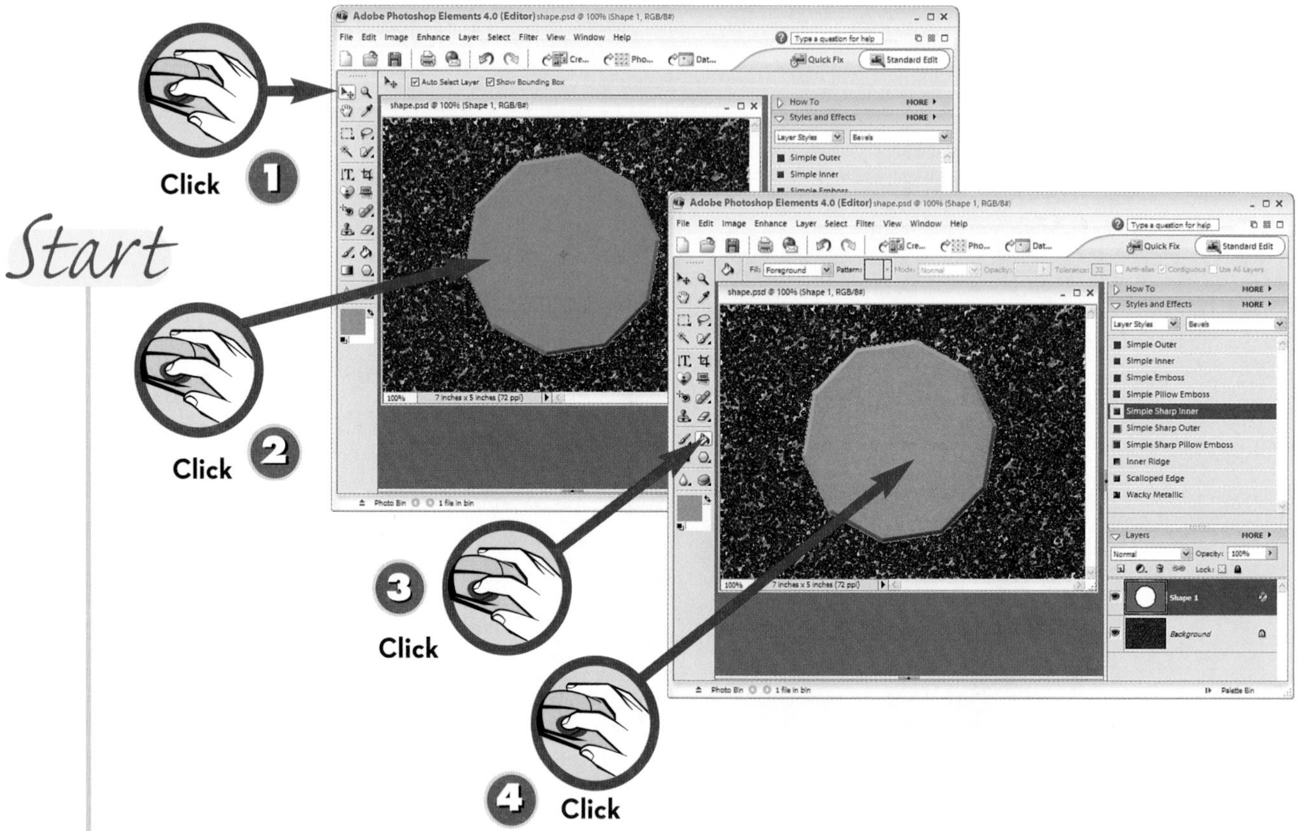

1. Having chosen the foreground color, switch to the **Move** tool or press **V**. (**Auto Select Layer** must be checked.)
2. Select the shape.
3. Switch to the **Paint Bucket** tool, or press **K**.
4. Click inside the shape to apply the color.

TIP

Change the Fill Color

Before you do step 1, click the **Foreground** color swatch at the bottom of the toolbar and make a selection from the **Color Picker**.

TIP

Fill with a Pattern

If you prefer a pattern rather than a color, before doing step 4, choose **Pattern** from the Fill pop-up menu in the Options bar; then make a selection from the **Pattern** menu.

CHOOSING A COLOR FROM THE IMAGE

Want to pick a color for a new shape or brush stroke that exactly matches some color in the image? The Eyedropper tool sucks up the color you click and loads it as the current foreground color. Whatever painting or drawing tool you use next applies that color.

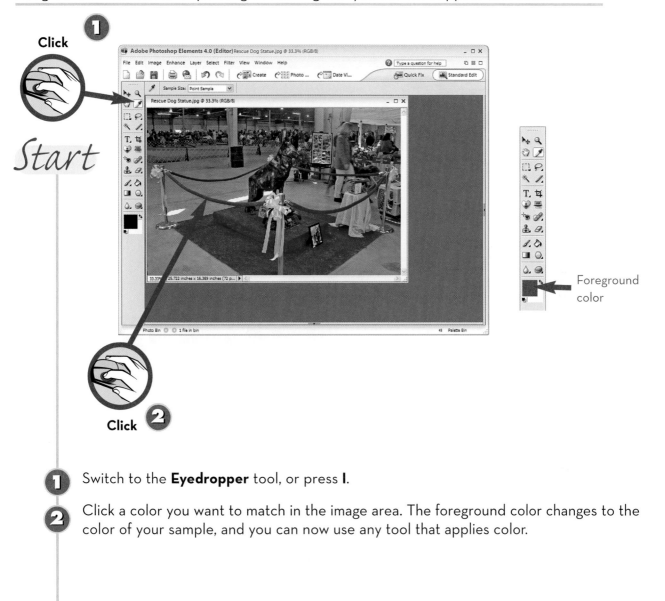

Click 1

Start

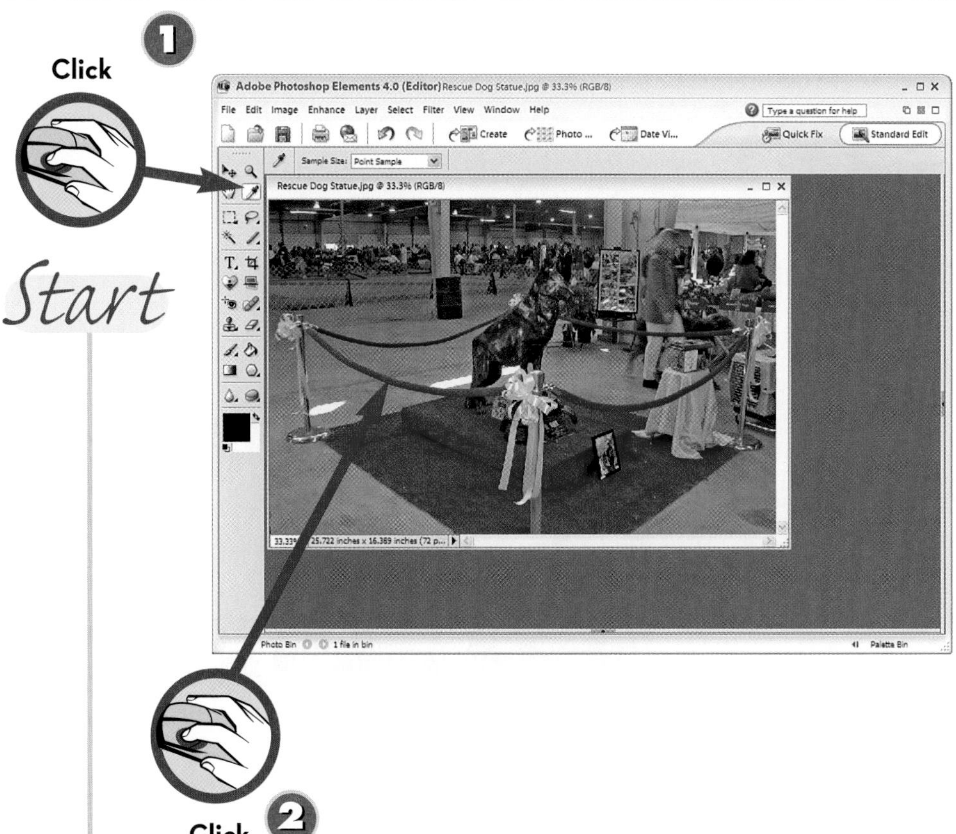

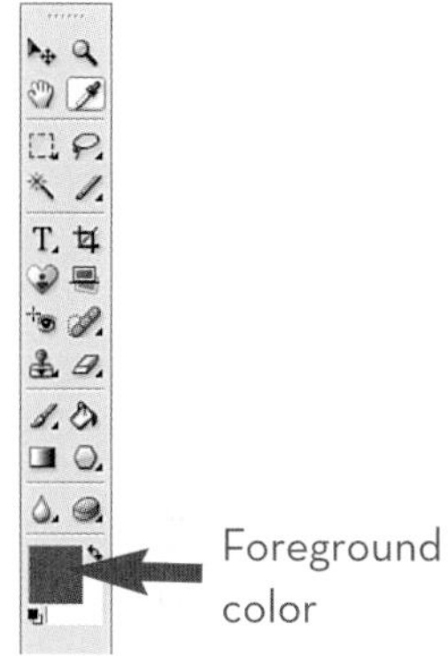

Foreground color

Click 2

1. Switch to the **Eyedropper** tool, or press **I**.
2. Click a color you want to match in the image area. The foreground color changes to the color of your sample, and you can now use any tool that applies color.

End

TIP

Changing Sample Size

Before step 2, you can choose **3 × 3 Average** or **5 × 5 Average** to set the number of pixels in the area the Eyedropper will sample. (It's an average, so the resulting color may be a blend of the sampled pixels.)

NOTE

Whenever You See It

Photoshop Elements uses the Eyedropper pointer in other places, such as the Color Swatches palette, and it always works as a color selector.

USING THE COLOR SWATCHES PALETTE

If you've ever browsed through color swatches at the paint store, you know how handy it can be to see a coordinated set of choices. It's generally quicker and easier to make a choice from preset Color Swatches than to use the Color Picker (which, for most folks, has way too many).

Start

1 Click

New Foreground color

2 Click

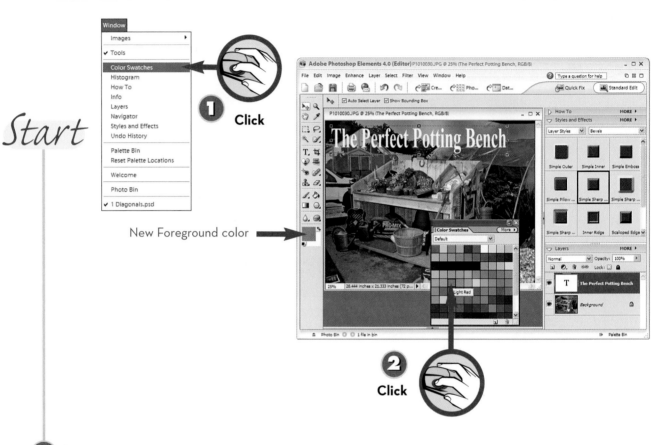

1. Choose **Window**, **Color Swatches**.
2. Click the color you want to use next. The foreground color changes to the color of your sample, and you are ready to use any tool that applies color.

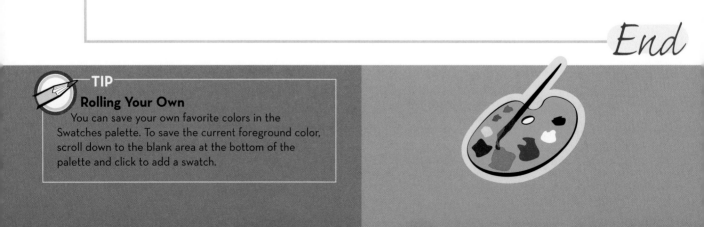

End

TIP

Rolling Your Own

You can save your own favorite colors in the Swatches palette. To save the current foreground color, scroll down to the blank area at the bottom of the palette and click to add a swatch.

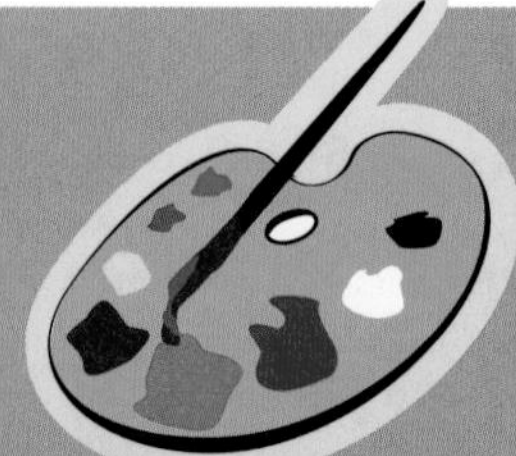

PAINTING AND DRAWING WITH A BRUSH AND PENCIL

Use the Brush tool to do freehand painting (or Impressionist Brush to paint over and blur an existing image). The Pencil tool right beside it in the toolbar works much the same, except pencil lines don't have soft edges.

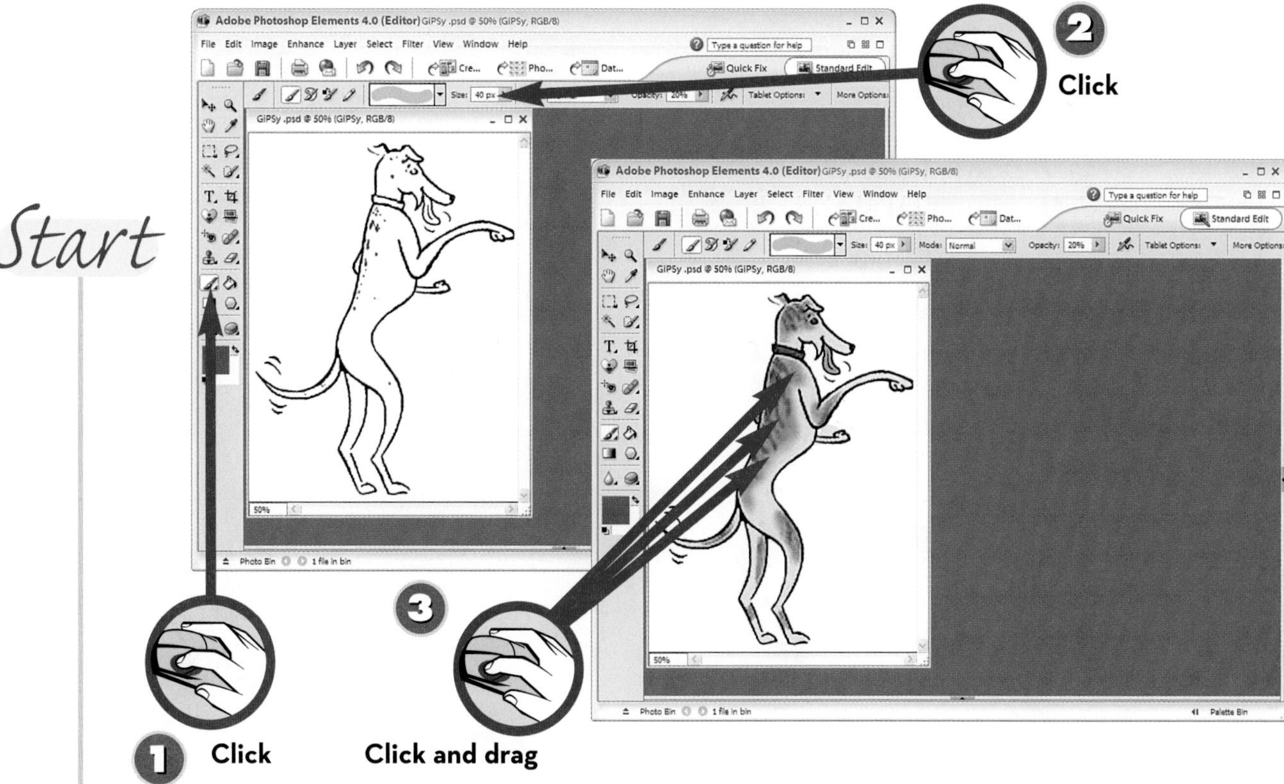

1. Choose the **Brush** tool.
2. Set brush properties in the Options bar, such as **Size**.
3. Click and drag in the image area to apply each brush stroke.

End

NOTE

Brush Stroke Technique

Keep holding down the mouse button and paint with a scrubbing motion to apply a single, continuous brush stroke. Or, click and release the mouse button frequently as you paint to apply dabs of color.

TIP

A Tip on Brush Tips

Choose the tip size and brush stroke properties in the Options bar before you do step 2. Pick one of the preset brushes or adjust the other options to create your own.

CONTROLLING HOW BRUSHES BEHAVE

If you really want to get arty with brush tips, you can make all kinds of adjustments in the Options bar, before you start painting. Also located there is the Airbrush button, which generates a spray of pixels at the brush tip. (Access the full range of options from the More Options pop-up menu.)

Start

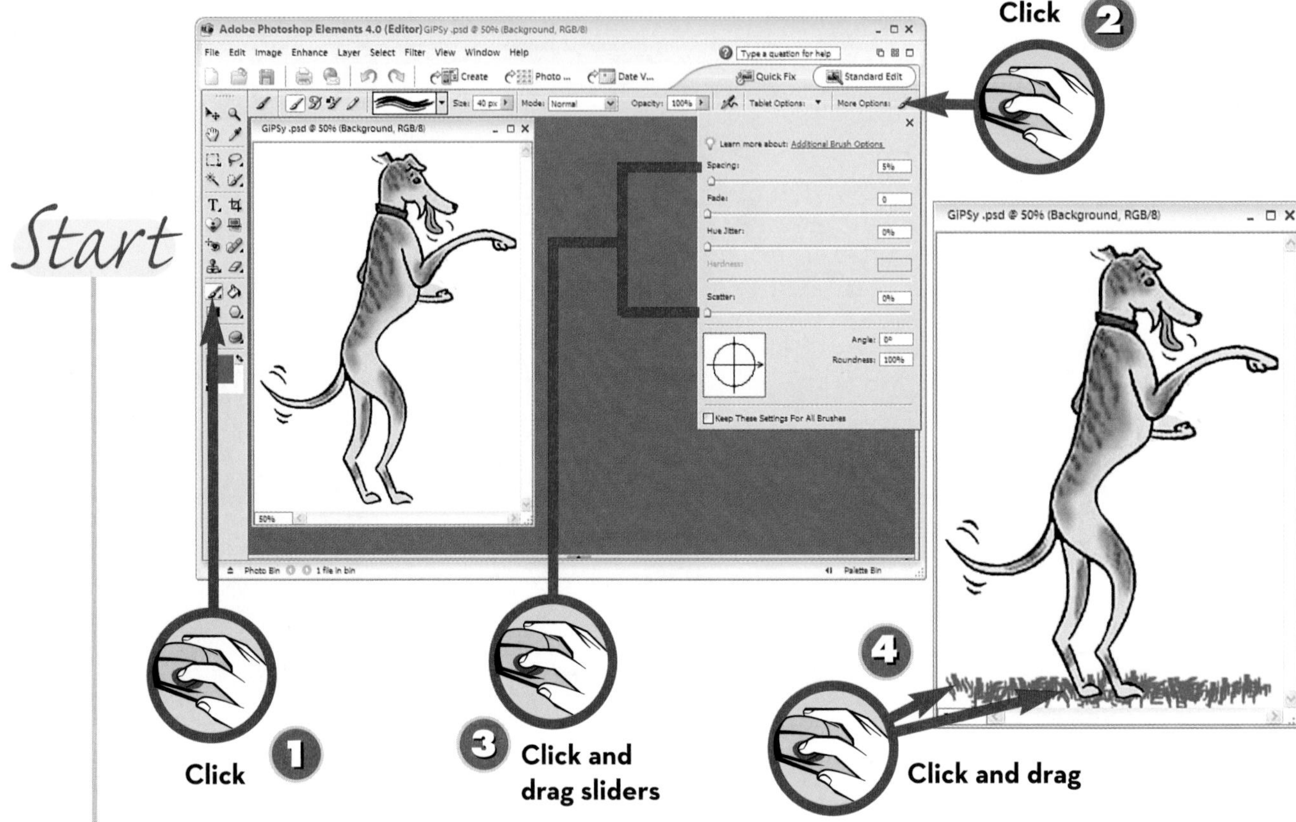

1. Switch to the **Brush** tool.
2. Click **More Options** in the Options bar.
3. Adjust how the brush works by dragging a slider or typing a new percentage for one or more options.
4. Click and drag in the image area to apply each brush stroke.

End

NOTE

Lots to Choose From

There are more than a dozen categories of preset brushes in the Options bar, and you have the choice of fine-tuning any of them by making adjustments using the More Options pop-up menu.

TIP

Still More Options

In the Options bar, Mode controls effects for artistic purposes, as well as for doing fine photo retouching. Opacity, in effect, is paint thickness—lower numbers are more like watercolor.

PAINTING WITH THE PATTERN STAMP

Painting with a pattern is lots of fun—and something you can't do nearly as easily with physical paint and paper. The result is more like making cutouts of wallpaper or fabric and pasting them down—much like art techniques collage and mixed media.

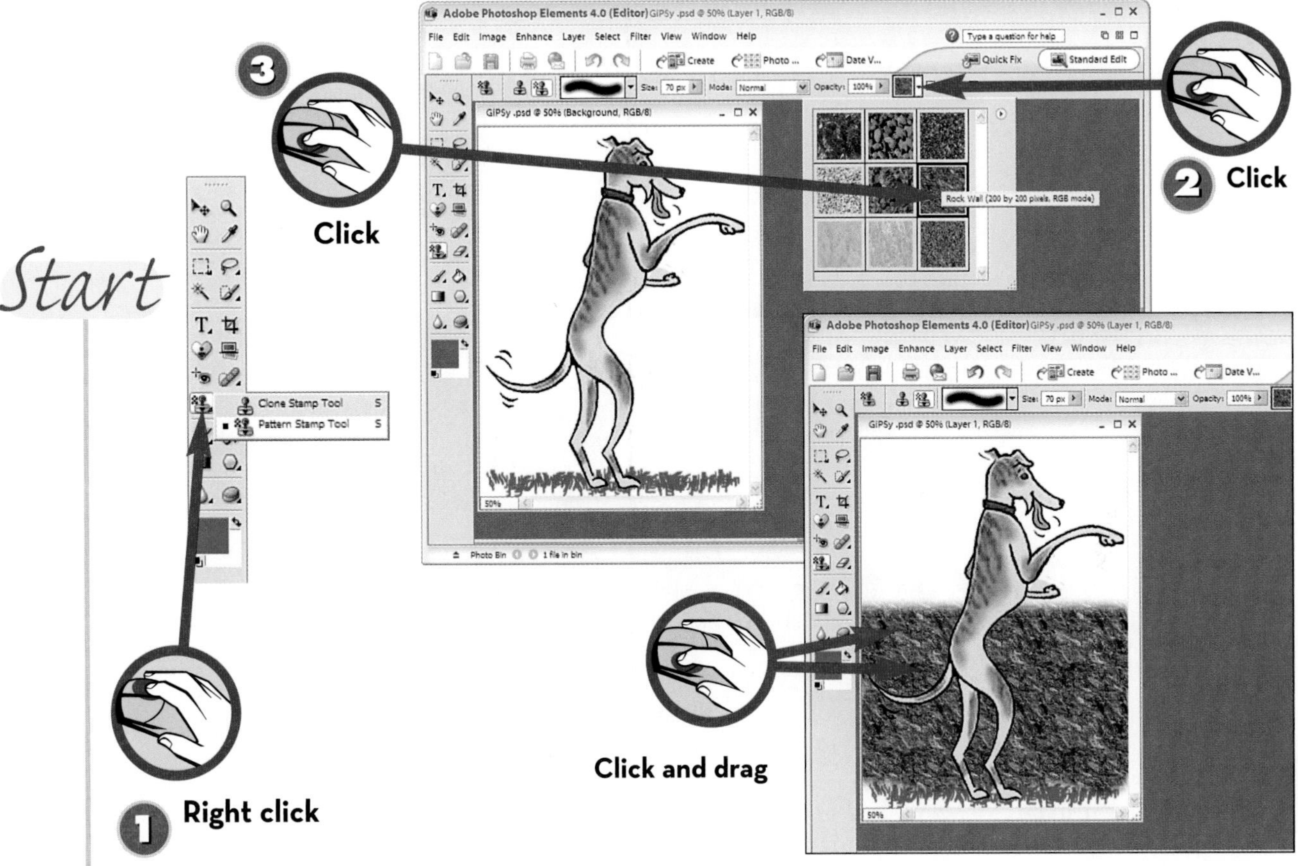

1. Right-click the **Stamp** tool and choose **Pattern Stamp Tool**.
2. Open the **Pattern** menu in the Options bar.
3. Click to choose a pattern from the Pattern pop-up menu.
4. Click and drag in the image area to paint, just as you would with the Brush tool.

End

NOTE

The Other Stamp Tool

The Pattern Stamp's roommate in the toolbar, the Clone Stamp, isn't so much for painting as it is a tool for removing unwanted details, such as facial blemishes, from photos.

NOTE

Options, Options

Notice that there are all kinds of choices in the Options bar. Make your selections before doing step 2, just as you would with a brush.

ERASING PART OF THE IMAGE

The Eraser tool works just like a brush—but removes pixels in its path rather than depositing them. It only affects shapes on the layer currently selected, so you may want to open the Layers palette first to get your bearings.

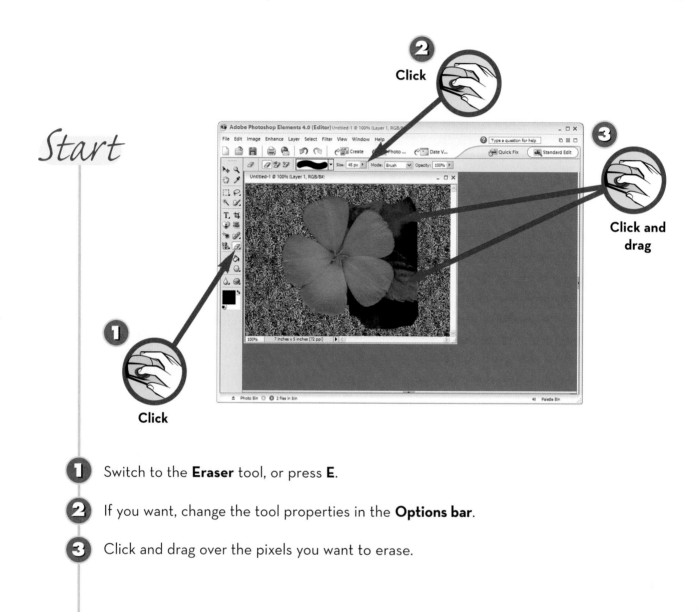

Start

2 Click

3 Click and drag

1 Click

1. Switch to the **Eraser** tool, or press **E**.
2. If you want, change the tool properties in the **Options bar**.
3. Click and drag over the pixels you want to erase.

End

TIP

Undo Instead?

Use the Eraser tool to partially erase objects in an image. To simply get rid of painting mistakes, **Edit**, **Undo** may be faster and cleaner.

TIP

Other Eraser Tools

Right-click in step 1 to choose **Background Eraser**, which deletes a single color sampled from the center of a brush, or **Magic Eraser**, which deletes areas of similar-colored pixels with a click (just as Magic Wand does for selections).

SMUDGING THE "PAINT"

Some of the painting tools can be used either for painting or for retouching details in photos, and the Smudge tool is one of these. Artists who've worked with pastels will be familiar with the technique of rubbing chalk edges to soften them.

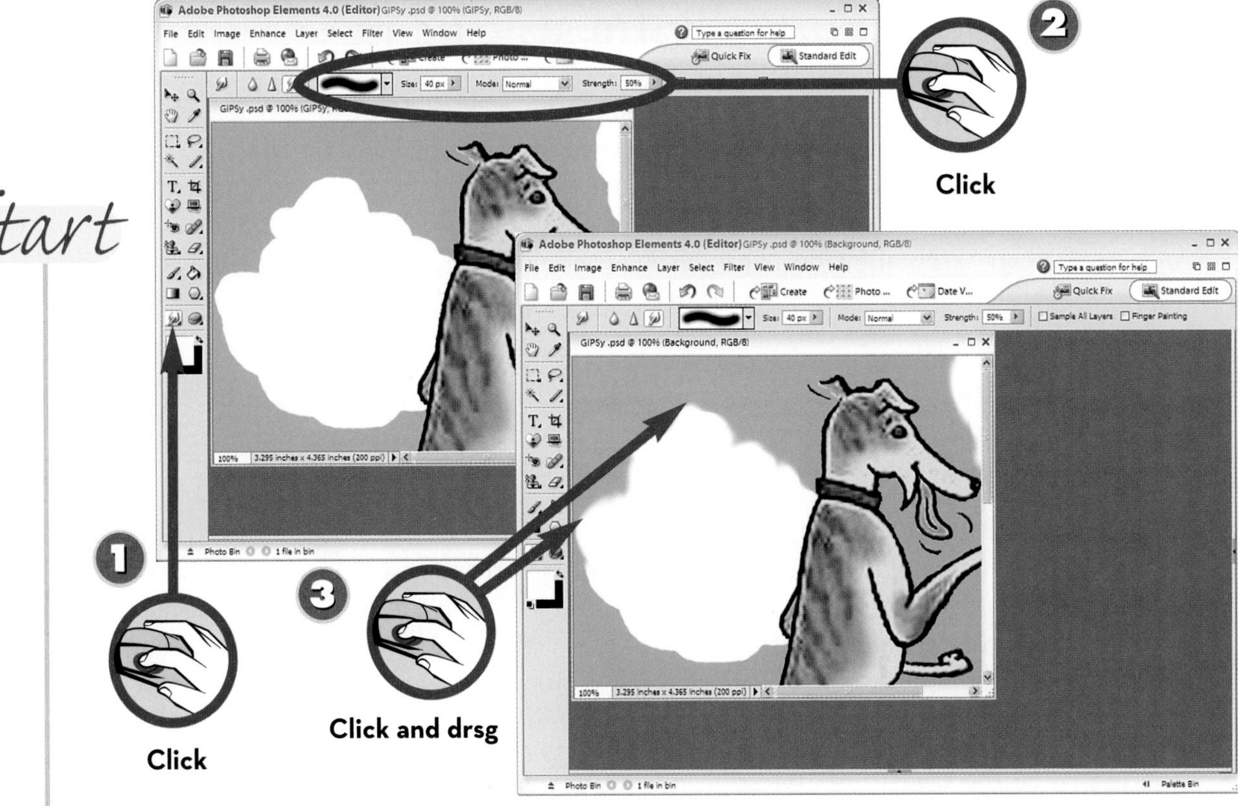

1. With the edge you want to soften zoomed in the image area, switch to the **Smudge** tool or press **R**.
2. If you want, change the tool properties in the **Options bar**.
3. Click and drag along the edge to soften it.

End

TIP

Finger Paint, Oh Boy!

If you're tempted to make a creative mess the clean, electronic way, check the **Finger Painting** box in the Options bar before you do step 3.

NOTE

Impressionist Brush Instead?

The effect of the Smudge tool may be too subtle for your taste. For more pronounced blurring, use the Impressionist Brush tool in one of the smaller brush sizes. Also try effects in the Filter, Blur submenu.

part 8

FLATTERING YOUR SUBJECTS

Okay, in other parts of this book we've talked about Photoshop Elements being your photo lab and your art studio—but why not also think of it as a one-stop health and beauty spa? Digital retouching, if not overdone, can perk up your friends and loved ones, making them appear to shed pounds, revitalizing their complexions, and putting that old sparkle in their eyes—all without risky fad diets, treatments, or pills!

But let's emphasize—*don't overdo it*. As a good rule of thumb, try to soften rather than erase. Leave some lines, freckles, and whatever other imperfections give your friend her unique character and winning charm. Go too far, and you'll have a slick beauty shot of a lifeless mannequin.

Many of the techniques described in this part were applied to the photo on the facing page. Retouching included correcting a color cast, softening facial lines with the Blur tool, removing a mole with the Spot Healing Brush tool, adding eyelight with the Brush tool, lightening shadows and darkening blown-out highlights with the Dodge and Burn tools, and intensifying lip and eye color with the Sponge tool set to Saturate.

The transformation took about 10 minutes—and it makes a lovely person even lovelier.

WHAT A DIFFERENCE A PIXEL MAKES

Before

After

SOFTENING WRINKLES

This one's sure to please—the wrinkle remover. Remember, the lines in the face convey expressiveness, so don't paint them all out. Ask yourself: Are these crow's feet or laugh lines? (To work in even finer detail, you can use the Blur tool much the same way.)

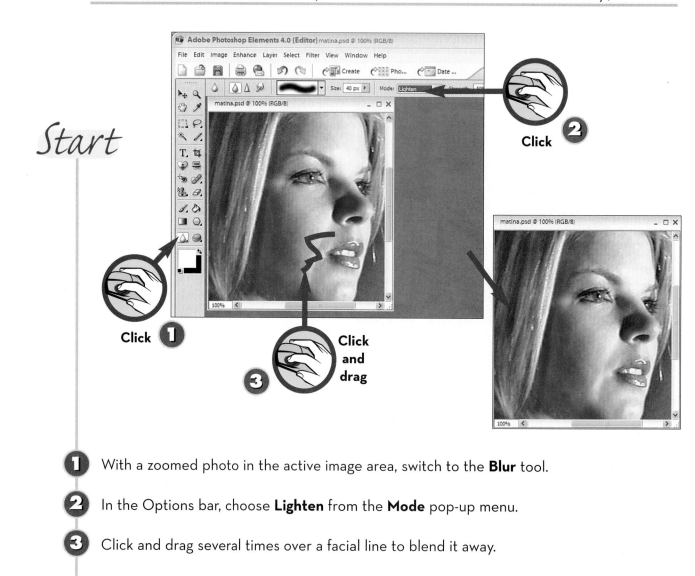

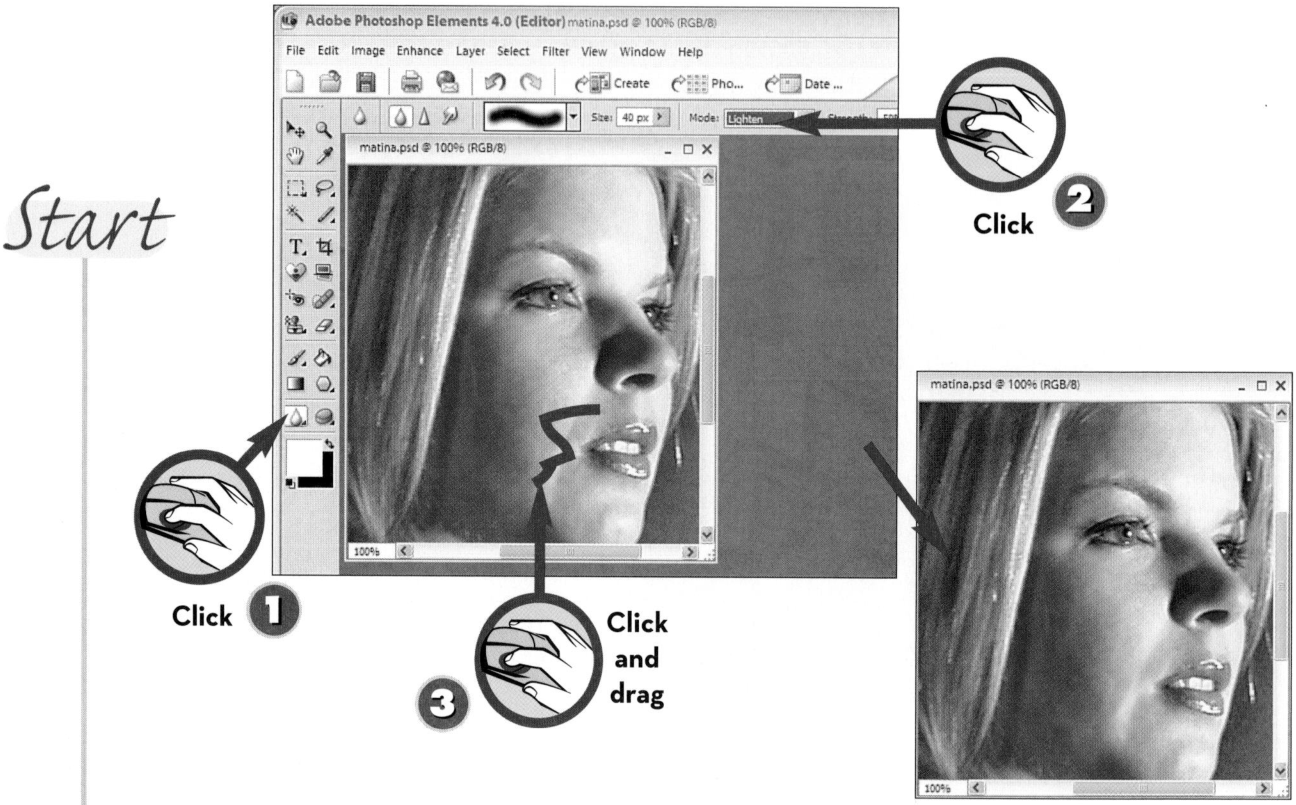

Start

Click 1

Click 2

Click and drag 3

1. With a zoomed photo in the active image area, switch to the **Blur** tool.
2. In the Options bar, choose **Lighten** from the **Mode** pop-up menu.
3. Click and drag several times over a facial line to blend it away.

End

TIP

To Be Precise About It

For best results, pick a Soft Round brush tip in the Options bar with a Size just slightly larger than the facial lines you're retouching—and trace along the line as you paint.

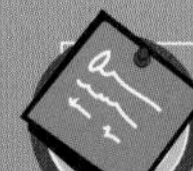

NOTE

Mode Options

The Blur tool can be versatile, depending on this setting. Besides Normal, Darken, and Lighten (used here), the effect can be confined to Hue, Saturation, Color, or Luminosity.

REMOVING BLEMISHES

That's right—the Spot Healing Brush tool is a painless zit zapper. But its marvels don't stop there. You can use it to cover up any part of a picture with textures Elements creates based on the surrounding pixels. Give it a try to get rid of spots on flower petals, lint on clothes, or any spot you can dab.

Start

1. With a zoomed photo in the active image area, switch to the **Spot Healing Brush** tool or press **J**.
2. Choose a brush size just slightly larger than the blemish you want to erase.
3. Click once on the blemish to remove it.

End

NOTE

The Big Jobs

The Spot Healing Brush works best on, well, spots! Use it to retouch small, "clickable" objects surrounded by relatively clear, flat areas of color, such as moles, pimples, and dust motes. Often, you'll want to retouch larger areas and objects that are right next to other objects you don't want to affect, such as tattoos and smudges. For these jobs, try using the Healing Brush tool instead. Turn to "Painting Problem Areas Away," **p. 144**, to learn more.

CHANGING HAIR COLOR

Being able to digitally recolor hair opens up all kinds of possibilities. Try on new looks and print them out to show the colorist at your hair salon. Change your Web photo because an ardent admirer has a thing for redheads. Or—go blue, pink, or green without fear of social stigma.

1. Switch to the **Lasso** tool, or press **L**.
2. Click and drag to trace the outline of the hair.
3. Choose **Layer**, **New Adjustment Layer**, **Hue/Saturation**.

Continued

NOTE

It's Cake, It's a Sandwich

There's a lot more about layers in a later part, but in these steps you're creating a special layer to contain just the Hue/Saturation effect. This adjustment layer doesn't contain any part of the image. By selecting the area you want to modify before creating the adjustment layer, you restrict its effects to that area.

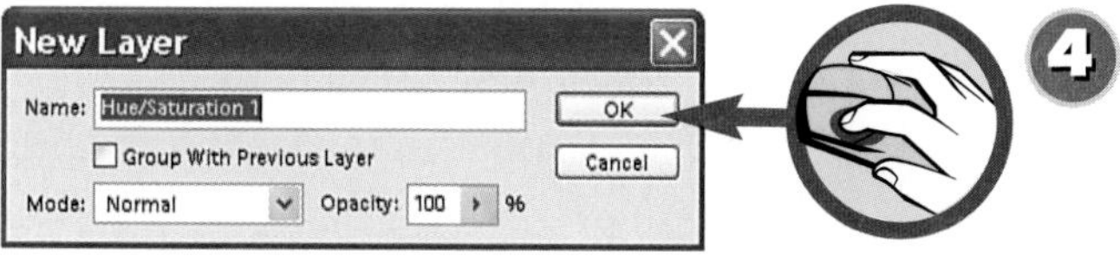

4. Click **OK**.
5. Adjust sliders to change the hair color.
6. Click **OK**.

End

TIP
Want Subtler Color?
To soften the effect of the Hue/Saturation layer on the underlying hair color, decrease the value of **Opacity** for the new layer in the Layers palette.

TIP
Keep Those Layers
To keep a version of the image that contains editable layers, save your file as a Photoshop (**.psd**) file.

PAINTING PROBLEM AREAS AWAY

Unlike the Spot Healing Brush, the Healing Brush tool requires you to paint back and forth across whatever you're trying to remove from the image. It's a better bet for fixing larger objects or areas that aren't completely surrounded by the same color or texture, such as tattoos, stray strands of hair, or distracting jewelry.

Start

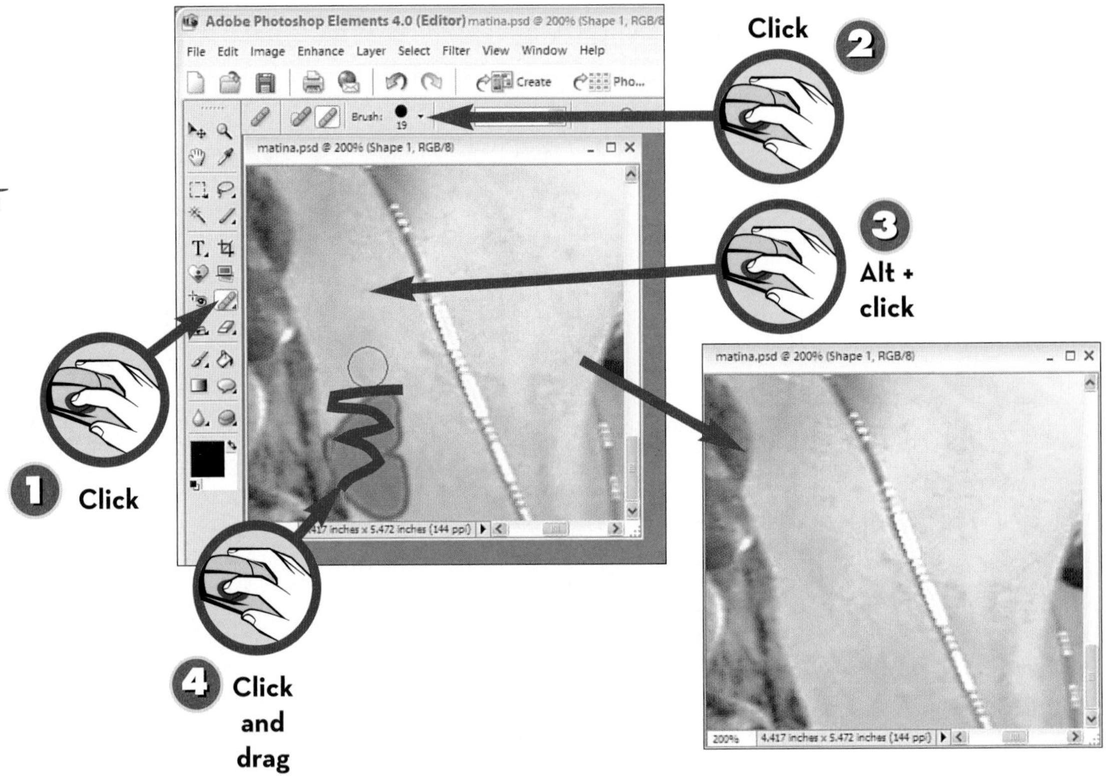

1 Click

2 Click

3 Alt + click

4 Click and drag

1. With a zoomed photo in the active image area, switch to the **Healing Brush** tool or press **J**.
2. Choose a brush size somewhat smaller than the area you want to fill in.
3. Alt-click in a clear area of skin to choose a source for the new pixels.
4. Click and drag across the area to paint it with texture copied from the source area.

End

TIP

Odds Are It'll Be Even

You can use the Healing Brush to even out skin tones. Alt-click to place your source point in the area whose color you want to reproduce; choose **Color** from the **Mode** pop-up menu on the **Options** bar.

ENHANCING OR TONING DOWN A COLOR

The Sponge tool doesn't actually change the color of a selection, it just intensifies (saturates) or reduces (desaturates) it. It can come in handy for brightening up a wardrobe, such as neck scarves, or for toning down a too-colorful background that's competing with your subject.

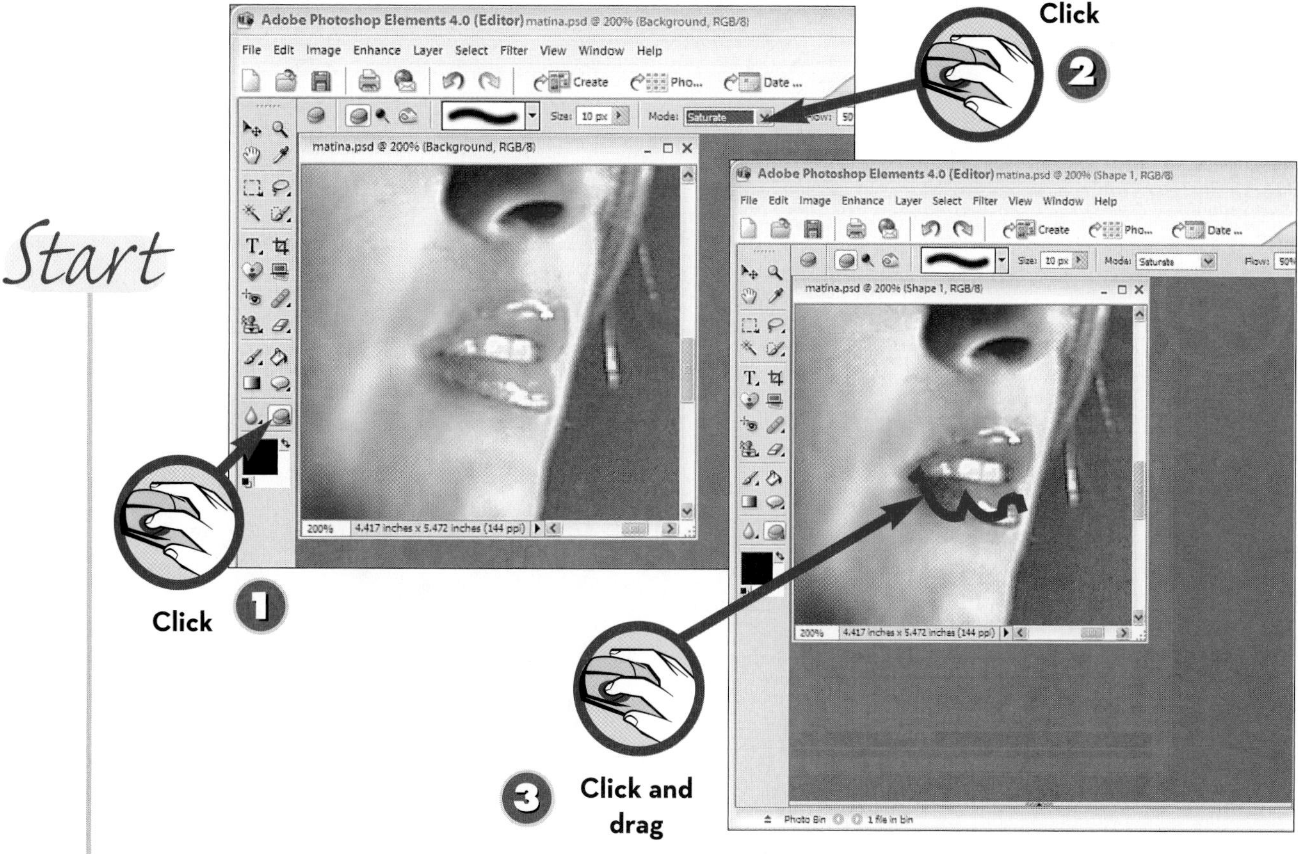

1. With a photo in the active image area, switch to the **Sponge** tool, or press **O**.
2. To enhance color, switch to **Saturate** from the **Mode** pop-up menu in the Options bar.
3. Click and drag over an area to heighten its color.

End

TIP

Sponge Options

As with many other tools, the Options bar offers a selection of brush tip sizes. The Flow setting controls the rate at which pixels become saturated or desaturated as you paint over them.

NOTE

Dishwater Results?

If you overuse the Sponge in Desaturate mode, you'll remove all color from the area. That's fine if you're going for a selective monochrome look—or to make skin look downright ghostly.

ADDING A SOFT GLOW

Ever notice the glow around starlets in black-and-white movies of the 20s and 30s? This *halation effect* was actually a flaw of early film, but audiences equated it with glamour. Soft focus is still a wonderful way to soften skin and hide pores.

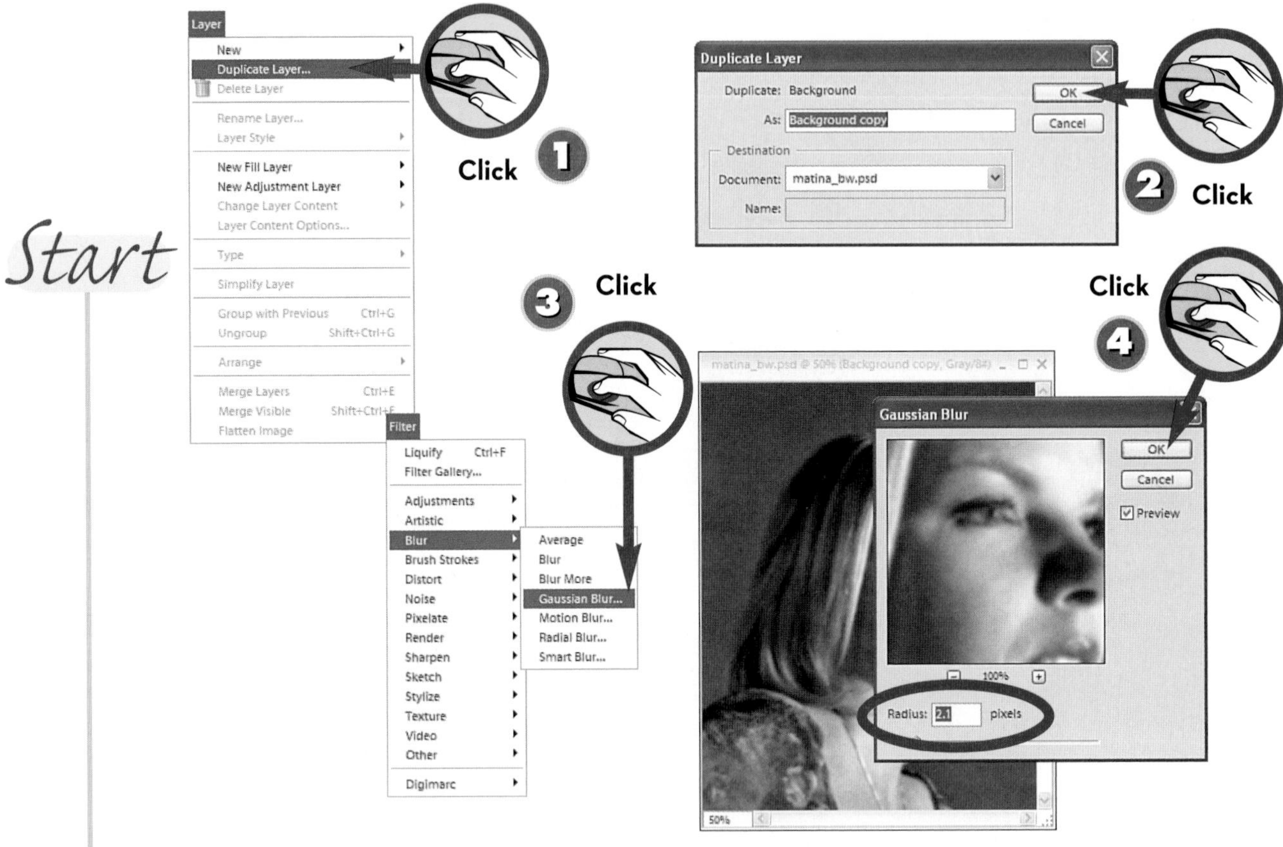

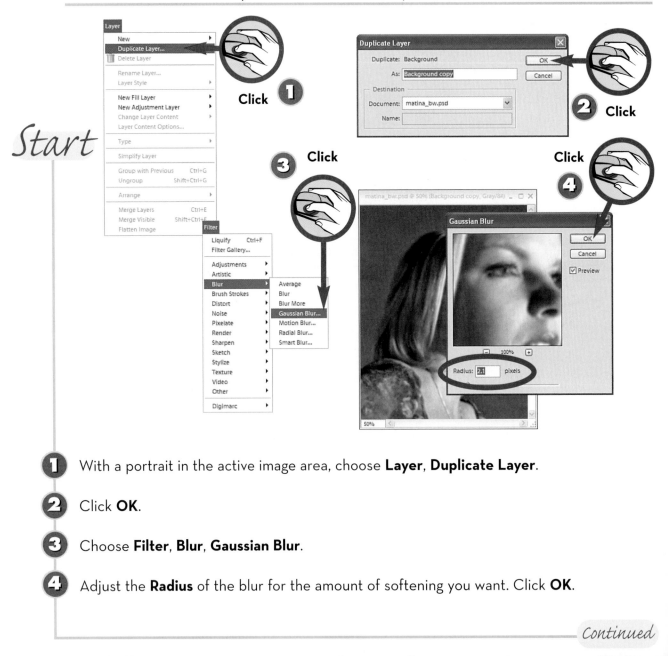

1. With a portrait in the active image area, choose **Layer**, **Duplicate Layer**.
2. Click **OK**.
3. Choose **Filter**, **Blur**, **Gaussian Blur**.
4. Adjust the **Radius** of the blur for the amount of softening you want. Click **OK**.

Continued

NOTE

Gaussian Blur Radius

The Gaussian Blur option controls the extent of blurring. The image changes as you adjust the slider. Make it blurred enough to lose unwanted detail, but sharp enough so the viewer can't immediately tell it's out of focus.

NOTE

Preserving Layers

To preserve editable layers so you can return to the original image, save your work as a Photoshop (**.psd**) file. TIFF (**.tif**) files also have an option for saving layers.

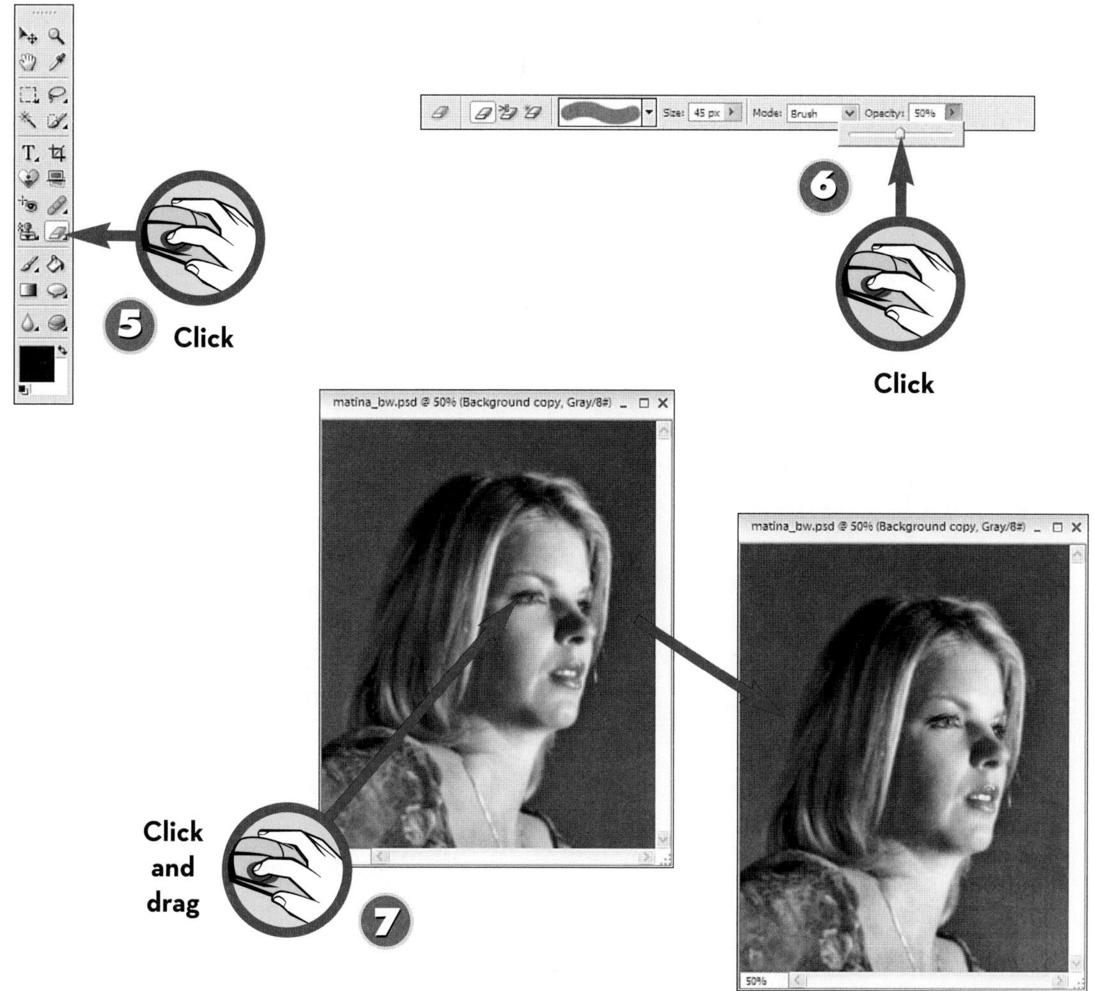

5 Click the **Eraser** tool, or press **E**.

6 Adjust **Opacity** to **50%**.

7 Click and drag in the image to paint over and reveal facial details you want to remain sharp.

End

NOTE

Clarify Important Details

If you sharpen facial features—such as eyes, nose, and mouth—viewers won't necessarily notice the rest is out of focus. Don't forget to sharpen important details, such as the necklace, in this case.

TIP

Do This Last

If you're doing a thorough retouching job on a portrait, use the other techniques described in this part first to reduce lines, and so on; then add the Gaussian blur last.

TRIMMING CONTOURS ON THE FACE OR BODY

We all have an unsightly bulge or two we wouldn't mind getting rid of, right? Well, forget diet and exercise—with the Liquify filter you can push that saggy skin right where you'd like it to be. No muss, no fuss!

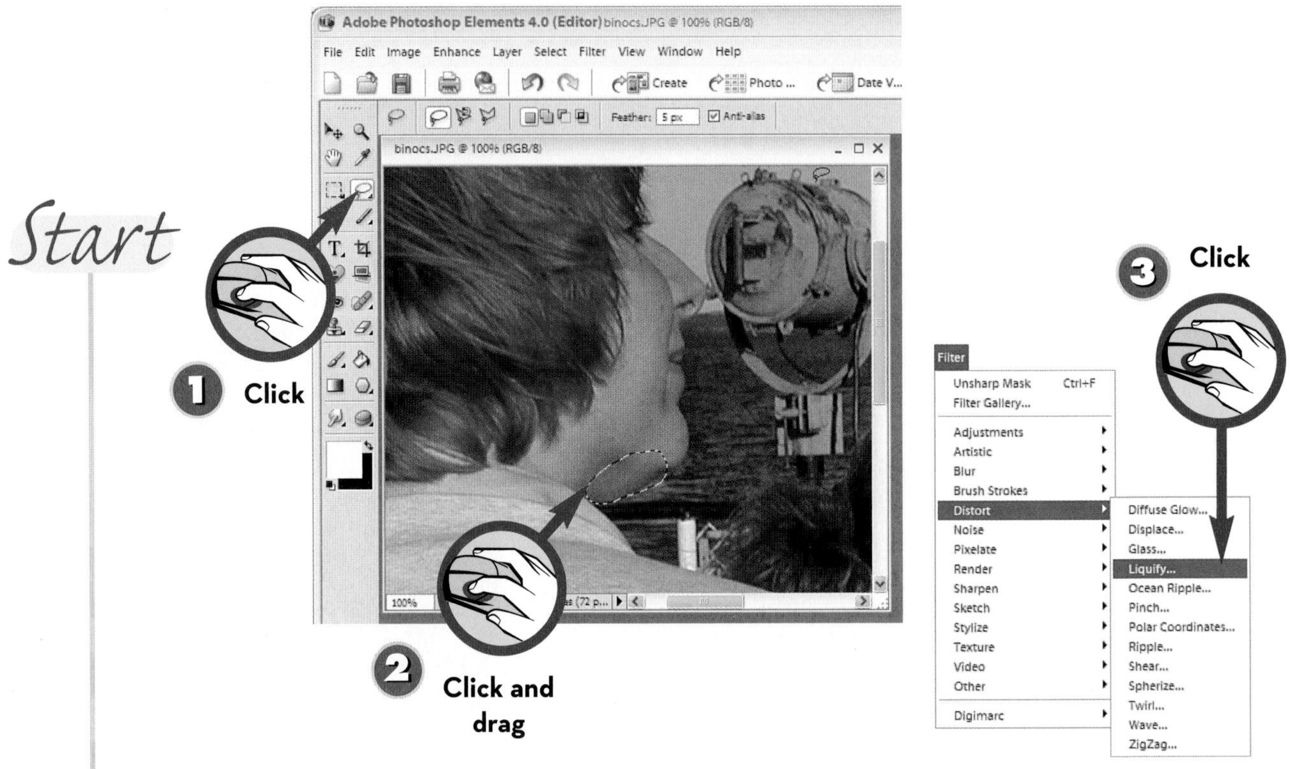

Start

1 Click

2 Click and drag

3 Click

1. Switch to the **Lasso** tool.
2. Click and drag around the contour to be reduced; make the inner edge of the selection along the line you want the contour to follow.
3. Choose **Filter**, **Distort**, **Liquify**.

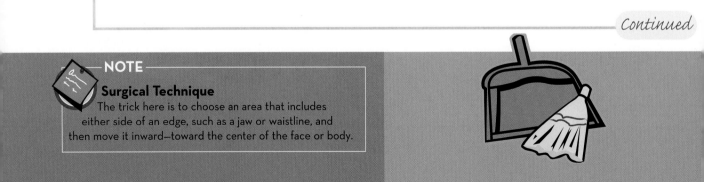

Continued

NOTE

Surgical Technique

The trick here is to choose an area that includes either side of an edge, such as a jaw or waistline, and then move it inward—toward the center of the face or body.

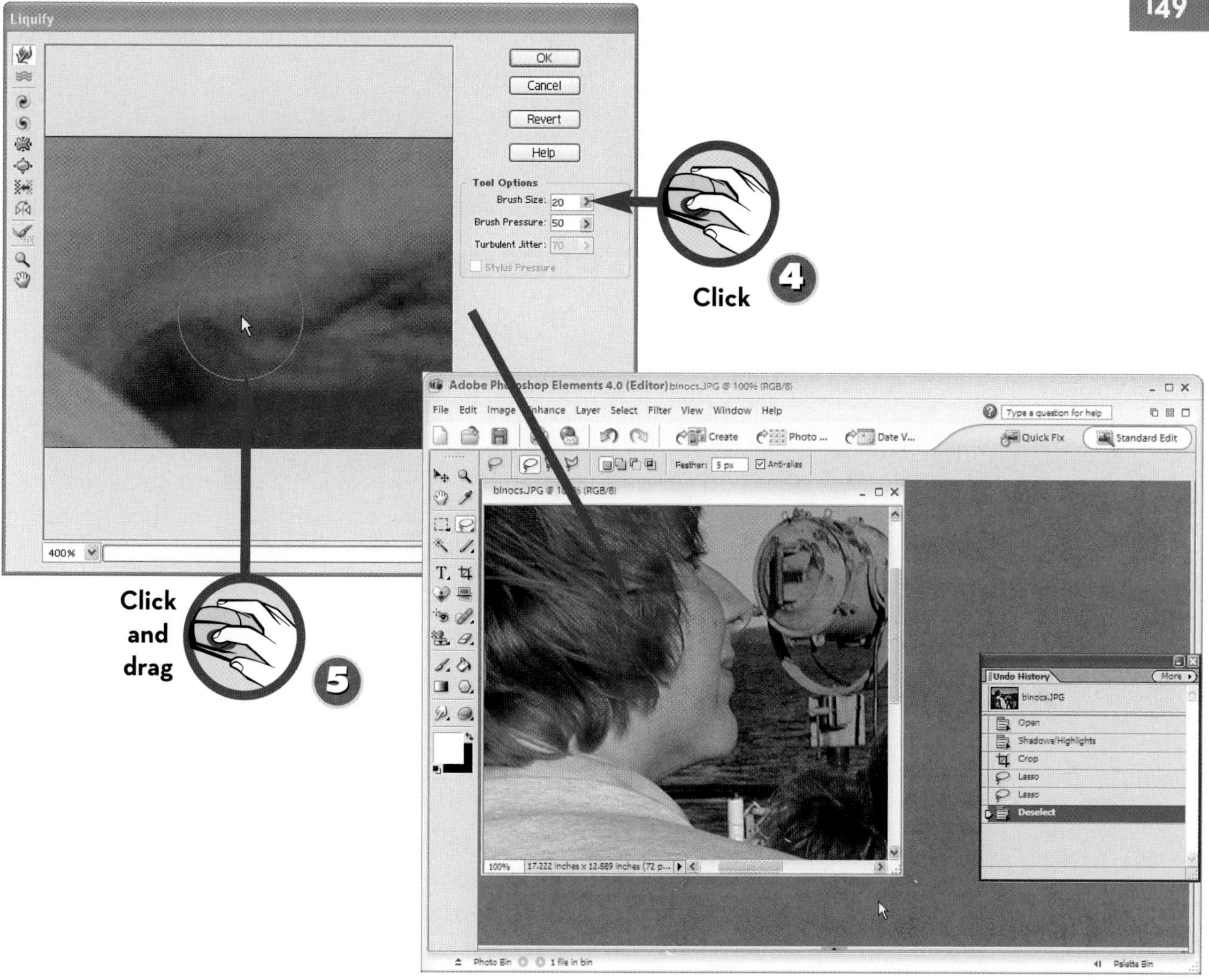

4. Choose a brush one third to one half the size of the area you want to "tuck."
5. Click and drag toward the inner edge of the selection to reposition the skin.
6. Click **OK**.

End

TIP

Move By Itty Bits

Take it slow and easy when using the Liquify tool. The smaller your movements with the mouse, the more subtle the effect will be. Watch out for adjacent objects—try to drag so they won't be distorted.

NOTE

Tidy Up

For a seamless transplant, you might need to use other retouching tools, such as Smudge or Clone Stamp, to clean up the edges.

6

part

ORGANIZING AND PRESENTING YOUR PHOTOS

Knowing how to crop, clean up, and print your photos is all very well and good—unless you can't find the images you want when you need them. That's what Organizer is all about. It's Photoshop Elements's "other half," the half that keeps track of what and where things are. You can use Organizer to catalog your photos and assign them categories and keywords, and it automatically places all your images in a timeline so you can easily locate the photos you *know* you took at last year's Fourth of July party.

Organizer has hidden depths, too; it's also a creative hub where you can turn your photos into slide shows, themed scrapbook pages, and Web photo galleries. After all, the whole point of taking wonderful photos is to be able to share them, right?

In version 4, Organizer has some new features that make it even more useful. For instance, it can recognize faces all by itself, so you can have it show you all the photos in your collection that include people. This makes for much faster tagging (tags are what Organizer calls categories). You'll also be intrigued by the new Bound Photo Book; you can lay out pages of photos and send them off to become a personalized, one-of-a-kind hardbound book.

THANKS FOR THE MEMORIES

Web Photo Gallery

Slide Show

Album Pages

CATALOGING YOUR PHOTOS IN THE ORGANIZER

Before you can access any of the Organizer's exciting features, you have to get your existing photos into an Organizer catalog. This is an easy process—just tell Organizer where the image files are located, and Elements takes it from there.

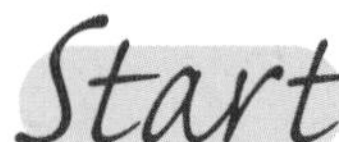

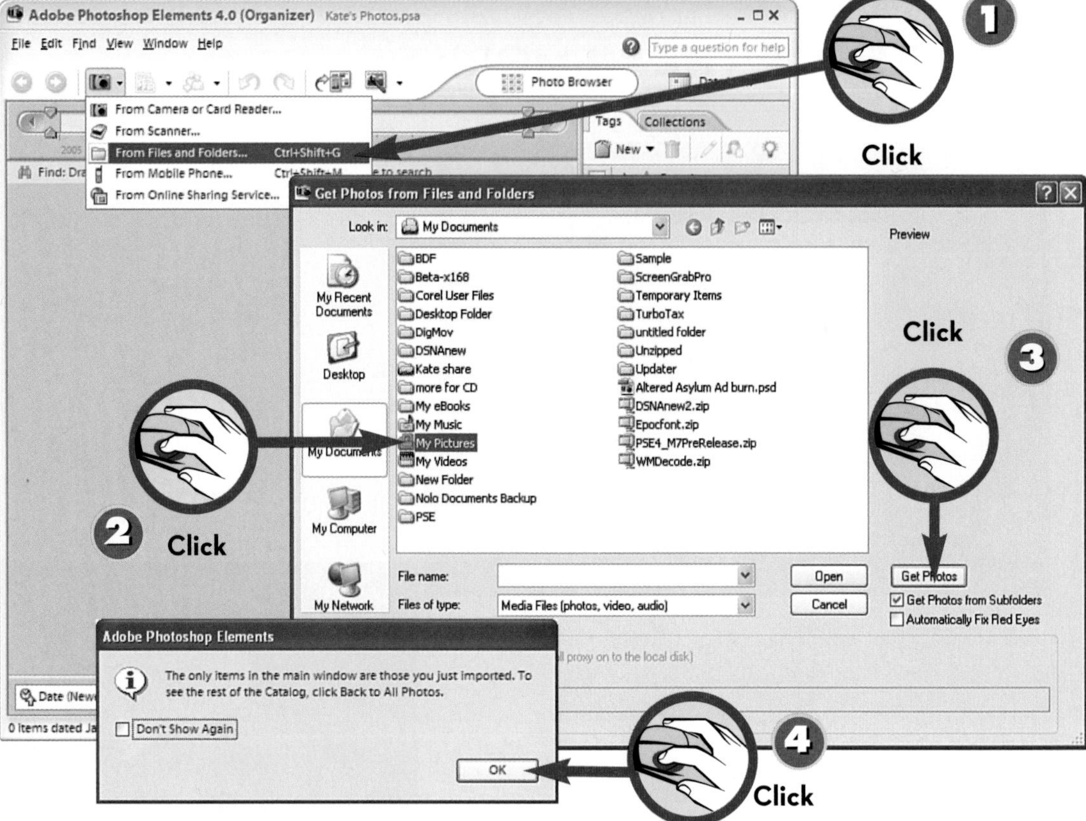

1. From the Organizer's **Get Photos** pop-up menu, choose **From Files and Folders**, or press **Ctrl+Shift+G**.
2. Navigate to the folder that contains your pictures, and click its thumbnail or filename.
3. Click the **Get Photos** button.
4. Click **OK**. The photos in the folder are loaded into your catalog.

Continued

NOTE

Where Do Photos Come From?

The Organizer is also the route that photos take on their way from your digital camera into your computer. Turn to ""Getting Photos into Your Computer"" in Part 2 to learn more.

TIP

Another Way of Looking at Things

Click the **Date View** button in the toolbar to see the photos you took each day in a month or a year. Click **Next Item on Selected Day** to scroll through the photos for a day.

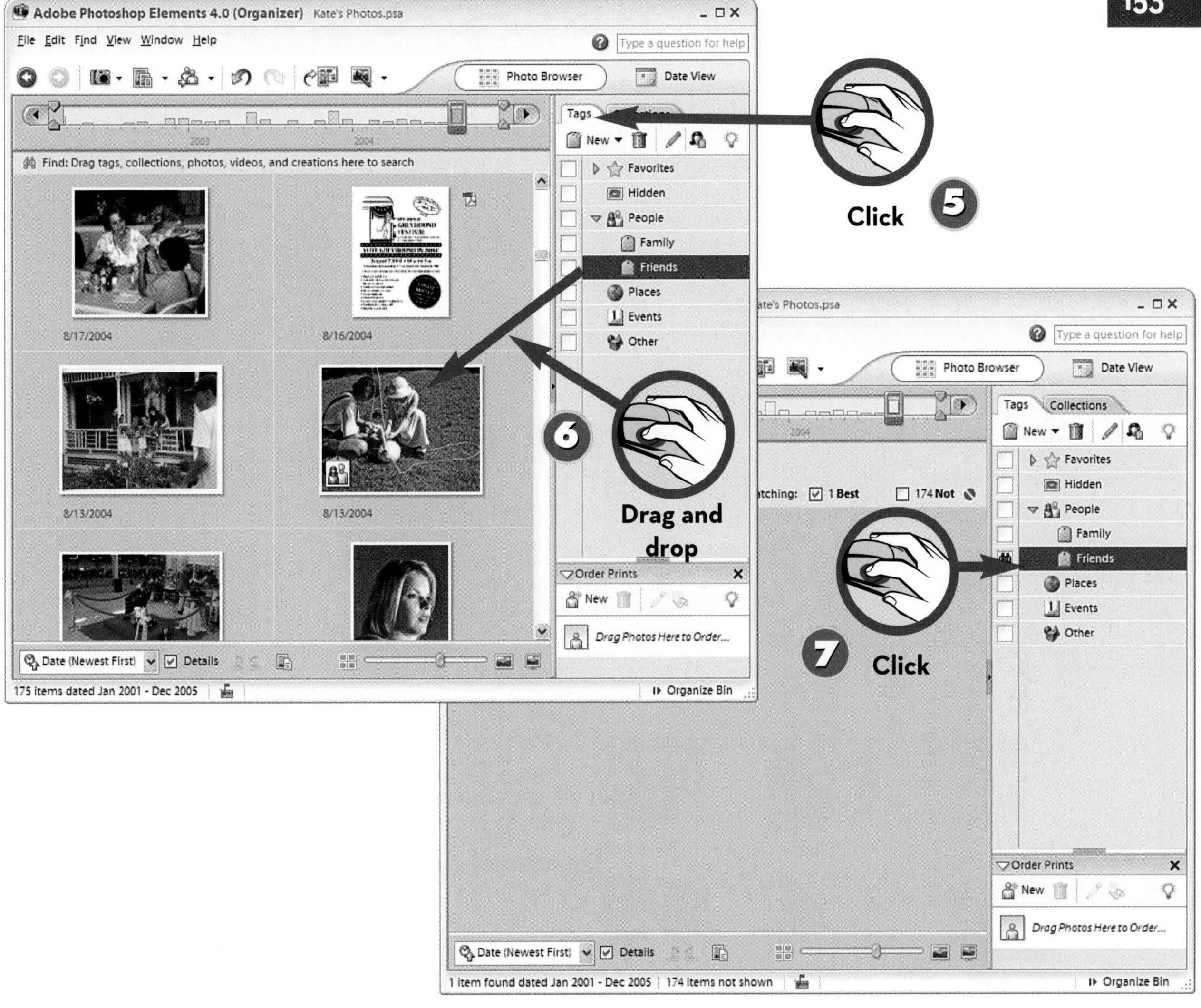

5 Click the **Tags** tab to view the list of available tags.

6 Drag a tag to a photo to apply it to that image.

7 Click the box next to a tag name to search for all images with that tag.

End

TIP

Tag Sale

Click the **New Tag** button at the top of the **Tags** tab to create your own tags. For example, you might make a tag for club activities, one for vacations, one for holidays, and one for pets.

TIP

Batch Tagging

You can assign a tag to more than one photo at a time. **Ctrl-click** to select the photos you want to tag, then drag the tag onto any one of them. The tag is assigned to all the selected pictures.

COLLECTING PHOTOS INTO STACKS

As your photo collection grows, you may find yourself wanting to consolidate similar photos in the Photo Browser. The Organizer provides a simple way to do that: stack them up. Stacking makes your Browser more useful because you can see more *different* photos at one time.

Start

1 Ctrl + click

2 Click

1. **Ctrl-click** to select the photos you want to stack.
2. Choose **Edit**, **Stack**, **Stack Selected Photos**.

TIP

Shuffling the Stack

To choose which photo shows on top of the stack in the Photo Browser, choose **Edit**, **Stack**, **Reveal Photos in Stack**. Click the one you want to use, then choose **Edit**, **Stack**, **Set as Top Photo**.

TAGGING PICTURES OF PEOPLE AUTOMATICALLY

Tagging your photos is an important part of getting them organized, but it's a lot of work. Elements can help out by finding people's faces wherever they show up in your photos and presenting them to you in a single window so you can tag photos of people efficiently.

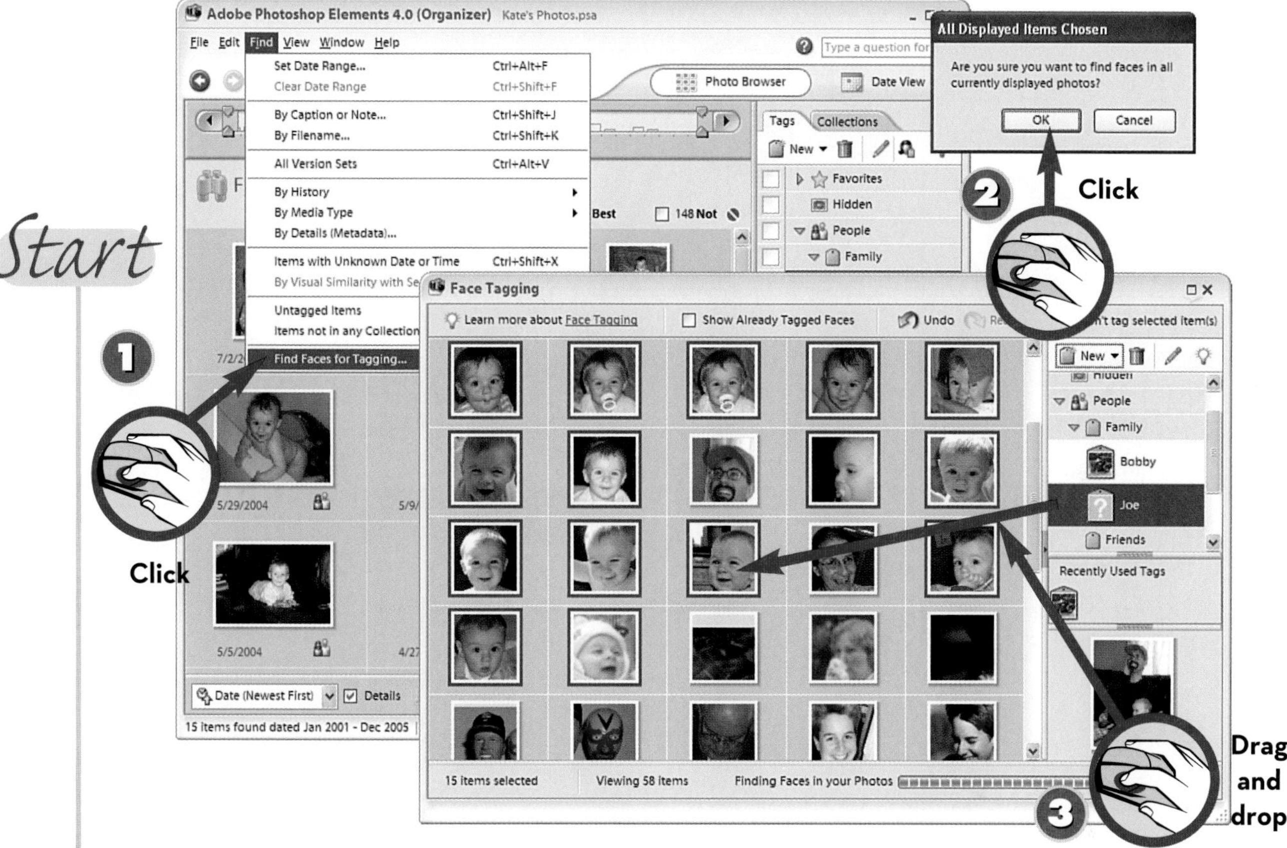

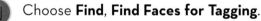

1. Choose **Find**, **Find Faces for Tagging**.
2. Click **OK**.
3. Drag a tag to a photo to apply it to that image.

End

NOTE

Your Choice

Don't forget, you can create as many tags as you like. You might want to tag photos with people's names, or perhaps you prefer a more streamlined approach and want to use just "Friends" and "Family." It's up to you!

TIP

Show Me

Click **Show Already Tagged Faces** at the top of the Find Faces window if you want to see all the faces, even the ones you've already tagged. When this box isn't checked, Elements hides photos as soon as you tag them.

BUILDING PRINTABLE ALBUM PAGES

A traditional-style printed photo album is just one of the creations available to you. The other selections that have much the same steps as Album Pages are Slide Show, VCD with Menu, Bound Photo Book, 4-Fold Greeting Card, Photo Greeting Card, Calendar Pages, Bound Calendar, and HTML Photo Gallery.

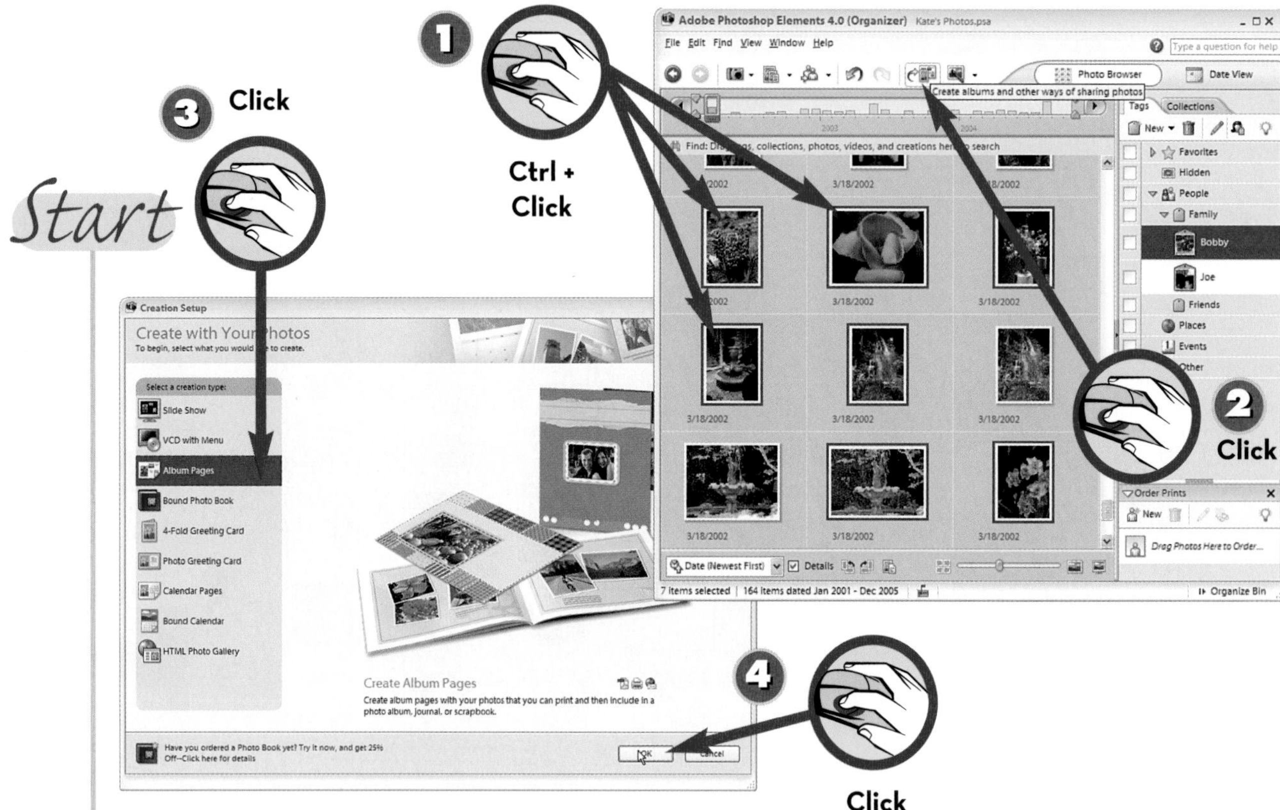

1. In the Organizer, select the photos you want to include in your printed album pages.
2. Click the **Create** button.
3. Click **Album Pages**.
4. Click **OK**.

Continued

NOTE

What's a VCD?

VCD stands for Video CD--it's a CD format you can write with your computer's CD-R or CD-RW drive and play in most DVD players. VCDs work much like DVDs, but they can hold only a tenth of the data.

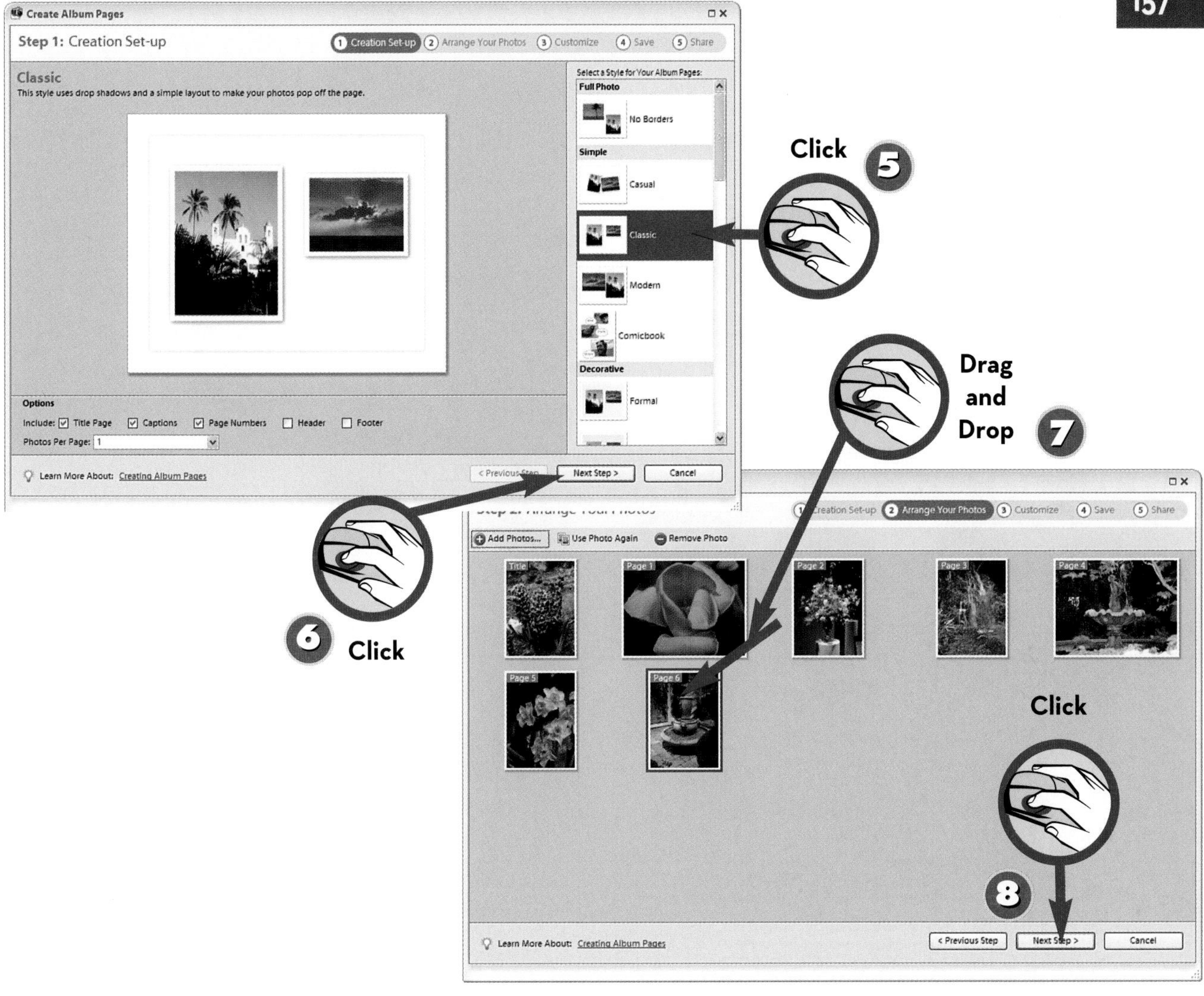

5 Choose an album style, such as **Classic**.

6 Click **Next Step**.

7 Drag and drop the photos into the order you want for the album pages.

8 Click **Next Step**.

Continued

NOTE

A 1000-Word Picture

The first photo in your grouping appears on your album's title page, so make sure it's one that reflects the spirit of the event, people, or places you're documenting in these album pages.

TIP

Selecting Photos

If you start by importing all the photos you need from a folder, you don't need to go looking for them in step 1. Regardless, you can use the buttons above the images to add, duplicate, or delete photos from the catalog in step 7.

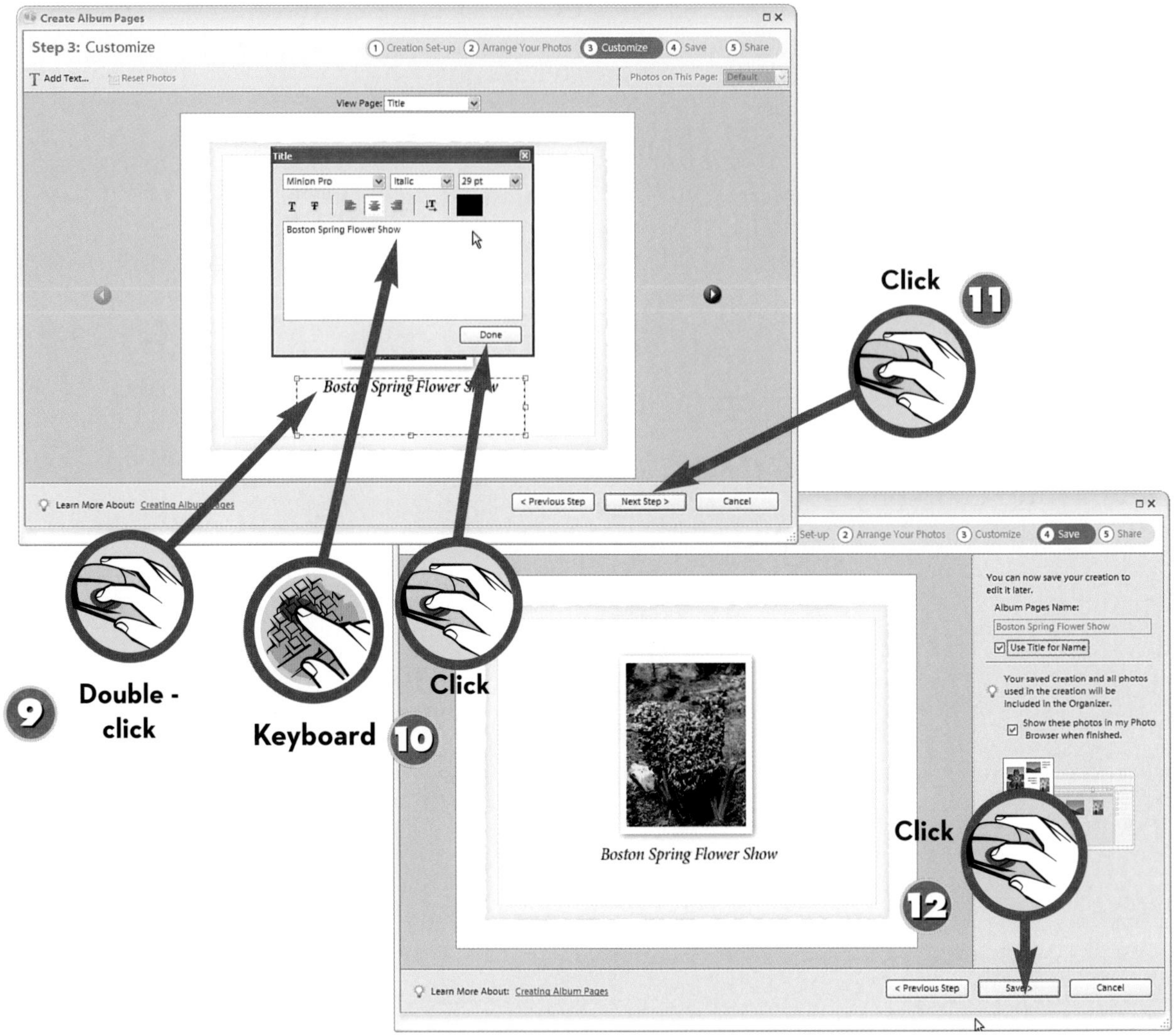

9. Double-click the album title placeholder to add your own title.
10. Type in the new album title and click **Done**.
11. Click **Next Step**.
12. Click **Save**.

Continued

TIP

Output Options

After you click Save in step 12, you have the options of printing your pages, saving them in Adobe Reader (PDF) format, sending the album as an email attachment, burning a CD, or ordering professional photo prints online.

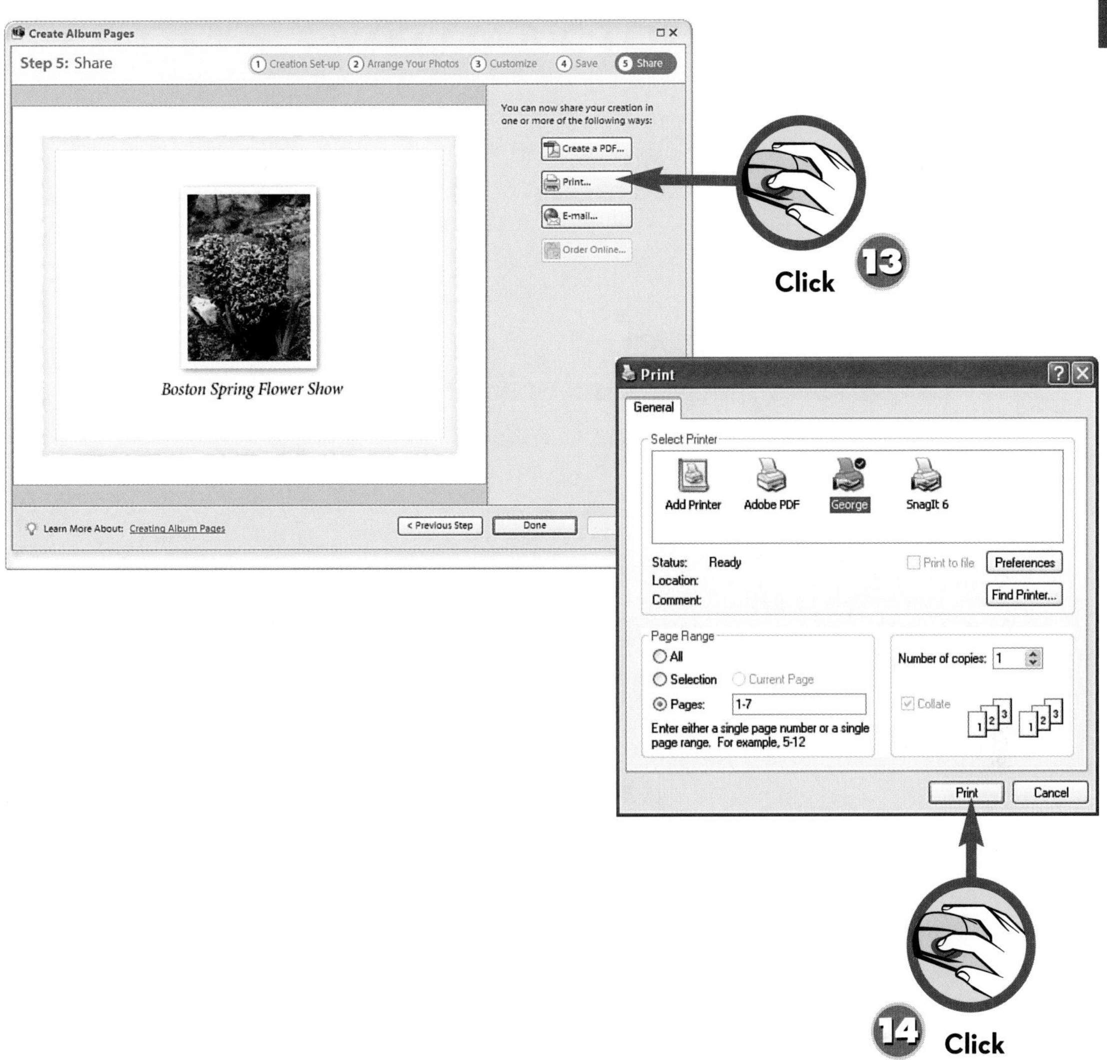

13 Click **Print** to create a printout of your album pages.

14 Click **Print**.

End

TIP

The Gift of Photos

Album pages are great for adding to your real-life photo albums or scrapbooks, and they make a nice gift for grandparents and family friends. If you'd like to create something a little fancier, try the Bound Photo Book option in step 3.

MAKING A WEB PHOTO GALLERY

Photoshop Elements includes a variety of designs for Web pages, and the program can automatically insert your photos and descriptive text into its templates with just a few clicks. It then generates completed pages ready for uploading to your Web hosting service or ISP.

Start

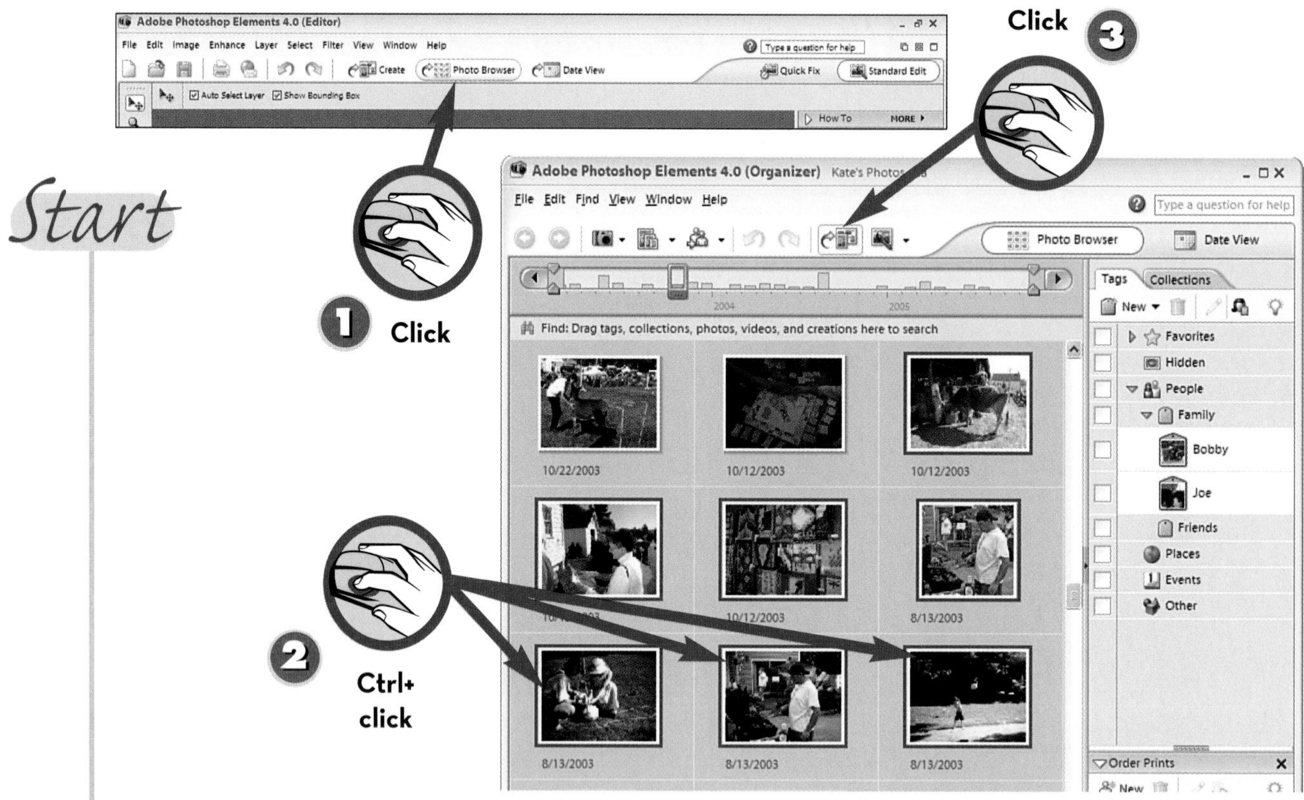

1. Click **Photo Browser** to switch to Organizer mode.
2. **Ctrl-click** to select the photos you want to include in your Web gallery.
3. Click **Create**.

Continued

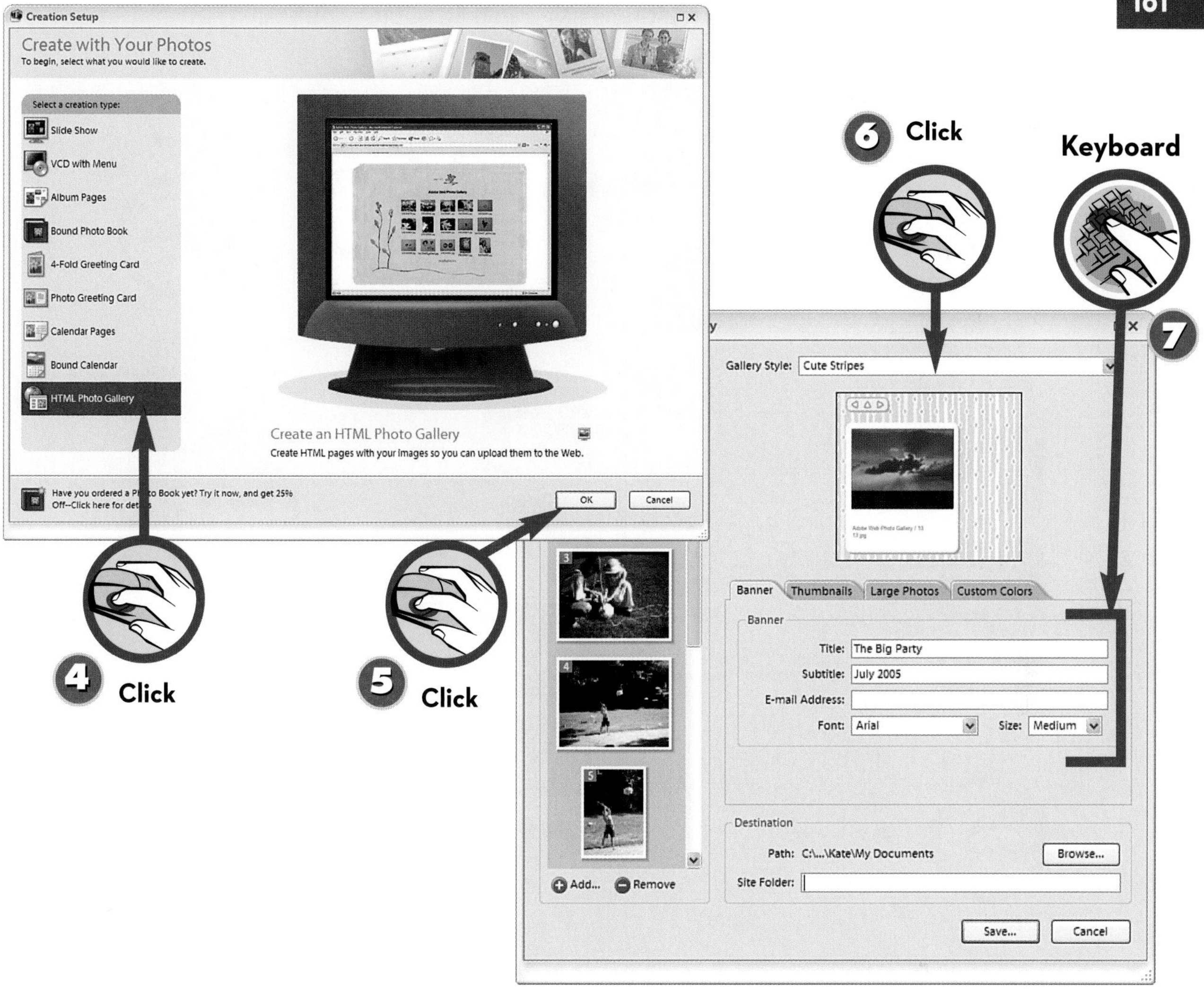

4 Click **HTML Photo Gallery**.

5 Click **OK**.

6 Choose an option from the **Gallery Style** pop-up menu, such as **Cute Stripes**.

7 Enter a title for the gallery and (if you like) your email address to receive comments from viewers.

Continued

TIP

Want Mail?

Entering an email address in step 3 isn't mandatory, so just leave it blank if you don't want site visitors to contact you. If the E-mail text box is grayed, the style you selected can't display an address.

Follow instructions of your Web hosting service for uploading—publishing—your files. The usual method is via the File Transfer Protocol (FTP). A handy and inexpensive program for doing this is GlobalSCAPE CuteFTP.

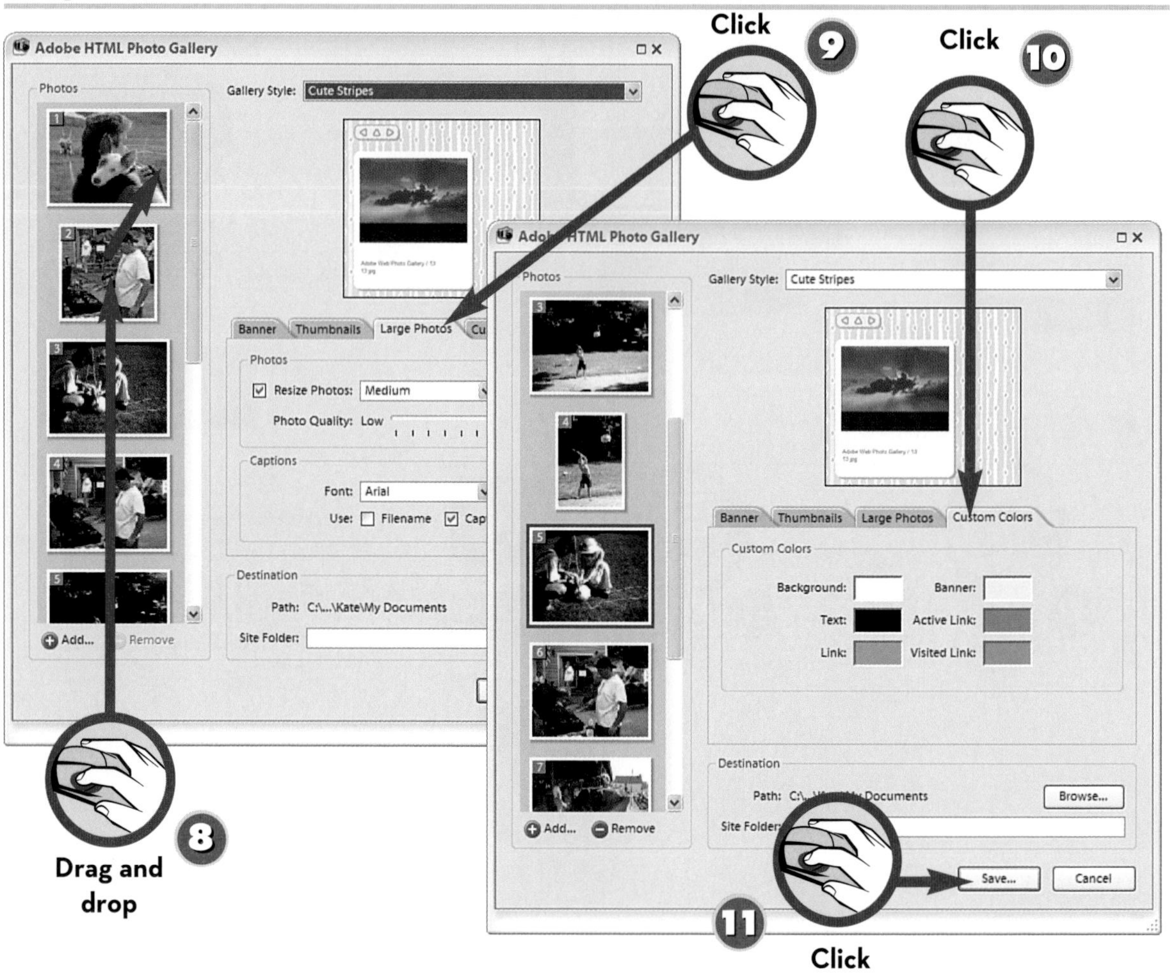

8 Drag and drop the pictures in the **Photos** area to change their order.

9 Click the **Thumbnails** or **Large Photos** tab and choose size, quality, and caption options.

10 Click the **Custom Colors** tab and click the color swatches to change the gallery's background and link colors.

11 Click **Save**.

Continued

TIP

What Is That Again?

To include captions, choose either **Filename** or **Caption** in the Captions area of the Thumb-nails tab; then choose a font and size. To store the caption, see "Adding and Printing Photo Captions" on **p. 78.**

TIP

Where's That Picture?

If you realize in the midst of setting options for your Web gallery that you've left out your favorite photo, click **Add** in the **Photos** section to return to the Organizer and select it.

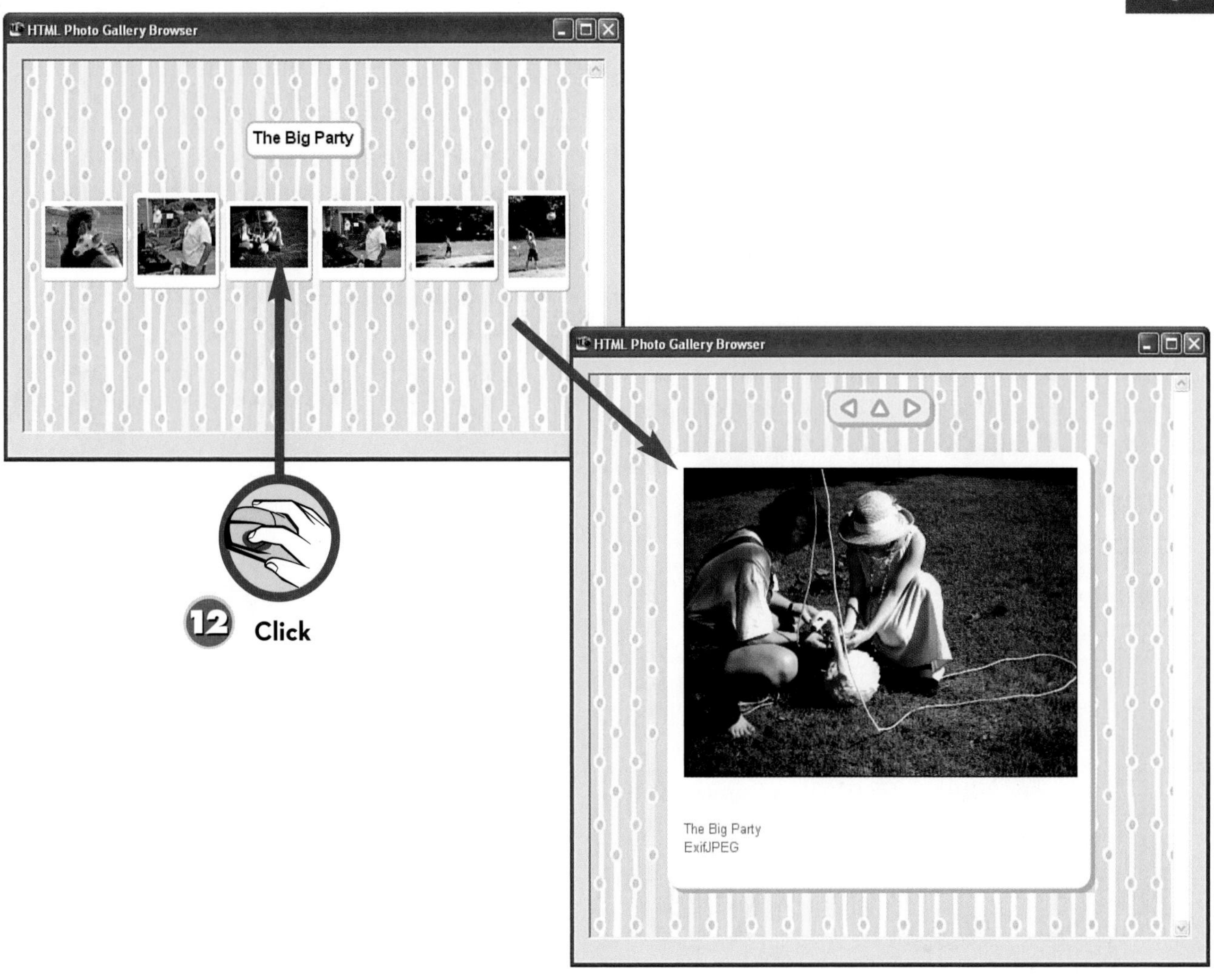

12 Click a thumbnail image to see the large version.

End

TIP

Oops!

If you don't enter a folder name in the Destination area before clicking **Save** in step 11, Elements reminds you politely to do so. This name is assigned to the folder that Elements creates to hold all the HTML and image files that make up the gallery. To upload the finished gallery to your Web site, just upload the entire folder with all its contents.

CREATING A SLIDE SHOW

What better way to get a good look at your photos—and share them with your friends—than to sit back and let them display themselves one at a time? But this slide show is not your granddad's musty slide carousel and projector with the burnt-out bulb. It's a PDF or a movie file that you can use in many ways.

1. **Ctrl-click** to select the photos you want to include in your slide show.
2. Click **Create**.
3. Click **Slide Show**.
4. Click **OK**.

Continued

TIP

Everything in Order

Elements places photos in your show in the order that they occupy in the Photo Browser. To change their order, drag and drop them in the preview area at the bottom of the **Slide Show Editor** window.

NOTE

Party Favor

Slide shows are fun to play at big events, such as anniversary or milestone birthday parties. Collect photos of the people being honored, choose one of their favorite songs, and go to town! The guests will love it.

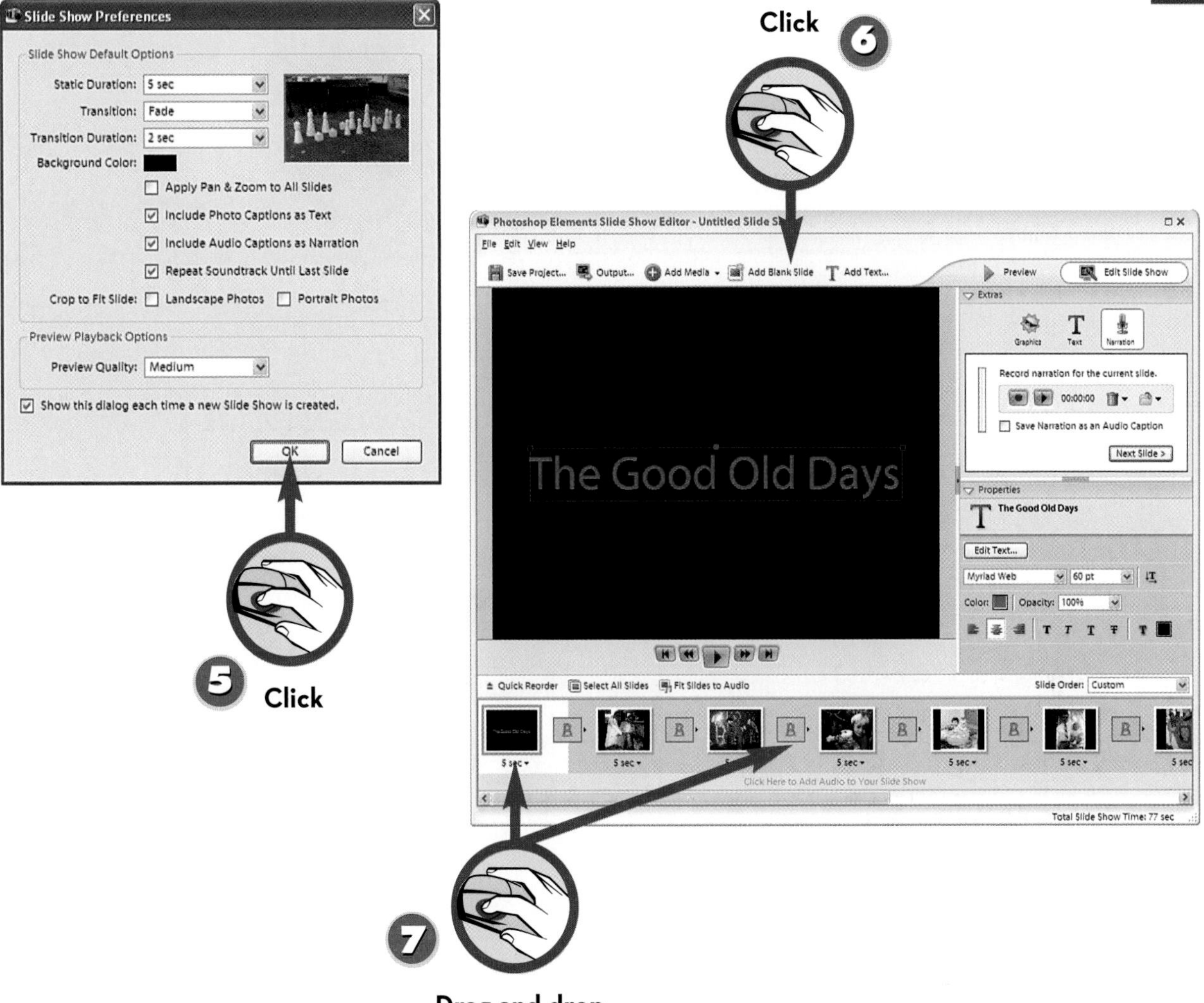

5 Set your slide show preferences and click **OK**.

6 Click **Add Blank Slide** to insert a blank slide for your title.

7 Drag and drop slides at the bottom of the window to change their order.

Continued

TIP

Talking About Photos

If your PC has a microphone, you can record a voiceover track for each slide. Click **Narration** at the top of the **Extras** palette, then click the **Record** button to add narration. Click **Stop** when you're done, and click **Play** to play back the recording.

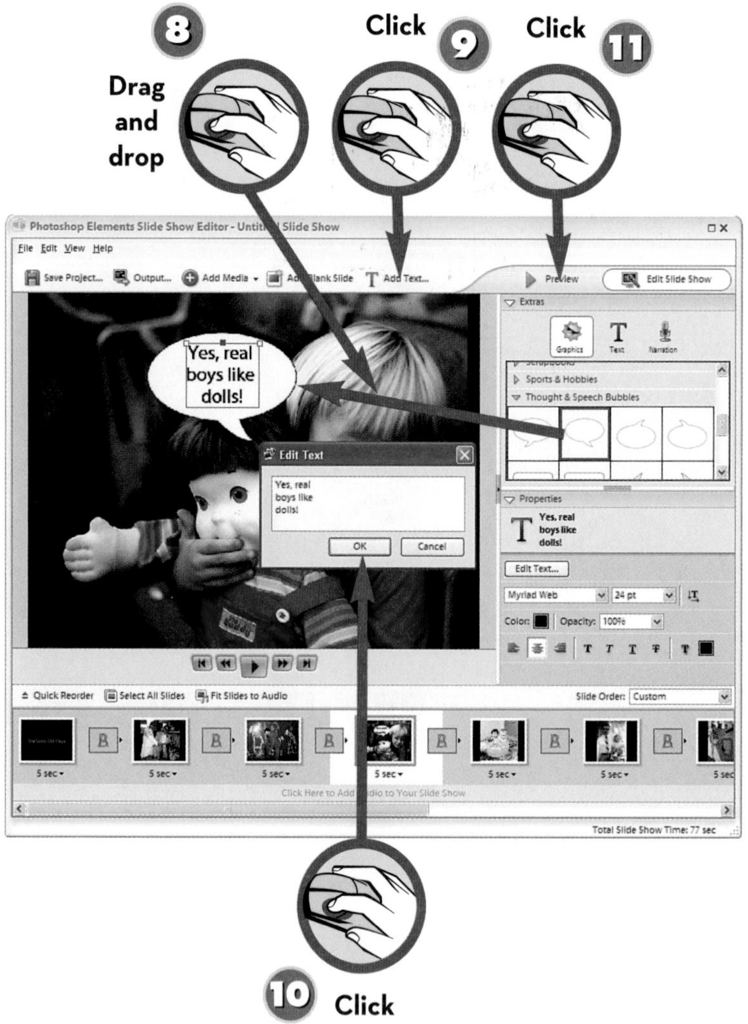

8 Drag and drop graphics from the **Extras** palette onto the slides.

9 Click **Add Text** to insert text on a slide.

10 Enter your text and click **OK**.

11 Click **Preview** to see what the slide show will look like.

Continued

TIP
Taking a Break

If you need to stop working on your slide show before it's finished, click **Save Project** at the top of the **Slide Show Editor** window to create a project file that you can re-open when you have time to complete the show.

TIP
PDF or WMV?

A PDF file can be opened in the free Adobe Reader on any computer, but it can't contain special effects such as Pan and Zoom. To use all the animation bells and whistles, save your slide show as a WMV file.

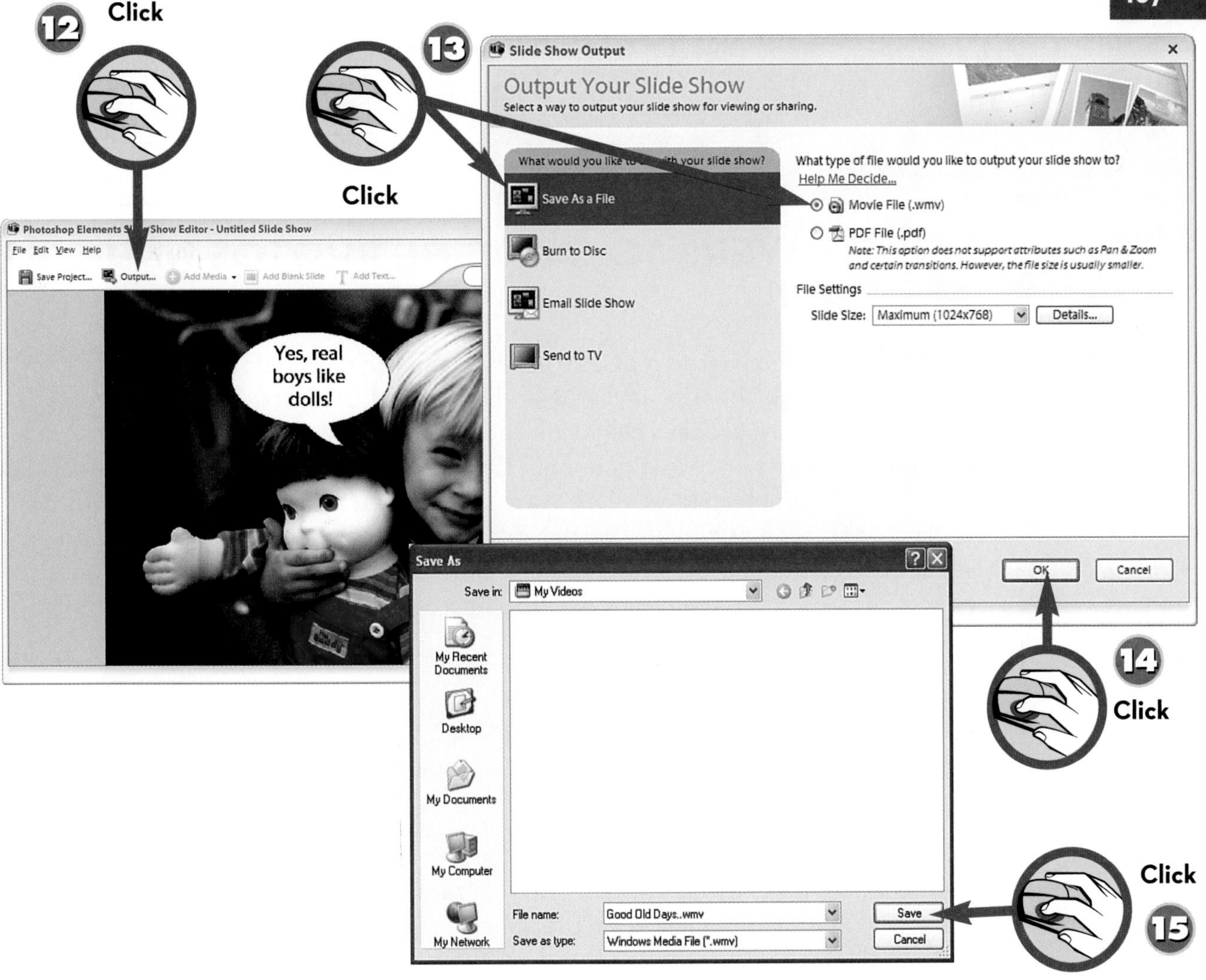

12 Click **Output**.

13 Click **Save as a File** and choose a file type option.

14 Click **OK**.

15 Give the slide show a name and click **Save**.

End

TIP

The Music of the Slides

To add a musical soundtrack, click **Add Media** at the top of the Slide Show Editor window and choose **Audio from Folder**. Choose a music file and click OK. Then, to make the slide show the same length as the song, click **Fit Slides to Audio**.

part 10

USING LAYERS TO COMBINE PHOTOS AND ARTWORK

If you know how animated movies were made in the days before computer generation, you're already familiar with the concept of layers. Animation artists traditionally used a process called ink-and-paint to draw cartoon characters on transparent sheets of celluloid, or cels. One new cel had to be created for each time a character moved. Cels were then placed over elaborate painted backgrounds, such as witches' castles or the decks of pirate ships. Painting on separate layers—the animated character on the cel and the background beneath—made it possible to reuse the same background throughout a long scene.

Layers in Photoshop Elements work much the same way. The image you begin with is the Background layer. Every layer you add starts out as transparent until you change its color, change its adjustment properties, or add objects to it.

If you've done any of the tasks in other parts involving shapes or text, you were working with layers, whether you realized it or not. Understand, building more complex layered images isn't for beginners. But you should learn some of this if you want to graduate to more ambitious tasks.

The postcard on the facing page is actually built from 10 layers, including the background. Photoshop Elements permits you as many as 8,000 layers—provided you don't run out of computer memory first!

A TEN-LAYERED IMAGE

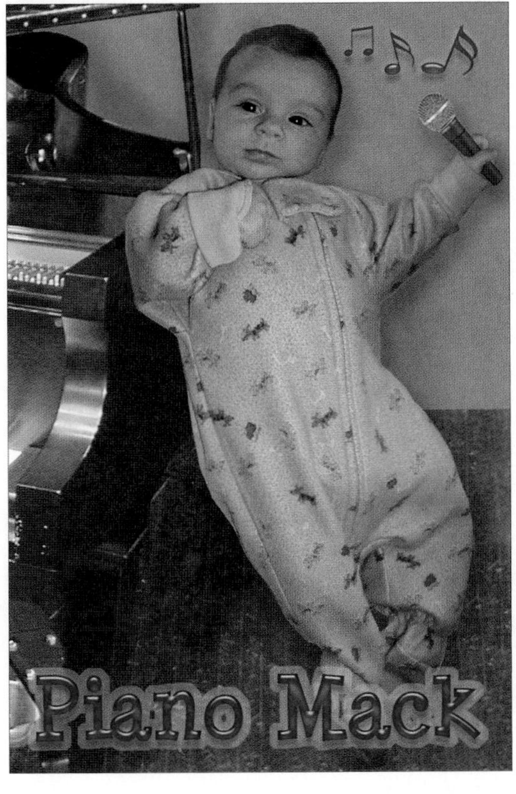

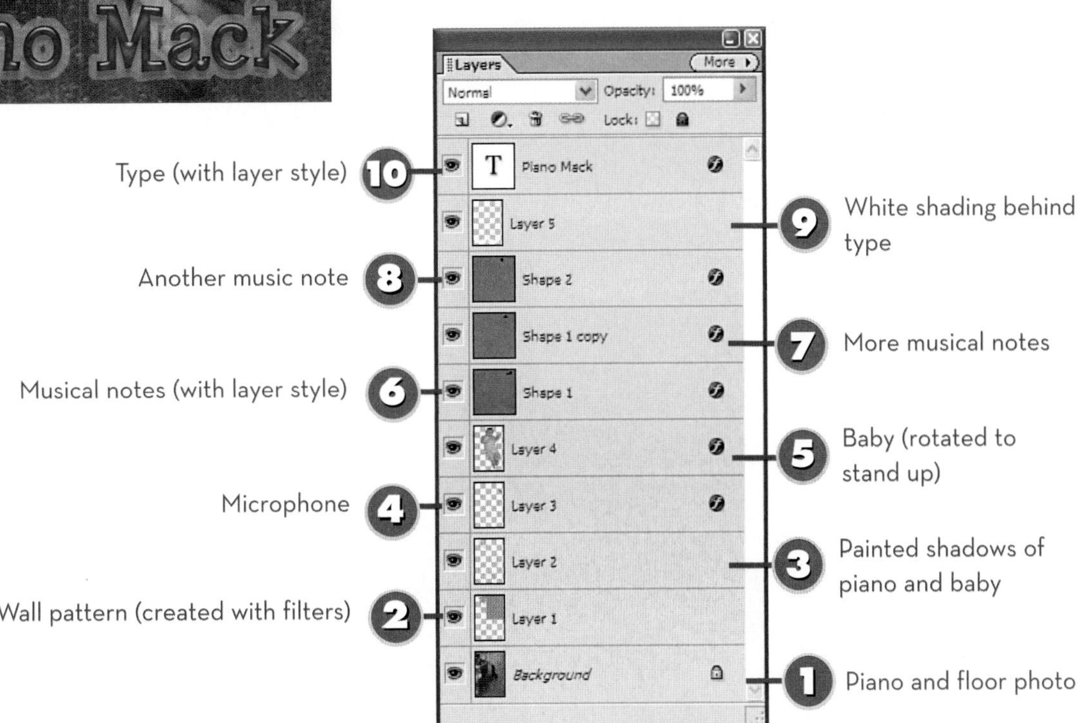

PAINTING ON A NEW LAYER

You should create a new layer for painting, drawing, or adding new shapes to your photo. However, a new layer is created automatically whenever you use the Shape or Type tools—also, whenever you paste (choose **Edit**, **Paste**) or choose certain other commands on the Layers menu.

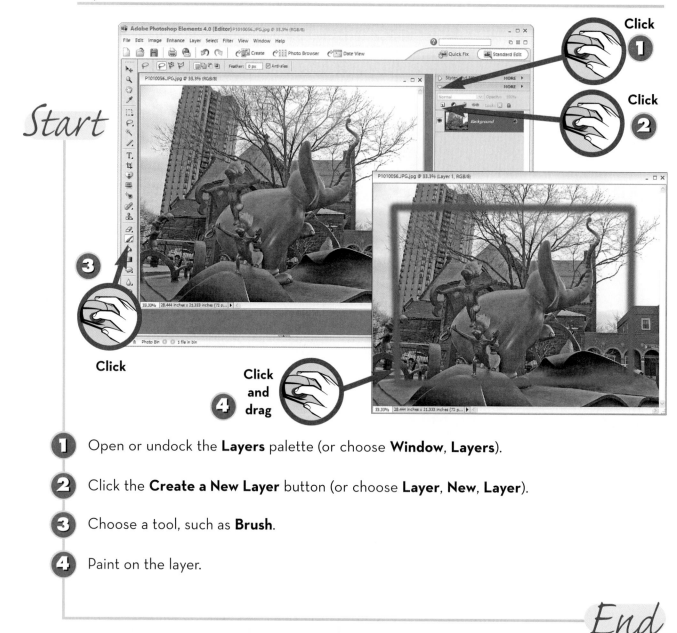

1. Open or undock the **Layers** palette (or choose **Window**, **Layers**).
2. Click the **Create a New Layer** button (or choose **Layer**, **New**, **Layer**).
3. Choose a tool, such as **Brush**.
4. Paint on the layer.

End

TIP

Simplify and Merge

Simplifying changes vector shapes and text (based on geometry) to pixels—editable as dots, not as shapes. Merging both simplifies the active (selected) layer and combines it with the layer beneath.

You can't manipulate text and shapes as objects after merging. If you see a warning that the layer must be simplified before proceeding with a tool, choose **Cancel** and create a new layer using these steps; then switch back to the tool and paint or draw.

COPYING AN OBJECT TO A NEW LAYER

Selecting an object on the background layer, making changes, and then saving your work, changes the original image forever. Instead, use these steps to copy a selected object to a new layer, leaving the background layer unchanged.

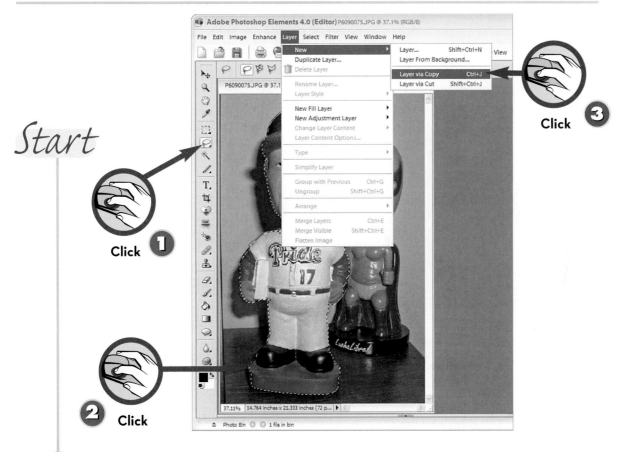

1. Click a selection tool, such as **Lasso**.
2. Select the object to be copied to a new layer.
3. Choose **Layer**, **New**, **Layer via Copy**.

TIP

Cutting a Selection

The command **Layer**, **New**, **Layer via Cut** works just the same way, but it also deletes the selection from the original layer. Especially if the original layer is the Background, use **Layer via Copy** instead.

TIP

Deleting or Hiding

As long as the original layer is intact, you can always hide or delete the copied layer (**Layer**, **Delete Layer**) to cancel all its changes with a click.

REPOSITIONING A LAYER

When you moved text and shapes in previous tasks, you might not have realized you were actually repositioning an entire layer, including not only the selection but also the transparent pixels surrounding it. In this image, the text and the baseball stadium are on separate layers, and the task moves the entire layer lower in the image.

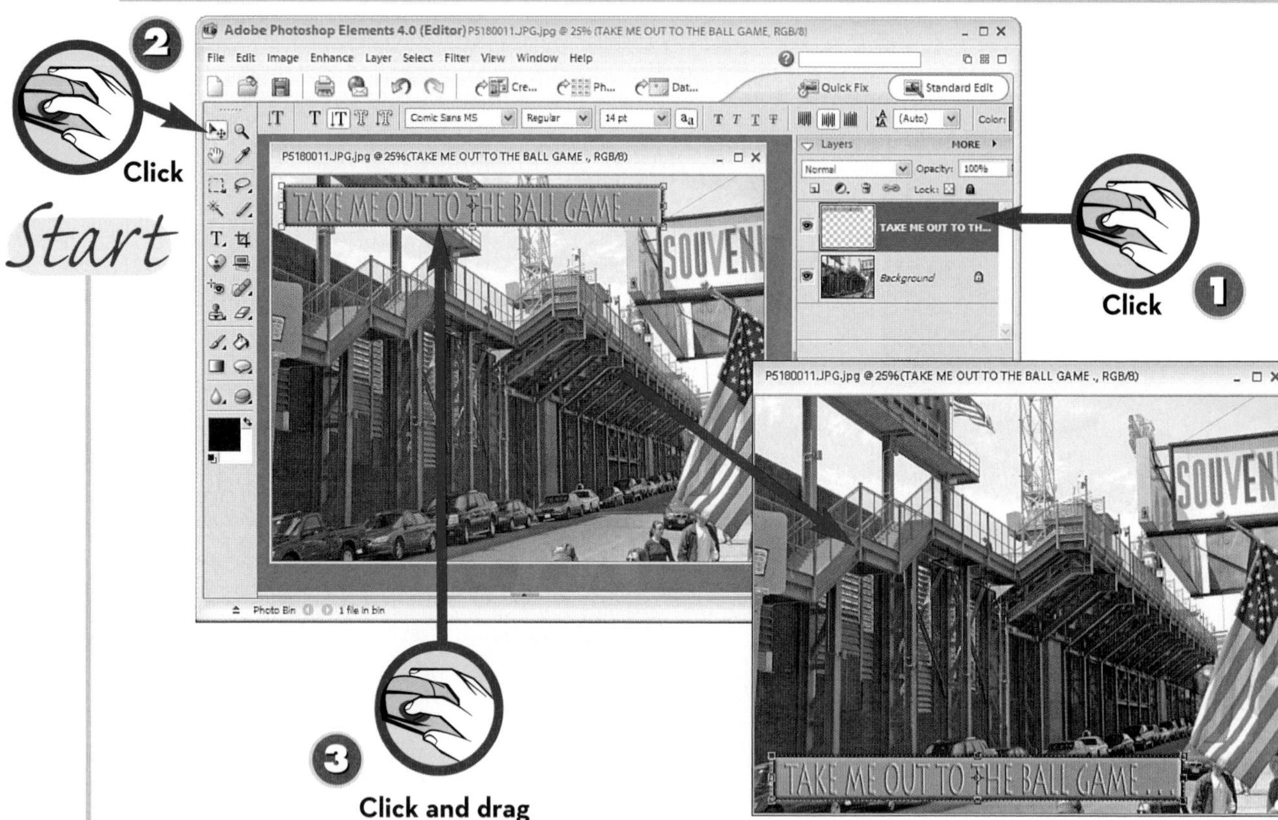

1. Click the name of the layer in the **Layers palette**.
2. Switch to the **Move** tool.
3. Click and drag the layer to reposition it in relation to the image area (or nudge it with the arrow keys, or **Shift-click** to constrain it as you drag).

End

TIP

Auto Select Layer

If Auto Select Layer is checked in the Move tool's Options bar, the layer selection (the active layer) changes automatically when you click an object that resides on it. Remember that doing so actually moves the entire layer, not just the object.

TIP

More Button

Clicking **More** in the top-right corner of the Layers palette brings up a menu of commands that affect layers (handy alternative to the Layers menu).

CONTROLLING LAYERS

The icons and buttons in the Layers palette control various layer behaviors such as locking a layer (preventing changes), creating and deleting a layer, hiding/unhiding a layer, new fill/adjustment layers, and linking layers.

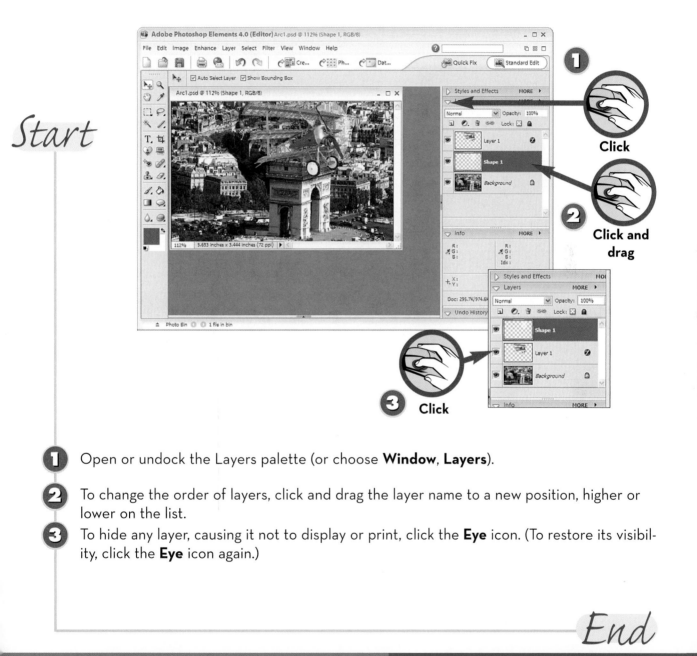

Start

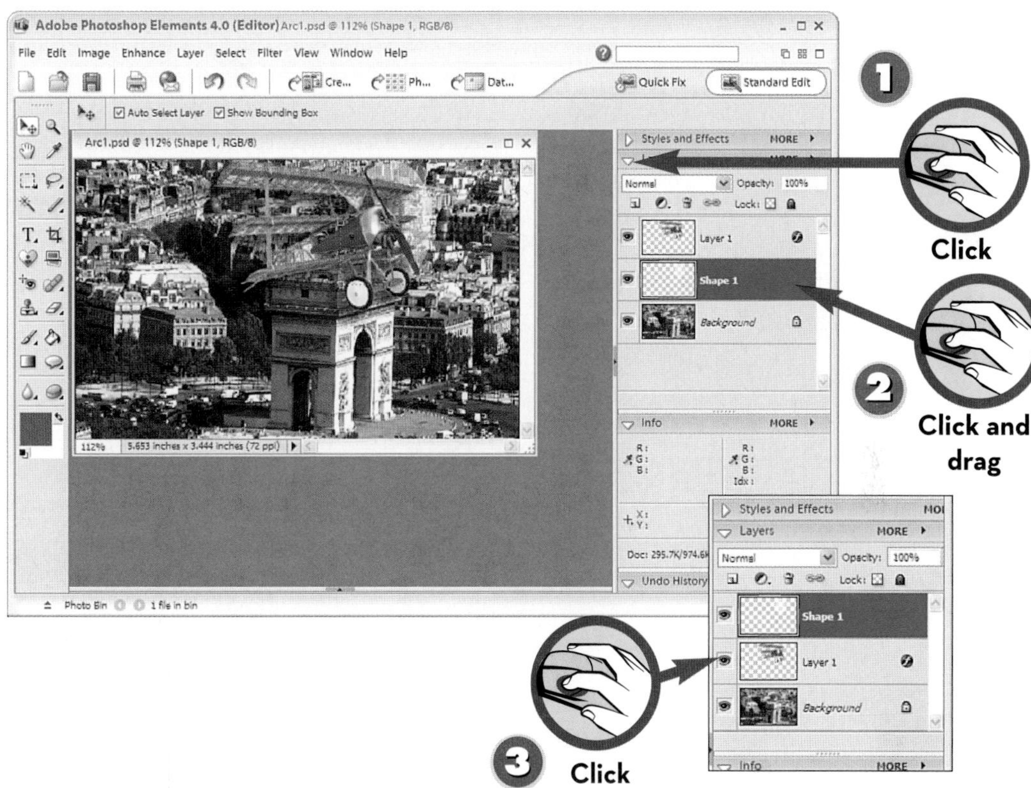

1. Open or undock the Layers palette (or choose **Window**, **Layers**).
2. To change the order of layers, click and drag the layer name to a new position, higher or lower on the list.
3. To hide any layer, causing it not to display or print, click the **Eye** icon. (To restore its visibility, click the **Eye** icon again.)

End

TIP

Linking Layers

Link any layer to the active one by Ctrl-clicking to select the second layer and clicking the **Link** button at the top of the Layers palette. A Link icon appears next to the layer's name. Some commands and tools, affect all linked layers at once.

TIP

Grouping Layers

The purpose of grouping layers is to control visibility of their objects according to a base layer. To group a layer with the one below, choose **Layer**, **Group with Previous**.

CREATING A FILL LAYER AND ADJUSTING LAYER OPACITY

One way to change how layers look is to adjust the *opacity* of a fill layer above them. Think of a *semitransparent* fill layer (less than 100 percent opacity) as a colored photographic filter—tinting and dimming the layers beneath it. (The more opaque, the less transparent, and vice versa.)

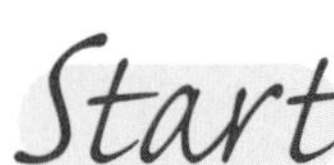

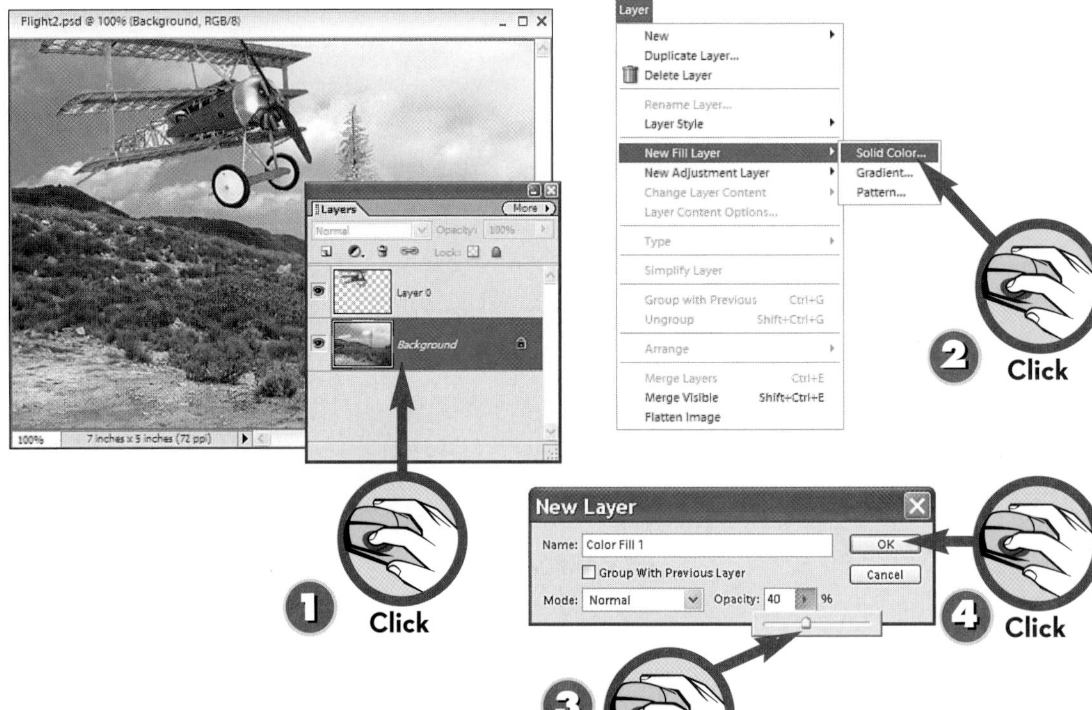

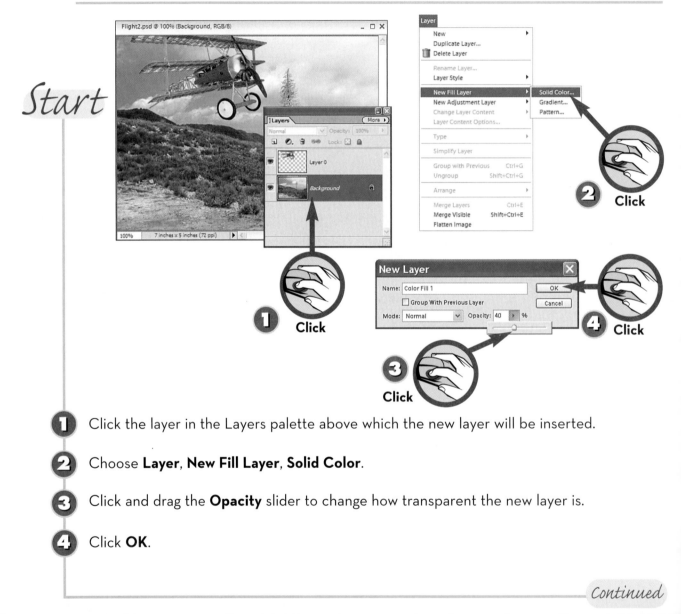

1. Click the layer in the Layers palette above which the new layer will be inserted.
2. Choose **Layer**, **New Fill Layer**, **Solid Color**.
3. Click and drag the **Opacity** slider to change how transparent the new layer is.
4. Click **OK**.

Continued

NOTE

To Bin or Not to Bin
Drag a palette out of the Palette Bin if you want to move it around on the screen. That way you can put it right next to the area of the image you're working on, or you can close the Palette Bin to enlarge your work area.

NOTE

Well Adjusted
Continuing to add other adjustment and fill layers, each with its own properties, will have a combined effect. Remember that an adjustment layer only affects the appearance of the layers *beneath* it.

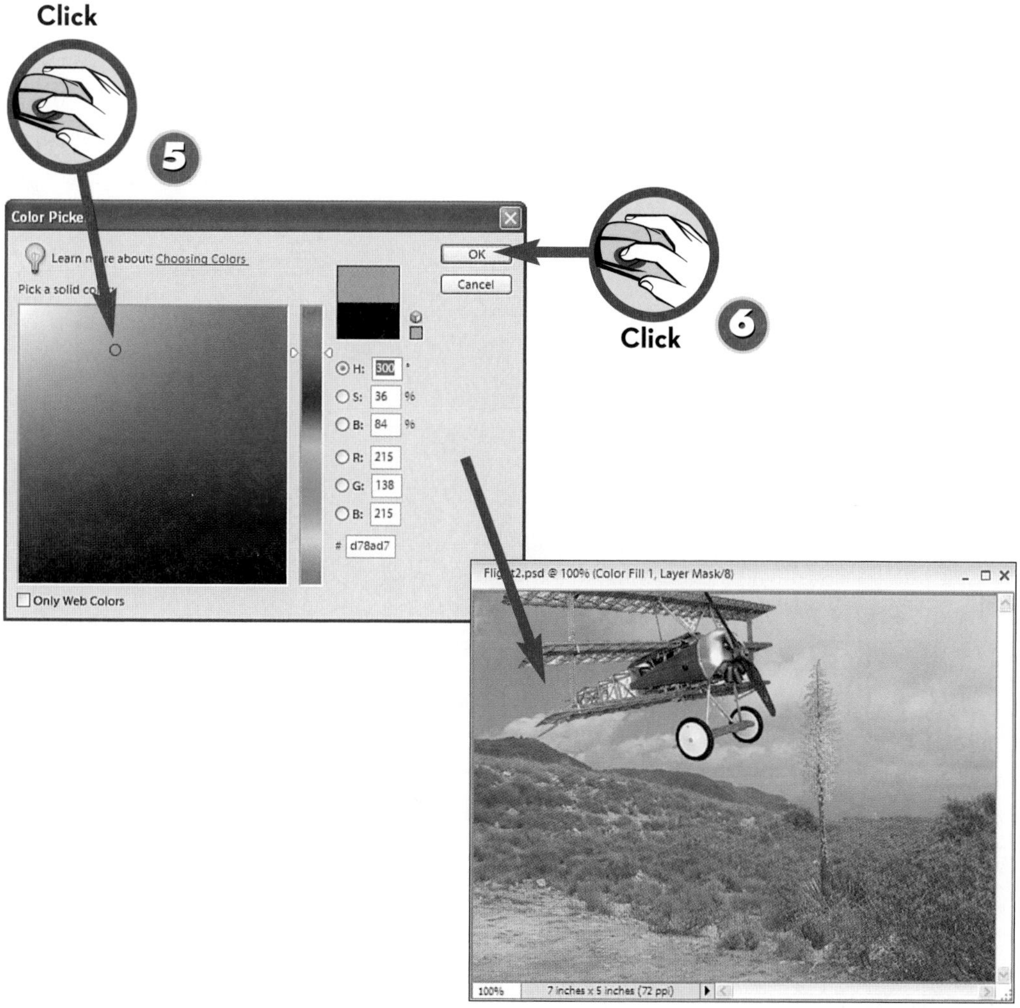

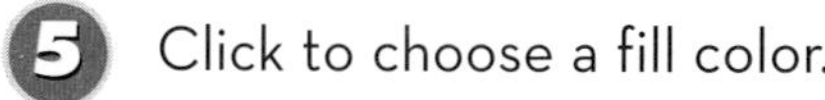

5 Click to choose a fill color.

6 Click **OK**.

End

TIP

Special Effects

By using either the Gradient or Pattern submenu commands instead of Solid Color, you can create variegated effects: Gradient could cause the filtration effect to fade across the background; Pattern could give it a texture, like a dust storm.

TIP

Gradient and Pattern Fills

Besides Solid Color, other submenu selections available in step 2 are Gradient and Pattern, which have the same options as the Gradient tool and the Pattern settings of the Paint Bucket tool.

FLIPPING OR ROTATING A LAYER

The purpose of flipping or rotating a layer can be either to change the position of the objects on the layer or to vary the effect of a gradient or pattern layer. The Image, Rotate command has a submenu section for such operations performed on entire layers.

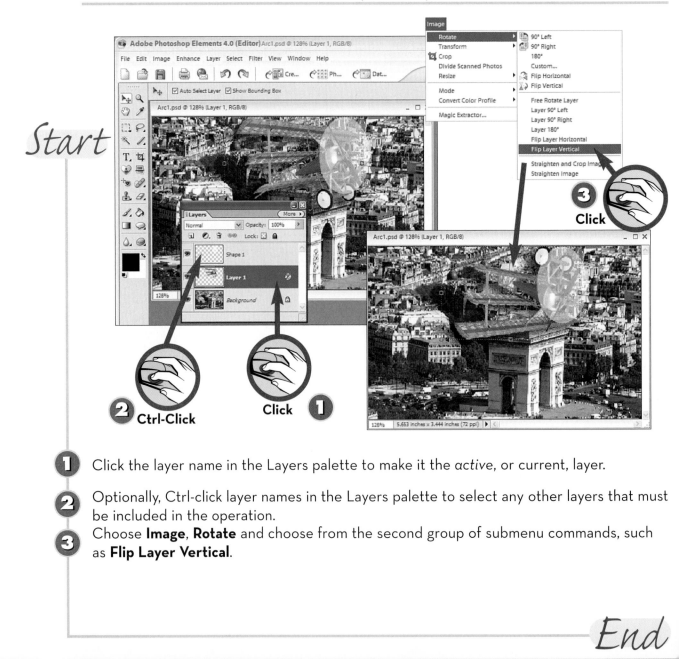

Start

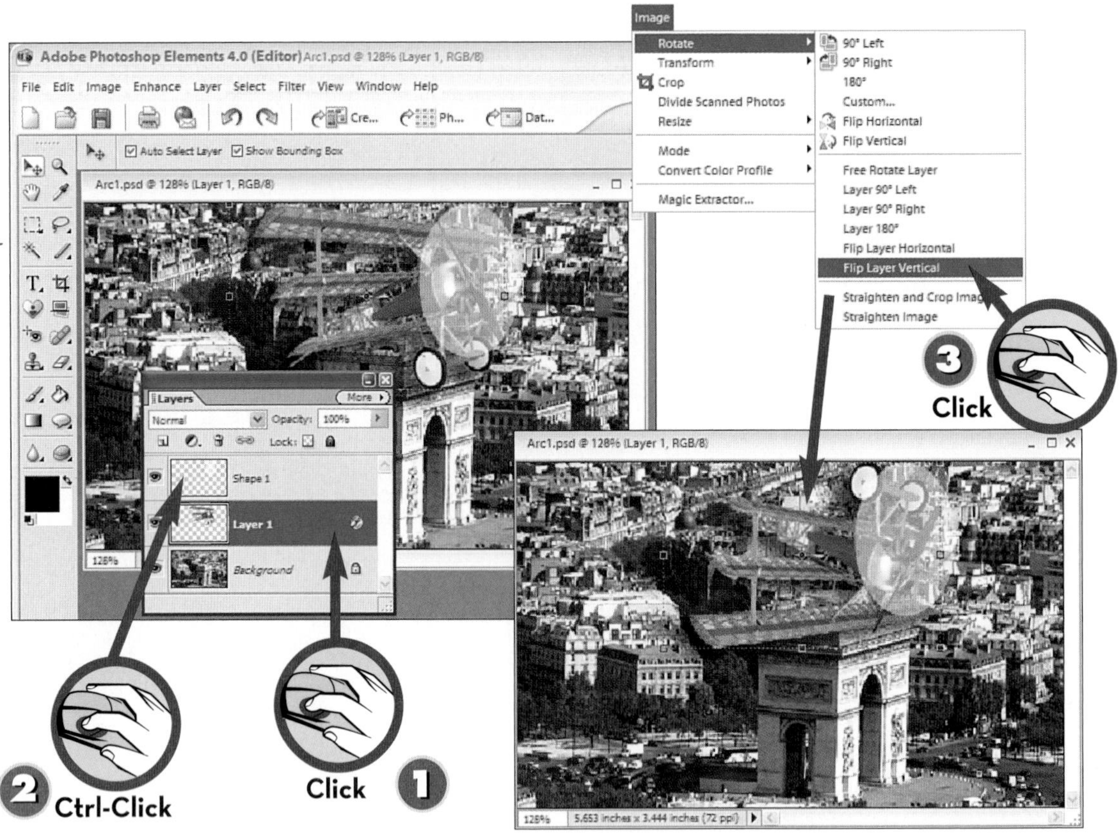

2 Ctrl-Click

Click 1

3 Click

1. Click the layer name in the Layers palette to make it the *active*, or current, layer.
2. Optionally, Ctrl-click layer names in the Layers palette to select any other layers that must be included in the operation.
3. Choose **Image**, **Rotate** and choose from the second group of submenu commands, such as **Flip Layer Vertical**.

End

TIP

Selections or Layers?

When part of the image within a layer—such as a shape or text—is selected, the second group of commands in the Image, Rotate submenu switch from Layer to Selection. They have the same effect but only on the selected area.

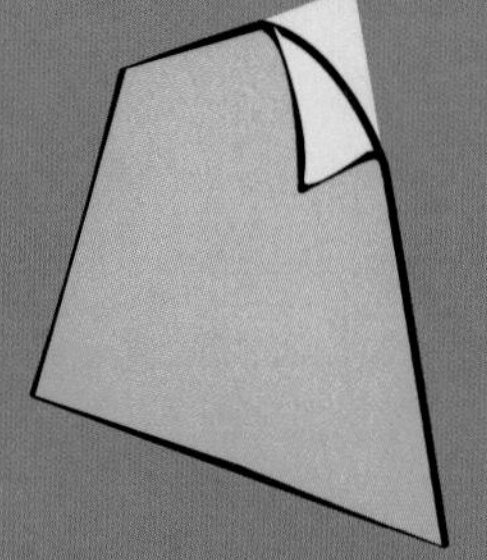

USING AN ADJUSTMENT LAYER

An adjustment layer has no color of its own but lets you control color, brightness/contrast, and other factors on layers beneath without making changes directly to them. The adjustment layer has no effect on layers above it.

Start

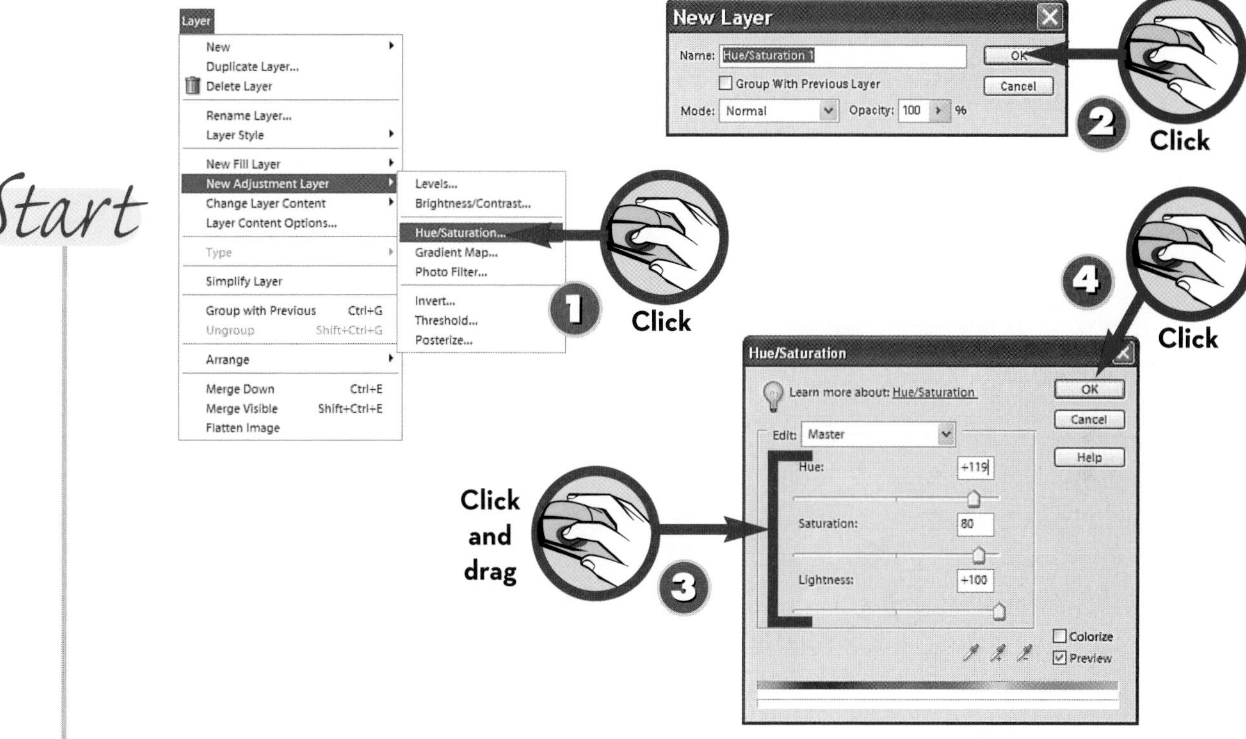

1 Having selected the layer you want to control, choose **Layer**, **New Adjustment Layer** and choose from the submenu commands, such as **Hue/Saturation**.

2 Click **OK**.

3 Make adjustments using the options in the dialog box and see the effect on your image in the background.

4 When you are satisfied with the effect, click **OK**.

End

NOTE

Blending Mode

As described in the next task, the effect of any fill or adjustment layer can also be controlled by choosing a blending mode from the Mode menu in the Layers palette (or Mode menu in the New Layer dialog box).

TIP

Select a Layer First

The new adjustment layer will be inserted just above the layer that's active when you begin step 1. So if you want to adjust the background image, select that layer first and then do these steps.

USING BLENDING MODES ON LAYERS

Blending mode controls how pixel values within a layer are blended with those of the layers beneath. The default is Normal. Other modes include Dissolve, several Dodge or Burn effects, quality of light (such as Soft or Hard), adding (Exclusion) or subtracting (Difference) pixel values, or individual elements of color.

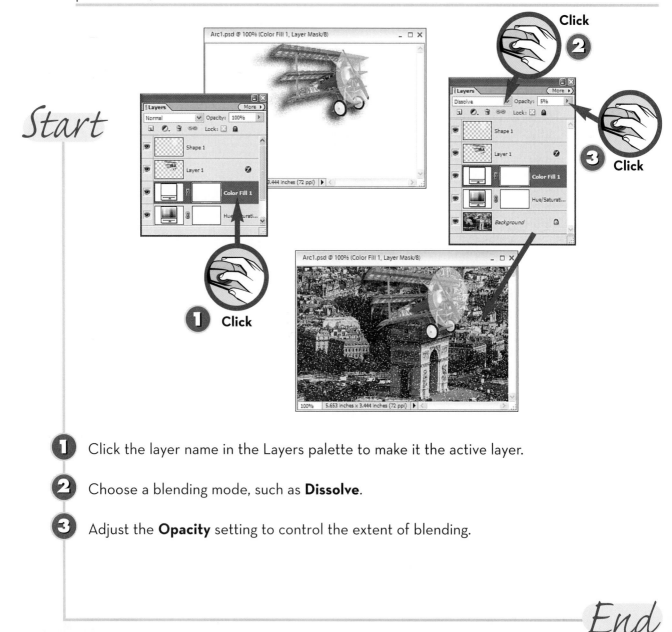

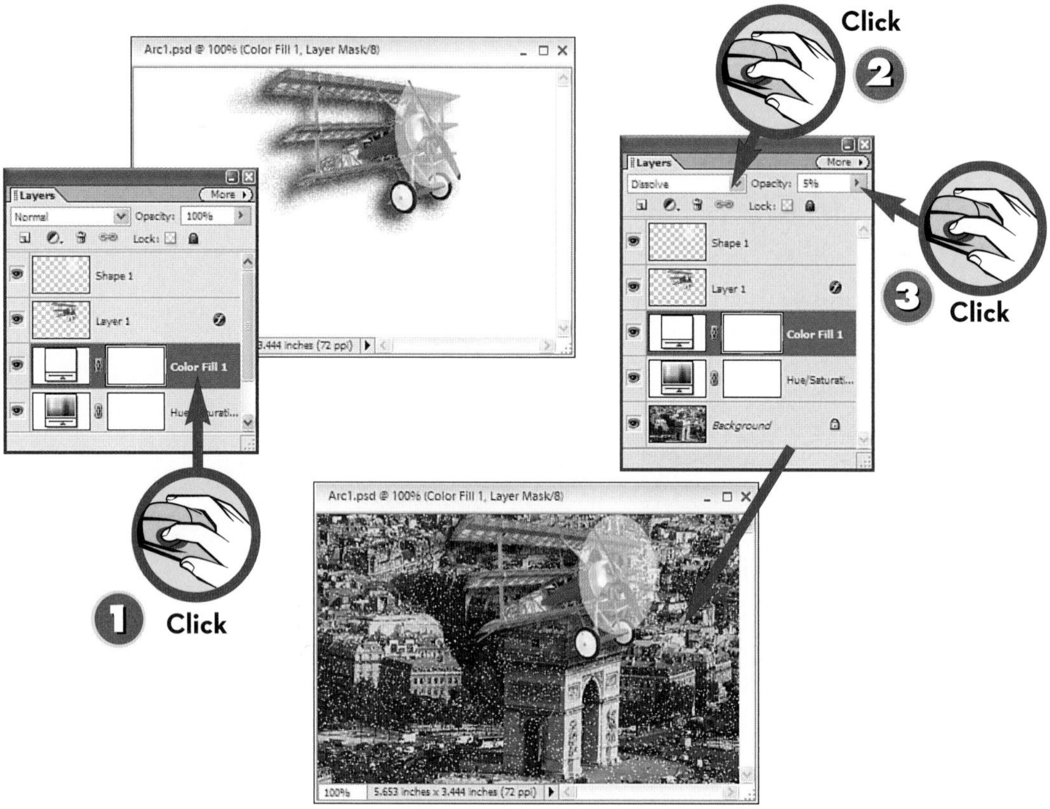

Start

1. Click the layer name in the Layers palette to make it the active layer.
2. Choose a blending mode, such as **Dissolve**.
3. Adjust the **Opacity** setting to control the extent of blending.

End

TIP

Try 'Em On

After making a choice from the blending mode list in step 2, press the **Up** or **Down** arrow keys to step through the other modes and preview their effects on the image.

TIP

Controlling Blending Mode

To turn off a blending mode, change the setting back to **Normal** for that layer in the pop-up menu in the top-left corner of the Layers palette.

COPYING AND PASTING A LAYER STYLE

Copying layer styles is particularly convenient when you've made several style changes on one layer and want to apply them with a click to all objects on another layer—also if you've taken pains to fine-tune a style, such as adjusted the angle of a drop-shadow.

Start

1. Click the name in the Layers palette of a layer that contains a layer style, such as **Drop Shadow**.
2. Choose **Layer, Layer Style**, **Copy Layer Style**.
3. Click the name of a layer to which the style will be applied.
4. Choose **Layer**, **Layer Style**, **Paste Layer Style**.

End

TIP

Fine-Tuning Styles

To fine-tune a layer style on the active layer, such as Bevel or Drop Shadow, choose **Layer, Layer Style, Style Settings**. Make adjustments by clicking and dragging the sliders, and then click **OK**.

PREPARING TO PUBLISH

With Photoshop Elements, a digital camera, a computer, and an inexpensive color inkjet printer, you can be your own one-stop shop for most of your photography needs. But there's a whole wide world out there—including a giant color printing industry—ready to serve you.

Need custom-printed tee shirts? Color posters? Banners? A thousand color postcards? These days, most commercial printers accept—and actually prefer—your Photoshop image files as source artwork for these kinds of printing jobs. You can even submit your orders online at sites such as **www.vistaprint.com**, **www.inkchaser.com**, and **www.kinkos.com**.

Admittedly, preparing files for commercial printing is a major reason why some serious graphic artists consider upgrading to "big Photoshop" (Adobe Photoshop CS 2). Specifically, that application has extensive *color management* capabilities that Photoshop Elements lacks.

But there's still a lot you can do in Photoshop Elements to improve the quality of the results when you decide to "send it out"—whether you're publishing on paper or via electronic media.

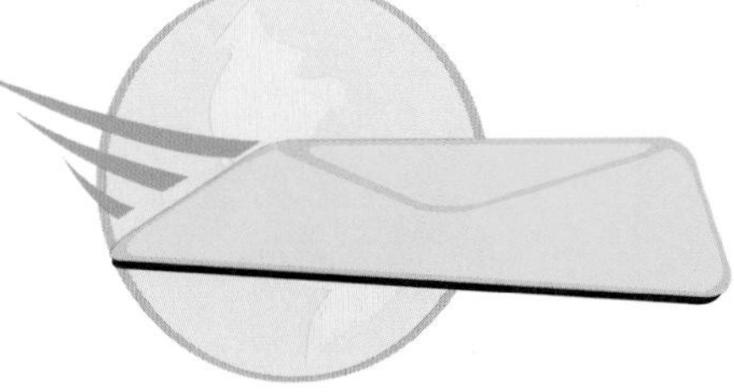

HOW DO I GET FROM HERE TO THERE?

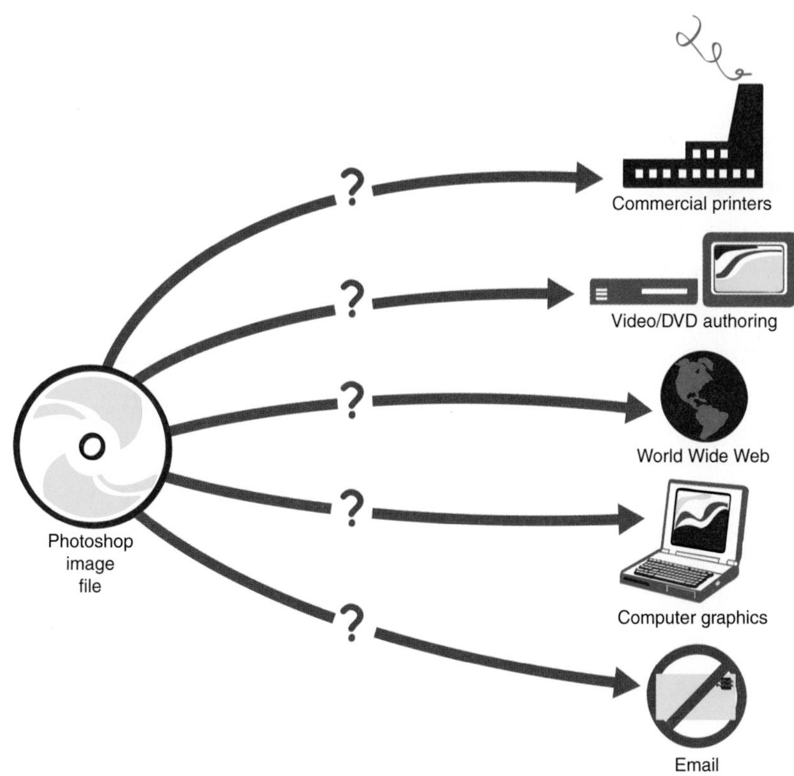

FIXING MULTIPLE IMAGES

Have a bunch of pictures that need fixing? You can have Photoshop Elements do the work while you refill your coffee cup. Enjoy a break while Elements adjusts the lighting, color, and sharpness of your images; resizes them; renames them; and saves them in your preferred format.

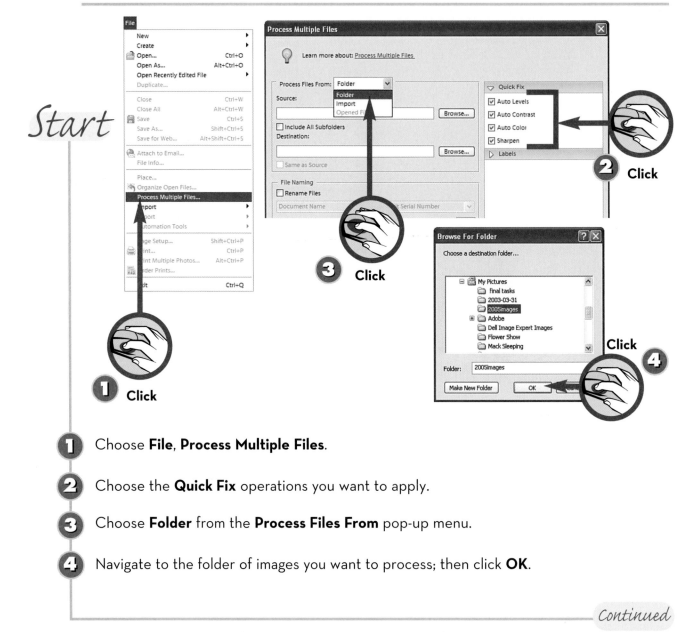

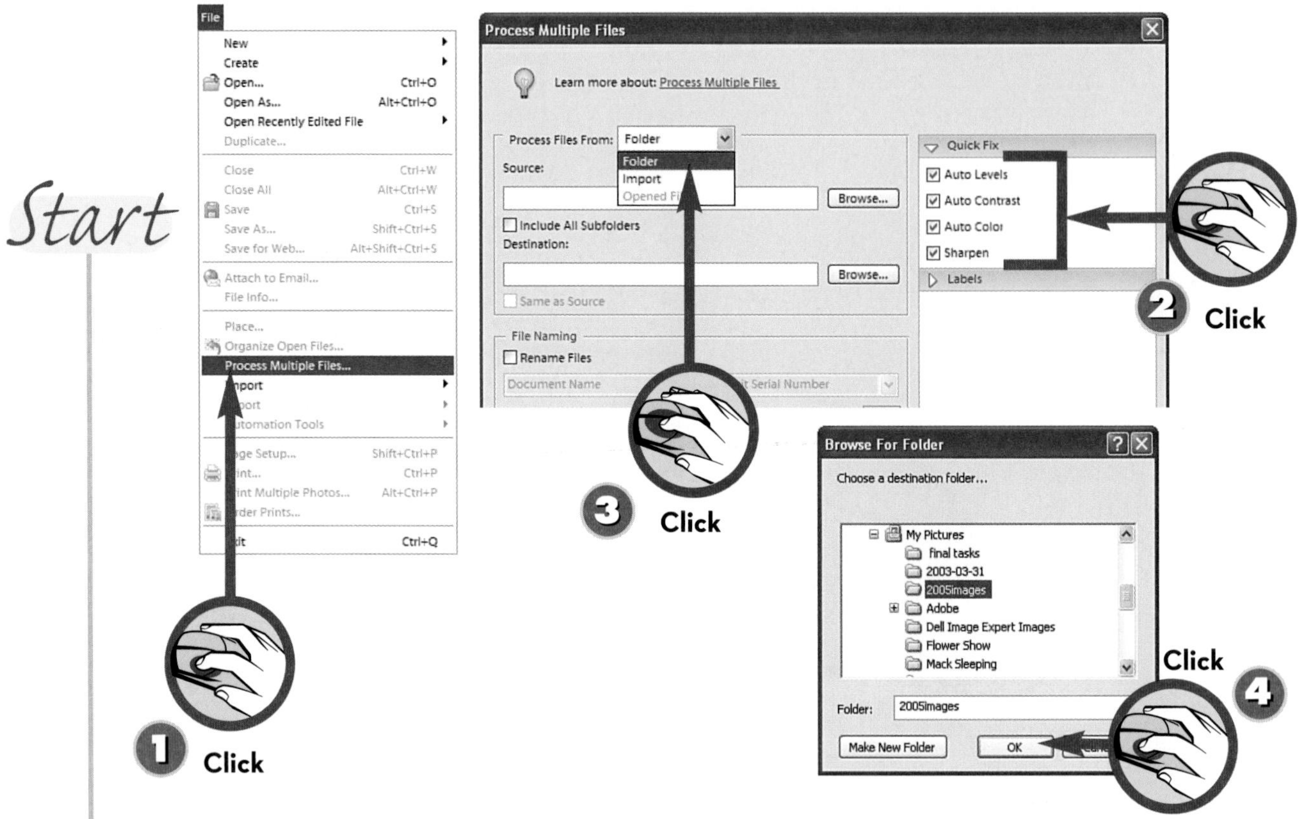

1. Choose **File**, **Process Multiple Files**.
2. Choose the **Quick Fix** operations you want to apply.
3. Choose **Folder** from the **Process Files From** pop-up menu.
4. Navigate to the folder of images you want to process; then click **OK**.

Continued

TIP

Get Organized First

Be sure to put all the image files you want to process in a single folder, so Elements will be able to find them.

TIP

You Have a Choice

After step 4, you get to choose a place for the revised files to be saved. Either click **Browse** to pick a destination folder, or check **Save As Source**.

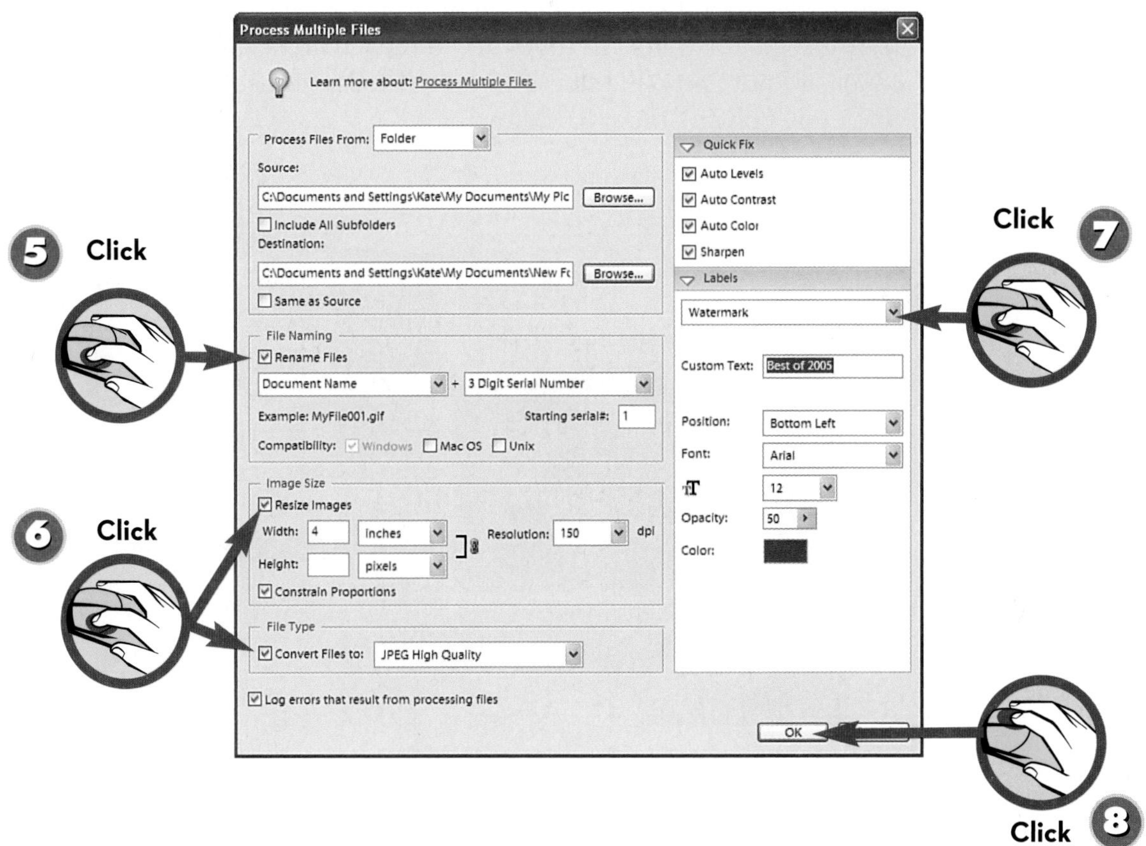

5 Choose **Rename Files** to automatically give the files consistent names.

6 Choose **Resize Images** and **Convert Files to** resize the images and save them in a different format.

7 Choose **Watermark** to add overlaid labels to the images.

8 Click **OK** to begin processing.

End

NOTE

What's a Watermark?

A *watermark* is a semitransparent design or line of text overlaid on an image to identify it. It's a great way to ensure everyone knows your pictures are yours without obscuring their details.

CAUTION

Be Careful

Don't choose **Same as Source** under **Destination** unless you don't want to keep your original files. With this option turned on, Elements overwrites the originals with the revised versions.

PREPARING A STILL IMAGE FOR VIDEO

A curious problem arises from the fact that computer images have square pixels, but in digital video they're rectangular. You might think this an odd technicality, but if you make video titles or DVD menus in Photoshop Elements and don't follow these steps, the images will look squished when you convert them to video.

Start

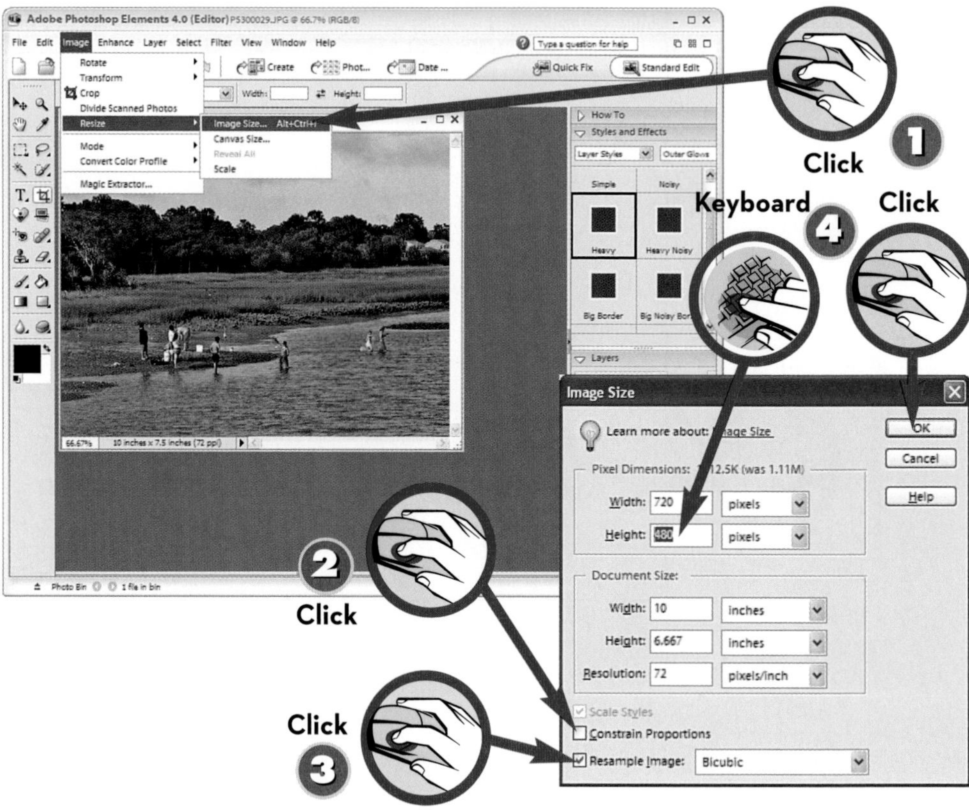

1. Start with an image that's 720×540 pixels open in the active image area. Choose **Image**, **Resize**, **Image Size**.
2. Uncheck **Constrain Proportions**.
3. Check **Resample Image**.
4. Keeping the Width at 720, change **Height** to **480** pixels and click **OK**.

Continued

TIP

What's Your System?

Digital video (DV) editing is coming to a PC near you. Windows Movie Maker, Apple iMovie, and Pinnacle Studio are examples of the many applications available for assembling your home movie footage in creative ways.

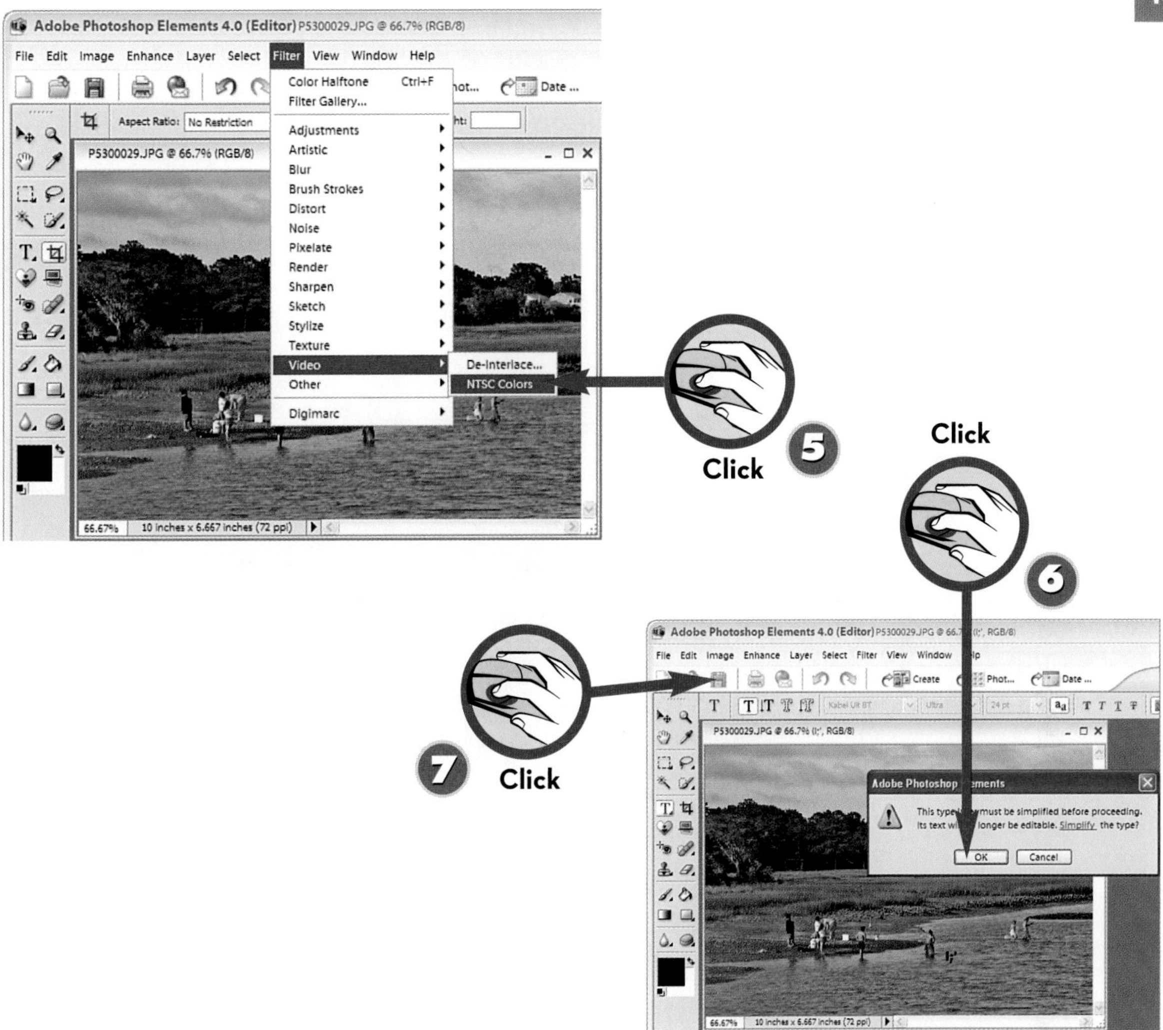

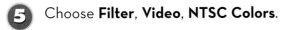

5 Choose **Filter**, **Video**, **NTSC Colors**.

6 If you see a simplify warning, click **OK**.

7 Click **Save**.

End

TIP

DVD Menus

One challenge of creating a DVD is to build the menu system by which users can make program selections. Many DVD authoring programs can use imagery you create as Photoshop files for menus.

NOTE

NTSC Color

This color model applies to broadcast television in North America. You'll need a different plug-in for the UK or France/Asia.

OPTIMIZING A PICTURE FOR THE WEB

Preparing an image for the Web involves converting its file type to JPEG, GIF, or PNG; restricting its colors to 256; reducing its size to a few inches wide; and limiting its resolution to 72 pixels/inch.

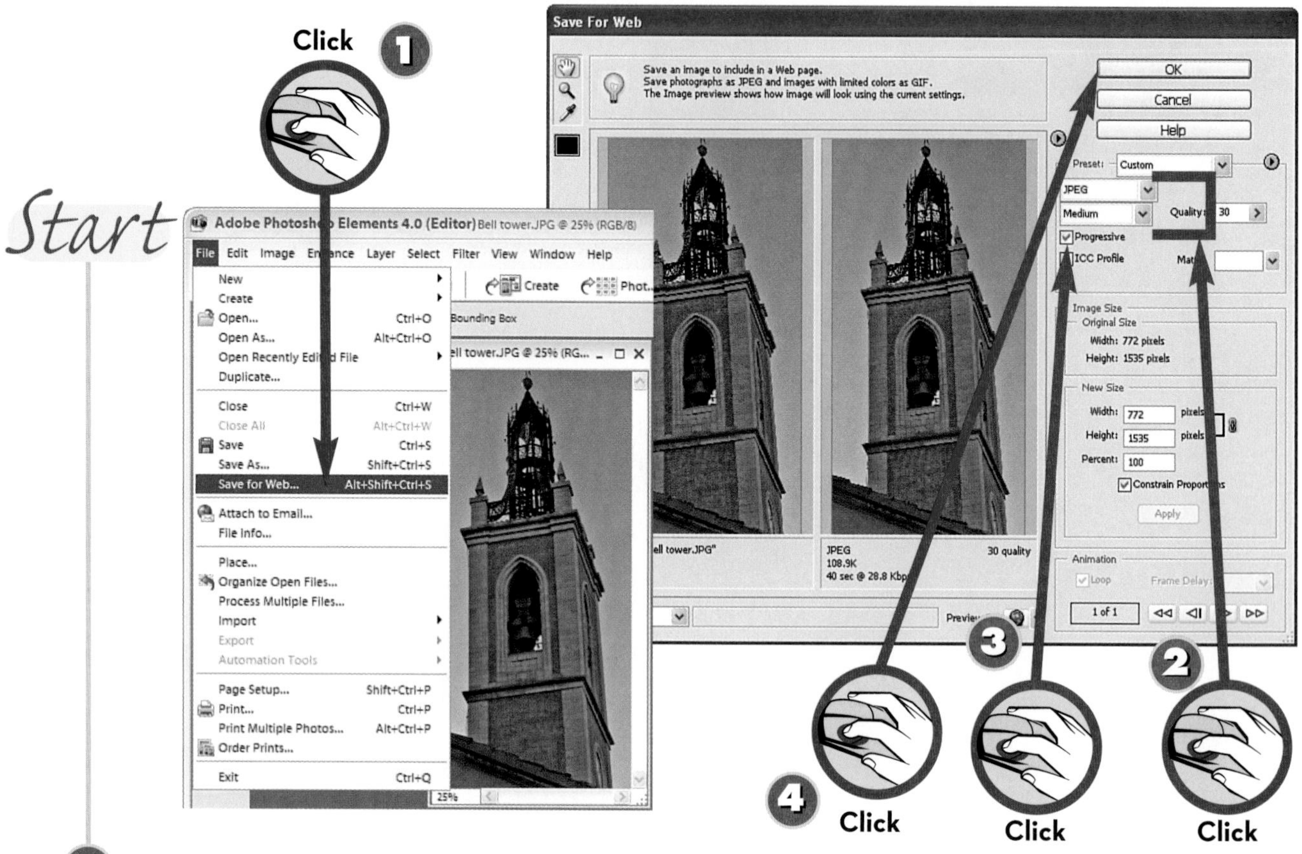

Start

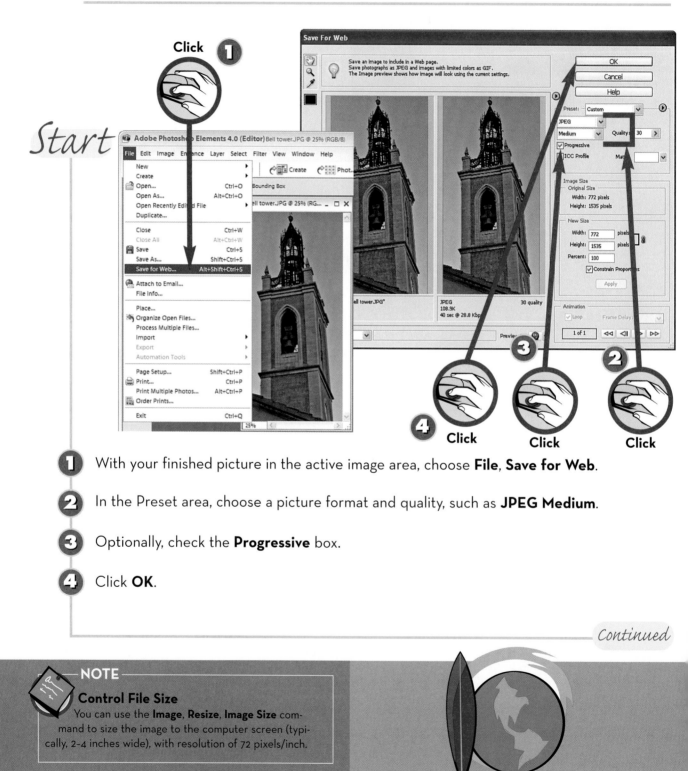

1. With your finished picture in the active image area, choose **File**, **Save for Web**.
2. In the Preset area, choose a picture format and quality, such as **JPEG Medium**.
3. Optionally, check the **Progressive** box.
4. Click **OK**.

Continued

NOTE

Control File Size

You can use the **Image**, **Resize**, **Image Size** command to size the image to the computer screen (typically, 2-4 inches wide), with resolution of 72 pixels/inch.

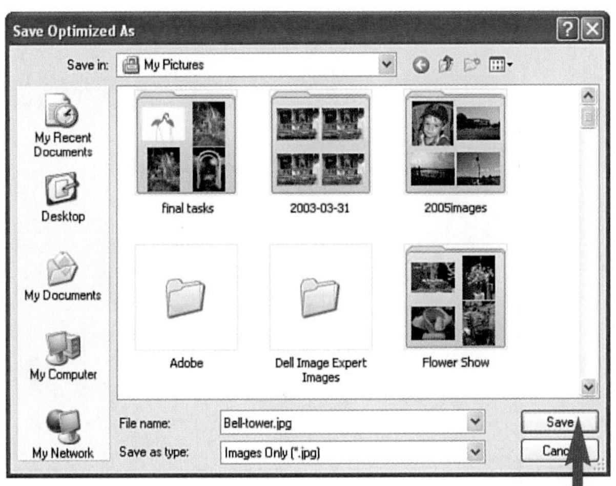

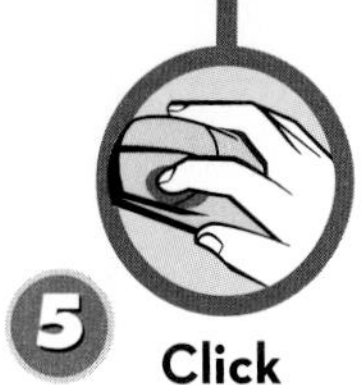

5 Click

5 Click **Save**.

End

NOTE

Control Image Size

To capture the interest of Web surfers, you want your home page to load as quickly as possible. Keep images there to thumbnail size; then permit interested viewers to click on them to download higher-resolution pictures.

TIP

Progressive Mode

Choosing **Progressive** mode for a JPEG file causes it to be displayed in stages as it downloads, resulting in a more pleasing experience for users with relatively slow (dial-up) connections.

SAVING AS AN ANIMATED PICTURE FOR THE WEB

These conversion steps take any layered file and convert it to a series of GIF frames (animated .gif file). Displayed on a Web page in rapid succession, a simple but effective animation sequence can be created. For example, text on successive layers appears to pop onto a background image.

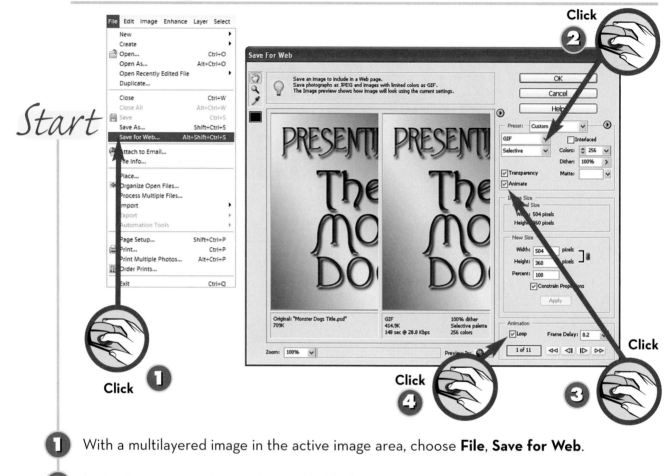

Start

Click 1 · Click 2 · Click 3 · Click 4

1. With a multilayered image in the active image area, choose **File**, **Save for Web**.
2. In the Preset area, choose **GIF** as the file format.
3. Check the **Animate** box.
4. In the Animation section, check the **Loop** box (for continuous playback).

Continued

TIP

Easy Animation

You can control the animated sequence by reordering the layers of your image in the Layers palette before you convert to GIF.

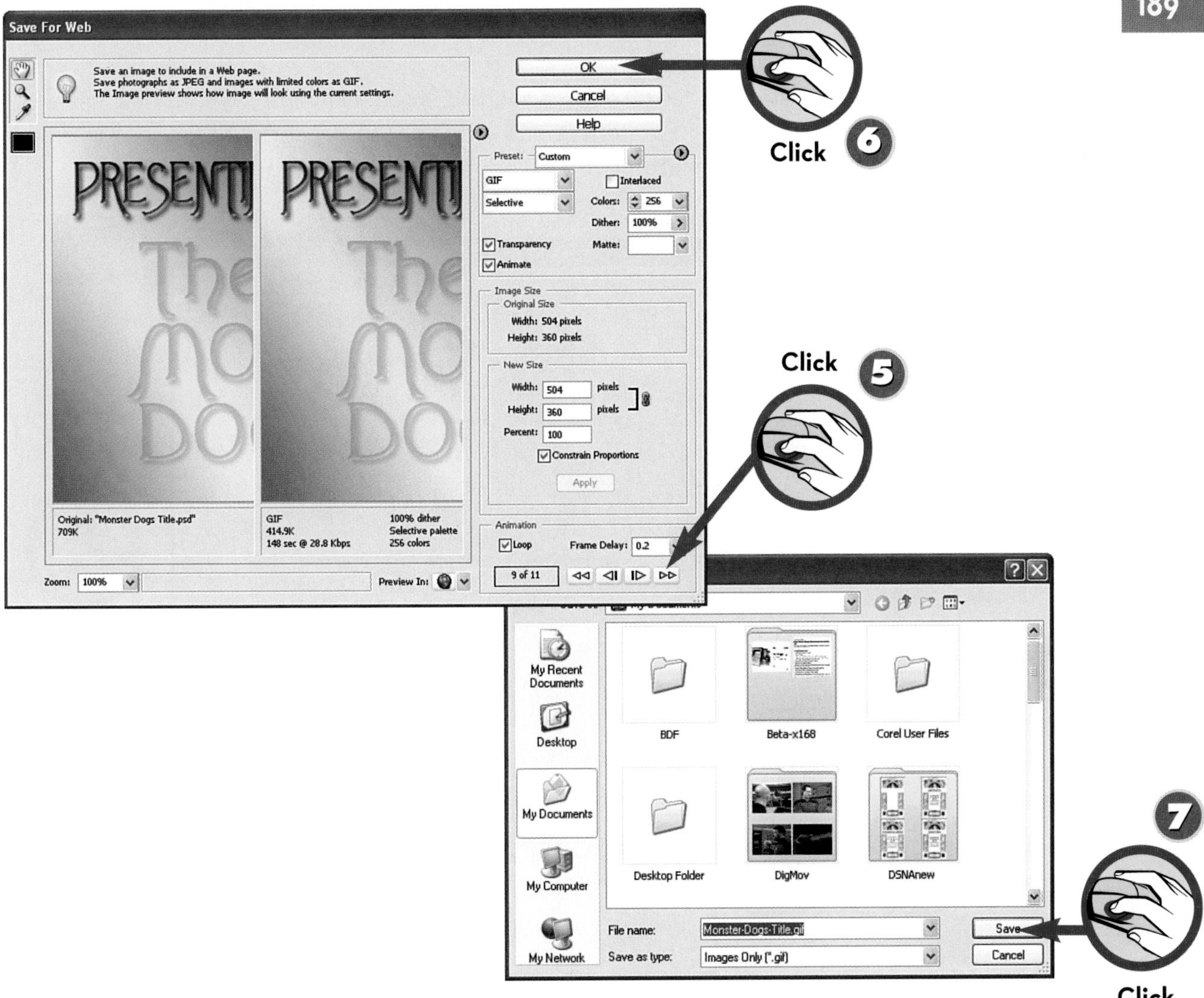

5 Step through to preview the animation by clicking the **Next Frame** button.

6 Click **OK**.

7 Click **Save**.

End

NOTE

Frame Delay

This option in the Animation section of the Save for Web window lets you vary the delay between frames (layers) from 0 to 10 seconds. If you don't check Loop, the sequence plays once and stops.

NOTE

Layered Imagery

Native Photoshop (**.psd**) files make excellent source material for this type of animation. For example, text can appear to pop onto a background. Creating different text layers can cause a message to be built up in steps.

SAVING FILES IN PHOTOSHOP FORMAT

If you've added Elements-specific features to a picture (such as layers, layer styles, shapes, or text), save the file in Photoshop Elements's native format to preserve those features so you can go back and change them later. Even if you're done working on an image, you should save a copy that includes all the layers and other stuff.

Start

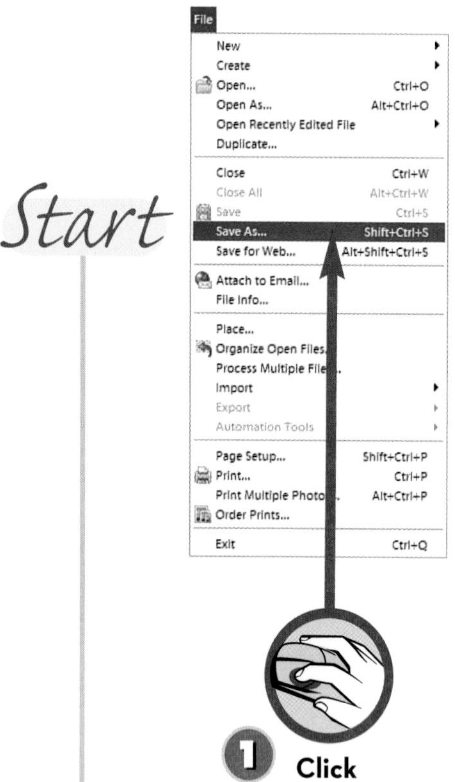

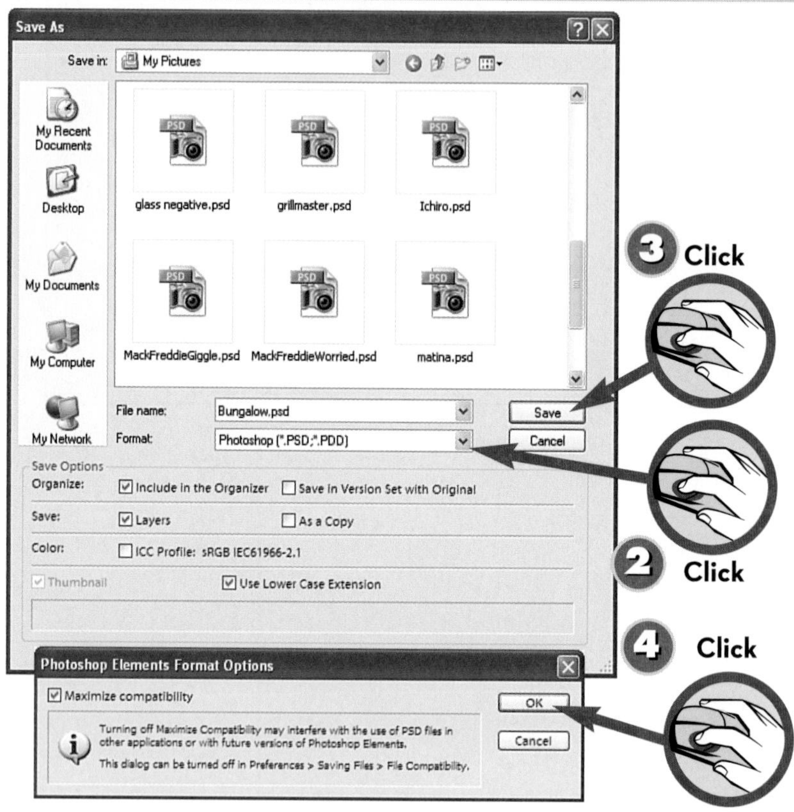

1. With an image open in the active image area, choose **File**, **Save As** or press **Shift+Ctrl+S**.
2. In the **Format** pop-up menu, choose **Photoshop**.
3. Navigate to the location where you want to save the file and click **Save**.
4. Click **OK**.

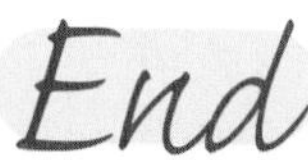

SAVING BEST-QUALITY PHOTOS FOR PRINTING

Of all the file formats, Tagged Image File Format (TIFF) is probably the best for saving a high-quality photograph that you intend to submit to a printer or publisher. The result is a file with a **.tif** extension.

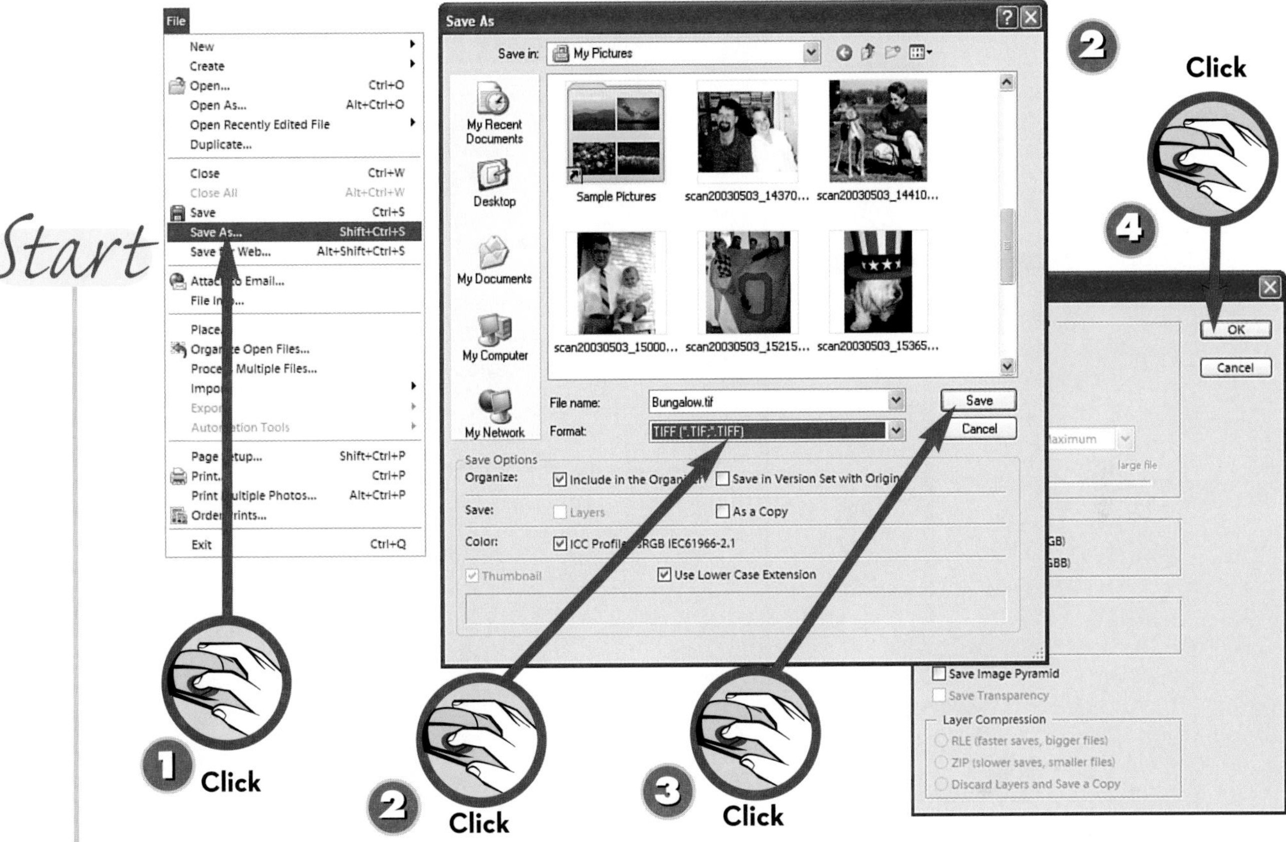

1. With an image open in the active image area, choose **File**, **Save As** or press **Shift+Ctrl+S**.
2. In the Format pop-up menu, choose **TIFF**.
3. Click **Save**.
4. Click **OK**.

End

TIP

Compression Options

Image Compression: LZW or ZIP are preferable to JPEG. LZW is the safest choice. ZIP can create smaller files, but some users won't be able to open them. Layer Compression: Select **Discard Layers and Save a Copy** unless the recipient needs to edit them.

SAVING DESIGNS FOR DESKTOP PUBLISHING

Adobe's Portable Document Format, or PDF, is the best choice for sharing finished-quality images and artwork with anyone anywhere, regardless of the computer make or model they happen to be using. When in doubt about which type of file your recipient can handle, this one is a safe bet.

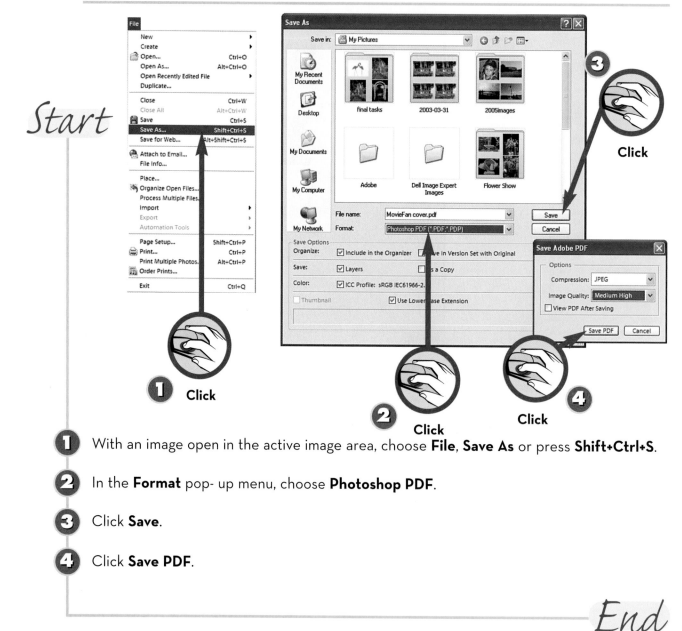

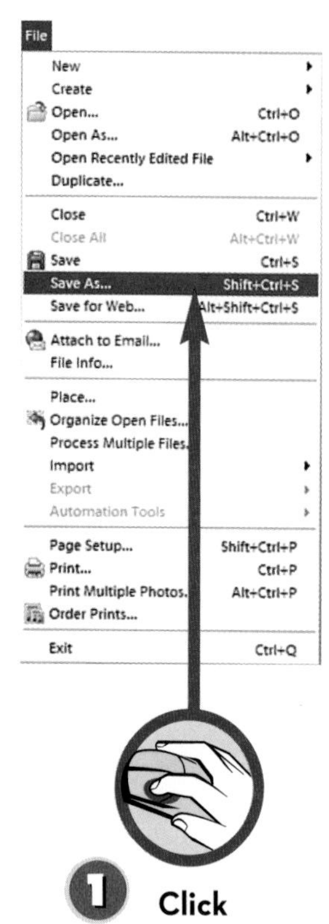

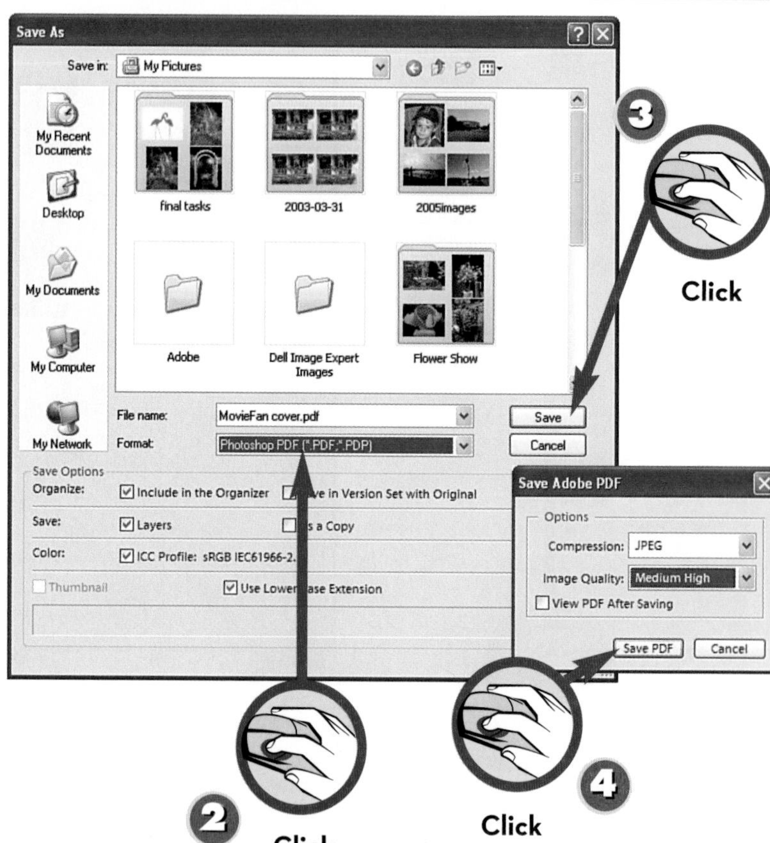

1. With an image open in the active image area, choose **File**, **Save As** or press **Shift+Ctrl+S**.
2. In the **Format** pop- up menu, choose **Photoshop PDF**.
3. Click **Save**.
4. Click **Save PDF**.

End

NOTE

Encoding Option

In the PDF Options window, even though JPEG is the default value, you'll get better picture quality (but a larger file) by choosing **ZIP** instead.

NOTE

PSD and Prepress PDF

Although you can convert from other files types when saving, starting with a Photoshop file usually gives the best results. To save as Prepress PDF, which contains print job information as well as image data, upgrade to Photoshop CS2.

APPLYING A COPYRIGHT NOTICE

For copyright purposes, a photographer is considered the author of the image and can hold intellectual property rights (IPR) to it—including licensing its use by others. This task shows you how to append a copyright notice to your images in the form of text data attached to the file.

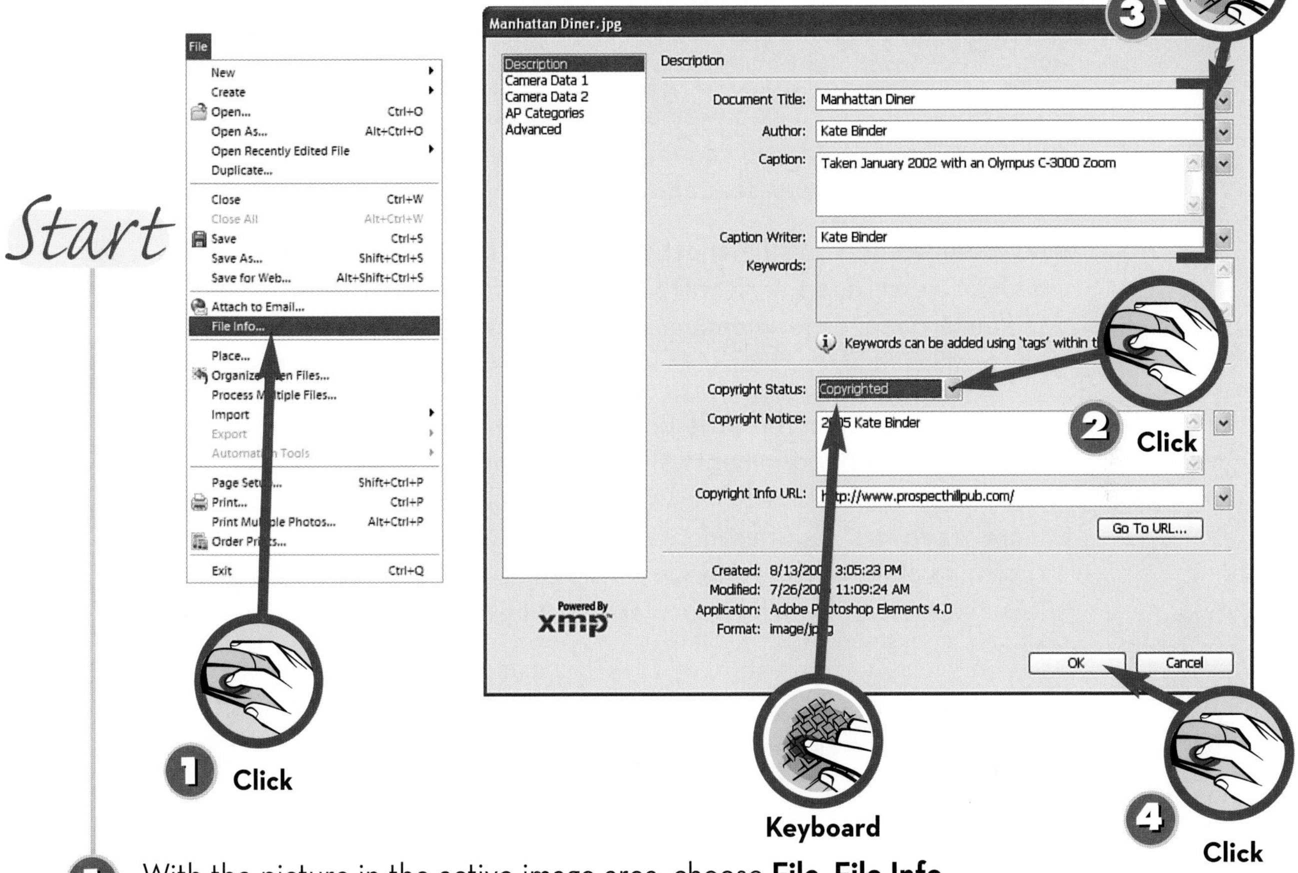

Start

1 Click

2 Click

3 Type

4 Click

Keyboard

1. With the picture in the active image area, choose **File**, **File Info**.
2. Choose **Copyrighted** in the **Copyright Status** pop-up menu.
3. Type information in the **Document Title**, **Author**, **Caption**, **Copyright Notice**, and **Copyright Info URL** fields.
4. Click **OK**. A copyright notice is included in the file information, and the © symbol appears in the image title bar.

End

NOTE

Getting Permission

If a file you downloaded is marked as copyrighted, the Go to URL button in the File Info dialog box takes you to the author's Web site, where you should find licensing and contact information.

NOTE

Proprietary Watermarks

Copyrighted images you download from the Web may also contain ownership information as *digital watermarks* in the image itself. To inspect a file for a watermark, choose **Filter**, **Digimarc**, **Read Watermark**.

part 12

JUST FOR FUN

It's only after you've mastered a set of tools that you can begin to take real joy in using them. Then, you can let the logical, step-by-step calculating part of your brain take a back seat and let your imagination do the driving.

If you've worked through most, if not all, of the preceding tasks, you're ready—and you've earned the right—to have some fun. Tasks in this part are all about fooling around, experimenting, and exploring ways of manipulating electronic images like collage artists use paper cutouts and a set of paints.

There isn't space in this little book to take you through all the things you can do with Photoshop Elements. (If, with so many possible choices and combinations, it's even possible.) But with the basic skills you've picked up here, the more your work with this incredibly rich and flexible computer application will seem like play. As you continue to explore, you'll sweat the technical details less and less, and you'll find a marvelous new outlet for your personal expression.

And if, perchance, some of your fantasies seem, er, just a bit bizarre—add a talk bubble or a clever caption and turn them into personalized greeting cards!

BRANCHING OUT

Ever wonder how to turn a simple portrait into a work of art?

Long ago, in a land far away...

PLACING ARTWORK IN AN IMAGE

Commands you may already have used for combining imagery are File, New From Clipboard; File, Import; and the pair Edit, Copy and Edit, Paste. Here's a handy alternative, a quicker way to insert artwork from an external file that's in one of the other Adobe formats (**.ai**, **.eps**, **.pdf**, or **.pdp** extensions).

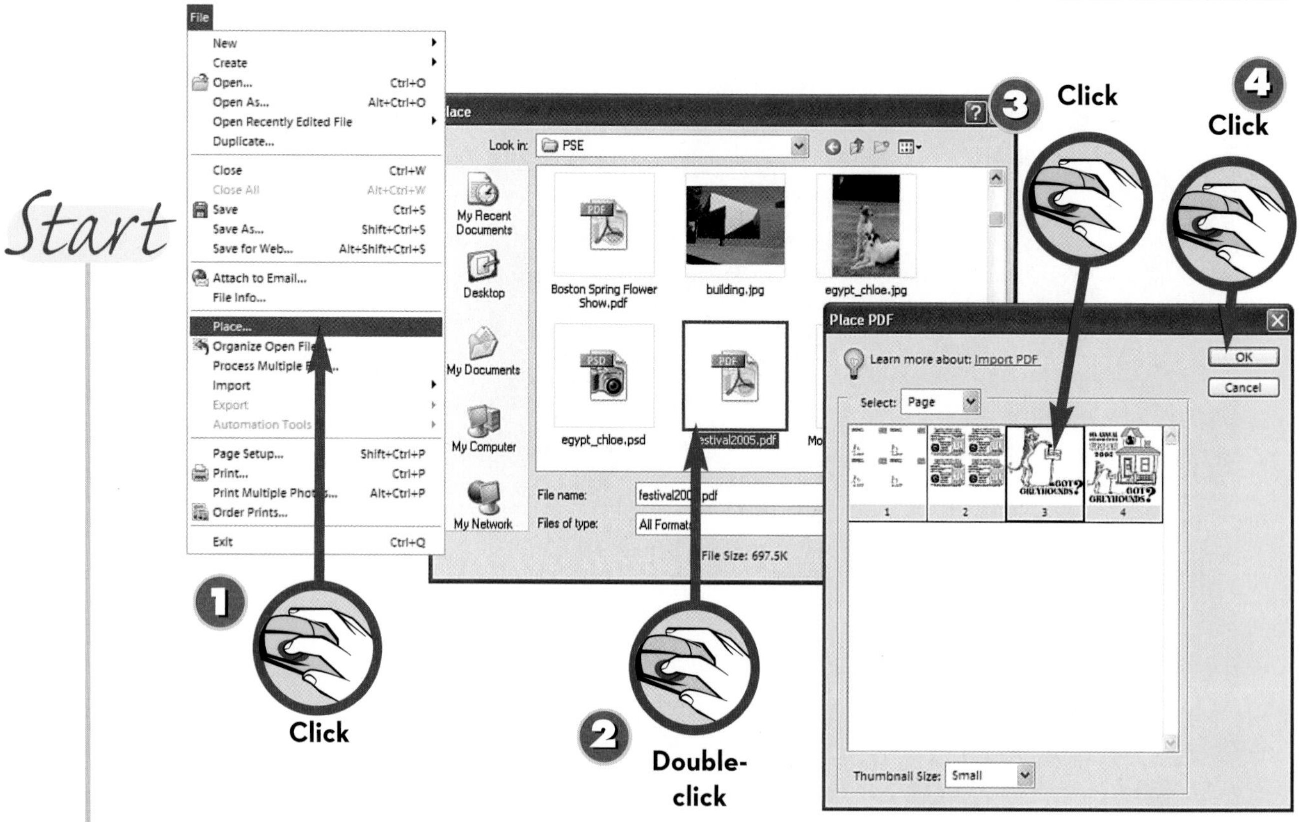

1. With a background image in the active image area, choose **File**, **Place**.
2. Locate and double-click the file that contains the artwork (or click it and click **Place**).
3. If the file contains multiple pages, choose the page you want to insert.
4. Click **OK**. The artwork or page is inserted into a new layer in the active image.

Continued

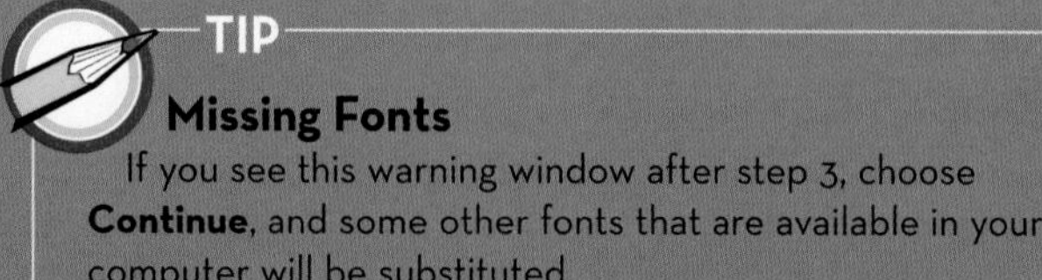

TIP

Missing Fonts

If you see this warning window after step 3, choose **Continue**, and some other fonts that are available in your computer will be substituted.

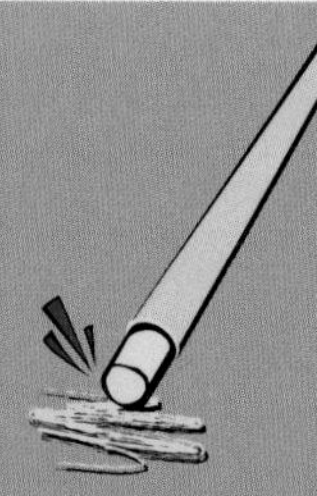

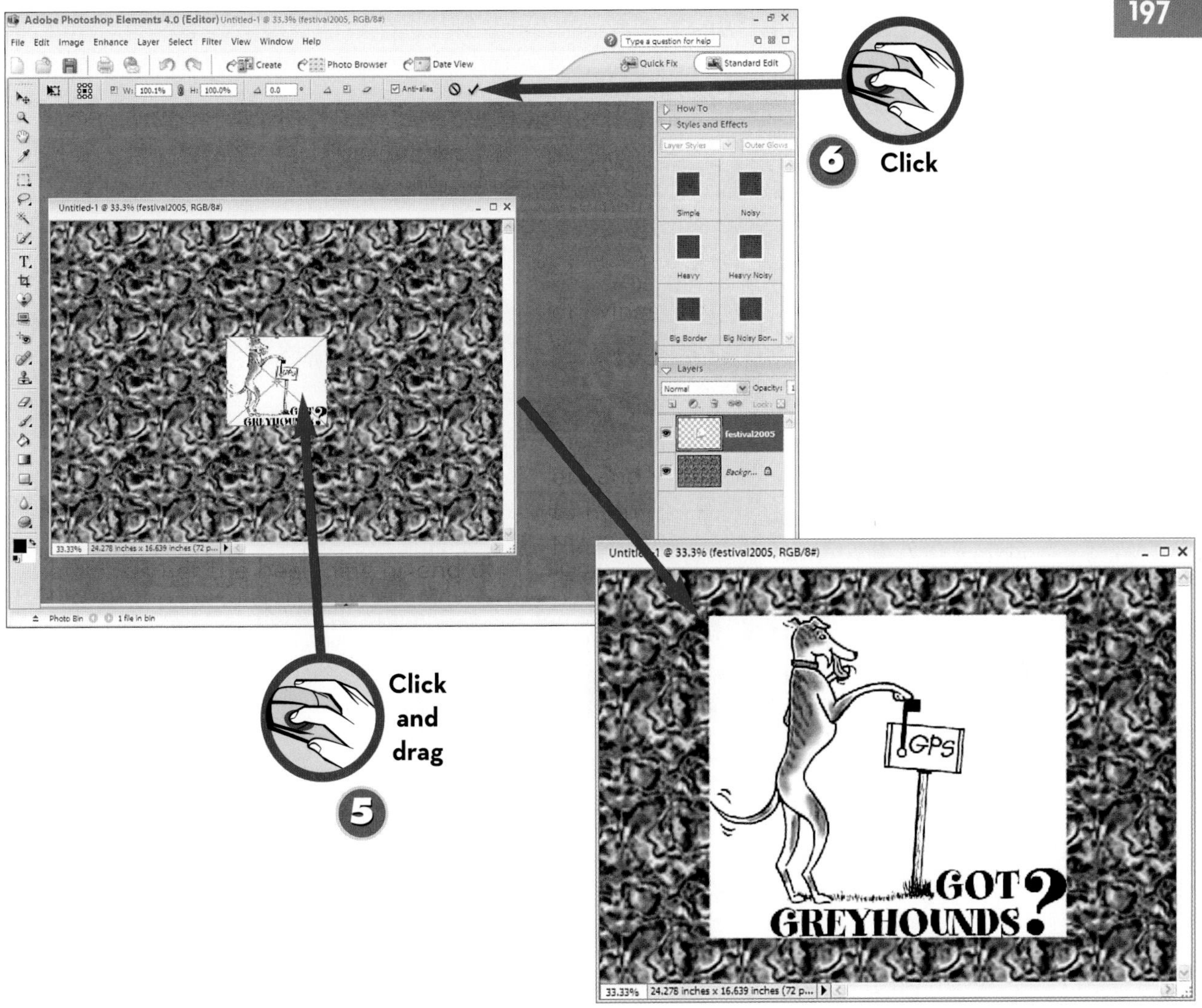

5 Optionally, drag a handle to move or resize the artwork to fit your canvas.

6 Click the **Commit** button, or press **Enter**.

End

NOTE

Vectors Get Rasterized

Vector graphics in the source file get simplified, or *rasterized* (converted to pixels), when you click Commit. The objects take on the same resolution as the target image.

MAKING MOSAIC TILES

Hand-painted tiles are so expensive—and you have to be a real artist to create your own. Unless, that is, you have Photoshop Elements. Here's a quick way to turn any photograph into a pretty convincing tile mosaic.

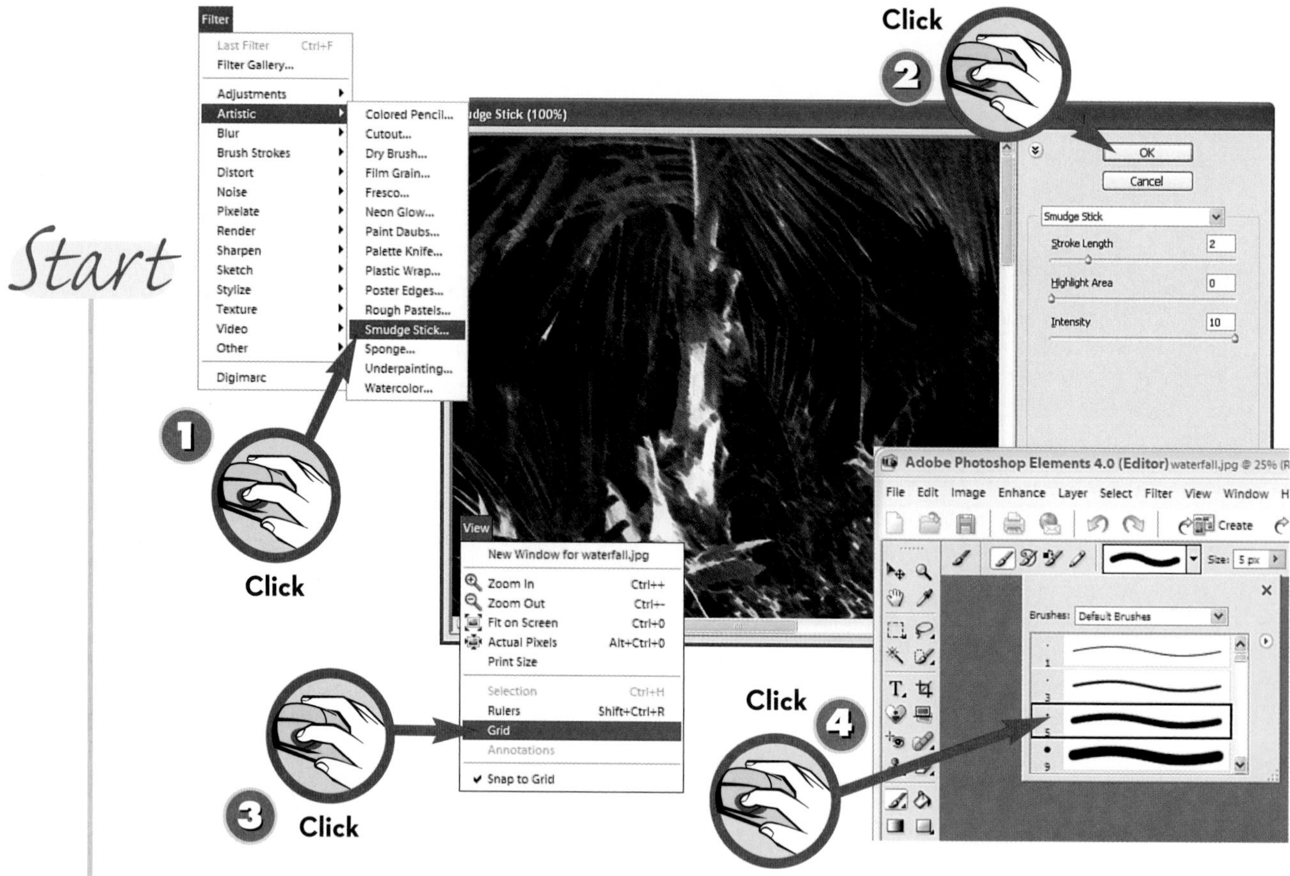

1. Choose **Filter**, **Artistic**, **Smudge Stick**.
2. Click **OK**.
3. Choose **View**, **Grid**.
4. Choose the **Brush** tool and pick a small, soft brush.

Continued

TIP

Making It Real

Mount your "tiles" on a tabletop using spray adhesive and a few coats of nonyellowing polyurethane varnish. Or put your mosaic on a wall—but mount the paper on a thin sheet of wood first, so you can take it with you when you move.

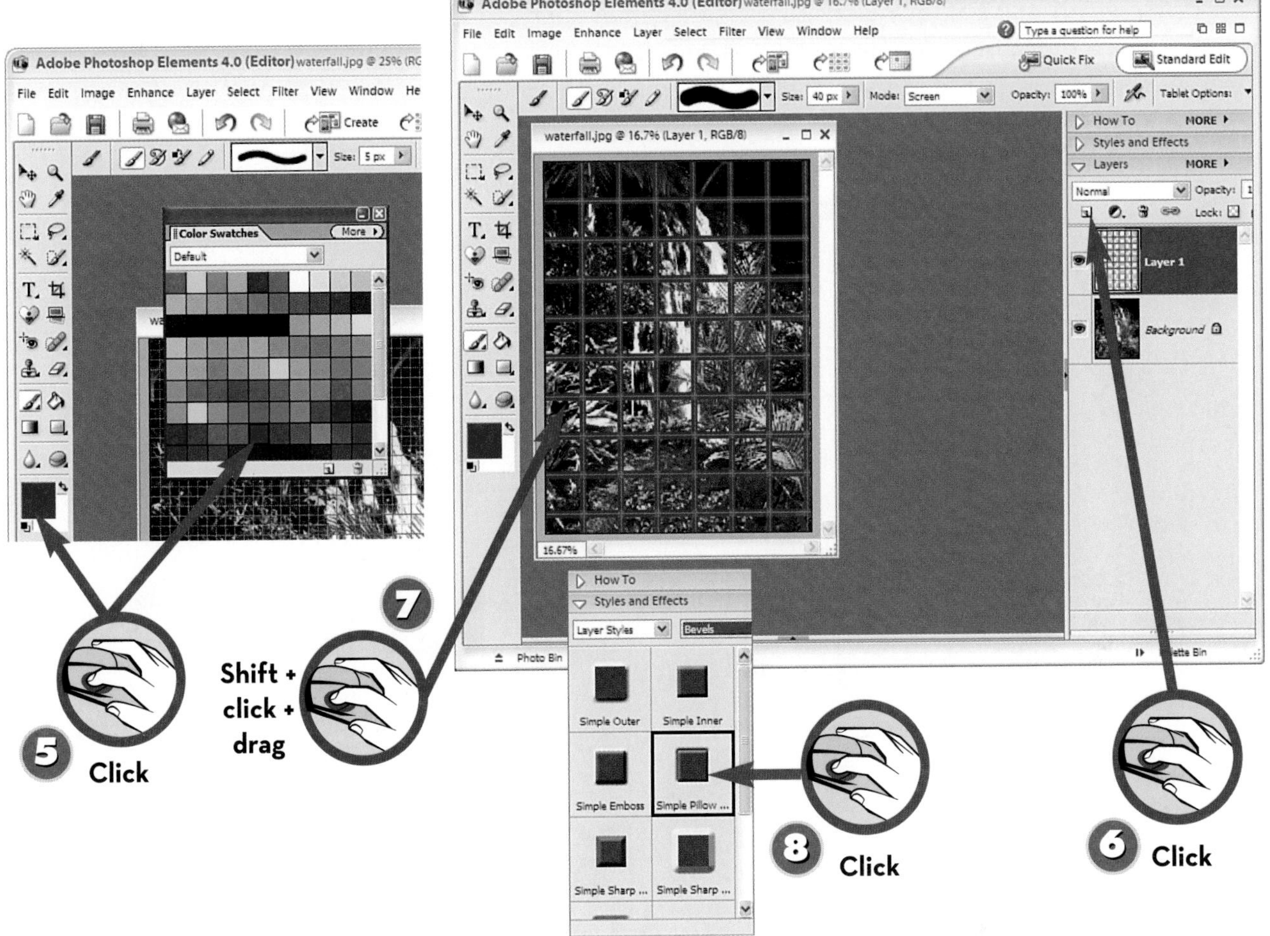

5 In the **Color Swatches** palette, choose a foreground color for the grout between the tiles.

6 Click the **Create New Layer** button in the Layers palette.

7 Hold down **Shift** and paint the grout lines along the grid.

8 Click the **Simple Pillow Emboss** style in the Styles and Effects palette.

End

NOTE

Get Creative!

Try any filter or combination of filters in step 1—you don't have to use Smudge Stick. You can also adjust the grout width (choose a different brush size).

TIP

Changing Your Mind

To change the grout color, make the grout layer active and choose a new foreground color. Click the **Preserve Transparency** check box at the top of the Layers palette, and then press **Alt+Delete** to replace all the layer's white pixels with the new color.

CREATING PANORAMIC VIEWS

It's truly amazing how sensitive digital cameras are, even in near darkness. These photos were taken in a moonless night, lit only by the glow of city lights. Photoshop Elements has the smarts to blend the edges of several scenic photos seamlessly into one gorgeous panorama.

Start

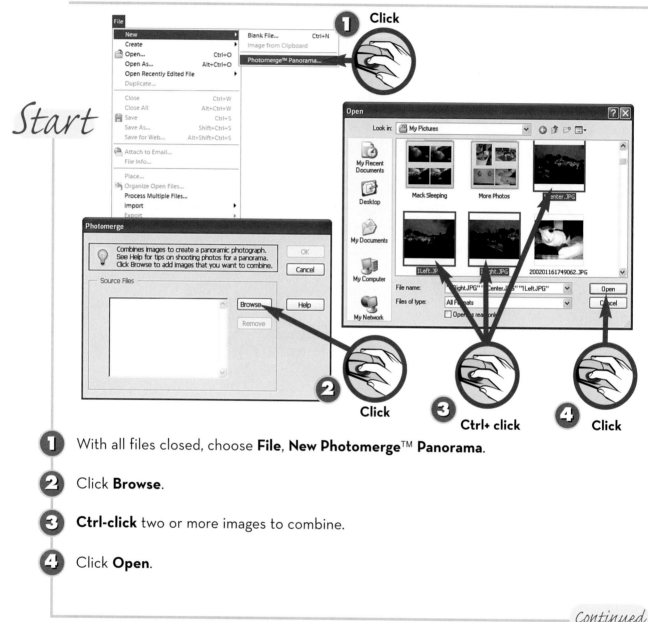

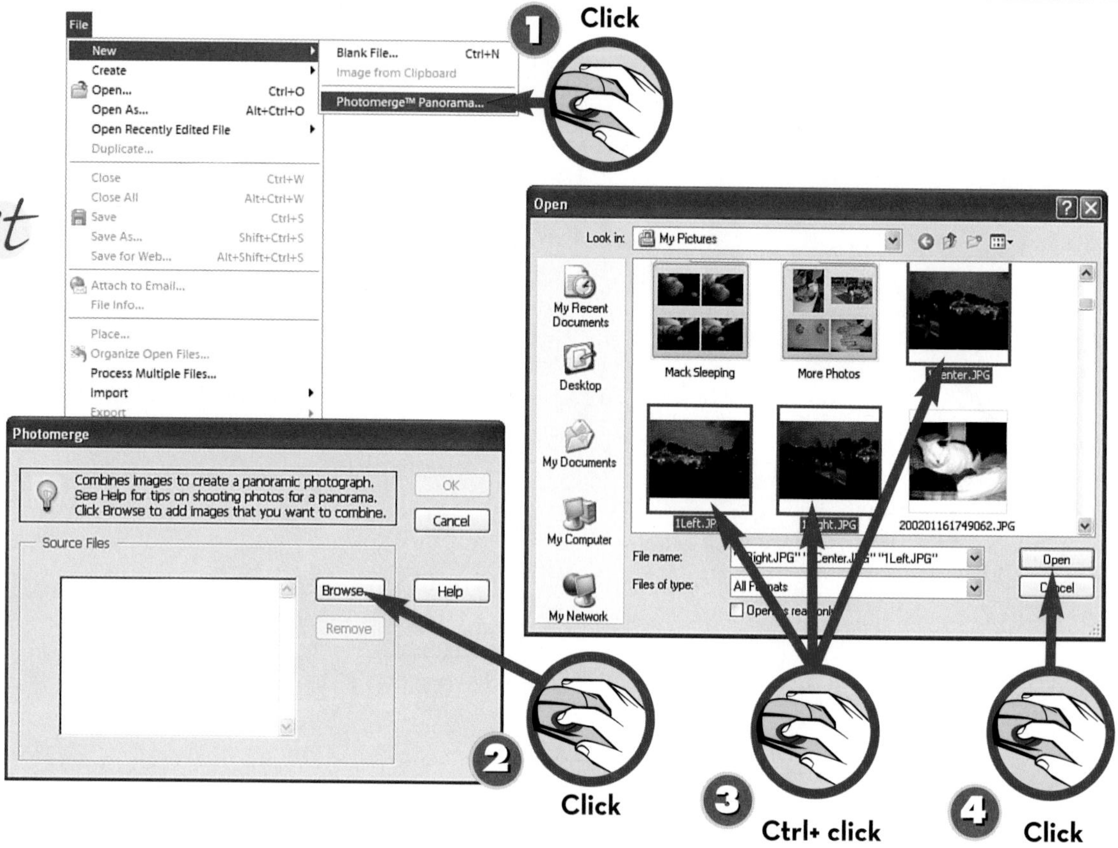

1. Click
2. Click
3. Ctrl+ click
4. Click

1. With all files closed, choose **File**, **New Photomerge™ Panorama**.
2. Click **Browse**.
3. **Ctrl-click** two or more images to combine.
4. Click **Open**.

Continued

NOTE

Pan Your Snaps

Shots must be adjacent so their edges align: Mount the camera on a tripod. Take your source photos all at the same vertical angle, *panning* from left to right, so that the edges overlap the scene.

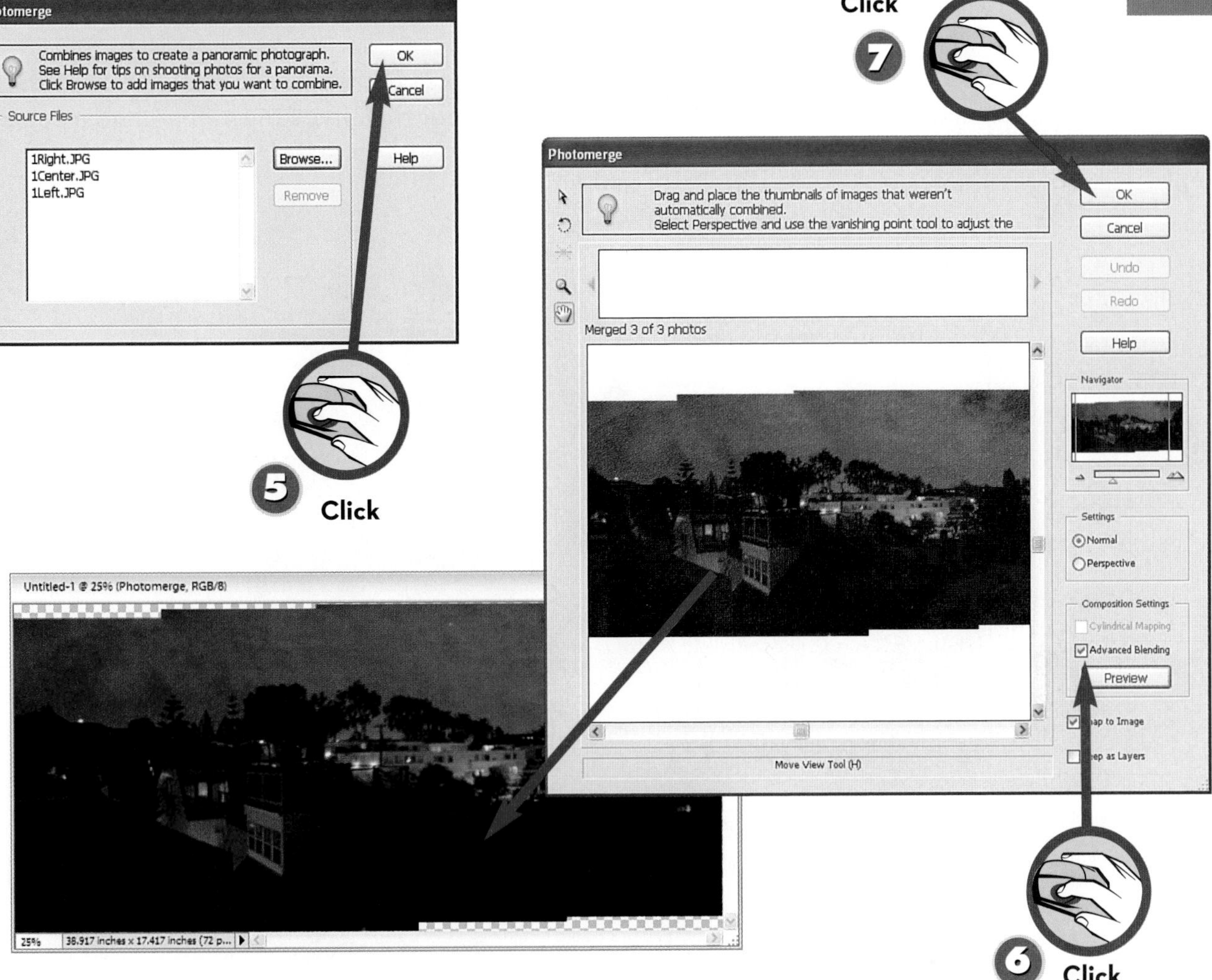

5. Click **OK**.
6. Optionally, check **Advanced Blending** to create seamless edges.
7. Click **OK**. The composite picture appears in the active image window.

End

TIP

Photomerge Options

Perspective can heighten the panoramic effect. Available in combination with this option, Cylindrical Mapping emphasizes curvature. Advanced Blending (recommended) not only aligns edges but also makes exposures match.

NOTE

Crop to Finish

Finish off by cropping the image, because no matter how careful you are, the horizontal edge of the composite image probably won't be smooth.

ACHIEVING A 3D EFFECT

Three-dimensional transformation opens up all kinds of creative possibilities. Think of the image you start with as being printed on a rubber sheet that you can wrap around a cube, a sphere, or a cylinder.

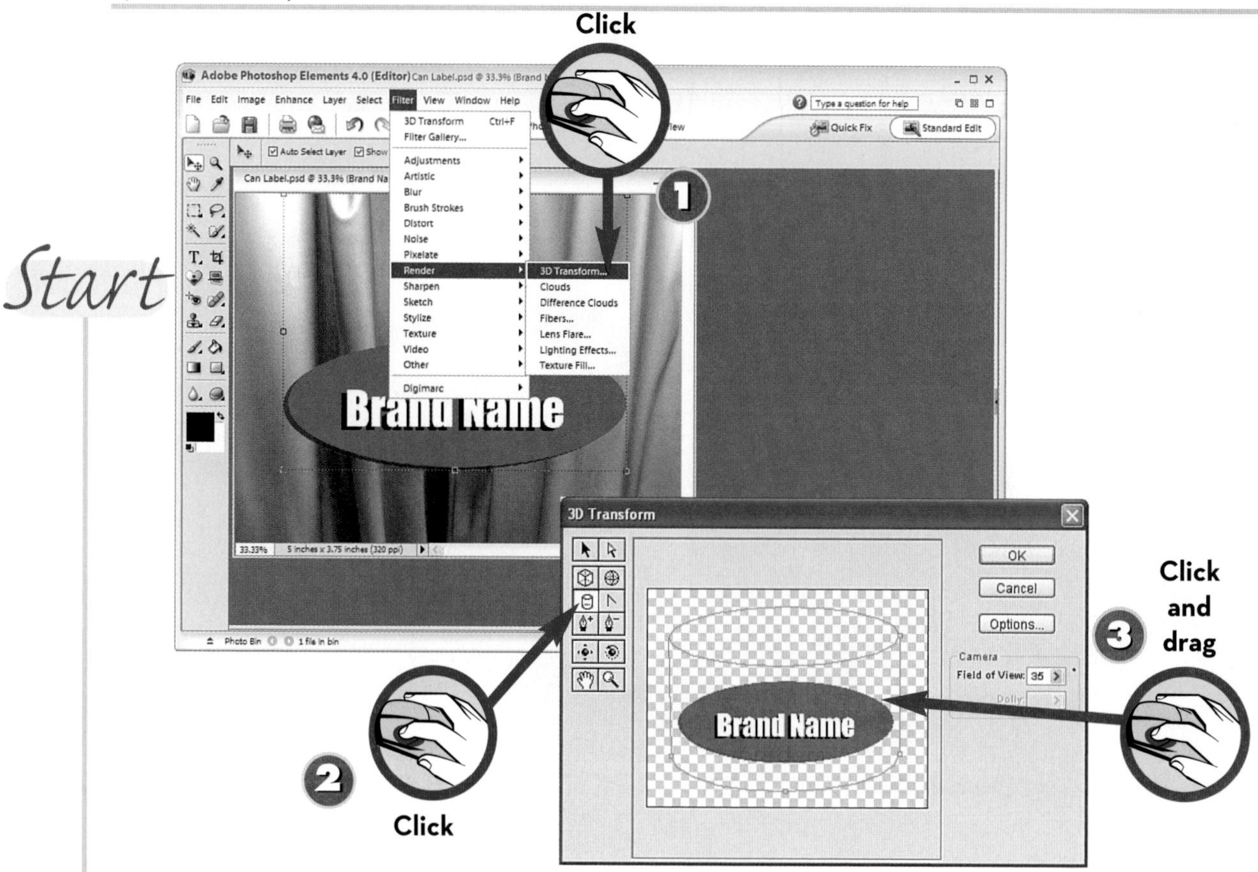

Start

1. With the object you want to transform selected, choose **Filter**, **Render**, **3D Transform**.
2. Choose a transformation shape, such as **Cylinder** (or press **C**).
3. Click and drag to size the shape in the 3D Transform preview window.

Continued

NOTE

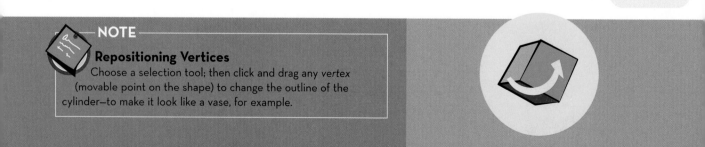

Repositioning Vertices

Choose a selection tool; then click and drag any *vertex* (movable point on the shape) to change the outline of the cylinder—to make it look like a vase, for example.

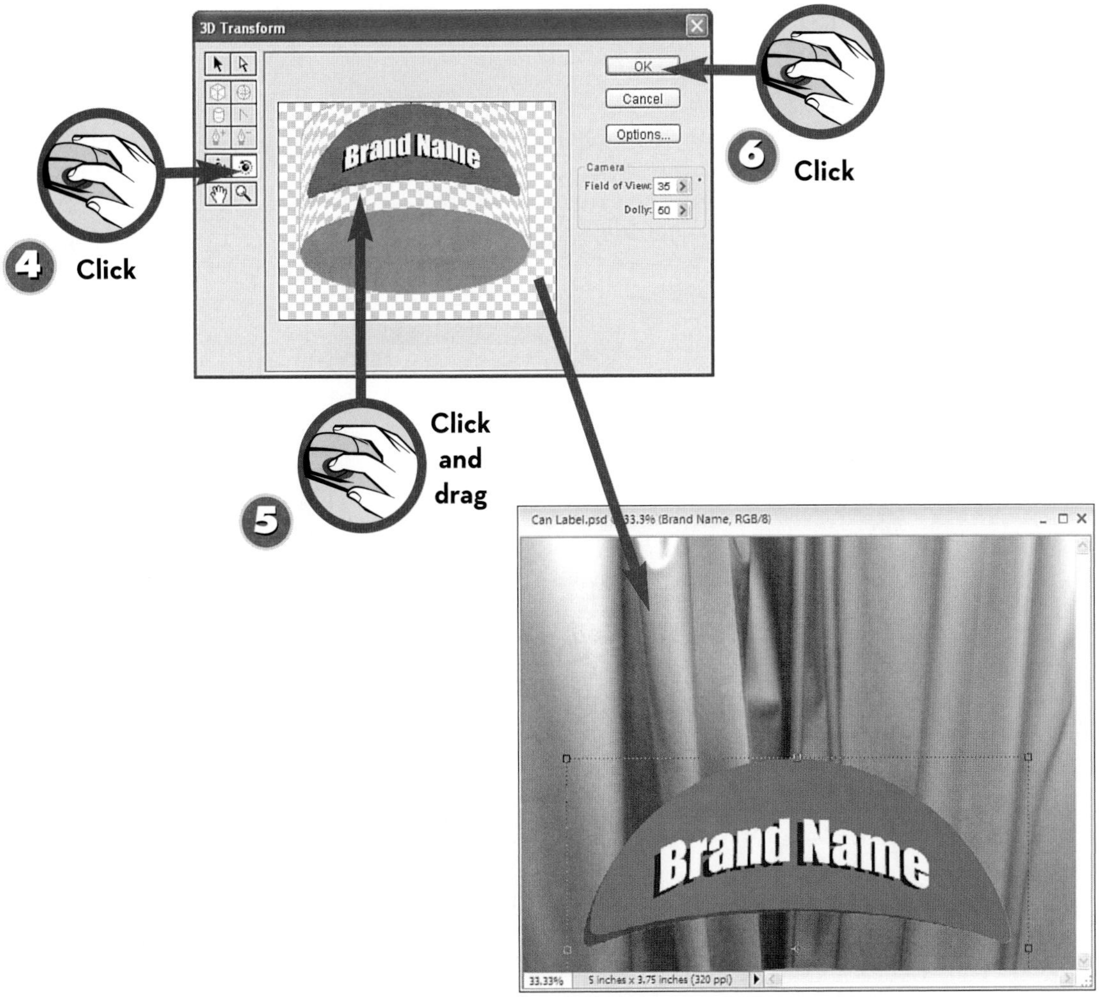

6 Click

4 Click

5 Click and drag

4 Click the **Trackball** tool (or press **R**). (You can also use the Pan Camera tool or press **E**.)

5 Click and drag to adjust the effect in the preview window.

6 Click **OK**. The transformed object appears in the active image window.

End

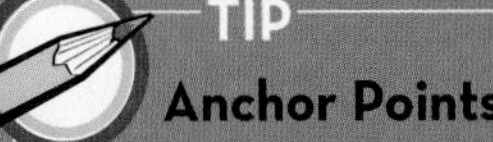

TIP

Anchor Points

The *anchor point* is a vertex on the shape to which the image can attach. For the Cylinder shape only, the Convert Anchor Point, Add Anchor Point, and Delete Anchor Point tools become available.

TURNING A PHOTO INTO A RUBBER STAMP

Rubber stamps are just plain fun to play with, especially once you get into all the fancy inks, embossing powders, and the like. And with Photoshop Elements, you're not restricted to the stamps you'll find at the store—you can make your own.

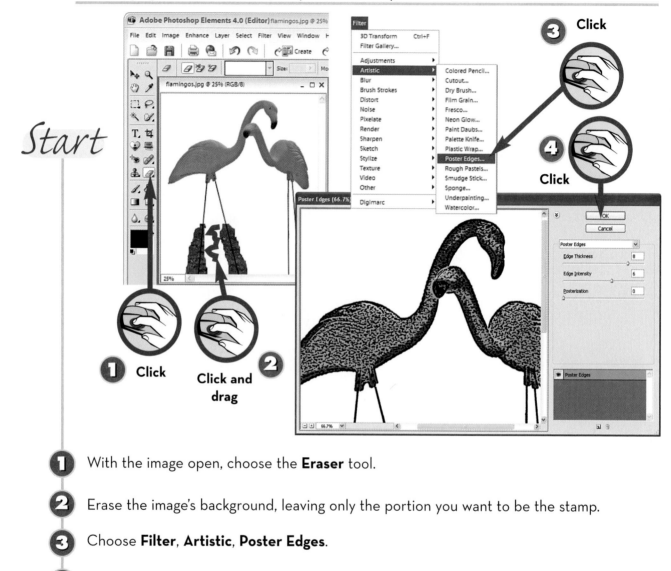

Start

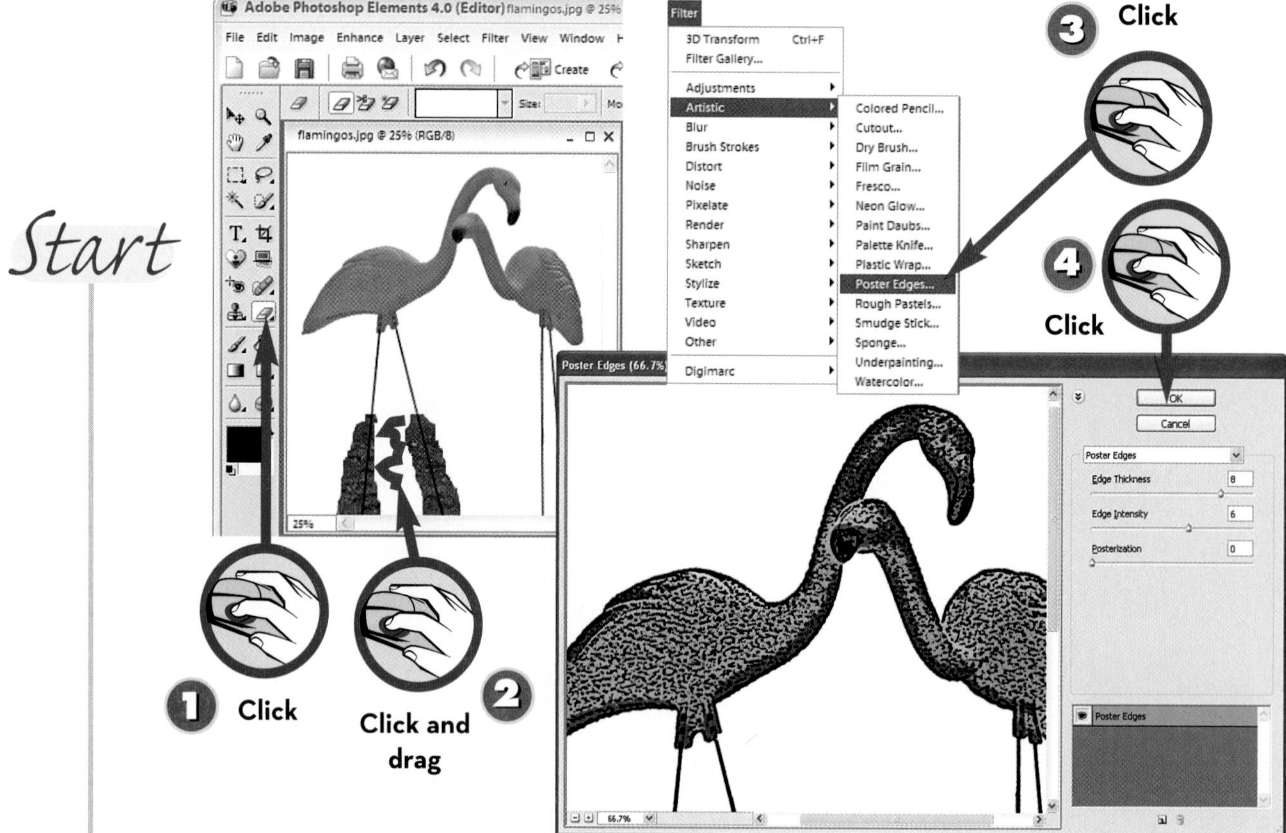

1. With the image open, choose the **Eraser** tool.
2. Erase the image's background, leaving only the portion you want to be the stamp.
3. Choose **Filter**, **Artistic**, **Poster Edges**.
4. Adjust the settings so the areas that will be the stamp are black; then click **OK**.

Continued

NOTE

From Concept to Reality

When your artwork is ready, convert it into a rubber stamp by Create a Stamp (**www.createastamp.com**), The Stampin' Place (**www.stampin.com**), Simon's Stamps (**www.simonstamp.com**), or other specialists.

TIP

Contrast Is the Key

For best results, choose a picture of an object against a contrasting background. It helps if there's some contrast within the object's outlines, too, unless it's recognizable merely from its silhouette.

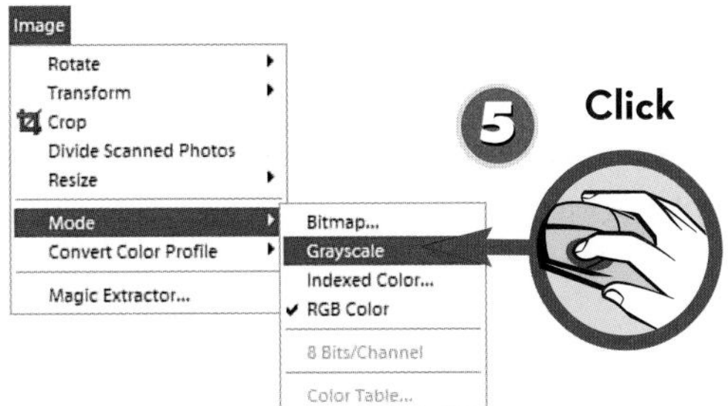

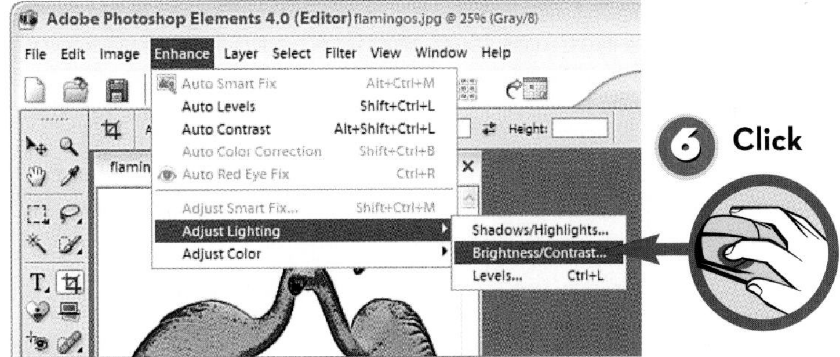

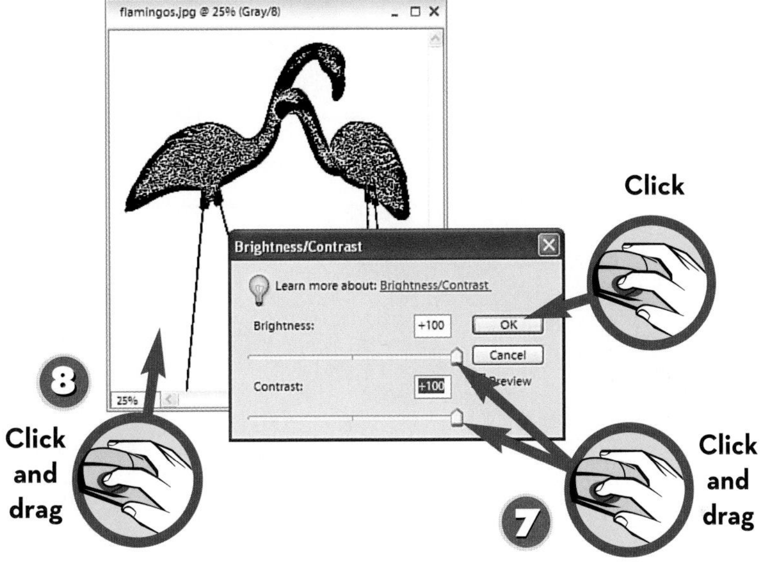

5 Choose **Image**, **Mode**, **Grayscale**.

6 Choose **Enhance**, **Adjust Lighting**, **Brightness/Contrast**.

7 Drag both sliders all the way to the right and click **OK**.

8 Use the **Eraser** to clean up around the stamp's edges if necessary.

End

TIP

Lighten Up

After step 5, if your picture has a lot of dark gray in areas that you want white, choose **Enhance**, **Adjust Lighting**, **Levels** and drag the middle slider to the left to lighten the midtones so they'll drop out to white in step 7.

NOTE

What Else It's Good For

This technique is also useful for making coloring pages for the kids, t-shirt artwork, or any kind of art that needs to be black on white.

FAKING IT LIKE THE PROS

Trick photography takes many forms, but most involve combining and reworking real images to create an unrealistic or improbable scene. This example creates a collage from three separate pictures and then adds some artwork to finish the job.

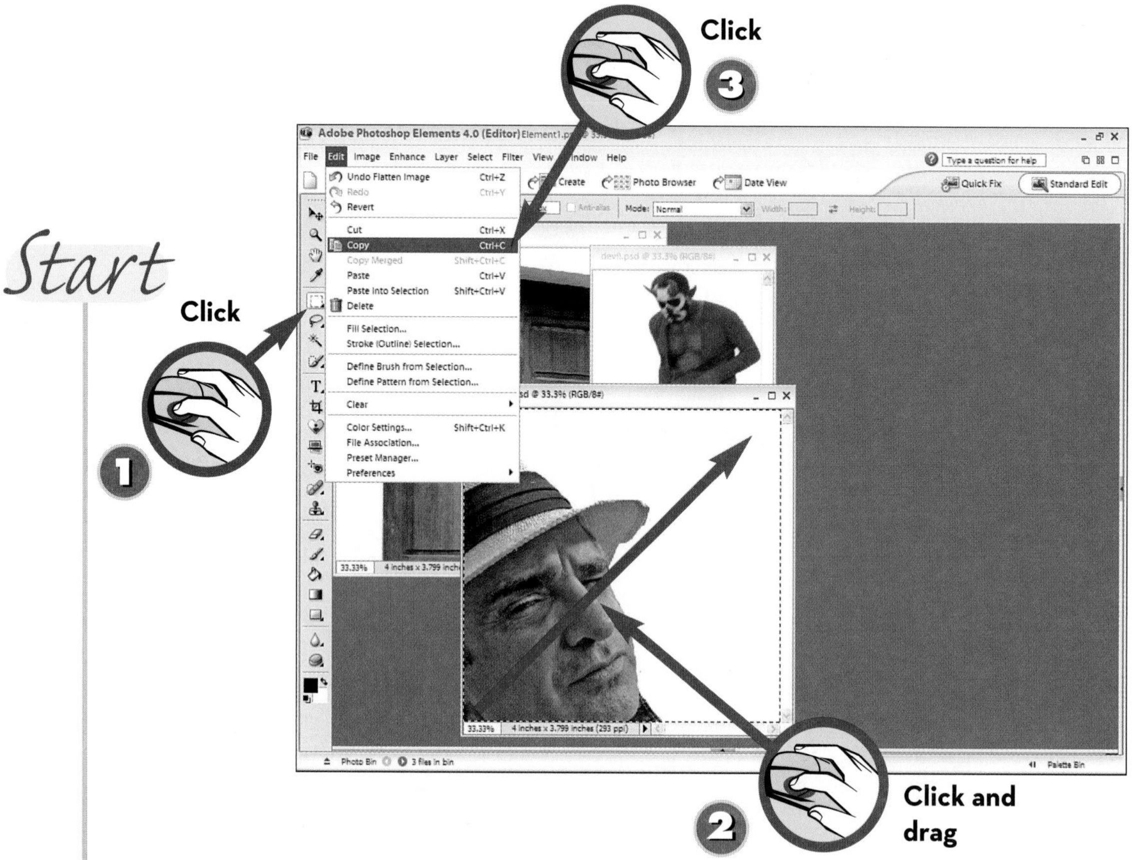

Start

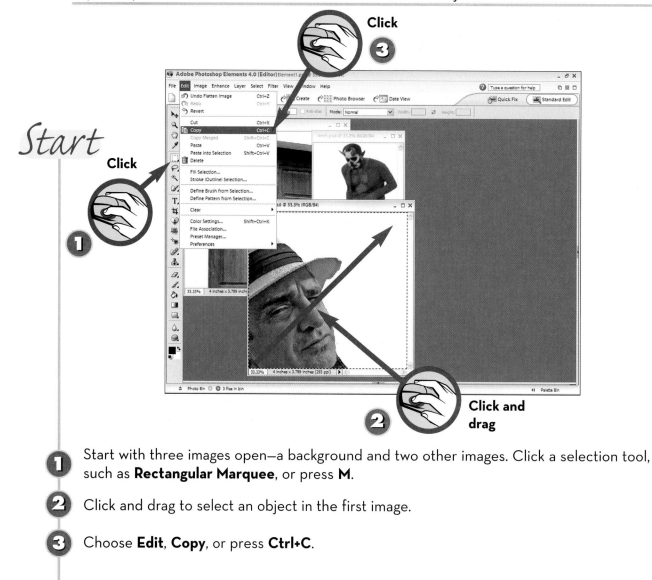

1. Start with three images open—a background and two other images. Click a selection tool, such as **Rectangular Marquee**, or press **M**.
2. Click and drag to select an object in the first image.
3. Choose **Edit**, **Copy**, or press **Ctrl+C**.

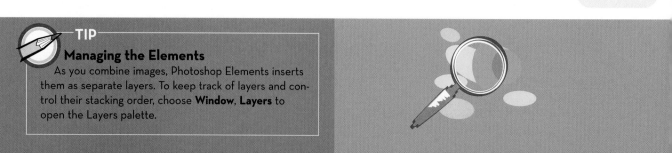

Continued

TIP

Managing the Elements

As you combine images, Photoshop Elements inserts them as separate layers. To keep track of layers and control their stacking order, choose **Window**, **Layers** to open the Layers palette.

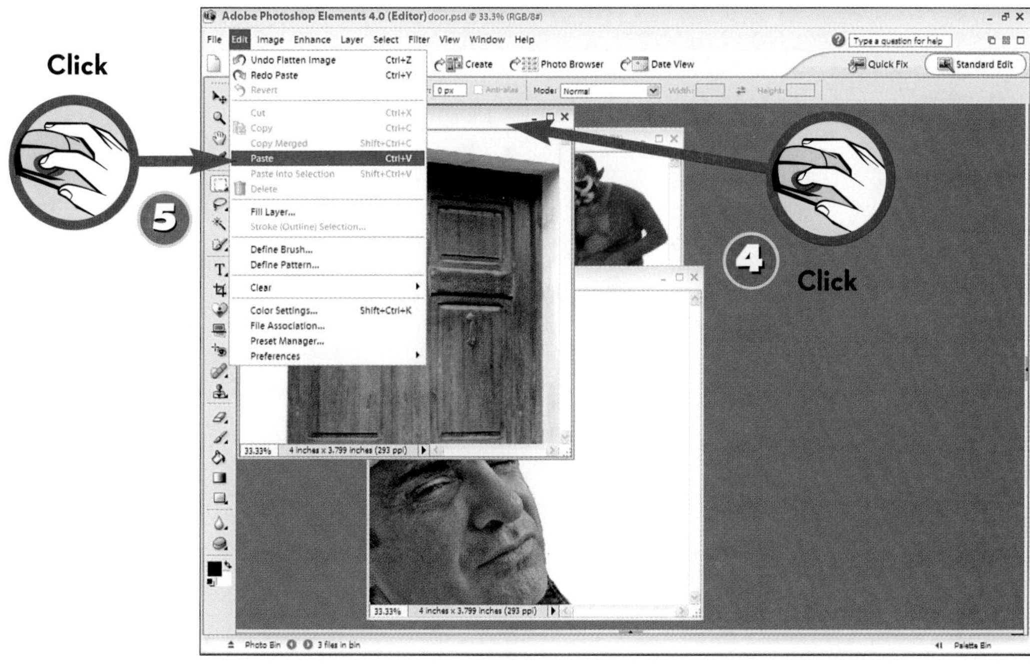

4 Select the background image by clicking its title bar.

5 Choose **Edit**, **Paste**, or press **Ctrl+V**. Repeat steps 2–5 to add more objects or images.

Continued

TIP

Merry Merging

After choosing **Edit**, **Copy**, a quick way to combine imagery, as shown in some previous tasks, is to use the **Edit**, **Paste Into** command. But remember, when you do this, the insertion does not create a separate layer.

The ability to combine images in improbable ways apparently brings out the humor in some people. If you use email at all, you've no doubt received pictures of pets doing superhuman feats, celebrities and politicians in compromising positions, or ordinary people with extraordinary physical characteristics!

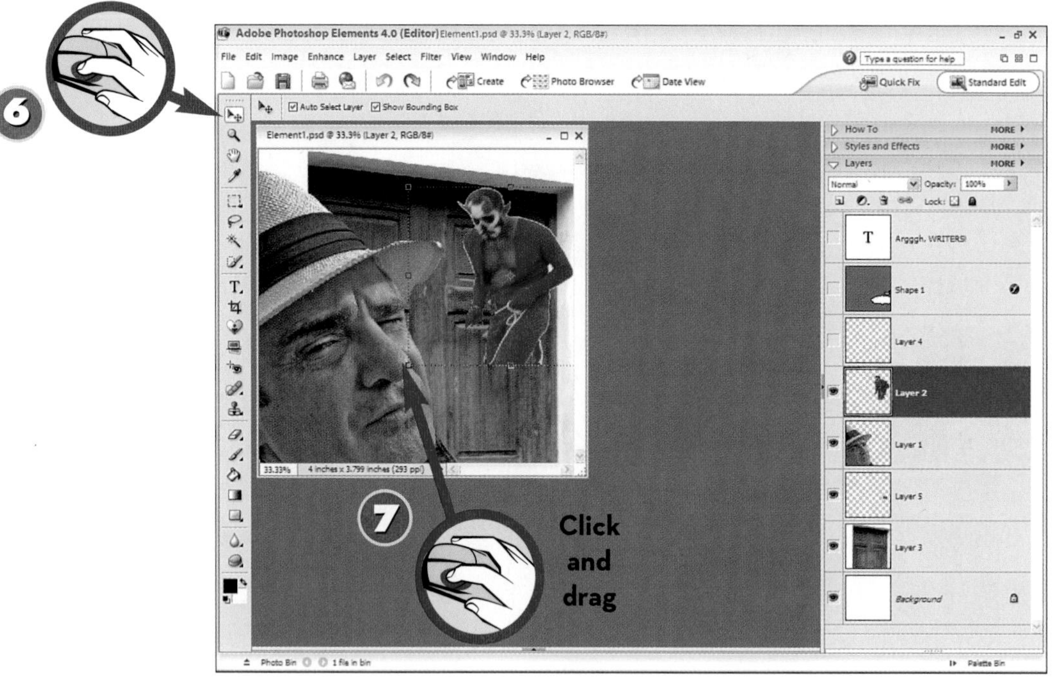

6. Choose the **Move** tool, or press **V**.
7. Click and drag object handles to move or resize the objects and compose the picture.

Continued

TIP

Shape Selection

In step 6, if the inserted picture contains multiple shapes, you can use the Shape Selection tool to select and manipulate them individually, as long as you haven't yet simplified or merged the layer.

Click

8

Click and drag

9

8 Switch to a **Brush** tool (or a **Shape** tool).

9 Click and drag to draw on the image. Repeat steps 8 and 9 to add more lines and shapes to your drawing.

End

TIP

Special Effects

After you've created a collage of images, you can go wild transforming them with any of the commands from the **Image**, **Transform**, or **Filter** menus.

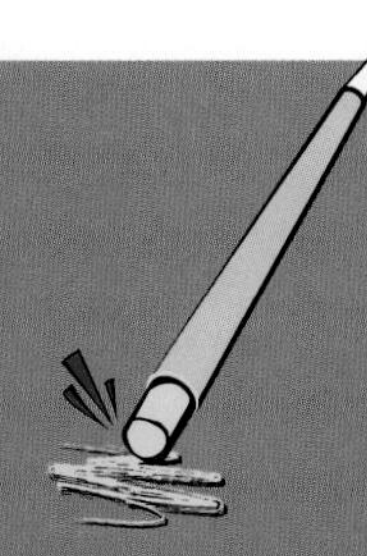

GETTING AN ANTIQUE LOOK

Of course, "antique" is relative to your age--or the ages of the relatives you want to transform. In this case, decreasing the saturation setting creates a look of old, faded Kodachrome. Adding Film Grain enhances the realism, and the Feather effect on the border adds to the impression of a faded snapshot.

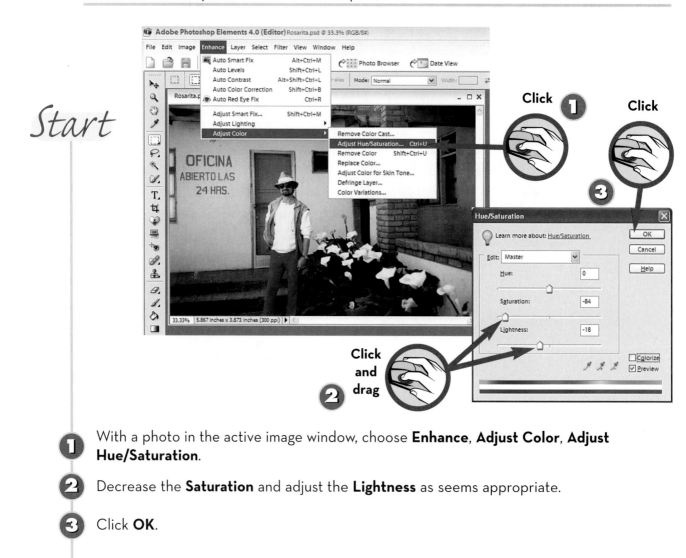

Start

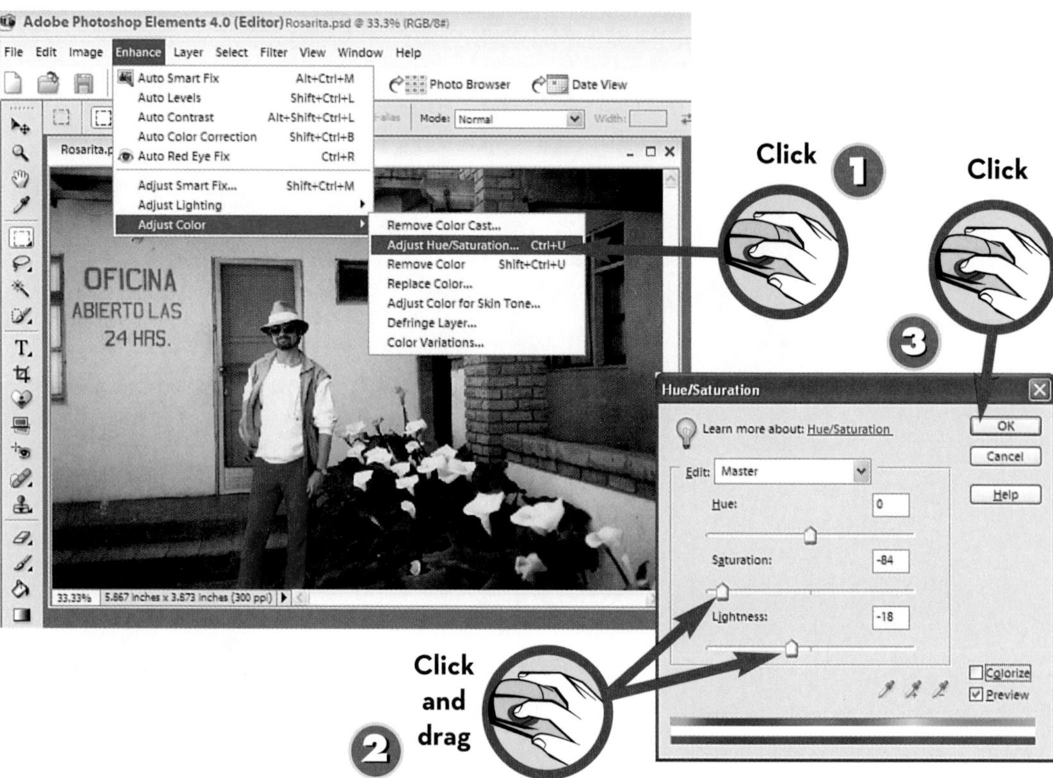

1. With a photo in the active image window, choose **Enhance**, **Adjust Color**, **Adjust Hue/Saturation**.
2. Decrease the **Saturation** and adjust the **Lightness** as seems appropriate.
3. Click **OK**.

Continued

TIP

Fading and Sepia

Decreasing Saturation can create a monochrome picture, but one that still contains color information. You can then apply Color Variations to get a sepia effect. By contrast, choosing **Image**, **Mode**, **Grayscale** discards all color.

TIP

Remove Color Command

An alternative conversion to grayscale that still preserves color information is the command **Enhance**, **Adjust Color**, **Remove Color**, which makes red, green, and blue values equal and reduces Saturation to zero.

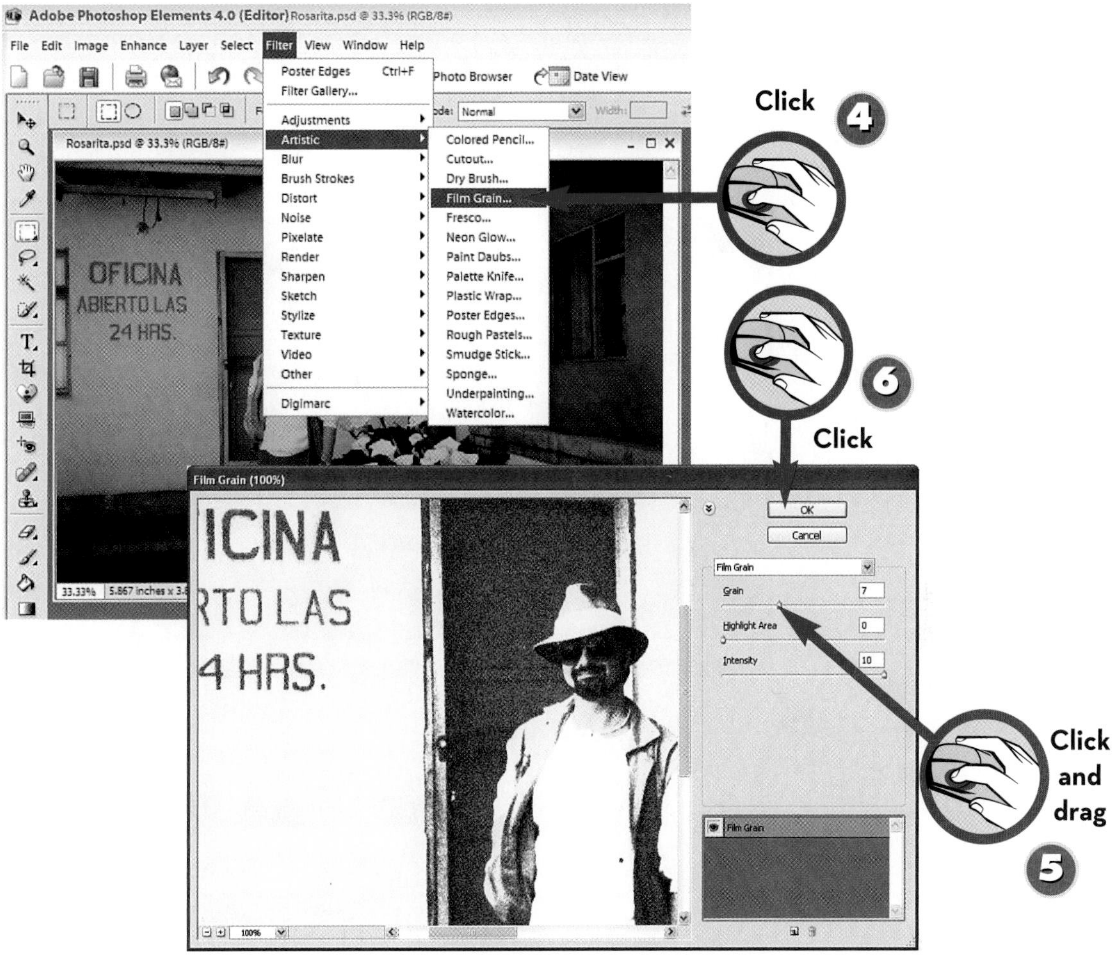

4. Choose **Filter**, **Artistic**, **Film Grain**.
5. Adjust the sliders for effect, such as increasing the **Grain** size.
6. Click **OK**.

Continued

NOTE

Film Grain

This same type of filter can be applied in the Adobe After Effects application to make your DV movies look like film.

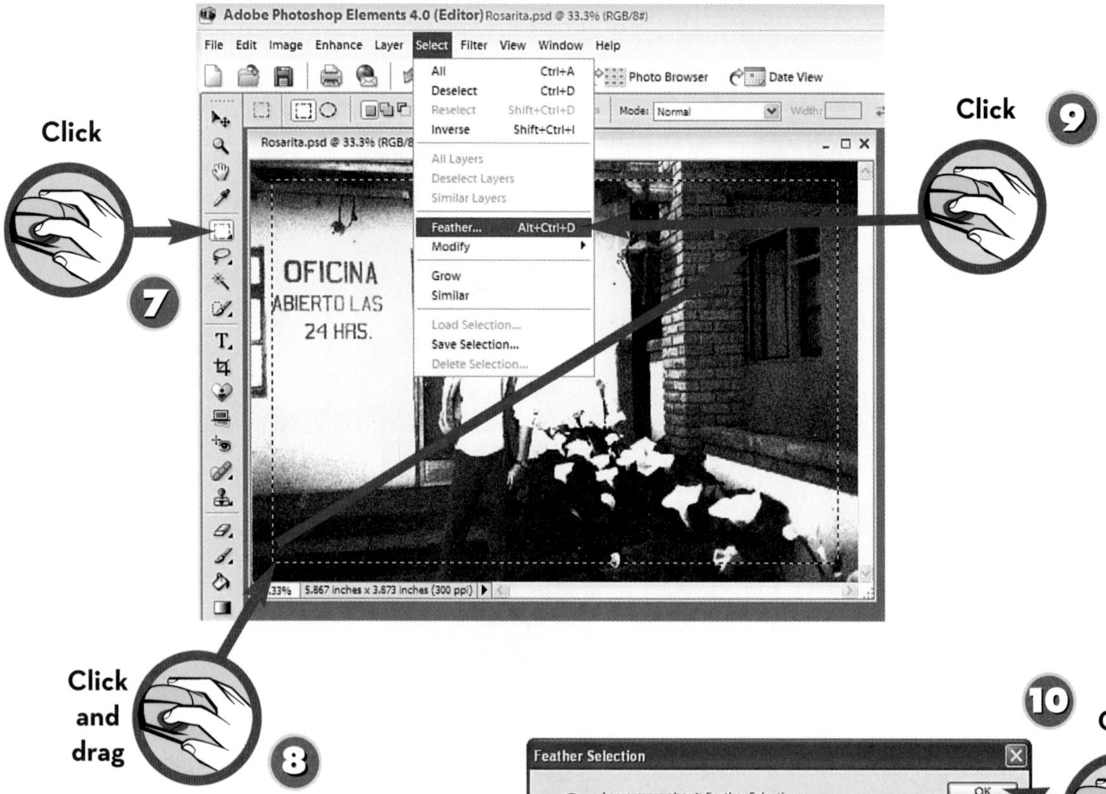

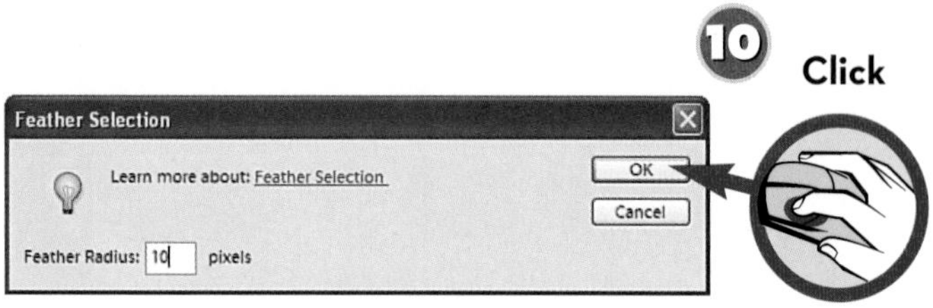

7. Choose the **Rectangular Marquee** tool, or press **M**.
8. Click and drag to size a border around the picture.
9. Choose **Select**, **Feather**.
10. Click **OK**.

Continued

TIP

Feather Radius

In step 10, remember that the size of the Feather effect is proportional to Image Size in pixels. For example, you may have to increase the Radius value to make the effect more obvious.

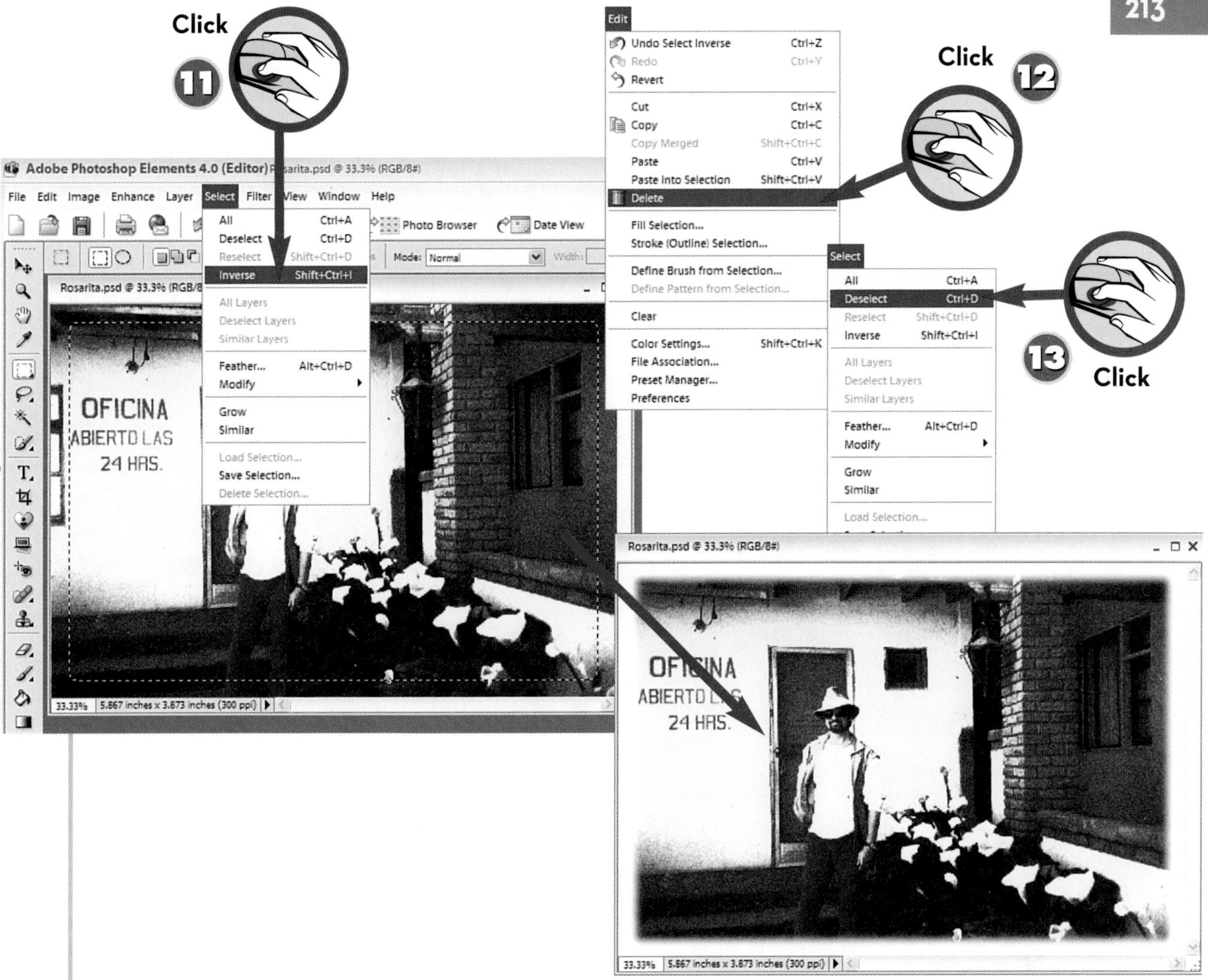

11 Choose **Select**, **Inverse**, or press **Shift+Ctrl+I**.

12 Choose **Edit**, **Delete**.

13 Choose **Select**, **Deselect**, or press **Ctrl+D**.

End

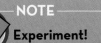

NOTE

Experiment!

This kind of experimentation with Photoshop Elements can bring into play any and all of the techniques you've learned in this book. Have fun!

CREATING POP ART

The biggest advantage of digital photo editing is that you can try dozens, hundreds, or even thousands of variations on a theme for each photo. And putting a few variations together in a collage format just happens to be a recognized art technique, one made famous by none other than Andy Warhol. Give it a try!

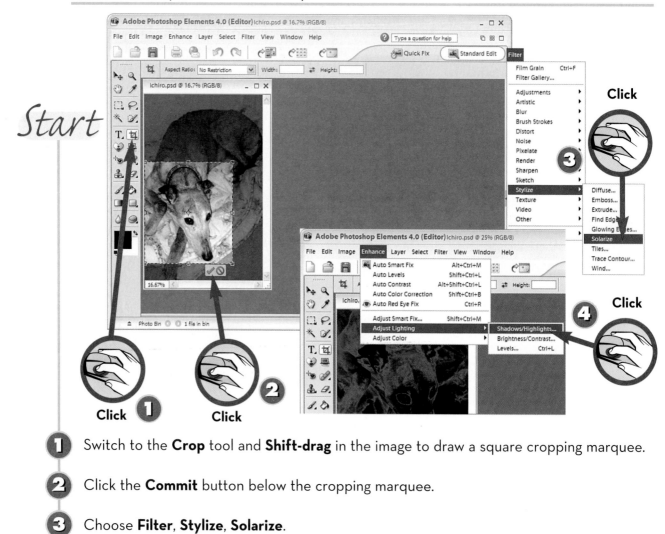

Start

1. Switch to the **Crop** tool and **Shift-drag** in the image to draw a square cropping marquee.
2. Click the **Commit** button below the cropping marquee.
3. Choose **Filter**, **Stylize**, **Solarize**.
4. Choose **Enhance**, **Adjust Lighting**, **Shadows/Highlights**.

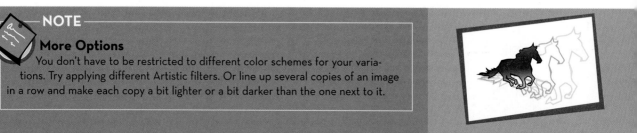

Continued

NOTE

More Options

You don't have to be restricted to different color schemes for your variations. Try applying different Artistic filters. Or line up several copies of an image in a row and make each copy a bit lighter or a bit darker than the one next to it.

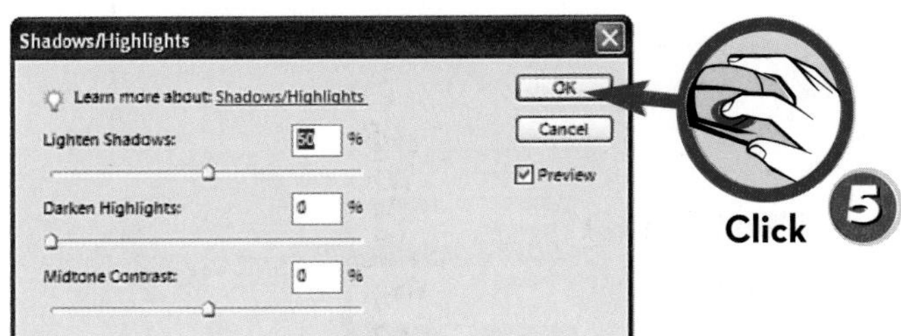

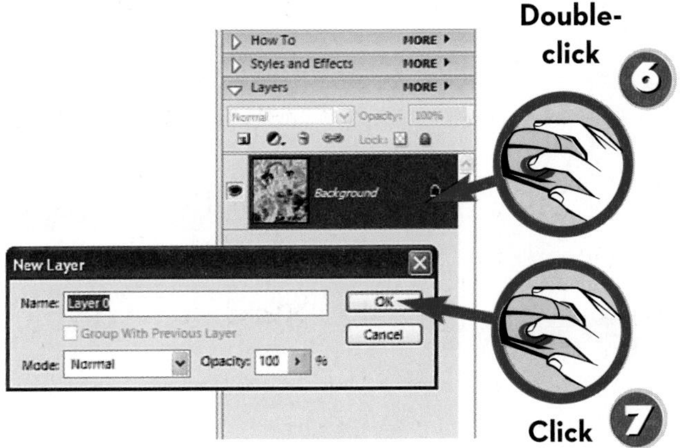

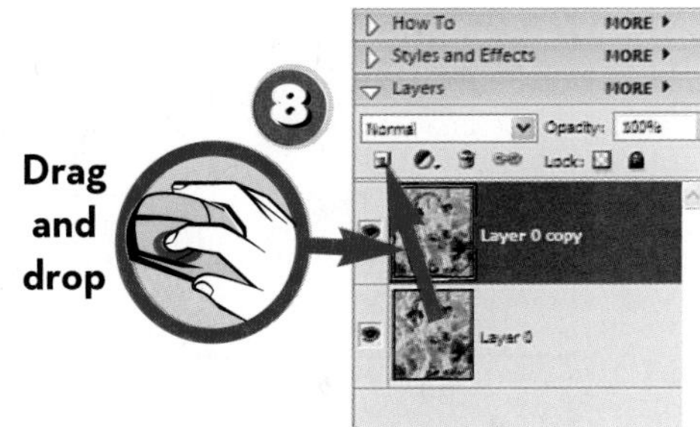

5. Click **OK**.
6. In the Layers palette, double-click the **Background**.
7. Click **OK**.
8. Drag Layer 0 onto the **Create Layer** button to duplicate it.

Continued

NOTE

Separation of Layers

Putting each copy of the image on its own layer makes moving it around and applying color changes to it easy.

TIP

Test Run

Make sure the picture you use has strong enough lines that you'll still be able to tell what it is after you run the Solarize filter. If you're not sure, test it before you spend any time cropping it by choosing **Filter**, **Stylize**, **Solarize**.

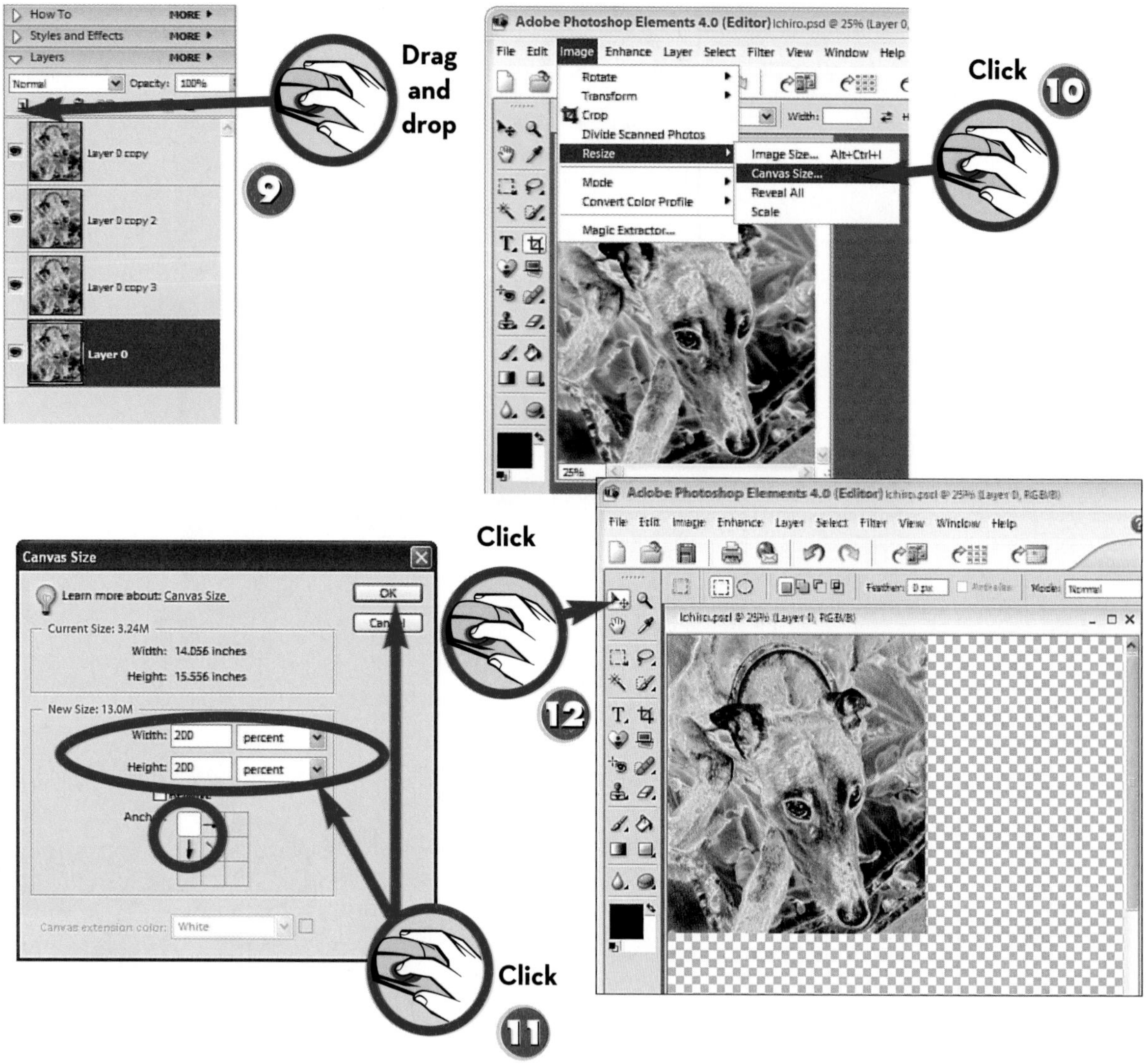

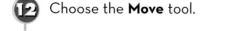

9 Repeat step 8 twice to create a total of four layers in the image.

10 Choose **Image**, **Resize**, **Canvas Size**.

11 Click the upper-left corner of the proxy grid and set the **Width** and **Height** to 200%; then click **OK**.

12 Choose the **Move** tool.

Continued

TIP

A Prerequisite

To select each layer with the Move tool, Auto Select Layer must be checked in the Options bar.

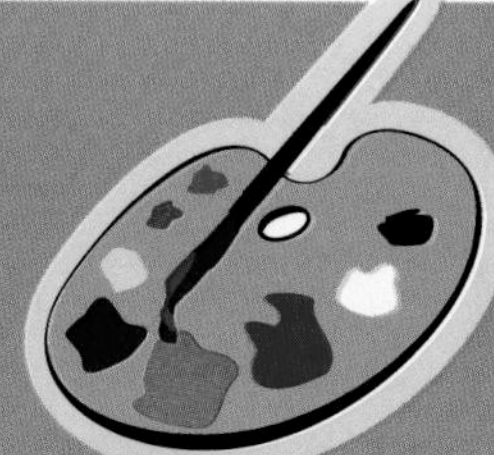

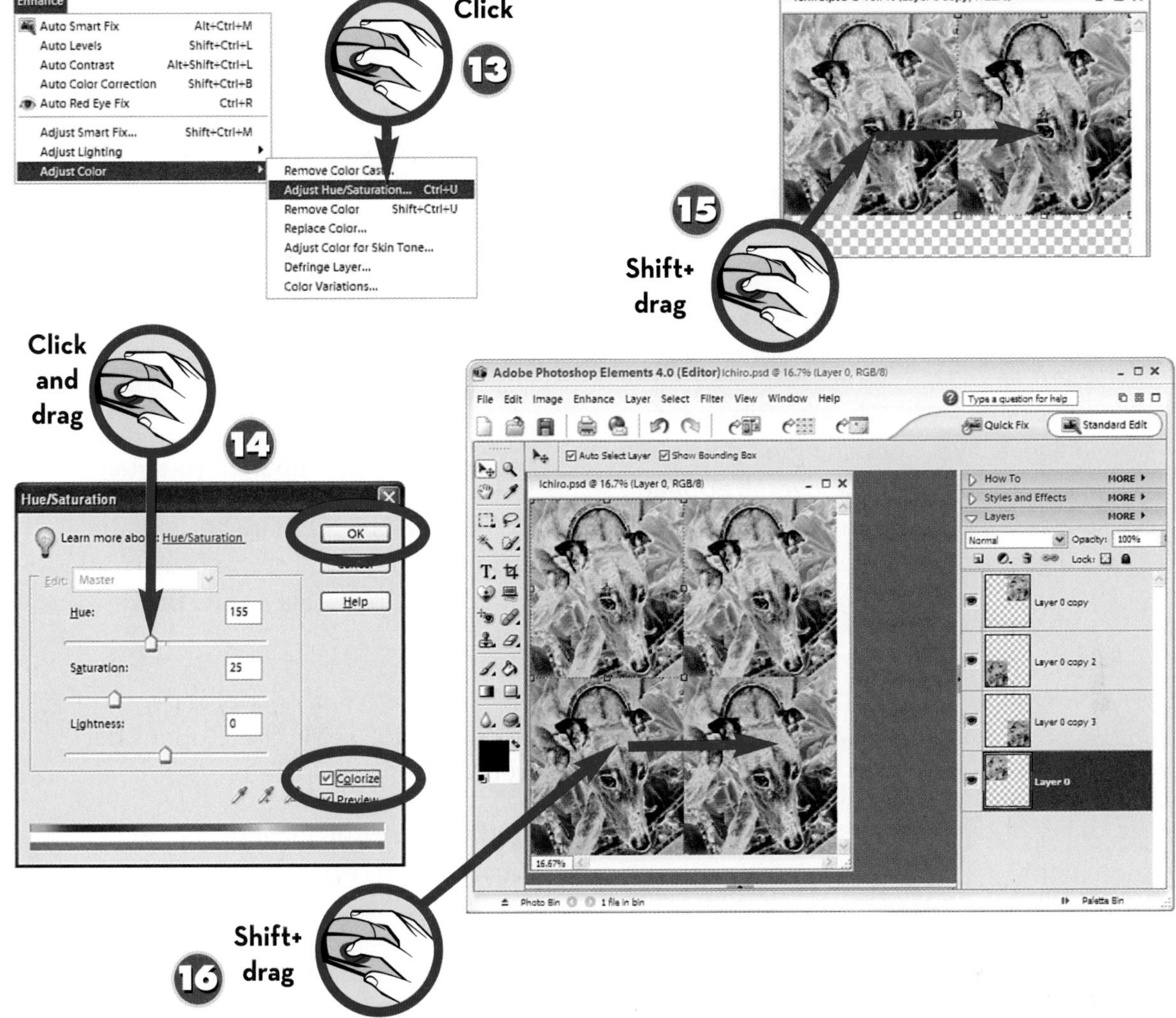

13 Click in the upper-left corner of the image and choose **Enhance**, **Adjust Color**, **Adjust Hue/Saturation**.

14 Click **Colorize** and drag the **Hue** slider until you like the image's color; then click **OK**.

15 Shift-drag the picture to the right side of the window.

16 Repeat steps 13–15 to move the other picture duplicates to the bottom corners of the window and colorize them with different colors.

End

NOTE

Enlarging Your Color Palette

In step 14, you can adjust the Saturation and Lightness sliders. Leaving these settings the same for all four images provides a more consistent look, but varying them enables you to use a wider range of colors and tints.

TIP

Lining Things Up

Press **Shift** as you drag the layers to constrain their movement to 45° angles: straight up and down, left and right, or corner to corner.

Glossary

A

active image area Application window that displays the image contained in the currently open file.

active layer Virtual drawing plane currently selected in an open image.

adjustment layer In a multilayered image, a layer containing no pixels, inserted to affect the overall appearance of all layers beneath it; in effect, a digital photographic filter.

Auto Select Layer Option whereby clicking a shape or text object with the Move tool automatically causes its layer to be selected.

autofocus Automatic focusing capability of digital cameras.

automatic white balance Digital camera function that reproduces colors based on the assumption that the lightest area in the frame is pure white.

B

backlight Photographic light source emanating from behind the subject.

base layer When layers are grouped, the bottommost layer that sets the boundaries of the upper ones, determined by the boundaries of a shape on that layer.

bitmap Digital image composed of pixels; raster image; pixel array; in Photoshop Elements color modes, a black-and-white image.

blending mode In a multilayered image, a layer option that determines how colors on different layers combine; an option for various tools and filters. Examples: Normal, Dissolve, Hard Light, Soft Light. Painting tools use blending modes, also.

blow out To totally overexpose an area of an image so that it is pure white and contains no picture detail.

brush dynamics Options for the size, shape, and behavior of the Brush tool that control the quality of its brush stroke.

brush tip Size and shape of the tip of the Brush tool, set in the Options bar after the tool is selected.

burn In traditional darkroom technique, to underexpose masked areas of a print as it's developed.

C

canvas size Paper or media size associated with an image file.

caption Printable text that describes the content of a picture.

capture To upload image data from a camera, camcorder, or scanner into a computer.

catalog In Organizer, a collection of image files from which a presentation can be created.

Clipboard Scratchpad memory area in Windows through which data, including graphics and images, can be exchanged between open applications.

Close box X button in the top-right corner of any Windows window by which it may be closed, or turned off.

collage Art term for a composition made from cut-out images pasted onto a board.

color cast Overall tint of a photograph, particularly noticeable and in need of correction when it creates unflattering flesh tones in the subjects.

color components Separate channels, or primary colors, within a color model; Red, Green, and Blue in the RGB color model; Hue, Saturation, and Lightness in the HSL model.

color management Coordination of color devices, such as cameras, computer screens, and printers, so that colors rendered on all of them appear to match.

color matching Fine-tuning the output of two or more color reproduction devices, such as a monitor and a printer, so that colors appear the same on both.

color space The range of all colors available in a color model.

composite Combination or merging of two or more images.

composition Artistic arrangement of subjects within the picture area.

compression Mathematical transformation of a digital file so as to describe its contents using less data, thereby creating a smaller file, and degrading its quality or accuracy as little as possible.

constrain To limit the repositioning or resizing of a shape or text to perpendicular angles; to prevent distortion; to maintain proportions (aspect ratio).

contact sheet Film photographer's reference print created in the darkroom by exposing filmstrips in direct contact with a sheet of print paper.

contrast Range of brightness between the highlights and shadows in a photograph.

crop To reframe an image, moving its edges to exclude unwanted areas.

crushed blacks Underexposed areas of a picture that are totally black and contain no picture detail.

D

default Preselected program option settings.

digital watermark Invisible copyright or proprietary notice within the image area of a photograph that can be read by Photoshop Elements or special reader software.

digitize To convert a film print or analog video clip to a digital file; to scan a photo.

discard layers To merge and simplify all layers in an image at once, rendering text and artwork uneditable as objects; see also **flatten**.

dither To render a subtle color by juxtaposing dots of two or more primary colors.

dodge In traditional darkroom technique, to overexpose unmasked areas of a print as it's developed.

dpi Unit of resolution of a digital printer; dots per inch; equivalent to pixels/inch.

duotone Two-color image.

DV Abbreviation of the Digital Video recording standard.

DVD Abbreviation for Digital Versatile Disc, optical recording medium for videos and movies.

DVD menu Onscreen selections of DVD chapters, each indicated by a button.

E

exposure Length of time light is permitted to strike a camera's film or sensors (called *CCD chips* in a digital camera).

extension In a computer filename, characters to the right of the rightmost period, indicating the file format; examples: .psd, .jpg, .doc, .mpeg.

eyelight Small photographic light source aimed directly into subject's eyes to make them sparkle.

F

feather Blurred edges of a shape; vignette.

file format Indicated by the extension in the filename, the type of file (such as a native Photoshop file).

fill Solid area or pattern within a shape, text, or image area.

fill flash Bright photographic light source used to supplement key light and fill in the area surrounding the subject. In Photoshop Elements, the ability to lighten the darkest (usually foreground) areas of a photo, leaving the bright (usually background) areas unchanged.

filter In Photoshop Elements, a prebuilt artistic effect that can be applied to an image; in conventional photography, a glass covering for a lens that changes the quality of light.

FireWire Apple trademark for the connection between a camcorder or other device and a computer, designated IEEE 1394; equivalent to Sony's iLINK.

flatten To merge and simplify all layers in an image at once; see also **discard layers**.

flip To create a mirror image of a shape, text, or image.

focus In Photoshop Elements, to sharpen or blur the edges of a selection; in conventional photography, to adjust the camera lens to achieve the same effect.

folder In a computer file system, a named directory that contains files.

font In typography, a typeface in a particular point size; in computer applications, a typeface.

f-stop Camera setting that controls how much light is admitted during an exposure.

FTP Abbreviation of File Transfer Protocol, a method of uploading files to the Internet.

G

Gaussian blur Named for mathematician Carl Friedrich Gauss, a filter that enables finer control over how an image is blurred than does Blur or Blur More.

gradient Blended color used to fill a shape or background.

grain Noise filter applied to a digital image to simulate the grain of photographic film.

grayed out Dimmed; refers to menu commands or dialog box options that are unavailable based on current settings.

grayscale Monochrome picture that contains shades of black and white.

group Combination of palettes or layers so they can be manipulated as a single palette or object.

H

halation effect Artifact of early film that created a beatific glow around closeups of movie stars.

halftone screen Dot pattern used in commercial printing to render shaded images using tiny, solid dots of black (B&W) or four primary colors (CMYK).

handle Corner on a selection that can be dragged to resize or reposition the object.

hard Quality of light that produces sharp edges and dark shadows.

hidden tool Any tool in the toolbar that can be selected by right-clicking a related tool.

HSL Color model and mixing scheme based on components Hue (primary color), Saturation (tint), and Lightness (light-dark value).

I

ICC Abbreviation of International Color Consortium, which promotes color standards for the printing industry.

Impressionist brush Tool used to lay down blurred brush strokes, after the technique of painters who rebelled against doing pictures in painstaking detail.

indexed color Restricted color tables for specific uses, such as Web or Windows system display.

ink-and-paint Conventional movie animator's technique of drawing a cartoon character's outline in ink on a clear sheet of celluloid and then filling in solid shapes with acrylic paint.

intellectual property rights (IPR) Copyrights, patents, and trademarks; copyright applies to photographs, to which the photographer is author and rights holder.

K

key light Main photographic light source aimed to highlight the subject.

keystoning Photographic distortion produced by aiming the camera at a steep angle, high or low, in relation to the subject.

L

landscape Rectangular image or printer orientation with the long dimension horizontal.

layer Separate drawing, painting, text, or image plane among multiple planes, or layers, in a Photoshop image.

layer style Options, such as bevels or drop shadows, that affect all objects on a given layer.

level Value of red, green, or blue, or black input or output channel to produce brightness and contrast.

linking layers Marking and associating layers so that they can be manipulated together.

lossless File compression that results in no perceptible loss of quality or accuracy.

lossy File compression that *does* result in a loss of quality or accuracy.

LZW File compression scheme based on a transformation named for mathematicians Lempel, Ziv, and Welch.

M

mapping Transformation that bends and spreads an image or texture over the surface of an object.

mask To cover part of an image so that that area is unaffected by changes made to other areas of the image.

menu bar Main pull-down program commands in an application such as Photoshop Elements, near the top of the program window, beginning with the File menu on the left and proceeding to the Help menu on the right.

merge To both simplify and combine layers in a single operation.

midtone Pixel values in the middle range between highlights and shadows.

mixed media Art term for works that may combine assemblage, collage, and painting or drawing.

mode Image rendering as either grayscale or color.

monochrome Single-color image, but not necessarily black and white.

multisession Describing a CD or DVD to which files can be written, or appended, at different times.

N–O

navigate Procedure for finding files and folders by exploring the file system, based on a hierarchy of files within folders (possibly within other folders) on a storage device (such as a disk).

negative Reverse image from processing camera film, resulting in shadow areas rendered as highlights, highlights as shadows, and color primaries as their opposites (red as cyan, blue as yellow, and so on).

nudge To move a selection by small increments by pressing the Arrow keys.

opacity Degree to which light is blocked by an object or layer; inverse of transparency.

Options bar Settings for a tool, such as Brush, that become available beneath the menu bar after the tool has been selected.

orientation Rotation angle of an image or printout; portrait or landscape.

P

palette Floating window containing effects, commands, and help grouped by category.

palette tab Handle by which a palette can be selected, docked, or undocked from the Palette Bin.

palette bin Storage location in the work area for frequently used palettes.

pan To rotate a camera, typically mounted on a tripod, from left to right or from right to left in the same horizontal plane.

panorama Scenic, wide-angle landscape; Photomerge output.

picture package Commercial photographer's offered assortment of prints in various sizes, from wallet-sized to larger sizes suitable for framing.

pixel Picture element; colored dot in a bitmap image.

pixels/inch Resolution of a raster image; equivalent to printer dots per inch (dpi).

place To insert artwork from an external file into an open image.

plug-in Add-on software module that extends the capability of an application.

point size Size of type.

Pointillize filter Limiting brush strokes to tiny dots of primary color; technique pioneered by Impressionist painter Georges Seurat.

port Input/output connector on a computer.

portrait Rectangular image or printer orientation with the long dimension vertical; headshot.

posterization Garish color effect produced by the command Image, Adjustments, Posterize.

preferences User option settings that override default values.

printable area Rectangular area of a printout that excludes margins where the printer grips the paper, and therefore where it can't print an image.

profile Stored color table used for color management.

progressive mode JPEG file setting that causes a downloaded image to be built up in visible stages, intended to improve the viewing experience over slow connections.

publish Upload files to the World Wide Web.

Q

Quick Fix Mode Interface view that simplifies and streamlines Photoshop Elements' features so that corrections can be applied more easily, but with limited user control. See also **Standard Editing Mode.**

R

rasterize To convert a vector shape or type object to pixels; to simplify.

red eye Undesirable reflection in a subject's eyes caused by flash photography.

redo Reverse the previous Undo command.

render To apply changes to a digital image and display or print it.

resample To change the resolution (pixels/inch) of an image.

reset To return to previous option settings.

resolution Measure of picture quality or degree of detail; pixels/inch; dpi.

retouch To use artistic techniques to improve the appearance of photographic subjects or scenes; in portrait work, to soften wrinkles, remove blemishes, and so on.

revert To cancel pending edits without saving and return to the original version of a file; see also **undo.**

RGB Color model and mixing scheme used in Photoshop Elements, based on components Red, Green, and Blue.

S

search field Text box in the top-right center of the Photoshop Elements work area into which a text description of a problem or task can be typed in order to search the Help files.

selection Active object or area within the image area to which the next command or operation will be applied.

sepia Brown-tinted monochrome image; typical of antique photographs.

shape Geometric object in Photoshop Elements; examples: Rectangle, Ellipse.

sharpen To increase pixel contrast at object boundaries; to bring into focus.

shortcuts bar Row of buttons with icons just beneath the menu bar, representing single-click activation of commonly used commands.

simplify To convert a vector shape or type to pixels; to rasterize.

skew To apply a spatial transformation to a selected object that causes its sides to be slanted.

slider Program control in some dialog boxes, toolbars, and palettes that can be adjusted by clicking and dragging.

soft Blurred; out of focus.

stacking order Priority of layers in a multilayered image that determines visibility of objects; objects on upper layers will obscure overlapping objects beneath.

Standard Editing Mode Interface view that enables access to all of Photoshop Elements' features. See also **Quick Fix Mode**.

still Single-frame photographic image (as opposed to a moving image created by a sequence of frames in a movie or video).

streaming video Video clip, usually low resolution, optimized for downloading over the Web.

superimpose To overlay one graphic object on another.

swatch A single, saved color; one of a table of colors coordinated for a specific purpose, such as Web-safe colors.

system colors Set of swatches containing only colors displayable without dithering on Windows computers.

T

texture Variegated surface or area; pattern.

thumbnail Small, low-resolution image used to preview file selections without having to spend time opening the full-resolution file.

title bar Top band on any Windows window showing the name of its selections (or filename of the image or document it contains, and by which the window may be moved by clicking and dragging.

tool One of the selection, drawing, and retouching tools found in the Photoshop Elements toolbar, located by default on the left edge of the work area.

tool tip Name or function of a tool or button, as well as its shortcut key (if any), which pops up when you hover the pointer over it prior to making a selection.

toolbox Collection of Photoshop Elements tools, located by default on the left edge of the work area.

transparency Degree to which objects and colors on underlying layers are visible; the inverse of opacity.

tutorial Training lesson available through the Help menu.

type mask Type-shaped selection area, typically used to create hollow text to let the Background or a lower layer show through.

U–V

undo To reverse or cancel the most recently executed command or change; see also **redo**.

undock To open a palette from the Palette Bin; see also **dock**.

ungroup To make a previously grouped set of palettes or layers accessible individually; see also **group**.

upload To transfer a digital file from a device, such as a camera, camcorder, or scanner, to a computer; to capture.

USB Abbreviation for Universal Serial Bus; a type of computer port that supports digital cameras and printers.

vector Mathematical description of a geometric object; a resolution-independent object description.

vignette Portrait with feathered edges.

W–Z

Web site index page Home page on the World Wide Web.

WIA Abbreviation of Windows Image Acquisition, a standard for connecting scanners and cameras to computers.

ZIP Lossless file compression scheme.

zoom To magnify the view of an image.

Index

A

B

C

Index

D

E

Index

G

H-I

K-L

P

Q-R

S

T

U-V

W-X-Y-Z